KU-615-739

Transforming the Center, Eroding the Margins

Studies in German Literature, Linguistics, and Culture

Edited by James Hardin
(*South Carolina*)

TRANSFORMING THE CENTER, ERODING THE MARGINS

ESSAYS ON ETHNIC AND CULTURAL BOUNDARIES IN GERMAN-SPEAKING COUNTRIES

EDITED BY
DAGMAR C. G. LORENZ
AND
RENATE S. POSTHOFEN

UNIVERSITY LIBRARY
NOTTINGHAM

CAMDEN HOUSE

Copyright © 1998 Dagmar C. G. Lorenz and Renate S. Posthofen

All Rights Reserved. Except as permitted under current legislation,
no part of this work may be photocopied, stored in a retrieval system,
published, performed in public, adapted, broadcast, transmitted,
recorded, or reproduced in any form or by any means,
without the prior permission of the copyright owner.

First published 1998
Camden House
Drawer 2025
Columbia, SC 29202–2025 USA

Camden House is an imprint of Boydell & Brewer Inc.
PO Box 41026, Rochester, NY 14604–4126 USA
and of Boydell & Brewer Limited
PO Box 9, Woodbridge, Suffolk IP12 3DF, UK

ISBN: 1–57113–171–x

Library of Congress Cataloging-in-Publication Data

Transforming the center, eroding the margins: essays on ethnic and
  cultural boundaries in German-speaking countries / edited by Dagmar
C. G. Lorenz and Renate S. Posthofen.
      p.   cm. – (Studies in German literature, linguistics, and
culture (Unnumbered))
    Includes bibliographical references and index.
    ISBN 1-57113-171-X (alk. paper)
    1. German literature—20th century—History and criticism.
2. German literature—19th century—History and criticism.
3. Multiculturalism in literature. 4. Minorities in literature.
5. Women in literature. 6. Jews in literature. 7. Literature and
society—Europe, German-speaking. I. Lorenz, Dagmar C.G., 1948-   .
II. Posthofen, Renate S. III. Series.
PT405.T683 1998
830.9'2069—dc21   98-3144
                                                            CIP

This publication is printed on acid-free paper.
Printed in the United States of America

This book is dedicated to
Sophia and Noah Palmieri Posthofen
and
Martha Cramer

Contents

Acknowledgments   xi
List of Contributors   xiii
Introduction   1

Dagmar C. G. Lorenz   21
More Than Metaphors: Animals, Gender,
and Jewish Identity in Gertrud Kolmar

Stephanie Hammer   29
In the Name of the Rose: Gertrud Kolmar,
Hélène Cixous, and the Poerotics of Jewish Femininity

Sigrid Bauschinger   44
Vindication through Suffering: Gertrud Kolmar's
Cycle of Poems "Robespierre"

Monika Shafi   62
Reconsidering Gertrud Kolmar through the Cycle
"German Sea"

Beate Schmeichel-Falkenberg   81
Women in Exile   81

Renate S. Posthofen   93
Claire Goll (1891–1977): Visionary Power and Creative
Symbiosis — Fictionalized Identity as Survival Strategy

Robert C. Fuhrmann   103
Masculine Form / Feminine Writing: The Autobiography
of Fanny Lewald

Neva Šlibar 115
Traveling, Living, Writing from and at the Margins:
Alma Maximiliana Karlin and Her Geobiographical Books

Alan Levenson 132
The Apostate as Philosemite: Selig Paulus Cassel
(1821–1892) and Edith Stein (1891–1942)

Dagmar C. G. Lorenz 146
History, Identity, and the Body in Edgar Hilsenrath's
The Story of the Last Thought

Deborah Viëtor-Engländer 155
Alfred Kerr and Marcel Reich-Ranicki: Critics and Power
in Germany in the Weimar Republic and the Federal Republic

Bernd Fischer 163
The Memory of Multiculturalism and the Politics of Identity

Matti Bunzl 169
Counter-Memory and Modes of Resistance: The Uses
of Fin-de-Siècle Vienna for Present-Day Austrian Jews

Neil G. Jacobs and Dagmar C. G. Lorenz 185
If I Were King of the Jews: *Germanistik* and the
Judaistikfrage

Renate S. Posthofen 199
Of Inclusions and Exclusions: Austrian Identity Reconsidered

Peter Arnds 215
The Fragmentation of Totality in Robert Menasse's
Selige Zeiten, brüchige Welt

Iman O. Khalil 227
From the Margins to the Center: Arab-German
Authors and Issues

Peter Werres 238
National Identity under Siege: Postwall Writing in Germany

Gernot Weiß 257
The Foreign and the Own: Polylingual Literature and
the Problem of Identity

Michael S. Bryant   268
I Say Coffee, You Say Inkwell:
Normalizing the Abnormal in Kafka's *The Castle*

Dagmar C. G. Lorenz   285
Transcending the Boundaries of Space and Culture: The
Figures of the Maharal and the Golem after the Shoah — Friedrich
Torberg's *Golems Wiederkehr*, Leo Perutz's
Nachts unter der steinernen Brücke, Frank Zwillinger's *Maharal*, and
Nelly Sachs's *Eli. Ein Mysterienspiel vom Leiden Israels*

Index   303

Acknowledgments

W E THANK ALL OF OUR COLLEAGUES whose work is represented in this collection of articles. Some of them participated in the 1996 ISSEI workshop in Utrecht, entitled "Transforming the Center, Eroding the Margins. Transcending Ethnic and Cultural Boundaries in German-speaking Countries," others joined the project at a later stage. Through their interest, expertise, and work, each of them has made a substantial contribution to the collection of articles.

Another person who has been central to our project is our copyeditor Sabine Barcatta who has devoted her untiring help and expertise to this book. She has gone far beyond her call of duty to ensure the consistency of the manuscript in terms of style, footnoting, endnoting, and spelling. She has also coordinated the individual contributions and standardized the manuscript overall. Sabine Barcatta has worked overtime, on weekends and through many nights to meet deadlines and get the book into its final form.

In addition, we are very much indebted to Peter Gerity, Vice President for Research, and to Joyce Kinkead, Associate Dean in the College of Humanities, Arts and Social Sciences, both at Utah State University. Joyce Kinkead was instrumental in reviewing the project in its grant-application phase for a New Faculty Research Grant (NFRG). She outlined the concepts and subsequent stages of editing and production for the project prior to its being funded by Utah State University. Her gentle, yet effective criticism helped to assure the final generous funding for the project. Furthermore we owe recognition and thanks to Peter Gerity for awarding a truly generous Research Grant to support our project. It ultimately made it possible for us to realize this project. We also thank Bernd Fischer, Chair of the Department of Germanic Languages and Literatures at the Ohio State University for granting us Research Associate support for the purpose of preparing the index.

Our sincere appreciation and gratitude goes to our publisher, James Hardin, at Camden House. He has been a constant source of advice, inspiration, and reliable feedback throughout the final stages of the project.

Finally, we thank our spouses, Mohsin A. Abdou and Robert A. Palmieri, for their encouragement, patience, and loyalty throughout the project.

Dagmar C. G. Lorenz
Renate S. Posthofen
April 1998

Contributors

Peter Arnds has been an assistant professor of German and Italian at Kansas State University in Manhattan, Kansas since 1995. He earned his M.A. from the Ludwig-Maximilians-University in Munich in 1990, and his Ph.D. from the University of Toronto in 1995. His main teaching and research interests include nineteenth and twentieth-century German literature. His research focuses on comparative and interdisciplinary issues: specifically on links between literature, philosophy, and psychology, contemporary German and Austrian literature, and Wilhelm Raabe and his nexus with Victorian writers. His most recent publication is *Wilhelm Raabe's 'Der Hungerpastor' and Charles Dickens's 'David Copperfield': Intertextuality of Two Bildungsromane* (1997).

Sigrid Bauschinger is professor of German at the University of Massachusetts at Amherst. She received her Doctorate in Philosophy from the Johann Wolfgang Goethe University in Frankfurt am Main in 1960. Her teaching and research interests include: nineteenth and twentieth century literature, German-Jewish authors, exile literature, and German-American literary relations. Her recent publications include: *Rilke Rezeptionen / Rilke Reconsidered* (1995) and *"Ich habe etwas zu sagen." Annette Kolb (1870–1967)*, (1993).

Michael S. Bryant is a doctoral student at the Ohio State University in Columbus, Ohio, where he earned his B.A. in English literature in 1985. He also received a Juris Doctor and Masters of Theological Studies degree from Emory University in 1990, and a M.A. in history from Ohio State in 1996. His research interests focus chiefly on issues of narrative and representation raised by Holocaust studies. His publications include *Entsetzliche Gleichgültigkeit* (1989), and *Hidden Religion in the Law* (1990).

Matti Bunzl is a Ph.D. candidate in the Departments of Anthropology and History at the University of Chicago. His research interests range from the anthropology of contemporary Austrian Jewry and the literature and culture of fin-de-siècle Vienna to the history of anthropology and questions of gender and sexuality. He has published articles in journals such as *History & Memory, The German Quarterly, Austrian Studies,* and *Cultural Anthropology,* among others.

Bernd Fischer is professor of German Literature at the Ohio State University. His areas of specialization include: eighteenth, nineteenth, and twentieth-century German literature and culture, intellectual history, and literary theory. Among his publications are: *Das Eigene und das Eigentliche: Klopstock, Herder, Fichte, Kleist; Episoden aus der Konstruktionsgeschichte nationaler Intentionalitäten* (1995); *Christoph Hein: Drama und Prosa im letzten Jahrzehnt der DDR* (1990); *Ironische Metaphysik: Die Erzählungen Heinrich von Kleists* (1988); *Kabale und Liebe: Skepsis und Melodrama in Schillers bürgerlichem Trauerspiel* (1987); and *Literatur und Politik: Die Novellensammlung von 1812 und das Landhausleben von Achim von Arnim* (1983).

Robert Fuhrmann is a Ph.D. candidate in the Department of Germanic Languages and Literatures at the Ohio State University. He earned an M.F.A. from the University of Iowa in 1992 and an M.A. from the University of Pennsylvania in 1996. His research interests include German-Jewish and Yiddish autobiographies, and ethnography.

Stephanie Hammer is currently Vice-Chair and associate professor of Comparative Literature at the University of California, Riverside, where she has been employed for the past 12 years. She received her Ph.D. in Comparative Literature from the University of North Carolina at Chapel Hill in 1982. She teaches and conducts research in the eighteenth century, the Holocaust, and in Women's Studies. Her essay on Margaret Atwood's *The Handmaid's Tale* is often used in college classrooms and has been reprinted in *A Practical Introduction to Literary Theory and Criticism* (1996). Since the publication of her book *The Sublime Crime: Fascination, Failure, and Form* (1993); she has divided her time between research on Friedrich Schiller, yielding an article entitled "Schiller, Time and Again" (1995), and on contemporary topics involving gender: her essay "Peter Handke, Roland Barthes, and Eddie Vedder's representation of the mother," appeared in the electronic journal *Postmodern Culture* (1995).

Neil G. Jacobs is associate professor in the Yiddish and Ashkenazic Studies Program in the Department of Germanic Languages and Literatures at the Ohio State University. His main areas of research and publication are Yiddish historical linguistics, Yiddish phonology, and Jewish geography. His research interests also include examination of post-Yiddish Jewish ethnolects of German and Dutch.

Iman O. Khalil has been an associate professor of German at the University of Missouri-Kansas City since 1988. She received her Ph.D. from the Ludwig-Maximilians-University in Munich in 1978. Her teaching interests include elementary and conversational German, composition, German culture, and nineteenth and twentieth-century German literature. Her research interests involve migrants' literature in Germany. Her last two publications are "Zur Rezeption arabischer Autoren in Deutschland," in Sabine Fischer & Moray McGowan (eds.), *Denn du tanzt auf einem Seil: Positionen deutschsprachiger MigrantInnenliteratur* (1997); and "Arabisch-deutsche Literatur," in Paul Michael Lützeler (ed.), *Schreiben zwischen den Kulturen: Beiträge zur deutschsprachigen Gegenwartsliteratur* (1996).

Alan Levenson, who received both his B.A. and M.A. from Brown University and his Ph.D. from the Ohio State University, teaches at the Cleveland College of Jewish Studies. He has been a visiting professor at the College of William and Mary and at Case Western Reserve University. His essays on German Jewry, modern Jewish thought, and pedagogy have appeared in *Jewish Social Studies, The Leo Baeck Institute Yearbook, Studies in Zionism* and *Shofar.*

Dagmar C. G. Lorenz is a professor of German at The Ohio State University in Columbus. She received her M.A. in English from the University of Cincinnati, and her Ph.D. in German at the University of Göttingen. She is the author of *Ilse Aichinger* (1981); *Franz Grillparzer: Dichter des sozialen Konflikts* (1986); *Verfolgung bis zum Massenmord: Diskurse zum Holocaust in deutscher Sprache* (1992); *Insiders and Outsiders: Jewish and Gentile Culture in Germany and Austria* (1994); and *Keepers of the Motherland: German Texts by Jewish Women Writers* (1997).

Renate S. Posthofen is associate professor of German at Utah State University in Logan, Utah. She studied at the Albert-Ludwigs-University in Freiburg in Breisgau, Germany, and received her M.A. in German from the University of Pittsburgh. Her Ph.D. in German was granted in 1993 by the State University of New York in Albany. She is the author of *Treibgut: Das vergessene Werk George Saikos* (1995), and a number of articles dealing with contemporary Austrian literature and culture, including such authors as Robert Schindel, Robert Menasse, Ruth Beckermann, Claire Goll, and György Sebestyén.

Beate Schmeichel-Falkenberg was born in Hamm, Westphalia, Germany. She is a journalist, writer, and translator. She has studied German and English literature in Göttingen and London, and education and psychology in Münster and Dortmund. She has worked as a moderator and script writer for German television, and as a lecturer in Germany and abroad, with the main focus on topics regarding exile under Hitler. In 1988 she founded the International Tucholsky Society. She also founded the Arbeitskreis Frauen im Exil as part of the International Society for Exile Studies, where she served as vice president in 1997. She organizes a conference on Women in Exile every year.

Monika Shafi is professor of German at the University of Delaware, which she joined in 1986. She studied at the Universities of Aachen and Freiburg, and in 1986 received her Ph.D. from the University of Maryland. She is the author of *Utopische Entwürfe in der Literatur von Frauen* (1989), *Gertrud Kolmar: Eine Einführung in das Werk* (1995), and articles on nineteenth and twentieth-century German literature, with special emphasis on women writers.

Neva Šlibar has been a professor of modern and contemporary German literature for the Department of Germanic Languages and Literatures at the University of Ljubljana, Slovenia, since 1979. She studied in Ljubljana, graduating in 1972. She received an M.A. degree from the University of Zagreb in 1981 and her Ph.D. in 1991 from the University of Ljubljana. Her research interests center around contemporary literature and literary theory with a focus on literary models and genres, biography, and narratology. Her recent publications include four articles on Ingeborg Bachmann (1990, 1995, and 1997); and books entitled *Im Freiraum Literatur: Literaturmodell, Textinterpretationen, Didaktische Hinweise* (1997), *Literary Theory* (1997), and *Biographical Discourse* (1998).

Deborah Judith Vietor-Engländer has taught at the Technical University of Darmstadt since 1992. Prior to that she taught at the University of Saarbrücken. She earned her B.A. from the University of London in 1968, and her Doctorate in Philosophy from the University of Tübingen in 1986. Exile literature is her main research interest. Currently she is the president of the International Arnold Zweig Society. Two of her recent publications are "Hermynia Zur Mühlen's fight against the enemy within: prejudice, injustice, cowardice and intolerance," in Charmian Brinson et al (eds.), *Hitler's Gift to Britain* (1997), and "'Ich kann in diesem Brief nicht tun, was ich als Anwesender hätte tun können': Arnold Zweig's letters in exile. The human dimension," in *Proceedings of the Fourth Arnold Zweig Conference 1996*, (1997).

Gernot Weiß is an independent scholar who has studied German literature, philosophy, and history at Heidelberg, Cologne, and Bonn. He received his doctorate in German literature at the University of Heidelberg in 1992. His dissertation on Thomas Bernhard's critics in philosophy was published with the title *Auslöschung der Philosphie* in 1993. His other works include articles on postmodernism (1995), and on Adelbert von Chamisso's *Peter Schlemihl,* entitled "Südseeträume: Schlemihls Suche nach dem Glück" (1996). His research currently centers on the problem of linear succession and simultaneity in literature, philosophy, and the arts.

DAGMAR C. G. LORENZ AND RENATE S. POSTHOFEN

Introduction

T HERE EXISTS A VAST BODY OF scholarship on German writers who were part of the traditional core canon of German literature. In the context of the recent debates about high culture(s) and low culture(s) and the discussion about postmodern concepts in contemporary literary theory, the focus has shifted from the writings of prominent mainstream authors to others who are less known. The literary canon is undergoing an almost unprecedented redefinition and expansion; in fact, its very raison d'être is being questioned. With the inclusion and examination of new texts, the recurring issues of marginality and centrality in the context of German-speaking culture(s) have come to the forefront of the literary debates. There is an increased awareness within the expanding and transforming field of German studies concerning the diverse histories and traditions, the theoretical foundations, and the cross-cultural context. Indeed, the concepts of center and margins are in the process of being reevaluated, so are the notions otherness and self, and, of course, identity. The articles in this volume explore and put to the test these notions in contemporary and historical configurations.

The concept of extracentrality relates to gender, ethnicity, culture, religion, and species. Recent scholarship has dealt with diverse forms and experiences of excentricity and challenged the bipolarity inherent in the discourse on gender and ethnicity, as it was typically expressed through the juxtaposition of two antithetically defined entities. This has been the case with gender studies, namely, the focus on the categories male and female, in German-Jewish studies, juxtaposing Jews and non-Jews — in both instances, the representations frequently relied on entrenched stereotypes — and the related problems of representation and identity formation. Beyond these more concrete social contexts, the same bipolarity governed the traditional discourses on reality and nonreality, mind and body, human and animal. By examining a variety of diverse texts that focus on difference, it is possible to reassess and transcend the model of one center and one margin suggested by the majority of discourses.

Relevant in this context are the most commonly used and much debated theories of postmodern philosophers (e.g., Jean-François Lyotard,[1] Félix

Guattari, and Gilles Deleuze[2]), who redefine the self, the other, nationhood, and culture in order to reevaluate occidental and oriental traditions. The reflections in which critics such as Edward Said,[3] Homi Bhabha,[4] and Benedict Anderson[5] engage have undermined, and to a large extent invalidated, the binary model and the hierarchical structures it implies. These are at the core of what has been referred to as the Cartesian way of thinking, the colonial eye, and the Age of Enlightenment.[6]

The concept of a minor literature articulated by Deleuze and Guattari was derived from an individual author, Franz Kafka. On the basis of Kafka's diary entries toward the end of December 1911,[7] Deleuze designed a theoretical framework pertaining to minor literatures, that is, literature written in the majority language by a member of a minority. The three constitutional elements characteristic of minor literature are, according to Deleuze, "the deterritorialization of language, the connection of the individual to a political immediacy, and the collective assemblage of enunciation."[8] The bond between the individual and his or her minority group is reflected on the literary level by the frequent discourse about the "community," the "territory" on an exterior scale while referring to the interior scale located within the illusionary self. Thus, the positioning and self-reflective nature of such concepts as the "self" and the "other" take on a much different perspective and notion when they are expressed by so-called outsiders as opposed to so-called insiders. The articles in this volume examine literature that deals with the experience of difference and its various expressions by Jewish, Arab, and women authors, German and Austrian writers who by all appearances are mainstream but nonetheless feel detached from or disenfranchised by the perceived centers of power for a variety of reasons not immediately visible, such as hidden disability or sexual orientation.

Many writers on the "margins," including Gertrud Kolmar, Robert Menasse, Edgar Hilsenrath, Franz Kafka, Claire Goll, and Fanny Lewald, dismantle the traditional dichotomies, since in their opinion, they represent the dominant cultural and linguistic expressions from which they are disenfranchised. Neither did they or their group shape the expression of these experiences in a significant way, nor do the mainstream models describe their experiences within and beyond the literary discourse. Minor writers develop their own paradigms and create their own individual and original metaphors on the basis of their cultural and personal resources, not for the sake of artistic innovation, but more important, with the goal to assert and reterritorialize the sphere of their linguistic imagination as something they create and occupy, as opposed to imitating and duplicating the textual strategies and discourses of the cultural mainstream. The construction and positioning of a literary "I" with its own specific narrative voice does not describe reality in absolute and static terms but rather reflects on the flux and change inherent in a relative and dynamic perspective. Negotiating between different centers, the texts of these authors fluctuate between environments within which different kinds of struggles of domination and subordination take place. They call into question the very existence of one single center, or mainstream. In part, this is a product of each author's own internal reference. Arab-German authors, for example, have at least two, but more likely several, major reference points, including the German language and culture, Arabic and often Muslim culture, the cities of the Middle East, but also, perhaps, the centers of the former colonizers: London, Paris, Istanbul. In addition, women negotiate the gender role expectations implied in the notions ranging from pious daughter to woman of the world to housewife and mother to caregiver to sexual object and agent. Centrality, in other words, is perceived differently by each author or group discussed in this volume, which illustrates constructedness of all positions, those of the supposed mainstream as well as those of the margins.

The examination of these diverse perspectives from which reality is being constructed is one of the most challenging facets in understanding the different components of "minor(ity) literature(s)." In addition to addressing these important issues, the book contains information on less-known works of the many German literatures and contributes to the knowledge in the field of *Germanistik*, German literary and cultural studies, by bringing to light emerging forms and traditions of communication.

While the majority of topics relating to contemporary literary practice are thematically connected to transforming the center and eroding the margins with regard to the transcending and redefined ethnic and cultural boundaries, historical dimensions are discussed as well. Rather than presenting a confined array of synchronous analyses of literary phenomena, authors, or topics, the assumptions underlying are also explored through theoretical considerations and by the interpretation of texts and the examination of broader movements. This approach makes it possible to show that it is possible to investigate the phenomena of alterity and positionality without placing the focus exclusively on the most recent literature. To draw conclusions about the processes of social and cultural diversification and the consciousness changes, it is useful to draw upon a large spectrum of texts and points of view, as is the case here.

Since the Second World War, cultural difference has become an issue of growing cultural importance and concern. This does not imply that in earlier times, none of these issues played a role. They were, however, more successfully contained by effective discourse regulation. The progressive democratization of the first half of this century (notwithstanding the interlude of barbarism in the German-speaking realm during the Nazi era) has made it increasingly impossible in Central Europe to privilege Germany and German culture and to repudiate otherness. In the 1990s, German texts transcending the boundaries of class, ethnicity, gender, country of origin, and traditional literary convention constitute a vast body of literature. The globally conceived German literature is no longer a marginal phenomenon. It has moved to the cutting edge not only because of its volume, but also because of the high intellectual and aesthetic qualities of many of its representative works to which the articles in this volume attest.

Today, it is more generally understood that any national literature despite its apparent unity and distinctive characteristics consists of more layers than those that historically and traditionally had been considered decisive until recently. Walter Benjamin's observations about the historians who always identify with the victor of any given political and cultural battle apply to literary scholars as well.[9] What was once considered a given set of characteristics, of dominating features defining German literature (i.e., its discursive and philosophical nature, the strict formal aspects, the absence of a strong comic tradition versus a dominating trend toward tragic constellations, and its ethnocentric traditions) must now be conceived as the fruits of the labor on the part of literary scholars, critics, historians, and philosophers in the service of a cultural agenda. Now it is their task to examine the foundations of their disciplines and to explore and write about formerly neglected and avoided discourses, which nonetheless are coming to the forefront — not only because they portray valid experiences, but also because they represent one of the most vital parts of the evolving contemporary German culture. Moreover, the articles in this volume show that the new writers and traditions belong into a long tradition of Central European diversity.

Within the framework of this collection of articles are issues and topics pertaining directly to literary texts situated on the "margins" as far as the dialectics of tradition and innovation are concerned. Several sections emphasize certain cultural reflections characteristic of any form of "minor(ity) literature(s)."[10] Referential questions regarding geographic, regional, economic, ethnic, religious, and linguistic margins are addressed in their respective contexts. The different contributors use various methodological approaches, including psychological, biographical, sociological, historical, anthropological, and ethnographic tools as well as close textual and deconstructionist readings within the context of postmodern thinking.

The first two sections of articles focus on perceptions of linguistic, cultural, ethnic, and geographic alterity of literary exile. Implied gender differences and their particular forms of representation as well as their current political implications are addressed in those articles focusing on women's writings.

The first four articles are devoted to one poet, dramatist, and prose writer: Gertrud Kolmar, who with her subtly iconoclastic views, her strong

Jewish and less obviously feminist voice, her expertise in different literary genres, languages, and schools of thought is one of the foremost representatives of the phenomenon of a minor literature in her era, the Weimar Republic and the 1930s under Nazi rule. Kolmar stands at the margins not only as a woman and a victim of Nazism, but as an early spokeswoman for the rights of the disabled and disempowered, women and animals.

Dagmar Lorenz's article on "More Than Metaphors: Animals, Gender, and Jewish Identity in Gertrud Kolmar" explores the interconnectedness of racially motivated violence, the oppression of women, and the abuse of animals as discussed in the works of Kolmar. The problem of killing and the use of animals as food that Judaism has wrestled with for centuries is put into context according to its literary dimensions and illustrations. Lorenz focuses on a comparison between the use and significance of animal imagery in selected works by Gertrud Kolmar as well as Elias Canetti and is able to demonstrate, by analyzing some of the animal motifs, that their use is more literal than metaphorical and that their function is philosophical rather than poetic. One aspect of transformation, as it pertains to classical mythology and Eastern religions, is the metamorphosis from human to animal and vice versa, a mechanism that Kolmar used as a literary device in many of her poems to express her animal advocacy and her identification with animals. Lorenz argues that Kolmar's conviction of this seamless integration of the concepts "man" and "animal" suggests the necessity to reevaluate the binary opposition between the two categories, ultimately calling into question the value hierarchy allowing one race to claim superiority over another.

Stephanie Hammer shows that Kolmar positions herself as a resident of the dark continent of otherness to which Freud relegated the psychology of women. She examines Kolmar's "Bild der Rose," a cycle of twenty poems, within the framework of the feminist philosophy created by Hélène Cixous and applies Cixous's theory of female writing strategies to Kolmar's poetry. Her article "In the Name of the Rose: Gertrud Kolmar, Hélène Cixous, and the Poerotics of Jewish Femininity" focuses on how Cixous and Kolmar offer an alternate understanding both of the Western literary tradition and of traditional heterosexual love as a general concept by calling into question the overarching system of binary values that separates the feminine from the masculine and reduces it. Drawing on lyric comparisons from Goethe to Rilke, Hammer shows that Kolmar redefines the symbol of the rose to fit her rather feminine imagery, entering the tradition and reworking it from within, while she herself represents a part of the complex and rich tradition of Jewish women's writing. Kolmar undercuts, according to Hammer, the oppositional masculine / feminine, aggressive / passive subject–object position implied by the rose trope as used by male poets, rejecting clear-cut identity in favor of a simultaneous blending of borders. She concludes that "Kolmar uses poetry to present continued, embattled attempts to posit alternative statuses for feminine consciousness."

In keeping with the first two articles, which suggest that conceptual and discursive patterns of otherness refer to clusters of ideas rather than being specifically and topically applied in isolation, Sigrid Bauschinger in "Vindication through Suffering: Gertrud Kolmar's Cycle of Poems 'Robespierre'" demonstrates Kolmar's concern for mis- and underrepresented figures in yet another context, that of the French Revolution. In her efforts to revise the established image of the revolutionary, Kolmar sides with the Robespierrists. For Kolmar, Robespierre is the just and pure man, the incorruptible seeker of justice with messianic traits in his struggle for the disenfranchised, while she does not talk about the "great terror" at all, making this aspect of her depiction of Robespierre the most difficult to understand for her critics. Subsequently, Bauschinger offers a close textual reading of the poems and examines the content of Kolmar's "Robespierre" cycle as to its shortcomings and reveals "how contemporary events are reflected in this cycle and how they impact Kolmar's understanding of Robespierre, who seems to be a figure of identification for her." Her identification with Robespierre through her own experience with suffering is, according to Bauschinger, historically connected to the context of the time in which it was composed.

Monika Shafi's article "Reconsidering Gertrud Kolmar through the Cycle 'German Sea'" explores Kolmar's propensity for crossing boundaries by examining the motif of travel. Shafi discusses how the poet blends themes from different cultural spheres and landscape images from different geographical areas. In defiance of the categories of space and time, Kolmar creates a subjective realm according to which individual perception and desire are the foremost forces. Shafi furthermore contends that Kolmar creates a new genre of travel literature by adapting "what is essentially a prose genre to a lyrical form." Indeed, a transgression against the radical view on ethnicity and race is already implied by the title "German Sea," meaning the Baltic Sea, which turns out to be anything but purely German but functions as a site of intercultural contacts. Kolmar's sense of Germanness is expansive, inclusive, and dynamic. Moreover, Kolmar imbues the politicized term "German" with intimate emotions and love motifs, which, in conjunction with the sea and water images, create an overall impression of fluidity in opposition to the static character of public discourse. It is precisely the creation of such a feminine space that is making Kolmar's work accessible to feminist critics, as Shafi notes.

The second group of articles is devoted to exile and contemporary relations. It reveals that similar motifs and topics are addressed in the works of women writers in exile. Implied gender differences and their particular forms of representation as well as their current political implications are addressed in the two articles focusing on women's writings.

Focusing on the situation of "Women in Exile," Beate Schmeichel-Falkenberg explores gender-specific aspects of exile as they shaped the experiences and writings of German and Austrian women who faced Nazi persecution during the 1930s and forties. She comments on first results of the research on emigrant women presented at the annual conference "Women in Exile." The multiple roles of women, their contributions to cultural life, and their ingenious survival strategies have become the topic of discussion. Some of Schmeichel-Falkenberg's observations point to women's flexibility in leaving their homeland, in adapting to unfamiliar conditions, and often in securing the family income. Bogged down by their responsibilities for others, only some of them were able to continue their writing. But even then, it was difficult for women writers to get published, a fact Schmeichel-Falkenberg exemplifies by analyzing the careers of Else Lasker-Schüler, Anna Seghers, Nelly Sachs, and Rose Ausländer.

One such case study of a woman writer's situation in exile, attempting to secure a home away from home, is included in Renate Posthofen's article entitled "Claire Goll (1891–1977): Visionary Power and Creative Symbiosis — Fictionalized Identity as Survival Strategy." The German-Jewish writer Claire Goll published her first poems and short prose pieces between 1917 and 1919 and was well on her way to establishing a promising career. In 1939, at the onset of the Second World War, she fled to New York, where she worked as a journalist for several newspapers and magazines. At the same time, she continued to pursue her own independent literary career. Posthofen focuses on the details of Claire Goll's life experience in exile and how it manifests itself and the search for an identity in her literary works. As particular examples of exile as a specific topic in her writings of that time, Posthofen discusses two of her stories in depth to demonstrate the extent to which the experiences of being removed from a sheltered environment and homeland dominate Goll's search for a multicultural identity and function as a strategy for survival for herself. Similar to Kolmar's perspectives, the two stories "Chinesische Wäscherei" and "Die Reise nach Italien," written in 1940 and 1942 respectively, reveal Goll's enormous empathy and advocacy for those with whom she was able to identify the best in her own situation at the time: the poor and the despised, the disenfranchised border figures of society, those who even in exile cannot make it.

The next section centers on the theme "Transcending Ethnicity and Cultural Boundaries: History and Culture." It includes historically based studies of pre–twentieth century minor literature and related problems: the transformation of individual and group identity through language and cultural interchange.

Robert Fuhrmann's article "Masculine Form / Feminine Writing: The Autobiography of Fanny Lewald" focuses on the concept of women's autobiography. He traces the history of the genre of autobiography and examines Lewald's work in the light of earlier texts. Fanny Lewald, converted from Judaism, entered the literary mainstream and became a bestseller author. Fuhrmann addresses the significance of a woman's "self-writing" as a form of self-representation. Fuhrmann reassesses earlier studies on the genre, namely, that women's autobiography represents a tradition, or a genre or subgenre, distinct from men's autobiographies. In his article, he points out several factors other than gender that are often overlooked by feminist critics. According to Fuhrmann, most early-nineteenth-century English Quaker autobiographies were virtually genderless. Moreover, he explains, Lewald used Goethe's *Dichtung und Wahrheit* as a model for presenting her life story. As a result, Fuhrmann writes, Lewald's autobiography reads like an account of various roles in search for a self. Critical reading, he suggests, has to proceed not from considerations of gender, but of genre.

Neva Šlibar writes about "Traveling, Living, Writing from and at the Margins: Alma Maximiliana Karlin and Her Geobiographical Books." Only recently has the world traveler, journalist, and writer Alma Karlin entered the collective memory through the increased interest in women's writing, particularly autobiographical writing. Šlibar traces multiple forms of marginality manifest in Karlin's life, travels, and books. She also stresses that there is a basic ambivalence underlying Karlin's writings, for instance, a surprising compliance with colonial discourse, mostly composed in German. Karlin's tendency to conform to mainstream expectations seem incongruent with her marginality. In her focus on Karlin's geobiographical books, Šlibar emphasizes the traveler's search for one's self and the exploration of foreign territory, the intertwining of biography and travel descriptions, resulting in the drive of the traveler to reach the other, the unknown, realized through the experience of space and movement.

The case studies about Lewald and Karlin reveal the interaction and intersection of different discursive and cultural traditions. This is also the case in Alan Levenson's article "The Apostate as Philosemite: Selig Paulus Cassel (1821–1892) and Edith Stein (1891–1942)." Levenson examines the lives of two Jewish apostates whose lives were fraught with the paradox typical of the German-Jewish experience. On the basis of these cases, Levenson discusses Jewish identity in Germany and the modern world. Having turned his back upon the synagogue, Cassel, baptized in 1855, led the Ministry of Christ Church in Berlin. He became a Protestant missionary and converted thousands of Jews to Protestantism, the dominant denomination in Imperial Germany. However, Levenson traces a theological residuum of Jewish identity: He explains that Cassel's millenarian desire to convert Jews was driven by the fear of universal secularism, not by fears of Judaization. Stein, a highly educated middle-class woman, on the other hand, was alienated from Judaism and Jewish life. Her conversion to Roman Catholicism in 1922 provided a spiritual outlet and connected her anew with the Jewish people. Deeply religious, she entered the Carmelite Order in 1933. In 1942, she was deported and murdered, dying in her own mind a willing martyr for the Jewish people.

Dagmar Lorenz's article "History, Identity, and the Body in Edgar Hilsenrath's *The Story of the Last Thought*" examines ways in which a Jewish Holocaust survivor reassesses humanism and spirituality against the backdrop of current animal rights philosophies, notably the Australian philosopher Peter Singer, who, like Hilsenrath, denounces a value system that elevates the heterosexual Christian human male to the most privileged position in the universe. By positioning his protagonists as other, as Jew, woman, and animal, Hilsenrath questions the Western hierarchy and assigns agency to those who have no voice. Lorenz discusses Hilsenrath's fantastic-historical novel *The Story of the Last Thought* foregrounding the author's body-centered concept of writing and his characters' physicalness, which shows the body as the target of the psychosexual aggression involved in genocide and warfare. It is the body, the outward manifestation of man's animal nature, that becomes the site of brutality. *The Story of the Last Thought* portrays persecution, exile, and the loss of cultural identity in a seemingly straightforward manner, which itself is directed against the abstractness of colonial and genocidal discourse.

Pre- and post-Shoah reality and the understanding of culture are likewise the issues in Deborah Viëtor-Engländer's comparative study of two important feuilletonistic writers. In "Alfred Kerr and Marcel Reich-Ranicki: Critics and Power in Germany in the Weimar Republic and the Federal Republic," she traces the careers of two prominent critics, one of the prewar, the other of the postwar era. Kerr was one of the most powerful of the Weimar Republic. Only after being forced into exile in 1933 did he become noticeably aware of his Jewish identity. Until then, he had viewed himself as a spokesman of German culture, viewing criticism as an art form in its own right. In contemporary Germany, Reich-Ranicki, who was born in Poland in 1920, plays a role similar to that of Kerr, being the foremost literary critic of the Federal Republic of Germany. Yet, Reich-Ranicki does not assume the status of a cultural institution, nor does he avoid subjective judgments. In contrast to Kerr, he considers criticism an auxiliary medium and believes that the critic's function is to serve literature.

The following group of articles is devoted to the theme of "Transforming the Center, Eroding the Margins." The articles in this section deal mostly with identity in terms of nationality, ethnicity, and gender, examining the diminishing differences between these categories while closely analyzing and relativizing the dominating traditional models per se.

Bernd Fischer's article "The Memory of Multiculturalism and the Politics of Identity" recaptures the debate about multiculturalism and cultural identity in the United States with reference to trends in literary criticism. He asserts that multiculturalist identity politics have circumvented the crucial problem of defining culture in an inclusive rather than exclusive manner. He questions in particular models that equate culture with ethnicity and, by defining ethnicity along the lines of racial categories, reproduce racism. Fischer suggests that to counteract the compartmentalization of constitutional democracies, one ought to reevaluate history, cultural conformity, ethnicity, and race and to remain receptive to modernism's central endeavors: the creation of a constitutional republic. According to Fischer, multiculturalism cannot succeed as a theoretical model for a pluralist society if it rejects the Enlightenment and modernist concept of the multicultural individual, the cosmopolitan citizen.

Taking contemporary Viennese Jewish culture as a case in point, Matti Bunzl examines post-Shoah identity constructs in his article "Counter-Memory and Modes of Resistance: The Uses of Fin-de-Siècle Vienna for Present-Day Austrian Jews." In a discourse-oriented anthropological approach, Bunzl investigates the representational dimensions of the past and reveals the functions and uses of oppositional modes of memory. In his discussion of the sociodiscursive dimensions of everyday life, Bunzl shows how present-day Austrian Jews can construct a counter-memory based on Vienna's fin-de-siècle literature. According to Bunzl, in the area of Austrian-Jewish relations since 1945 ruptured historical continuities have provided contemporary Austrian Jews the potential to sustain an affirmative sense of ethnic self in an anti-Semitic environment. On the basis of his interviews with young Viennese Jews, Bunzl analyzes the components of present-day Viennese-Jewish identity configurations with Vienna's urban and social space as their central site. Austria's metropolitan cultural landscape can sustain Jewish life. Institutions such as the *Kaffeehaus* offer continuities to young Jews, and narratives and geographic linkages keep cultural traditions alive.

The situation of minor studies and perspectives in academia are explored in Neil Jacobs's and Dagmar Lorenz's article "If I Were King of the Jews: *Germanistik* and the *Judaistikfrage*," which deals with the representation of Jewish studies within the field of German literary, cultural, and linguistic studies. In a historical continuum, the emergence of certain phenomena in Jewish culture is contextualized with non-Jewish movements, for instance, the Enlightenment and its Jewish counterpart, the *Haskole,* or *Haskalah.* Lorenz and Jacobs argue that Jewish-internal dynamics triggered counter-movements and developments as much as, if not more so than, emerging trends in the Christian sphere, religious or secular. An overview over Jewish, Yiddish, and Ashkenazic studies makes major paradigms transparent that have shaped the Jewish discourses on Jewish phenomena as opposed to the views derived from the Gentile perspective. In addition, the authors address to which — marginal — extent "Jewish concerns" were represented by Gentile academics. Overall, the study analyzes the representation of Jewish culture from the point of view of Gentile literature and scholarship by ostensibly neutral or even well-intentioned authors, some of whom use Jewish themes and characters to their own ends. Ultimately, Lorenz and Jacobs call for a more balanced and leveled exchange and approach between the fields of Jewish, Yiddish, Ashkenazic, and German studies so that it is possible for *Germanistik* to avail itself and profit from the insights and perspectives of its sister disciplines.

Renate Posthofen's investigation "Of Inclusions and Exclusions: Austrian Identity Reconsidered" examines the shifting paradigms indicating the formation of a "New Europe" at the turn of yet another century while specifically considering the present situation in Austria. Posthofen explores public representations of the Austrian nation in its historical and current context as it reflects cultural self-understanding, and she presents an analysis of a fictional text, Robert Menasse's novel *Schubumkehr*, with an eye toward the fictional representation of contemporary Austria from a "minor" and a "major" point of view. With the recent publicity Austria's image has received in conjunction with joining the European Union in 1995, its fiftieth anniversary of the liberation from National Socialist rule, the fortieth anniversary of the signing of the Austrian State Treaty in 1955, and the celebration of the Austrian millennium in 1996, Austria's national identity has also been called into question. The myth of the small and vulnerable country, pronounced innocent of its war crimes because it had fallen victim to the powerful Nazis, appears now largely constructed. Menasse, one of Austria's most prominent critics and analysts of current cultural affairs, takes up these issues in his novel *Schubumkehr*. The events in the novel take place in Bohemia and are centered around a protagonist of Austrian-Jewish descent whose dysfunctional presence and existence as a marginalized intellectual in 1989, ultimately unsuccessful to exist in the small Austrian town, leads to his final departure. With his text, which presents a fictional microcosm closely modeled after current events in Austria, Menasse advocates a critical examination of xenophobic trends and anti-Semitic tendencies while pleading for a more open and inclusive attitude toward multicultural and marginal perspectives in contemporary Austria.

Peter Arnds's focus rests on another novel by the same author. In "The Fragmentation of Totality in Robert Menasse's *Selige Zeiten, brüchige Welt*," Arnds argues that Menasse's work transcends strictly delineated cultural and chronological barriers because it uses a great variety of intertextual references. Of the novel's subtexts, he discusses primarily those that refer to historical

biographies, literary and philosophical texts, film, art and generic components, showing that Menasse creates a transcultural and intertextual work
while at the same time fragmenting his fictional world. According to Arnds,
Menasse deconstructs the categories of the realist Bildungsroman on a fictional level, but by the novel's sinister conclusion, he demonstrates the profound fragmentation of the modern individual and his / her world. Menasse
has lived in Austria and Brazil. In his novel, he succeeds in describing these
vastly different cultures, thereby eroding the narrow cultural margins of his
readers by exposing them to Brazil.

A similarly radical cultural difference is overcome by the authors discussed
by Iman Khalil, who addresses concerns and misperceptions about migrant
authors in Germany. Her article "From the Margins to the Center: Arab-
German Authors and Issues" focuses on Arab-German authors originating
from several different Arab countries. These authors portray different regions
of the Arab Orient and speak in the voices of minorities to the majority in
their host country. Khalil writes that Arab-German authors refute the misperceptions concerning the Arab world and challenge clichés they face in the
West. Still, they encounter discriminatory attitudes, which they counter by
portraying the diversity of Arab life, and they challenge the notion that the
Arab world and the Arab peoples are homogeneous. Arab-German authors
discuss cultural codes, local customs, popular beliefs, and superstitions that
shape everyday life in Arab societies, compelling their readers to consider
non-Western perspectives from the viewpoint of oriental protagonists,
thereby engaging the German reader in questioning the traditional division
between the Orient and the Occident, which is perpetuated by the notion of
Western supremacy. Khalil underscores the great intellectual and aesthetic
potential of these texts and calls for their serious treatment by scholars.

Peter Werres undertakes the daunting task of examining the literary scene
in Germany since reunification. According to him, contemporary German
culture faces the end of the age of reading. His article entitled "National
Identity under Siege: Postwall Writing in Germany?" combines the question
of cultural diversity with a discussion of literary genre, including forms of
popular culture. This approach allows him to discuss the challenges to traditional concepts of national identity while considering their impact on
emerging literary trends. Werres observes that German reunification did not
yield a unifying theme but rather seems to have precipitated the loss of consensus. Regionalism is, according to him, the primary new force in popular
culture, and he observes that artists increasingly rely on regional dialects.
More and more, popular culture genres and fringe genres carry the messages
of the margins, of disadvantaged and dispossessed groups. Werres considers
the current situation of German writing the reflection of the most significant
German identity crisis since 1945. In view of violent public controversies,

Werres believes that there is a need to develop new community paradigms and to redefine the cultural center and the margins.

The final group of articles deals with configurations of tradition and innovation, and examines the mystical and the uncanny as challenge and dissent. The focal point is the interplay between esoteric and exoteric modes of perception and representation, past and present. Whether in the works of conservative or revolutionary authors, the concept of reality has been repeatedly challenged in an attempt to gain a deeper understanding of the human condition within and beyond the limits of human understanding.

Gernot Weiß explores perceptions of "The Foreign and the Own: Polylingual Literature and the Problem of Identity." He begins by investigating the concept of polylingual literature in an attempt to establish the connection drawn between language and identity. Then he proceeds to analyze the concept of polylingualism and the aesthetic views on polylingual texts by nineteenth- and twentieth-century scholars. Finally, he focuses on Tristan Tzara and Hugo Ball to show how these authors apply polylingualism to propose alternative concepts of identity contrary to the dominant nineteenth-century views. With Zurich Dadaism as his example, Weiß notes that blending languages implied doing something self-contradictory that indicated for the mainstream a schism within identity. The authors in question followed Henri Bergson, whose philosophy proposed a new concept of identity in opposition to any hierarchy of human perception. According to Weiß, Ball's practice of using words that carry meaning in more than one language, his incorporation of shamanism and magic in his search for a language of original purity, and his use of trance and mystical experiences in his poetry recitals ultimately constitute an attempt to show the hidden unity of the human tongue — "a unity never touched by questions of ethnic or individual identity."

In his article entitled "I Say Coffee, You Say Inkwell: Normalizing the Abnormal in Kafka's *The Castle*," Michael Bryant challenges traditional theological interpretations by Kafka scholars such as Max Brod and Thomas Mann, who impose figurative readings to texts such as *The Castle*. According to Bryant, both the theological and more recent Marxist interpretations share a common emphasis on the symbolic character of the novel. He argues all of these attempts are premised on a tropological reading of *The Castle*: "Whether it is God, repressive bourgeois authority, or an archaic hierarchy that has outlived its time, the castle is a sign referring to something other than itself." Bryant, in contrast, contends that the castle is precisely what it is, no more and no less. Developing his arguments along the lines of Wolfgang Iser's theories, Bryant points to the fact that the reader strives for closure at the end of a literary work. Basing his conclusions on a concrete reading of *The Castle*, Bryant demonstrates that and in which way *The Castle* is a work

that resists the implied reader, and he points to the lack of extratextual refer-
ents. According to Bryant, Kafka did not resort to mysticism in order to resolve his own ambivalences, in contrast to many of his contemporaries —
Schönberg, Kandinsky, Strindberg, Kubin, Meyrink, and Brod — who tried
to overcome the fragmentation of modern life by turning to the occult
teachings of Theosophy, Anthroposophy, parapsychology, alchemy, and
Eastern mysticism. In Bryant's view, it is this very position that shielded
Kafka against any propensity for Nazi radicalism.

Finally, Dagmar Lorenz's article entitled "Transcending the Boundaries
of Space and Culture: The Figures of the Maharal and the Golem after the
Shoah: Friedrich Torberg's *Golems Wiederkehr*, Leo Perutz's *Nachts unter
der steinernen Brücke*, Frank Zwillinger's *Maharal*, and Nelly Sachs's *Eli. Ein
Mysterienspiel vom Leiden Israels*" is concerned with the exchange and modi-
fication of literary and historical themes across cultural borders. Lorenz looks
at figures of the Maharal (Rabbi Loew) and the Golem, both of which played
an important role in Christian literature as well as in Jewish folk traditions
and mysticism. Moreover, these motifs also mirror changes in Central European Jewish culture, including that of Prague, to which these figures are tied.
Lorenz traces the transformation of the Maharal and the Golem from the
medieval tradition, the widely popularized versions of the fin de siècle, an era
receptive to modern and medieval ideas alike, to the post-Shoah era. Lorenz
argues that figures such as the Golem have traditionally provided discursive
models for diverse ideological positions, pro-Jewish and anti-Semitic. Gustav
Meyrink's fantastic novel *Der Golem* and several Golem versions of the interwar and postwar era serve as examples. With her focus on the texts of Torberg, Perutz, Zwillinger, and Sachs, authors of Jewish descent, Lorenz argues that post-Shoah authors reconfigured the Maharal, the Golem, and
Emperor Rudolph II into paradigms of the destroyed Jewish culture. There
are marked differences between the Golem and Maharal representations prior
to the Holocaust and thereafter. However, the Holocaust did not produce a
unified literary expression. Rather, the works by different authors discussing
the Shoah and its aftermath portray the destruction from different points of
view.

The articles in this volume reveal an intricate network of textual inter-
plays, including those between authors and critics, and authors past, present,
and future. Of these diverse forces, the text, read and interpreted, remains
the key element. In the framework of this volume, works of literature are examined in their function as multiple referential systems and in view of their
cultural contexts. The most frequently asked questions include the role of individual memory and cultural memory, the relationship between individual
and society — how do they correlate with issues such as identity formation,
and how does a "minor" literary voice make itself heard, considering its diffi-

culties of establishing itself in the larger societal context? Likewise important is the relationship to the past, the individual or collective past, depending on the author's point of view, in light of a prolonged collective memory.

Examinations of selected literary themes and visual images pertain to this issue. Some of them attest to the postmodern perplexity and the inability to affirm and implement conventional modes. Here one may think of protagonists characterized as being in constant motion, traveling to distant locations — Brazil, the Orient, the United States — fundamentally homeless characters in a fragmented world. These questions point to new directions and modes that have emerged in contemporary literary criticism as well as other seemingly unrelated disciplines such as ethology and anthropology. They address the need of expanding interdisciplinary scholarship able to analyze the conditions that link late modern and postmodern concepts to their origins in the Age of Enlightenment and beyond. Moreover, the broad range of literary and cultural trends that are investigated in the context of German literature clearly convey that different intellectual paradigms and research methods are needed to deal with the wealth of new forms, voices, and positions.

With the millennium approaching, we may find the conditions for a complete reorientation. In retrospect, the succession of issues and developments of the past decades in the course of which time-honored concepts were questioned and dismantled — of course not without reactions and backlashes — appear almost like preparatory steps for greater change.

The civil rights and the women's movements brought the issue of identity, configured in terms of race, ethnicity, and sexuality, into the foreground of the political and eventual academic debates and influenced significantly the literature and films of the respective eras, the 1960s and the 1970s. In the German-speaking countries — East and West Germany, Austria, and Switzerland — debates similar to those in the United States were taken up, albeit under different auspices, with different issues, and for different reasons.

Since the 1960s, the domestic and international problems of the most powerful of the Second World War allies, the United States, were covered in depth and with a certain glee by the German and Austrian media. West Germans and Austrians who refused to deal with the Nazi past experienced media coverage of the problems — the Vietnam War, race riots, and the economic and class-related inequities — regarding the victor nation as a respite from the *Vergangenheitsbewältigung,* which they had been called upon to undertake since the end of the war. The obvious shortcomings within the United States, which had assumed an international leadership role in the Western bloc in military, economic, and moral terms, for instance during the trial at Nuremberg, were used as a subterfuge to downplay the crimes of the German military and civilian institutions during the Nazi era. As far as the

German Democratic Republic was concerned, the problems faced by the United States added fuel to the Cold War.

Partly as a result of the European revolutionary movements of the late 1960s, of which the German student movement was a part (the riots at the German universities coincided roughly with the American anti-Vietnam protests, the Hippie movement, and the 1967 "Summer of Love"), the events of the Second World War, Germany's Nazi past, and the Nazi legacy in the postwar republics became the focus of attention for the student generation in West Germany. Informed by the Frankfurt School, critical debates centered on class issues and power in economical and ideological terms. Only later, in a reaction to the male-dominated revolutionary scene, did women assert themselves and protested against the patriarchal structures that the leftist dissenters had left largely unquestioned. Young Jewish intellectuals began to distance themselves from the Marxist movement, with which many of them had sympathized or in which they had taken part early on.

There are parallels and, of course, differences between the debates of the civil rights and anti-Vietnam movements in the United States, and the way in which European students and feminists expressed their discontent with their countries' social and political structures. In both cases, however, camps of insiders and outsiders were defined by the use of terms such as "establishment," "APO" (außerparlamentarische Opposition=extraparliamentary opposition), "antiauthoritarian," and "antipatriarchal." New terminologies came into existence, describing the phenomena of being a part of or taking a position outside of what came to be referred to as the mainstream, for example *Aussteiger*, someone who gets out. In Germany and later in Austria, a new Jewish literature emerged, written by Jews "in" Germany or Austria, the qualifier "in" underscoring the separateness of the writers from the assumed majority culture of Germans or Austrians. Around the same time, the German-speaking public became aware of the fact that the foreign workers from Mediterranean countries (they had been coming to the Federal Republic since the 1950s) and their children would remain in their countries of employment, which had become their countries of residence. It had proven impossible to carry out the earlier plan of limiting their stay to the duration of their contracts and have them return to their countries of origin thereafter. In addition, growing numbers of persons seeking asylum from persecution entered German-speaking countries, some settled permanently. Central Europe was developing into an increasingly and obviously multicultural, multiethnic area.

None of these developments, the mobility of groups and populations worldwide, the influx of people from so-called underdeveloped or Third-World nations into technologically and industrially more advanced countries was unique to the German-speaking sphere. Yet, wherever these develop-

ments occurred, they were contextualized internally and externally in different ways, in post-Shoah Germany and Austria with Nazi history and the Holocaust as the background. In addition, these processes were analyzed and discussed in light of international debates and from the point of view of different perspectives and methodologies, including Critical Theory, sociology, psychoanalysis, deconstructionism, feminism, comparative studies, diverse theories on multiculturalism, and interdisciplinarity. Some of these approaches were designed to create group affinities in opposition to the traditional focus on the individual and individual identity. The latter had been prevalent during the postwar era, inspired by Existentialism and the skepticism toward collectivism the recent past had fostered. Counterbalanced by Marxism during the cold war era until the collapse of the Eastern bloc, ethnic, national, and gender identity concepts dominated the discourse in the early 1990s. However, since the fall of the Berlin wall and the demise of the Eastern bloc, leftist theories have come under attack, as the great victorious ally in the East was discredited as had been the case with the United States earlier, although by far to a smaller extent. Some of the identity and reality models and constructs are addressed in the anthology at hand: Jewish identity and literature in German-speaking countries, Arab-German writing, alongside cultural debates regarding, for example, the separateness of Austrian culture within the German language sphere, as well as the identity formation caused by particular historical experiences such as those of exile and surviving the Holocaust.

The concepts of center and margin, center and periphery, insider and outsider, presuppose the existence of at least two definable entities and two distinct groups. Considering the degree of multiculturalism in German "culture," the question arises as to who represents the "center," or even "the center of power," as Klaus Theweleit confidently put it when he began his gigantic enterprise entitled *Buch der Könige* (1988, "Book of Kings").[11] Or, at least in the case of culture and literature, the question may be reformulated to read: Who is a mainstream author and of which mainstream? In addition to being associated with German-speaking culture, many authors writing in German are connected with and write in reference to one or more other cultures and languages. In the case of a Jewish writer, additional implied reference languages can be many: Hebrew, Russian, English, French, Bulgarian, as is the case with a multilingual author such as Elias Canetti. Issues of class or, more important even, of gender will play a role as well so that ultimately not only the concept of a more or less static center but also that of a homogeneous margin becomes untenable.

Furthermore, the articles in this anthology reveal that there is nothing new about multiculturalism and cultures in contact except the current terminology and focus. European men and women have sought to explore other countries through travel and interacted — successfully or unsuccessfully, with more or less prejudice — with individuals outside of their cultural sphere of origin, and they have communicated the process and the results of these contacts to their society. Likewise the categories of gender as they relate to status, power, and economy: They have been, and continue to be, the fundamental elements of the Judeo-Christian-Islamic discourse and are basic to Central European thought and practice.

Notwithstanding differences from case to case, the notion of cultural and ethnic cohesion does not hold: Except in the imagination of Nazis or other chauvinists, the German-speaking countries of Central Europe never constituted a homogeneous population in linguistic, intellectual, or cultural terms, nor was the Jewish minority the only minority (although it was for ideological reasons the most visible and most discussed). It would be equally difficult to point to any specific group that at any point represented "the center." Instead, the discussions of writers, travelers, exiles, emigrants and immigrants, men and women reveal a multitude of internal and external reference points, some of which individual writers affirm, some of which they reject or ignore. Overall, the study of literary and cultural texts reveals the fluidity of various positions and, as a consequence, reveals notions of identity, regardless of how they are designed, to be synthetic.

At this point, it is a fact that even the most "elemental" concepts and organizing principles such as sex, gender, and species, whose actual existence is increasingly questioned, are functions in a complex network of meanings and constellations. Not a single element can be isolated from the whole and identified on its own terms. Rather than asking about the nature of center and margin, it would be more productive to ask about the function of these terms and the effects of their widespread acceptance. Rather than trying to define the relationship between an author and his or her protagonists vis-à-vis the cultural mainstream or his or her respective margins (these would differ from case to case), it might be more useful to examine the motivation and the effects of assigning this relationship in this particular way. On the surface, this is a more modest, less concrete approach, which might prove more realistic nonetheless, because it could help to remove the limitations imposed on the way in which we Westerners process our perceptions and consolidate them into our respective view of reality.

The established binary patterns, most of them oppositional, are also expressed in terms of margin and center, both of which ultimately represent nothing more than a variation on the more basic pair of self and other, which is also played out as male and female, German and Jew, citizen and noncitizen, native and foreigner, white and black, human and animal. This binarism is also reflected in the function of the familiar vis-à-vis the unfamiliar, of the foreign and that which is one's own — the former is rejected, the latter loved in most cases. Involved in all of these instances are issues of power, domination, attachment, and aversion.

Reifying these reactions and attitudes, consolidating them into static concepts, creates fronts, not only rhetorically but also in terms of actions and behavior. Literature relying on stereotypes is not only bad literature, it is unimaginative, because it closes paths toward a greater world openness. It is damaging because it distorts the human experience. Aware of the limitations of language, which comes replete with an armory of stock phrases, characters, residues of older and more recent attitudes and texts, writers have made attempts to transcend in their works the confining cultural material their immediate environment has offered them: They have created imaginary creatures and made them their protagonists, and working with the limitless possibilities of the mind, they disregarded the categories of space and time. They chose the path of language mystics or prophets, the dialogue with legendary figures and voices of the dead whom they invited to assume a supratemporal function in their works. Although specific to certain cultures, Jewish and Christian motifs have moved between the cultures and times because a part of the reality language is capable to contain, reproduce, and modify.

Experience is for the most part communicated and mediated through language and images. Whether biographical or imagined, transmitted by a person or writing, it affects the recipient and establishes connections, more or less profound, more or less lasting. Communication represents a constant attack on identities and solidified fronts, and it requires of those involved in the process to revise their positions, deliberately or intuitively. Although on the macrolevel it may seem that communication involves the masses, even entire populations, the ultimate recipient is the individual, elusive, ever changing, both in the physical makeup and his or her responses. The articles in this anthology are devoted, for the most part, to individual authors or groups of individual authors with certain comparable experiences. Yet, the fascinating thing about them is not their sameness, but rather their multiplicity, the difference between them and their paths although some of them lived at the same time and in the same place. The smallest site of the conflict of center and margin is the individual in its loneliness and its connectedness.

With their particular experiences of marginality as well as their endurance, the authors discussed have created lines of communication through which others participate in their memories and visions, and through which they open themselves up to new impulses and intellectual avenues.

Notes

[1] Jean-François Lyotard, *Das postmoderne Wissen* (Vienna: Edition Passagen, 1993).

[2] Gilles Deleuze and Félix Guattari, "What Is Philosophy?" in *The Deleuze Reader*, ed. Constantine V. Boundas (New York: Columbia UP, 1994).

[3] Edward Said, *Orientalism* (New York: Vintage Books / Random House, 1994) and *Kultur und Materialismus. Einbildungskraft und Politik im Zeitalter der Macht* (Frankfurt am Main: Fischer, 1994).

[4] Homi K. Bhabha, *The Location of Culture* (London: Routledge, 1995); Homi K. Bhabha, ed., *Nation and Narration* (London: Routledge, 1994).

[5] Benedict Anderson, *Imagined Communities* (London: Verso, 1991).

[6] Theodor W. Adorno, *Notes to Literature*, vol. 2., trans. S. W. Nicholson (New York: Columbia UP, 1992); Max Horkheimer and Theodor W. Adorno, *Die Dialektik der Aufklärung* (Frankfurt am Main: Fischer, 1982).

[7] Gilles Deleuze, "Minor Literature: Kafka," in *The Deleuze Reader*, ed. Constantine V. Boundas (New York: Columbia UP, 1993), 152–64.

[8] Ibid., 154.

[9] Walter Benjamin, "Über den Begriff der Geschichte," in *Gesammelte Schriften*, ed. Rolf Tiedemann and Hermann S. Schwepphäuser (Frankfurt am Main: Suhrkamp, 1974), 693–704.

[10] Lawrence W. Levine, *Highbrow Lowbrow: The Emergence of Cultural Hierarchy in America* (Cambridge: Harvard UP, 1990).

[11] Klaus Theweleit, *Orpheus und Eurydike* , vol. 1 of *Buch der Könige* (Basel: Stroemfeld / Roter Stern, 1988).

DAGMAR C. G. LORENZ

More Than Metaphors:
Animals, Gender, and
Jewish Identity in Gertrud Kolmar

D URING AN INTERVIEW ON THE Dick Cavett Show, Isaac B. Singer, an
avowed vegetarian, dismissed the show host's suggestion that a chicken
feast might be an appropriate way to celebrate his 1978 Nobel Prize, because
such a meal might benefit him, but hardly the chicken. In all likelihood, this
statement was taken less seriously than the laureate intended. Singer's vegetarianism must be viewed as a reaction to the fact that meat consumption requires killing.

Judaism has wrestled with the problem of killing for centuries, as is evident from the various regulations concerning ritual slaughter. The *shoykhet* is
allowed only one attempt at cutting the animal's throat. If he fails, the animal
lives. Other examples are the separation of *milkhik* and *fleyshik* food in kosher
households, bringing constantly to mind the origins of the food and the laws
regulating food processing. The origin of the meat and the fact that an animal was killed to provide it must not be obscured. Singer's refusal to associate himself with the process of killing and to use animals as food represent
the logical conclusion to an ethical dilemma central to his culture.

Another Jewish Nobel Prize winner, Elias Canetti, placed killing and
eating into the context of power, mass-murder, survival, and the psychology
of the paranoid leader. In his treatise *Masse und Macht* (1960, "Crowds and
Power"), he established the connection between oppression and ingesting.
He writes:

> Wer über Menschen herrschen will, sucht sie zu erniedrigen; ihren Wider-
> stand und ihre Rechte ihnen abzulisten, bis sie ohnmächtig vor ihm sind wie
> Tiere. Als Tiere verwendet er sie; wenn er es ihnen auch nicht sagt, *in sich*
> hat er immer Klarheit darüber, wie wenig sie ihm bedeuten; seinen Vertrau-
> ten gegenüber wird sie als Schafe oder Vieh bezeichnet. Sein letztes Ziel ist
> immer, sie sich "einzuverleiben" und auszusaugen. Es ist ihm gleichgültig,
> was von ihnen übrigbleibt.[1]

Rather than distinguishing between human beings and animals, Canetti differentiates between beings who exploit and dominate others, and those who do not. A large number of his epigrams in his *Aufzeichnungen* (1993, "Notebooks"), particularly "Das Geheimherz der Uhr" (1982, translated and published as *The Secret Heart of the Clock*, 1989), suggest that the traditional differentiation between man and animal is unproductive, for example, in the following aphorism with its peculiar use of the term "friend": "Du hast unter Tieren nicht einen einzigen Freund. Nennst du das Leben?"[2] Similar statements about animals pervade Canetti's entire œuvre, beginning with the chapter "Ein Irrenhaus" in his novel *Die Blendung* (1935, translated as *Auto-da-Fé*, 1946), whose protagonist is a human male trying to transform himself into a gorilla who physically and emotionally interacts with human beings.[3] This creature is reminiscent of Franz Kafka's protagonist in "Ein Bericht für eine Akademie," an ape aspiring to be like a human being, a scholar, whereas in Canetti the opposite is the case.[4]

Critical studies tend to steer clear of Canetti's statements about animals, or they focus on their metaphoric character, although most of these passages leave little room for elaborate literary interpretations. At a loss as to how to read them, most critics reacted with embarrassed silence or superficial commentaries. Richard Lawson, for example, observes: "Repeatedly Canetti condemns human cruelty to animals."[5] This rather innocuous explanation fails to come to terms with statements that demand love and intimacy between human beings and animals, for instance, in Canetti's lament of 1982: "Kein Tier habe ich umarmt. Ein ganzes Leben habe ich mit qualvollen Erbarmen an Tiere gedacht, aber kein Tier habe ich umarmt."[6]

Gertrud Kolmar's animal imagery, the animal advocacy expressed in her animal poems, and her identification with animals are no less amazing than those in Canetti's texts. Indeed, they reveal a kindred spirit. Both authors shared a similar background — that of the educated European Jewish middle class — and belonged to the same generation. Kolmar was born in 1894, Canetti in 1905 — which may in part explain the similarities of their views concerning this central aspect of their works. Moreover, both of their lives were profoundly affected by National Socialism. Kolmar remained in Berlin after Hitler's rise to power and was subsequently deported and murdered in Auschwitz in 1943. Canetti left Vienna after the annexation of Austria and went into exile in London. In 1994, he died and was buried in Zurich, the exile city of Kolmar's sister Hilde Wenzel. A brief analysis of some of the animal motifs in Kolmar's *Susanna* (first published posthumously in 1959)[7] and selected poems of *Die Frau und die Tiere* (1938, "The Woman and the Animals"), a collection that appeared only briefly in 1938, shows (1) that the meaning of the animal images is more literal than metaphorical and (2) that their function is philosophical rather than poetic. A comparison between the use and significance of animal imagery in Kolmar's and Canetti's works will test the range and meaning of these themes.

"Du weißt viel von den Tieren, Susanna," says the governess, one of the protagonists in the novella *Susanna,* to the young woman under her care, whereupon Susanna replies: "Ich bin doch ein Tier." Startled, the narrator comments: "Sie sagte es ohne Lächeln, wie eine Frau, wenn von Völkern die Rede ist, feststellen würde: Ich bin doch Polin" (19). Less than a page later, in answer to one of her teacher's questions, Susanna says: "Ich bin doch die Königstochter. ... Ich bin eine Tochter vom König David oder von König Saul. ... Aber die vielen anderen Leute stammen nicht von Königen ab. Bloß ich. Denn ich bin eine Jüdin" (20).

There is an obvious parallel between this seamless integration of the concepts animal, woman, aristocrat, and Jew in Susanna's response, and Canetti's concept of transformation, *Verwandlung,* which he discusses in *Masse und Macht,* stating that according to African mythology, the body of one and the same bushman turns into the body of his father, of his wife, that of an ostrich, and a gazelle.[8] Claudio Magris correctly extracts the concept of transformation from Canetti's biography, but the biographical context is not the only plane on which the term can be applied.[9]

One aspect of transformation is the metamorphosis from human to animal and vice versa, which includes an interconnectedness as physical beings. This phenomenon is of cardinal importance in classical mythology as well as in Eastern religions, one example being the Indian elephant-god Ganesh. Canetti was familiar with both. During his time in Vienna, he and his wife had studied Buddhism. In modern Europe, metamorphosis is of no significance except in children's literature, fairy tales, and science fiction. Being an animal, rather than being *like* an animal, speaking with the voice of an animal, rather than speaking *as if* with the voice of an animal, is the basic situation in a number of Kolmar's poems, namely, in the *Rollengedichte,* role poems, in "Tierträume" as part of the cycle "Das weibliche Bildnis" in *Die Frau und die Tiere.* Kolmar lived in the outskirts of Berlin, taking care of the garden and the animals owned by her family prior to her forced relocation to a *Judenhaus,* a ghetto house, to which the Nazis assigned Jewish citizens. Kolmar was familiar with animals and knew their physical and behavioral makeup as well as their evolutionary history.

Kolmar's poems express empathy with their animal protagonists, but not in the usual patronizing manner in which animal lovers discuss their pets. Her speakers take the side of the animals as equals — as creatures who are downtrodden like the Jews in Hitler's Third Reich. Those animals who are the most despised by human beings, amphibians and spiders, arouse the speaker's most ardent compassion. These animals are persecuted like herself, and they are, so-to-speak, Jews among animals. To express the injustice done to them, the speakers highlight those parts of their bodies that resemble the human anatomy, particularly in its fetal form. For example, the frog in "Teichfrosch" ("Frog in a Pond") is ascribed a *Gnomenhand,* the hand of a dwarf, which knows *die Erde,* the earth, and in "Arachne," she perceives the *zwergige Hand,* the dwarfish hand, of a spider.[10]

"Legende" ("Legend") expresses compassion with the ghosts of the dead animals and together with them accuses the human being, a man who lies sleeping in bed. Like all civilized people, this man has made use of the parts of animal bodies — their hide, their wool, their feathers — to furnish his place. These elements surround him in his comfortable bedroom (148–49). Similarly to the killed animals in the vision of *Bhagavad-Gita,* one of the most important texts of Vedic literature, the murdered animals in Kolmar hold the man accountable for their suffering and their deaths, and they demand satisfaction. In the man's nightmare, animal products such as down pillows transform themselves back into ducks, and so forth:

> Den kleinen fellgewirkten Teppich riß
> Der Wolf, geschunden, häutig, blutendrot,
> Aufröchelnd, zuckend mit gefletschtem Biß:
> Dies war mein Kleid! Und darum bin ich tot? (149)

The last lines of the poem allude to the naked human body, exposing the animal nature of man along with his physical and psychological inferiority — he is shown as the most helpless creature and, at the same time, as the exploiter and murderer of his fellow creatures. Alone in nature, it is suggested, he is clearly inferior to most animals — he would die of exposure were it not for the animal bodies that he uses as raw material (148–49).

Canetti's observations about human survival read almost like a comment on the characterization of the naked human body and man's isolation and vulnerability in Kolmar's poem. He writes: "Der Leib des Menschen ist nackt und anfällig; in seiner Weichheit jedem Zugriff ausgesetzt."[11] Kolmar conveys this very message in "Der Tag der großen Klage" ("The Day of the Great Lament"), a poem about the "Gerichtstag totgeplagter Tiere" ("Judgment Day, Held by Animals Tortured to Death"), which ends with the ominous lines:

> Und eine neue Gottheit spie wie Drachen
> Die Flamme einen neuen Horizont. (167–68)

The new god, spitting forth fire like dragons, as well as the fire image itself suggest an apocalyptic ending to man's reign and a day of reckoning that will be quite unlike the Christian judgment day, for neither God the father, nor the son, but animals shall sit in judgment. At the same time, the image of the dragon, an imaginary creature born of human imagination, suggests a synthesis between man and animal. Endowed with an animal's body, created by the human mind, and, as most legends allege, killed by a human warrior, the dragon, Kolmar suggests, must live and the warrior be overcome for the sake of global survival.

Like the poems discussed thus far, numerous other texts in "Tierträume" express Kolmar's condemnation of the use of animal products for food, clothing, and luxury goods, the capture of zoo animals, and the torture of animals for scientific experiments. More intensely personal yet are the texts in which the speaker assumes the role of an animal and speaks as an animal. This is the case in "Die Kröte" ("The Toad"). The assertion "Ich bin die Kröte" — I am the toad — occurs at the beginning of the first and third stanzas. It is made with the same self-assurance with which Susanna states that she is an animal, and with the same pride that she takes in being a Jewish woman. The poem ends with the lines:

> Mag ich nur ekles Geziefer dir sein:
> Ich bin die Kröte
> Und trage den Edelstein (159–60)

The speaker proudly assumes the role of the "repulsive" toad and by asserting its inherent value, devalues the mainstream culture and its opponents. Yet other poems are written entirely from the point of view of the animal, among them "Lied der Schlange" ("Song of the Snake"), the opening lines of which seem strangely incommensurate with the traditional image of snakes: "Ich durchschritt zierlich das hölzerne Gatter" (161–62).

These texts are too serious to be dismissed as witty role play. Rather, they set forth the conviction that it is necessary to reevaluate the categories man and animal. Kolmar's point of view is informed by a variety of experiences and discourses: Kolmar was a pedagogue for disabled children and a keeper of animals, and she belonged intellectually to Walter Benjamin's circle. As a persecuted Jewish woman intellectual, she was a penetrating critic of the European mind.

The aforementioned motif of the dragon is the focal point of the poem "Der Drache" ("The Dragon," 199–200), which begins with the dragon's complaint that it was driven from its native territory by human beings and ends with a critical comment on the dualism inherent in Western philosophy. It questions the conventional concepts of death, immortality, and the concept of the soul by evoking images of living sand and stone. They suggest that beyond the apparent oppositions of life and death, matter and spirit, there is, must be, a third reality, unknown and inescapable. Kolmar configures it as the dragon, a synthetic entity created by imagination to signify the synthesis of physical and mental reality.

The dragon represents the third option, a metaphysical and physical option, which constitutes the missing link in the manichaeistic patterns of European thought, including Hegelian and Marxist dialectics. The dragon asserts that a solution reaching beyond the binary patterns of Western philosophy must be found for the sake of global survival about which Canetti raises serious doubts. He maintains that the human race is becoming ever more impoverished to the point that it may find itself in complete emptiness and destitution, and he goes on to lament the fact that no other animal species prevented the ascent of mankind.[12]

Kolmar's line of argument follows Benjamin's observations on history, but Kolmar is more radical. Benjamin questions the validity of the dominant culture because it is made possible by acts of barbarism, and he denounces the fact that it presupposes the silencing of the victims and the socially weak.[13] Kolmar questions the conceptual boundaries on which modern science relies by including nonhumans into the category of the victims and the oppressed. Her awareness of the fact that the discourses of modern Europe were formulated to produce answers and ideologies that preserve the status quo lead her to question humanism and its foundation, the Judeo-Christian concept of the universe. Kolmar's involvement with the problems of race, gender, and mental health opened her eyes to the fact that early twentieth-century science was constructed to condone the persecution and murder of disabled persons, Jews, and women as well as animals to the same degree as had been the case in medieval church doctrine and popular medieval superstition. Insofar as her animal images and characters reflect her experience of racist anti-Semitism, they are metaphors. Yet, they also articulate her concern for and identification with animals as fellow creatures and shed doubt on the assumed superiority of one species over another.

Kolmar's work shows that the disregard for life no matter the form is the first step in the abuses perpetrated by human beings against members of their own species. Particularly her later works, the novella *Susanna* and her poems in "Das weibliche Bildnis," show that the degradation of animals is the first step toward the degradation of human beings, or, in other words, that brutality against animals is the last social and intellectual frontier. Her unspoken case in point are the Nazis, who considered Jews animals, or less than animals — in Auschwitz they were, like the animals in Kolmar's "Gerichtstag totgeplagter Tiere," reduced to raw material. Kolmar's urgent call for a third option between thesis and antithesis is derived from her realization that the existing dialectic patterns allow for such notions as "subhuman," which open the door to the mass extermination of lives "unworthy of living." The value hierarchy allows one race to claim superiority over another and offers intellectual tools to those who wish to justify their exploitation of all other creatures, humans and animals.

Kolmar's call for a third option also questions what the Torah and the Christian Bible proclaim as God's command, namely, that Adam seek domination over the world and its creatures. Cognizant that the concept of humanity in the Western tradition includes man's control over nature, Kolmar, unlike most other antifascist intellectuals, refrains from calling for more humanity. The history of Jew-hatred and misogyny, the medieval witch and cat hunts, and the extermination of entire species illustrate that neither the Judeo-Christian religions nor the ensuing secular philosophies managed to instill their adherents with the love of life.

To illustrate the future consequences in which the current attitudes toward life result, Canetti predicted in 1979 that in a thousand years only a few select animal species will have survived, and they will be considered rare and precious. Humans will worship them like gods.[14] Canetti places this emphasis on the fate of the animals, since the racist and misogynist excesses of the first third of the twentieth century have already been the topics of much debate. Nevertheless, the study of these phenomena, including the Holocaust, has not resulted in an improved global situation. Canetti's and Kolmar's works suggest that such an improvement will not occur, unless the preservation of animal life is considered an integral part of survival. Neither author exhibits any optimism in view of the fact that, in contrast to Hinduism and Buddhism, the killing of animals is deeply rooted in Western cultures. In their examination of the relationship of man and animal, they assert that a viable third path must be found and that the axioms of modern European civilization must be abandoned. Voices such as Kolmar's, Canetti's, and Singer's are few. Dismissed or misinterpreted, they have carried no weight in cultural debates, perhaps because the conclusions they draw question deeply ingrained taboos. They constitute a direct assault on man's creature comforts, consumerism, and love of gratuitous violence, but most of all, man's arrogance — the same arrogance that caused the destruction of Kolmar in the Holocaust.

Notes

1. Elias Canetti, *Masse und Macht* (Frankfurt am Main: Fischer, 1981), 231.

2. Elias Canetti, *Aufzeichnungen von 1942–1985* (Munich: Hanser, 1993), 516.

3. Elias Canetti, *Die Blendung* (1935; reprint, Frankfurt am Main: Fischer, 1965), 436–58.

4. Franz Kafka, "Ein Bericht für eine Akademie," trans. as "Report to an Academy," in *The Penal Colony*, trans. Willa Muir and Edwin Muir (New York: Schocken, 1948), 173–84.

5. Richard H. Lawson, *Understanding Elias Canetti* (Columbia: South Carolina Press, 1991), 91.

6. Elias Canetti, "Das Geheimherz der Uhr," *Aufzeichnungen 1942–1985:* 480.

7. Gertrud Kolmar, *Susanna* (Frankfurt am Main: Jüdischer Verlag, 1994). Further references to this novella will be contained parenthetically in the text.

8. Canetti, *Masse und Macht*, 378.

9. "Der große Dichter der Verwandlung bleibt Canetti auch in seiner Autobiographie, die ihn verbirgt, während sie ihn zu enthüllen scheint." Claudio Magris, "Ein Schriftsteller, der aus vielen Personen besteht," *Hüter der Verwandlung* (Munich: Hanser, 1985), 271–72.

10. Gertrud Kolmar, *Das lyrische Werk* (Munich: Kösel, 1960), 157 and 155 respectively. As mentioned previously, *Die Frau und die Tiere* was first published in 1938. The poems were reprinted in *Das lyrische Werk*, and all in-text citations are to the latter volume.

11. Canetti, *Masse und Macht*, 250.

12. Canetti, *Aufzeichnungen 1942–1985*, 66.

13. Walter Benjamin, "Über den Begriff der Geschichte," in *Gesammelte Schriften*, ed. Rolf Tiedemann and Hermann S. Schweppenhäuser (Frankfurt am Main: Suhrkamp, 1974), 693–704.

14. Canetti, *Aufzeichnungen 1942–1985*, 455.

STEPHANIE HAMMER

In the Name of the Rose:
Gertrud Kolmar, Hélène Cixous, and
the Poerotics of Jewish Femininity

> ... yet I would remind you ... of our past happiness.
> Many wreaths of roses and violets you placed beside you at my side.
>> — Sappho, "To Atthis," poem #24

> a rose is a rose is a rose is a rose
>> — Gertrude Stein, "Sacred Emily"

THE FEMINIST PHILOSOPHER HÉLÈNE CIXOUS has argued that the source of women's powerlessness lies in Western civilization's construction of a vast, overarching system of binary values, which both separates the feminine from the masculine and reduces it — transforming it into an unequal, invisible partner to the supreme and supremely sexual masculine:

> *où est-elle?*
> Activité / Passivité
> Soleil / lune
> Culture / Nature
> Jour / Nuit
>
> Homme
> -------
> Femme

Toujours la même métaphore: ... que dans la philosophie la femme est toujours du côté de la passivité. ... Du vouloir: désir, autorité, on interroge ça, et on est ramené droit ... au père.[1]

Through arrays of references to literary, philosophical, and psychoanalytical sources that buttress bare schematic lists such as the one given above, Cixous's most famous exercise in feminist deconstruction, *La jeune née* (coauthored with Cathérine Clément in 1975), is at once creative writing and "serious" scholarship. Like Heinrich von Kleist's *Penthesilea* (to whom she devotes considerable analytical space), Cixous's own text is armed with an impressive artillery of Western thinkers and writers. With this variegated arsenal, Cixous maps out the phalanx of phallogocentricism and her inferior position vis-à-vis that considerable force.

But, taking her cue from Kleist's heroine, she neither accepts this position as an insurmountable given and undeniable truth, nor does she attempt to detonate its power in favor of some other, similarly monolithic model that should be erected in its place. Instead, Cixous considers the system carefully and then meticulously dismantles it from within, using her own ambiguous autobiographical identity as a wedge to dismantle the superstructure of patriarchal values in the West. She negotiates a difficult balancing act between feminist creative writing and a philosophical history that seeks to legitimize her thinking by placing it against and within the Western tradition. She veers between a language of vision that borders on the spiritual and a critical language of politics and economics: a metaphysics of *her* and a historiography of *him*.

Cixous repeatedly displays a classical humanistic erudition to ground observations which prove to be supremely subversive interpretational acts. Note, for example, the weaving together of intertexts that informs her writing.[2] Using mixtures of Grimm's fairy tale, and classical mythology, modern and ancient Western literatures, and a work by such seminal thinkers as Hegel, Nietzsche, and Freud, Cixous unpacks the insidious ideological formation at work in our most dearly beloved narratives — of both high and low culture.[3] At the same time, she alters them — suggesting that new stories could be told if the director of the tale were not a man or were able to see beyond the phallocratic constraints of the official story of male-female relations.[4]

This imagistic reversal allows for a second, more radical move — that of focusing on women: on their dreams, aspirations, and possibilities. These are, at first, not easy to determine or to understand, because the feminine is hard to find in our narratives and in our culture at large — placed at once outside and inside culture, in what Cixous calls "un dehors domestique," a domestic outside (124). This space is both internal and external, at once the home and the dark continent, at once an architecture and a physiology in which woman finds herself a stranger and within whose boundaries she is commanded to hate herself as well as other women in a move of "antinarcissism" (125).

Cixous assumes charge of this dark continent — a gesture laden for her, because of her Sephardic, Algerian roots — and rather than resigning herself to its opacity, explores it and proclaims its importance; taking on a woman's version of the orphic role — namely that of Persephone, the negotiator of life and death and the renewer of the circle of life. Accordingly, she leads women back from what is at once their neocolonial banishment to the dark continent of female subjectivity and their imprisonment within the home — addressing them / us as a collective, using an emphatic *nous*, us. She calls upon them to return from their places of hiding and banishment, their positions as witches and outsiders to "culture," and asserts that "we are black *and* we are beautiful" (126).[5]

Through her own writing, Cixous suggests that the crippling effects of a male-imposed feminine consciousness can be surmounted only by a radical therapy of a creative imagination that embraces "blackness" — i.e., an understanding of gender as race — thereby rebelling against the legacy and the destiny of passivity that tradition has called for.

Explicitly linking writing to pleasure and to sexual self-pleasuring, which includes pregnancy and giving birth, Cixous refuses the traditional Western split between maternity and female sexuality.[6] Through her own commentary on canonical male writers, Cixous demonstrates that within the patriarchal matrix — a seemingly paradoxical juxtaposition — lurks an untapped subversive possibility, precisely because the masculine cannot entirely suppress the feminine; she offers her own example — the present work — as a guidepost, as the Ariadne thread *(fil)* to our way out of the patriarchal trap so that femininity and its heterogeneous voices may at last run free.

Cixous's theories of women's writing as at once sexually, psychologically, politically, and spiritually empowering explicate retroactively the contribution of another great Jewish writer of feminine agency, the German poet Gertrud Kolmar. Together they build upon a complex, rich, and still only partially understood and reconstructed tradition of Jewish women's writing in Europe and in the United States.

This writing was private rather than public, written in vernaculars rather than in Hebrew, and was created by women for women; anecdotal, autobiographical, at once visionary and pragmatic, writing by Jewish women was often mosaic in character; fragmentary, it first took the forms of prayers, letters, and diary entries and only later entered the mainstream of officially "literary" formats. This tradition was particularly strong in Germany and includes the writings of baroque-era businesswoman Glückel of Hameln, or Glikl Hamil, the salonières of Berlin Romanticism, notably Rahel Varnhagen, and the popular nineteenth-century novelist Fanny Lewald.[7]

The considerable counterweight of this countertradition represents one powerful reason for the achievement of twentieth-century Jewish intellectual women — in politics, in letters, in the theater — of Emma Goldmann and Rosa Luxemburg, of Gertrude Stein (arguably the mother of modernism and an anticipator of postmodern) and visionary philosopher Simone Weil.[8] In the U. S. postwar era, we see the overweening presence of Jewish women in

American cultural life — the artist Judy Chicago, the performance artist co-median Sandra Bernhardt, writers Wendy Wasserstein and Erika Jong, di-rector-actress Barbara Streisand, feminist activist Betty Friedan.

Most important, this legacy also testifies to the long-standing ability of Jewish intellectual women to bring with them and weave together a richly paradoxical mass of intellectual threads. They inherit the scholastic meticu-lousness of the Talmudic tradition predicated upon close, philologically based readings of master texts and subsequently upon accounts of interpre-tative debates that must — legalistically — be rehearsed, reiterated, and dis-cussed before any new ground can be broken. Similarly, Jewish women writ-ers are able to employ the capacity already implied within the forgoing de-scription of the Talmudic tradition — namely, classical Judaism's astonishing, if imperfect, ability (in comparison with Christianity) to tolerate, protect, and encourage informed dissent and a resulting wide divergence of opinion. Fi-nally, there is the subversive possibility of the Torah itself (as witnessed by popular contemporary readings of the story of Ruth and Naomi as being a tale of female bonding and, possibly, lesbian love) and of the religious tradi-tion in its more mystical and folkloric manifestations. The possibility for many opinions about texts and about truth itself, and the submerged but stubborn presence of female characters and figures in the sacred writing, has recently empowered feminist theologians to undertake radical revisions of traditional Jewish religious principles and practices. These resulted in Judith Plaskow's tale of Eden in which Eve and Lillith leave and eventually return to the garden "bursting with possibilities, ready to rebuild it together"[9] and in Rabbi Lynn Gottlieb's revision of Judaism toward matriarchal rituals based on the renaming of G-d: She replaces the masculine *Adonai* with the femi-nine, cabalistic *Shekinah,* she who dwells within.

An understanding of the tradition that relies upon a conflated dialectic of suspicion and remembrance — i.e., the regarding of the Torah tradition as an (historically and ideologically constructed and constrained) authority, but not as the ultimate authority[10] — and, with this, the move to create a femi-nist vision of individual transcendence clearly mark Cixous's writing, as we have already seen. But this dual movement is even more characteristic of the aesthetic efforts of Gertrud Kolmar. As an almost, but not quite, survivor of the Holocaust and as at once a resolutely German, Jewish, and female writer, Kolmar stands at a crucial juncture in the development of this legacy, as she stands at the juncture of pre- and postwar literature, and of pre- and postfas-cist German identity.[11]

Like Cixous's writing, the work of Gertrud Kolmar is Janus-faced, albeit more subtly so. Kolmar looks simultaneously forward and back — both re-lying upon and attempting to dismantle the classical European tradition gov-erning the (masculinist, heterosexist) literary iconography of romantic, sexual relations. At the same time, she is also influenced by a partially erased Jewish identity, which she covertly attempts to bring back to the surface by a Spinozean love of nature, which sees in it a reflection of the divine.

These multiple aims account for the extreme complexity of her work. Kolmar writes consistently about a feminine consciousness under fire, about desires constricted and trapped or banished to a fierce, savage "African" realm on the margins of society, and about a marginal gaze of longing that must be given voice and words. But her choice of literary form is crucial; out of the rich storehouse of Western genres, she selects the most formal, the most literally classical, and the most ancient of the Western literary arts, namely, lyric poetry — one of the three Aristotelian modes of literary address. Again, Cixous gives us a hint as to why lyric — as opposed to epic or drama — should be the form of choice for Kolmar. She maintains that in feminine speech and writing, there is a resonance of subtle, yet profound emotions, of perceptions preserved as if in song. This songlike quality is kept alive by the woman writer.[12] For Cixous, the primordial feminine voice is the voice of song — the orphic voice, which is at once music and poetry. A modernist "Devorah" — the charismatic female chief who sings a song of triumph with her man-at-arms, Barak (the song of Devorah constitutes, significantly, one of the earliest composed portions of the Torah[13]) — Kolmar brings the feminine song into play in the by then male-dominated realm of poetry.

In pursuit of this goal, Kolmar's poetry presents continued, embattled attempts to posit alternative statuses for feminine consciousness; these veer toward the science fictional, as Kolmar shape-shifts between life-forms of animals or humans of a different race, sometimes even turning into monsters. But before she can imagine herself free, Kolmar must — as must Cixous — state the reality of the matter: a feminine poetic consciousness in chains, laid low by masculine tradition — a poetic speech that can just barely assert itself as such. Nowhere is the challenging nature of this preliminary struggle more poignant and, arguably, more powerful than in the "Bild der Rose" ("Rose Sonnets"), a cycle of twenty poems — primarily sonnets — thought by Henry A. Smith to have been composed probably in the early 1930s.[14] Here the images of woman-as-plant disseminate a muted, yet evocative voice that comes to the fore in miniature poems, which — like the flowers they replicate — contain a dense, multipetaled structure, a rich imagistic color, and a heady imaginative perfume.

Much needs to be made of the choice of subject and of form. The subject is typical of Kolmar, who was fond of the small and seemingly insignificant creations of nature, as Michael Eben has noted.[15] It is common knowledge that the rose is a deeply freighted flower symbol; even in postmodernist, late-twentieth-century America, roses are the romantic gift of choice surrounding such special occasions as Valentine's Day and wedding anniversaries; they still usually are present in wedding bouquets. The rose is the world's most popular and prized flower,[16] although the origins of its importance have Western, predominantly pagan, rather than Judeo-Christian sources. Roses appear rarely in the Bible,[17] but seem to have been present from the beginning in Greco-Roman culture. Grown first in Crete (images of roses graced the palace walls of Knossos) and subsequently in Greece (Sappho called them the "queens of flowers"),[18] they were even more popularized by the Romans, whose legions brought them to northern Europe.

The burgeoning iconography of the rose was further complicated in the ever powerful discourse of romantic heterosexual love relations, which took root in the courtly love tradition. The seminal work for this tradition is the celebrated *Roman de la Rose* ("The Romance of the Rose," volume 1 written by Guillaume de Lorris ca. 1225–1230 and volume 2 written by Jean de Meaun ca. 1267–1278), an allegorical novel in which the man's desire for sexual fulfillment with the beloved woman takes the form of a knight's quest for possession of the rose. Significantly, behind this seemingly innocent, arcadian imagery lurks the language of war, as Denis de Rougemont notes[19] — a presence that explains the aggressive stance taken by male poets using the rose / woman image, as we shall see shortly. Since their central appearance in the courtly tradition, roses have abounded in Western and in German poetry, from Goethe to Rilke to Arp.

The rose is clearly a symbol at once of erotic love and femininity, of beauty, and of fragility, but it is important to remember that this icon plays a key role in a masculine — rather than feminine — imagination. This system employs the flower as a means to encode woman as a thorny, yet fragile object of cultural cultivation, decoration, and eventual, careless annihilation.

Robert Herrick's injunction "gather ye rosebuds while ye may"[20] clearly implies such a point of view, but Goethe's famous ballad "Heidenröslein" ("Rock-Rose") offers an even more insidious take on the real power relations that lie, only partially concealed, behind the picturesque use of the rose image in heterosexual love poetry. The poet justifies the rapelike actions of the *wilder Knabe,* the wild youth, who, as a young male, cannot be expected to control his urges to take violent possession of the beautiful rose. Although the speaking rose resists her "desirer" — albeit ineffectively — the tonal emphasis is on the youth, and our sympathy is drawn to his suffering rather than to hers despite the fact that once picked, the rose must quickly die. It is his subjectivity that is of interest to Goethe, and consequently to us. A similar, if more refined, point of view invests the rose imagery of Rainer Maria Rilke — where, as in one of the sonnets to Orpheus, the rose is invoked in terms of female death, and this provides a spectacle of pleasure for a male viewer / poet. Indeed, Rilke's notion of the *Dinggedicht* (literally, thing poem — a poem that focuses on a material object) does nothing more or less than theorize the gesture already implicit in the poetic use of rose iconography from the beginning; the rose serves as an erotic emblem to make woman into "a thing ... recreated within the poem into an 'art-thing' ... [which] impresses the reader with a clarity and plasticity of subject."[21]

Thus, Kolmar assumes the weight of a heavy literary legacy by choosing the rose (she will do this elsewhere in her poetry, as Cooper argues). And she chooses an equally daunting legacy in her choice of the sonnet — a dense, compact, rigidly rhymed and organized fourteen-line poem, which has been employed by an intimidating host of great male poets: Petrarch, Shakespeare, Gryphius, the British metaphysical poets, Baudelaire, Yeats, Rilke, and e. e. cummings.[22] But using a strategy much like that of Cixous, she neither denies the ideological force of the traditional image and traditional form, nor attempts to substitute another system of meanings and formal requirements in their place; fully recognizing the value of the art that has gone before, Kolmar enters the tradition and reworks it from within, using her own version of Plaskow's remembrance and suspicion.

Thus, Kolmar's poetics offer a powerful corrective to the psychoanalytic theory of Harold Bloom, which assigns to male writers an "anxiety of influence" that prompts them to "kill off" the father through the oedipal act of writing. Instead, Kolmar reveres the father and subverts him at the same time, placing him in an unlikely marriage with her own feminine sensibility. From this point of view in particular, the choice of subject is perfect; the rose is a hybrid, a product of unlikely, difficult, opposing parentage. The result is a life-form that is at once unique, legitimate, and racially suspect — a situation that neatly encapsulates the situation of the Jew in Germany as well as Kolmar's problematic "hybrid" position as a German, Jewish woman poet.

The poems themselves recognize their complex heritage, which they then employ to achieve even greater imagistic complexity. Kolmar uses both titles and subtitles in most of her poems, which — as in the use of the *Stadtwappen* images for the poems in the cycle "Preussische Wappen" ("Prussian Coats of Arms") — reveal a playful, simultaneous recognition and deconstruction of and on a number of levels. This titular interplay blends the boundaries between the binary categories of power / knowledge, which dominate Western masculinist thinking; often her titles pertain at once to specific hybrids of the flower and to something or someone else altogether, as in "Traumsee / Captain Harvey-Cant" ("Sea of Dreams / Captain Harvey-Cant") and "Rose in Trauer / Etoile de Hollande" ("Rose in Mourning / Star of Holland"). This practice pays homage to and mocks the intricate, encyclopedic practice of hybrid naming and the self-consciously erudite fascination with the development of ever improved rose plants; the interplay also suggests that the poem may well designate a person and / or a place as well as a plant — an implication that in turn minimizes the borders of identity, which cause us to differ between such seemingly basic life-forms.[23] On a more subtle level, Kolmar deconstructs the distanced, biologically superior position of the male poet — particularly the sonnet writer — and his human role vis-à-vis the botanical, feminine, and seemingly inferior rose.

This act of deconstruction is particularly evident in the first poem, entitled suggestively "Die schönen Wunder" ("Beautiful Wonders"):

> Die schönen Wunder aus den sieben Reichen,
> Die bald Zitronenenfalter, groß an Stielen.
> Bald Zwergflamingos, die in Büsche fielen,
> Bald Muscheln sind aus zauberstillen Teichen.

The poem follows the Petrarchan, or Italian, model of two quatrains (one octave) and one sestet using the rhyme scheme *abbaabba cdecde*. In the first quatrain, Kolmar offers the reader her impressive classical poetic credentials. Her symmetrical use of anaphora, repetition, consonance, and assonance demonstrates her mastery of the rhetorical tricks of the trade. The opening is reminiscent of Baudelaire's "L'invitation au voyage" ("Invitation to a Voyage"). The poet invites the reader to a lush, utopian, and exotic world of abundance where fruits, flowers, and animals of the air and sea mingle together in union of sight and smell, as her invocation of the seven wonders of the world places the poem in a classical poetic context. The second quatrain marks both a sudden change of style and mood:

> O meine Rosen. Herzen. Mögt ihr bleichen,
> Erschlafft, erschöpft von weißen Sonnenspielen,
> Verzehrt vom Überschwang, dem Allzuvielen;
> Tragt singend euch zu Grabe, süße Leichen!

The style becomes abrupt and abbreviated; where we had two sentences in four lines, we now have three. The first two are extremely short and telegraphic as opposed to the detailed descriptiveness of the opening; the third seems incongruous with the first; it dominates the quatrain, invading the first line and encroaching upon the two small, but crucial utterances that precede it; then the sentence winds through the rest, divided into two clauses of very unequal length. The first two sentences establish, by physical proximity, a metaphoric relation between roses and hearts, which, by inference, extends to the *schönen Wunder,* the beautiful wonders, referred to in the opening lines, which we now understand are "wonders" of a very different order than the architectural / natural monumental wonders referred to in classical antiquity. These are marvels of smallness, not of bigness, of an internality that does not choke off the external, and of an emotional center that is as marvelous as a bridge or statue. The metaphor becomes more complex as Kolmar addresses these hearts / roses / wonders with the familiar *ihr*, you, as though she were one of them and they were her intimates — family or friends; through an unexplained use of personification, Kolmar suggests the unbounded connections between the animal and the vegetable, between the exterior object of the gaze and the internal workings of the gazer. At the same time, the second quatrain contains an important concession to the rose tradition — the recognition of the fragility of roses, their certain death under the heat of the sun. As is typical for the Petrarchan sonnet, the first two quatrains present the central problem or unified process of thought, while the sestet introduces the *volta*, or turnaround.[24] Here and only here does the *ich*, the "I," explicitly enter in:

> Ich will euch doch vom lieben Zweig nicht trennen,
> Euch nicht im engen, lauen Glase wissen,
> Die kurze Spanne Blühn euch kunstreich dehnen.

Clearly rejecting the dramatic scene in Goethe's poem discussed earlier, the female poet refuses to separate the roses from their branches; unlike his *wilder Knabe*, she will not cut them. Here Kolmar reverses the Goethean image even further: The poet, who is also the mistress of the home and the garden, argues that the preservation of the roses ensures only false life — imprisoned in the vase, which will serve as decoration within the domestic space (implied but never mentioned in this poem), or squeezed into a desiccated existence as a pressed flower. Again, as in Cixous, we have here an indirect reference to Snow White and her living death within the glass coffin. The coda makes Kolmar's philosophy clear:

> O gut: an unermessenem Glanz verbrennen,
> Statt, von der heißen Erde fortgerissen,
> Ein langes schales Leben hinzusehnen.

Kolmar's final lines reiterate the odd sentence structure of the second quatrain. These sentences, devoid of main verbs, suggest possibility and futurity rather than fact and actuality. Kolmar's roses are then most emphatically *not* the roses of patriarchal poetry, although she admits their generic relation. Her roses of the heart are also the wonders of a female sensibility, which — at once earthy and spiritual — longs for its roots in the earth and dreams of living its short life to the fullest underneath the sun of desire and emotional vibrancy. In this manner, Kolmar revises the standard *carpe diem* imagery of much love poetry in the West; her roses / hearts / women recognize the brevity of human existence as well as the evanescence of emotional fulfillment. But rather than attempting to master or evade time, they accept it, and Kolmar, as their empathic guardian,[25] frees them in her imaginative garden to run rampant, to live to the fullest, and to expire connected to the elements, which nourished them in the first place.

In this first poem, Kolmar implicitly unpacks the Edenic garden as the problematic, porous, and therefore fertile boundary separating public from private, the civilized from the savage, the masculine world of commodified labor and production from the feminine world of childbirth, nurture, conservation, and interior decoration. The move into the garden marks Kolmar's move away from the unspoken house of which she is the proprietor — fetishized only as the narrow glass — and away from Cixous's Africa — the domesticated dark continent, where woman has been imprisoned by and within herself. It is the first step "out." To find the seven wonders here is, indeed, to work miracles.

Kolmar's garden grows larger and more variegated with each poem, incorporating more ideas, growing more expansive, wilder, increasingly subversive. Racial hybridity becomes the measure of beauty in "Mulattenrose" ("Mulatto Rose"); the poet herself becomes a rose that blooms in "Traumsee / Captain Harvey-Cant"; and a young girl contemplates the imprisonment and eventual emancipation of the exotic bird / flower in "Kanarienrose / Ville de Paris" ("Canary Rose / City of Paris"). In inclusive, fluid movements of thought, which look forward to Cixous's description of *écriture féminine*, Kolmar's contemplations of the different, yet similar flowers transform themselves into occasions to rethink images, cultural differences (in particular as they relate to Orientalism), stories, and flavors — most of which (but not all) relate explicitly to women and to female sensibility,[26] as in "Ägyptische Rose / Madame Ravary" ("Egyptian Rose / Madame Ravary"), where Kolmar by association links the rose with the pharaoh's daughter and by implication with the famous and crucial scene from Exodus, in which the princess discovers Moses in the bulrushes.

Emotionality and sexuality gradually magnify in these later poems, and Kolmar makes explicit the heart / flower connection articulated in the cycle's first poem. If "Die schönen Wunder" emphasizes the external side of the metaphoric relation, it is the internal, emotional, and psychological aspect that is established and explored in "Uneingestandene Liebe / General Superior Arnold Janssen" ("Love Not Professed / General Superior Arnold Janssen)." The internal difficulties attending the desire of the feminine subject to live beyond the scope of "im engen lauen Glase" of "Die schönen Wunder" are dramatized with terrible simplicity. Here a fragile, erotic "desirer" attempts with great trepidation to express herself, to find her voice, even as she explores the complexities of her own physical terrain:

> Dies ist das Herz: die Knospe, halb erschlossen,
> So zag, so rot, sich schämend, Glut zu sein,

So voller Angst verhaltend schmalen Schein,
Der schon sie netzt und bald sie ganz durchflossen.

Sie fühlt ein fremdes Glück, noch nie genossen,
Das, ihrem Kelch entboren matt und klein,
Nun über seine Ränder stürzt wie Wein,
Von ungezähmter Hand ihm eingegossen.

Was ist das? Kind? Sie kann es nicht mehr töten,
Und ist es Frucht, sie kann es nicht mehr sammeln,
Doch wie es heiße, Zauber, Flamme, Fluß:

Das blüht auf einer Wange als Erröten
Und findets eine Kehle, wird es Stammeln,
Und eine Lippe rührt es an als Kuß.

This deeply intimate, self-revelatory piece enacts a series of subtle metamorphoses. The metaphoric connections are dense: The blooming of the rose (described in the poetic equivalent of accelerated photography) replicates at once the feeling heart, which first feels love, an organic and delicate female sexual body experiencing arousal and pleasure (graphically suggested by the moistened calyx and the overflow of a never before experienced *Glüeck* — imagery that verbally captures the visual impact of Georgia O'Keefe's erotic flower paintings), and the burgeoning imagination of the poet herself.

Kolmar uses the trope of female sexuality / sensibility as rose nowhere more powerfully than here, as she proceeds to reverse the dynamics of the *Roman de la Rose*. While the allegory's male protagonist eventually takes possession of the flower (which swells — with either pleasure, pregnancy, or both), Kolmar depicts the flower's point of view in an erotic relation that removes the dominance of male sexuality; indeed, except for the presence of the general in the subtitle, the masculine agent is absent. Again, this poem may be seen as a direct repudiation of Goethe. Unlike the *Röslein* of the famous ballad, this feminine subject is not cold and unwilling, but rather deeply desirous of the untamed hand, which replaces the wild youth and which may or may not be that of a man; indeed, it may or may not be the hand of someone else. In addition, we have a sly, disjunct play on the proverb "zwischen Lipp' und Kelches Rand schwebt der finsteren Mächte Hand" — the dark powers here being the unconscious powers of sexuality, the unspoken potential and power of a seemingly frail femininity coming into the language of desire. Also referred to and definitively refused is the *Kindermörderin* tradition exemplified by Gretchen in *Faust I*, in which a young girl fatally succumbs to her own desire and then murders the offspring that pleasure has produced.

Through these simultaneous evocations and rejections of the images that have dominated the masculine imagination regarding feminine desire, Kolmar undercuts the oppositional masculine / feminine, aggressive / passive subject-object position implied by the rose trope as used by male poets (again one thinks of Herrick's "gather ye rosebuds while ye may"). Clear-cut identity is also rejected in favor of a simultaneous blending of borders: of hands and cups, of productions of the self, which are neither autonomous beings — children — or indifferent, if beautiful, by-products; the poem describes a ripeness that is not death, an erotic action that supersedes possession *(sammeln)*, and a seduction that is nonviolent, but sensuous, powerful, graceful, and possibly autoerogenous. This poetic experience of blossoming approaches the *jouissance* described by Jane Gallop reading Roland Barthes as a metapleasure, which is "shocking, ego-disruptive, and in conflict with the canons of culture"[27] and which displays a "vibrant, androgynous creativity."[28]

The last two poems complete the organic, floral life cycle imaginatively rendered in the series. Kolmar thereby suggests that our organic existences do indeed resemble those of flowers, and the process of the poems documents this awareness; they mirror an evolution of growth, bud, bloom, ripeness, which then fades away into an unspectacular death that will furnish the raw material for the lives of others. In keeping with this procedure, the last poem self-consciously eschews grandiose closure; rather, it brings the articulation of the persephonic poetic voice to its appropriate resolution while once again resonating with and rejecting Goethe:

> Ja, neige, neige dich du Rosenrot,
> Du kleine Ampel, Alabasterstern!
> Dir will ich dienen, meinem Ruhm und Herrn,
> Dir Opfer bieten, Wein und süßes Brot.
>
> O nimmt mich ein. Ich führe, sanftes Boot
> Mit deinem Wind in tiefen Abend gern;
> Er wiegt dich sacht, und du bist doch schon fern
> Und gleitest scheinend nieder in den Tod.

Revising Gretchen's despairing prayer to the Holy Mother, Kolmar intertwines the sacred ritual emblems of the *sabbat* meal ("Wein" and "Brot") with the pagan image of the boat that ferries the dead across the river Styx. Kolmar positions herself at once as the ferryman and the orphic survivor of the beloved who has passed on. At the same time, she indirectly invokes yet another pagan image, this one feminine: the saddened Demeter — appropriately, the goddess who governs all that grows. Here, however, she does not hear the cries of the abducted Persephone crying for help. Instead, she represents the fecundity of spring and summer ("Sommertagsgesicht"):

> So ohne Flackern schwindest du, o Licht,
> So sinkst du, Nachen, ohne Hilfeschrei.
> Ich hör dein Schweigen: hör den Jammer nicht,
>
> Ich sehe dich an: die Erde rollt vorbei.
> Du bist gestorben, Sommertagsgesicht;
> Ich lebe, daß ich trauern mag: verzeih.

Seen from this point of view, Kolmar mourns the loss of the beloved but also tentatively suggests that the erotic — in all its senses — persists beyond death, to be reborn once again in its unending cycles of life; such a reading is already implied in the first strophe with its adoration of the "Rosenrot" — signifying the divine and therefore immortal nature of that which is at once flower, heart, and female sensibility, as we have already seen in the other poems. This interpretation would account for the poem's last word, "verzeih," signifying a demand on the part of the poet that the beloved understand and allow that she will both mourn and love again. In this manner, Kolmar positions herself as both masculine and feminine, as mediatrix between death and life, as devotee of the sacred ethos of love that transcends the lover himself (although he is clearly the object of sadness and loss), and as an aspect of the divine mother of / daughter to herself.

Kolmar's complex gesture of affiliation with the entwined masculine traditions of sonnet writing and writing about roses dramatizes the complicated and powerful kinship of Jewish women's writing in the West to the masculine canon, which it criticizes but must, perforce, remain intimately connected with. Acting as both bad and dutiful daughter, the author of the rose poems grafts her texts to the patriarchal genus from which they stem while the poems make claim to an independent and alternative set of identities. Through these strategies, "Das Bild der Rose" grows a multipetaled vision that celebrates a feminine poe(ro)tics tied to the seasons and to the earth, a sensibility that invites the female reader to explore her own feelings / body / mind and offers an alternate understanding both of the Western literary tradition and of the tradition of heterosexual love as a whole. These alternatives offer themselves, like the writing of Cixous, as the seeds of revelation and revolution — the tropes and metaphors the feminine subject can use to grow a radiant, multivalent sense of self, of personal power, of pleasure, and of potential.

Notes

For Lilian Furst, Ruth Klüger, Gail Hart, Martha Nussbaum, and Erika Suderburg.

1. Hélène Cixous, *La jeune née* (Paris: Union Général d'Editions, 1975), 115–17.

2. "Les belles dorment dans leurs bois, en attendant que les princes viennent les réveiller. Dans leurs lits, dans leurs cercueils de verre, dans leur forêts d'enfance comme des mortes. ... Ce sont les hommes quie aiment jouer à la poupée. Comme on le sait depuis Pygmalion. Leur viex rêve: être dieu la mère. La meilleure mère, la deuxième, celle qui donne la deuxième naissance" (Cixous, 120).

3. Morag Shiach, *Hélène Cixous: A Politics of Writing* (London: Routledge, 1991), 7.

4. "Il se penche sur elle. ... On coupe. Le conte est fini. Rideau. Une fois réveillé(e) ce serait une toute autre histoire. Alors il y aurait deux personnes peut-être. On ne sait jamais, avec les femmes" (Cixous, 122).

5. "Plus une minute a perdre. Sortons. Elles reviennent de loin: de toujours: du 'dehors', des landes, où se maintiennent en vie les sorcières, d'en dessous, en deçà de la "culture."... Nous, les précoces, nous les refoulées de la culture ... nous les labyrinthes, les échelles, les espaces foulées; les voilées, — nous sommes "noires" *et* nous sommes belles" (Cixous, 126).

6. Cixous writes: "Pulsion orale, pulsion anale, pulsion vocale, toutes les pulsions sont nos bonnes forces, et parmi elles la pulsion de gestation, — tout comme l'envie d'écrire: une envie de vivre dedans, une envie du ventre, de la langue, du sang. ... La femme qui fait l'épreuve du non-moi, comment n'aurait-elle pas à l'écrit un rapport spécifique? ... Il y a un lien entre l'économie de la fémininité, la subjectivité ouverte, prodigue, ce rapport à l'autre où le don ne calcule pas son coup et la possibilité de l'amour; et entre cette 'libido' de l'autre et l'écriture aujourd'hui" (166–68). See also Adrienne Rich, *Of Woman Born* (New York: Norton, 1986), 119.

7. Dagmar C. G. Lorenz, "The Unspoken Bond: Else Lasker-Schüler and Gertrud Kolmar in Their Historical and Cultural Context," *Seminar* 29, no. 4 (1993): 349–69.

8. Cathy N. Davidson and Linda Wagner-Martin, ed., "Gertrude Stein," in *The Oxford Companion to Women's Writing in the United States* (Oxford: Oxford UP, 1995), 847.

9. Ellen M. Umansky and Dianne Ashton, *Four Centuries of Jewish Women's Spirituality* (Boston: Beacon, 1992), 216.

10. Judith Plaskow, *Standing Again at Sinai* (New York: HarperCollins, 1991), 15.

11. Lorenz, 367.

12. "Dans la parole féminine comme dans l'écriture ne cesse jamais de résonner ce qui de nous avons jadis traversé, touché imperceptiblement, profondément, garde le pouvoir de nous affecter, le *chant*, la première musique, celle de la première voix d'amour, que toute femme préserve vivante" (Cixous, 172).

13. Judah Gribetz, Edward L. Greenstein, and Regina Stein, *The Timetables of Jewish History* (New York: Simon and Schuster, 1993), 11.

14. Henry A. Smith, trans., *Dark Soliloquy: The Selected Poems of Gertrud Kolmar* (New York: Seabury, 1975), 28.

15. Michael C. Eben, "Gertrud Kolmar: An Appraisal," *German Life and Letters* 37, no. 3 (1984): 204.

16. "Rose," Encarta 95, Microsoft Home Software (1992–94).

17. D. G. Hessayon, *The Rose Expert* (London: Expert, 1995), 110.

18. Ibid.

19. Denis de Rougemont, *Love in the Western World* (New York: Pantheon, 1940), 245.

20. This poem is from the Hesperides collection and appeared in 1648. See Robert Herrick, "To the Virgins, to Make Much of Time," in *The Poetical Works of Robert Herrick* (London: Oxford at Clarendon, 1915).

21. Michael C. Eben, "Rainer Maria Rilke and Gertrud Kolmar: Das Dinggedicht — Two Poems," *Neophilologus* 73, no. 4 (1989): 633.

22. "Sonnet," in *Princeton Encyclopedia of Poetry and Poetics,* ed. Alex Preminger (Princeton: Princeton UP, 1974), 782–83.

23. Monika Shafi, "'Mein Ruf ist dünn und leicht' — Zur Weiblichkeitsdarstellung in Gertrud Kolmars Zyklus 'Weibliches Bildnis,'" *The Germanic Review* 66, no. 2 (1991): 83.

24. "Sonnet," 781.

25. Eben, "Rilke and Kolmar," 636.

26. Shafi, 85.

27. Jane Gallop, "Beyond the *Jouissance* Principle," *Representations* 7 (summer 1984): 111.

28. Lorenz, 351.

SIGRID BAUSCHINGER

Vindication through Suffering: Gertrud Kolmar's Cycle of Poems "Robespierre"

GERTRUD KOLMAR'S CYCLE OF POEMS "Robespierre" is usually seen in the context of another cycle, "Das Wort der Stummen" ("The Word of the Silenced"). Both works were written in the same time frame, between 1933 and 1934. "Das Wort der Stummen" includes two poems on Robespierre, which could just as well be included in the other collection. Both cycles also show a reaction to the events surrounding the rise of Hitler's dictatorship.

In "Das Wort der Stummen," this can be taken for granted as it is a collection of poems with a contemporary topic: the political and racial persecution by the National Socialist regime, beginning immediately after January 30, 1933. But in "Robespierre," too, impressions of contemporary events have left their traces. Both cycles are after all connected by the same intention: to give voice to those who were forced into silence through dictatorial persecution as well as to Robespierre, who was sentenced to silence by historical accounts that distorted his political role. This voice calls out the one word that is of vital significance in the work of this poet: "Gerechtigkeit!" — justice.[1]

Nevertheless, we must not look at "Robespierre" too narrowly and only in the context of its date of origin. Gertrud Kolmar's interest in this figure as well as in the French Revolution and in French history dates back much further. In her essay "Das Bildnis Robespierres" (written in 1933), she alludes to a poem on the revolution written by Theodor Fontane, which she memorized enthusiastically when she was only sixteen years old.[2] The essay strongly suggests that Kolmar must have been occupied with the literature of the French Revolution for years. She was able to read this literature in the original French language as she had been educated to be an English and French language instructor. She passed an exam for military interpreters during the First World War and subsequently worked as a mail inspector in a prisoner of war camp. In 1927, she took a summer course for foreign students at the University of Dijon.[3]

"Das Bildnis Robespierres" is an attempt at finding an answer to the question of how it was possible that this revolutionary's portrayal, created by the partisan hatred of his time, could be maintained over a period of almost a century and a half. The author finds traces of this portrayal in an abundance of more or less reliable historical accounts and supports her statements with exact literary references. In the process, she notes innumerable differences of opinion about Robespierre. His birth, his appearance, and his character are described and interpreted in completely different terms by French and German authors. Only one thing remains clear: that there were considerably more accusers than defenders. Evil motives are imputed even to his good deeds, and his virtues are distorted beyond recognition and presented as the manifestation of repulsive character traits. Kolmar's analysis of the scholarship on Robespierre comes to the following conclusion: The image that the world created of this man is that of the petty bourgeois, suspicious of all that is out of the ordinary. They distrust Robespierre's moral austerity, his modesty, his temperance. "Redliche Leute," says Kolmar, hereby revealing herself as a Berliner, eat "Eisbein with Sauerkraut" (569). Danton, however, strong and dedicated to any and all pleasures that life had to offer, was the revolutionary of the Philistines, which he could not help" (573).

When Kolmar was occupied with her studies of Robespierre and the French Revolution, new historiographers such as Albert Mathiez and other experts on Robespierre appeared on the scene. In his many studies of individual aspects of Robespierre, which he derived from source material and which were published in *Études robespierristes* as well as in collections of his articles, Mathiez hoped to fundamentally revise the accepted image of the revolutionary. Mathiez (1874–1932) taught at various French universities, at Dijon among others, from where he was called to the Sorbonne in 1926. He considered Robespierre a great democrat who under no circumstances should be held solely accountable for the terror and bloodshed of the revolution. To the contrary, according to Mathiez, his temperance and persistence vis-à-vis his opponents in the revolutionary movement brought about the triumph of the republican ideal.[4]

Mathiez's influence can be felt also in the Danton play by Romain Rolland, which Kolmar saw in 1920 in the *Großes Schauspielhaus* in Berlin under the direction of Max Reinhardt. Herbert Ihering, however, made less than flattering comments about the role and the actor interpreting Robespierre: He maintained that Werner Kraus's physical intensity brought to the stage a Robespierre that resembled a petty and fanatic flea. According to Ihering, the actor came dangerously close to debasing the language through his repeatedly shrill and harsh tone.[5] Another critic, however, recognized Rolland's attempt to give Robespierre a "more human" face. Paul Wiegler observed the incongruence between Robespierre, the "fanatic of virtue," and the harmless and modest tenant of Mrs. Duplay, a widow whose young daughter loves him platonically and guards the threshold of his room.[6] Wiegler did think, though, that the characters in Rolland's drama were not as strongly drawn as those in Georg Büchner's play *Dantons Tod* (first published posthumously in 1835, "Danton's Death"). Reinhardt had brought this play to the stage of the *Deutsches Theater* four years earlier in a performance that had achieved fame through its lighting effects. Kolmar saw this performance, too, and she could still feel the effects of the fabulous Reinhardt production for weeks after. She quoted complete scenes from Romain Rolland's *Danton* and from Büchner's play *Dantons Tod*.[7]

Gertrud Kolmar's image of Robespierre, however, was formed predominantly as a result of her readings of the Robespierrists. Mathiez emphatically pointed out Robespierre's humanity and his struggle for all the disenfranchised. "Il ne s'est pas borné à prendre en toute occasion la défense des tous les déshérites, des juifs, des comédiens, des esclaves."[8] Also Mathiez believes that Robespierre intervened with remarkable understanding against the new oligarchy, which used the revolution as a means to enrich itself. Kolmar characterizes him as a just and pure man who looks at everything unclean and unjust as not belonging to humanity. He wants to eradicate these flaws where he finds them, just as one would pull weeds from a flower bed (577). In order to understand the terror, one must, according to Mathiez, put oneself into "l'atmosphere de l'époque"[9] — the spirit of the times — which did not leave the revolutionaries any other choice. Friedrich Sieburg shares this opinion. He evidently read the Robespierrists and wrote his book about Robespierre (it was published in 1935) at the same time as Kolmar wrote her works on the French Revolution. Sieburg argues that Robespierre fought relentlessly against the senseless cruelty and violence committed in the name of the terror. However, Sieburg also believes that Robespierre upheld the basis of the terror with complete awareness and without qualification. "One must give him his due and admit that the harshness of the law does not work only against the innocent. There *are* traitors, there *are* conspirators, there are circles connected to the enemy outside. ... There is corruption which ate its way through to the innermost circles of the Revolution, ... there are speculators who earn fortunes from the hunger of the people."[10] According to Kolmar, terror was a tool made only for him and his followers, which — fatefully — fell into the hands of the wrong people: "others were not able to wield the blade without abusing it, without letting it fall casually on head after head" (578). This aspect of Kolmar's depiction of Robespierre is the most difficult for her critics. The difficulty applies also to her cycle of poems, because she does not mention the "great terror" at all; instead, Robespierre is seen as *the* victim of the revolution. He is the victim who throws himself into the abyss "not to close it, but to keep it open," as if it were the permanent revolution (580). At the end of her essay, Kolmar shies away from proffering a true portrayal of Robespierre as refutation of the many false ones. She finds it quite impossible to do so, leaving Robespierre the enigma he has always been. In her cycle of poems, she attempts to make out the enigma Robespierre by casting him as an incorruptible seeker of justice with messianic character traits.

With only a few exceptions, Kolmar's poetic work appears in cycles. In her two historical cycles, "Napoleon und Marie" ("Napoleon and Marie"), an early work, and in "Robespierre," the poetic voice speaks with the same passion as in "Weibliches Bildnis" ("Female Portrait"), "Mein Kind" ("My Child"), or "Tierträume" ("Animal Dreams"). The historical backdrop and its costume neither distance nor diminish the intensity with which she writes. The cyclical arrangement of individual poems also allows the poet to promote her theme with ever increasing intensity by means of contrasts and ritardandos, or through repetition and variations of a motif. Were one to follow Joachim Müller and his treatise on "Das zyklische Prinzip der Lyrik,"[11] "Robespierre" would constitute an "open cycle" with experience as its motif and the poet's objective as the main theme. Epic elements change in a lyrical process and simultaneously develop the theme more elaborately, motifs run into one another, are taken up and carried over through isolated poems.

Gertrud Kolmar proves her mastery in all forty-five poems. Strict stanzas and rhymes are saturated with an abundance of rhetorical figures highlighting the bold metaphors and sound images. The metric structures are overlaid by a multitude of rhythms. Kolmar shows perfect mastery of the five-line stanza[12] that follows the rhyme pattern *abaab* and includes an added fourth verse whose ritardando renders the "dynamic force" of an "intensifying principle," as becomes evident in Walther Wiegler's excellent formal analysis of "Rue Saint-Honoré."[13] Kolmar utilizes this type of stanza with great finesse: She adds an especially strong last verse to the fourth — only seemingly final — verse, thereby fulfilling the conditions under which this stanza is successfully composed. Kolmar also writes stanzas of two, seven, and nine lines as well as tercets, sonnets, and octaves. Her octaves are not simply two stanzas of four lines put together, but her rhyme pattern *ababcdcd* bears the mark of the artfully composed "ottave rima." The majority of the "Robespierre" poems, however, is written in stanzas of four verses, in which Kolmar prefers to use alternate rhyme, a form which has fallen into increasing neglect in the twentieth century.

Following a brief overview over Kolmar's "Robespierre" cycle, the portrayal of Robespierre will be examined with an eye to its shortcomings and the poet's intent. For clarification and further elucidation, we will also examine Kolmar's unpublished play *Cécile Renault*. This will show us how contemporary events are reflected in this cycle and how they impact Kolmar's understanding of Robespierre, who seems to be a figure of identification for her.

The largest group of poems in the Robespierre cycle is devoted to the biography of the revolutionary. It takes us from his school days at the Collège d'Arras in that city where Maximilien-Marie Isidore de Robespierre, the son of a lawyer, was born in 1758 ("Arras"), to the Collège Louis le Grand in Paris ("Ludwig XVI., 1775"), where he received a scholarship. His mother had already died in 1767 and his father had left the country. Robespierre's visit to Rousseau in Ermenonville probably did not take place the way Kolmar describes it in "Rousseau und der Jüngling" ("Rousseau and the Youth"). Kolmar skips Robespierre's study of law in Paris and his professional life as a lawyer in Arras. We see him next at the National Convention, where his political career started.

Robespierre is shown in public as well as in private situations, wherein he is called upon to make historic decisions. In her poem "Camille," we see him struggle toward the decision to have his friend and fellow revolutionary Camille Desmoulins (with whom he attended the Collège Louis le Grand) executed in order to save the revolutionary movement from disintegrating. Desmoulins and Georges Danton were executed together. "Mit aufmerksamen Augen, unbewegt," (426)[14] Robespierre watches the execution in the poem "Dantons Ende" ("Danton's End").

On May 8, 1794, in "Das Fest des höchsten Wesens" ("The Feast of the Highest Being"), Robespierre elevates the belief in the immortality of the soul to the level of state religion. For Kolmar, this act constitutes a turning point in his career: He had become intoxicated with power, ecstasy, and death (433). His speech before the convent on July 26 ("Am achten Thermidor," "On the 8th Thermidor") would be his last. After the executions of thousands of people in the preceding weeks and since allowing the judges to judge at their own discretion according to the "Law of the 22nd Prairial," Robespierre had come to be considered by his contemporaries as exceedingly powerful and terrible. Before Kolmar arrives at the climax in this series of biographical poems, she interjects a poem about Eléonore Duplay, the daughter of Robespierre's landlord. Old and alone, she still mourns him after decades, her image being evoked again in the poem "Jener Abend" ("That Evening"). She and Robespierre are strolling through the park on a warm summer evening: she, the "young bride"; he, disquieted by the anticipation of his death. Only the night from the 9th to the 10th Thermidor (July 27 to July 28) separates him from his end after his arraignment ("Die Nacht"). In this poem, Kolmar paints his defeat, drawing on "Beschwörung" ("Incantation"), a poem from the beginning of the cycle. In the earlier poem, she writes: "Nimm die Waage. Nimm das Schwert" (376). Now it says:

> Der Balken seiner Waage hing zerstört.
> Er hielt des Schwertes Scherbe in der Hand. (442)

Robespierre has become a defeated symbol of justice, a fallen Archangel Michael.

Kolmar depicts Robespierre's end in three poems and shows his tortures with brutal candor in "Der Tisch" ("The Table"), on which the mortally wounded man was placed after an attempted suicide — he shot himself in the jaw but failed; in "Der Sessel" ("The Armchair"), which shows the half-dead revolutionary being carried away from the Tuileries to the Conciergerie, where he was sentenced to death; and in "Rue Saint-Honoré," the street through which he was led to his execution.

In between her poems sketching Robespierre's biography, Kolmar intersperses several portraits of other revolutionaries and figures of the epoch. She has a particular predilection for Saint-Just, not only because he was Robespierre's most loyal disciple, who was executed at his side; she likes him because of his classical beauty. Saint-Just was celebrated as an enthusiastic orator and as victor in the battles of the revolutionary army. Kolmar depicts this young revolutionary, who in so many ways was the opposite of Robespierre, as a man prepared to sacrifice. "Der Anbeginn Saint-Justs" ("The Beginning of Saint-Just") shows him controlling his youthful licentiousness and embarking on a new life, a luminous figure but at the same time ice cold. He is contrasted with the volcanic Napoleon in "Begegnung" ("Encounter"). No character in the whole cycle is shown as more radiant and charming than Saint-Just, a "Jüngling der in Blitzen stand" (429), who is victorious even on the scaffold.

Marat, on the other hand, is conjured up in all his ugliness: as animal, dirt, amphibian, cur, and toad. From his body, disfigured by illness and wracked with pain, he projects his great utopian model. He wants to put "in alle Hungerhände Brot" (394), and so, against all odds, he stands before the convent as "Marat Triumphator." Danton remains the only one for whom Gertrud Kolmar did not write a poem, except the one about his death. For her, he may have been praised enough. In the poems "Danton und Robespierre" ("Danton and Robespierre") and "Dantons Ende" ("Danton's End"), she contrasts him with his opponent Robespierre. Danton is characterized as one of those strong men who live their lives without regard for others, who never repent, and who laugh when they die (391). His end is captured in imagery radiating sexual energy. Danton clings on to his last hour, envisioned as female, grabs her black mane of hair and then throws her before the barrier of the scaffold, "glühend, stark und nackt" (426).

Eléonore Duplay and two other women, Marat's widow, Simone Evrard, and Marat's murderess, Charlotte Corday, are the only female characters in the cycle. Corday is the only female figure — aside from the anonymous "Girondist" — from the opposing camp of the revolution to whom Kolmar dedicated a poem. She, too, could not escape the fascination emanating from this "luminous figure"[15] so often depicted in poetry, prose, and drama. In her description of Corday, she even uses the same metaphor that she uses for Robespierre, calling her an "ash blond candle." Like all women characters, she is drawn according to Kolmar's conservative understanding of women. Inge Stephan notes that should there be a woman who could be depicted as heroine, Kolmar will let her appear as a victim. In "Der König" ("The King"), rather than rendering a portrait of Louis XVI, Kolmar gives a verdict condemning the monarchy. The poem is part of the small group of texts that complete the panoramic picture of the revolution: "Paris," "Die Nationalversammlung" ("The National Assembly"), "Die Hébertisten" ("The Hébertists"), and as coda "Alte Jakobiner" ("Old Jacobins").

At a prominent place right at the beginning of the "Robespierre" cycle, at the end, and in irregular intervals throughout the cycle there are poems that differ from the ones mentioned so far. They are less descriptive, but evocative: They are incantations, as the title of the first poem indicates. They convey Kolmar's intent. Going far beyond reminiscences about the French Revolution, they serve as the poet's yardstick for doing complete justice to history (and to the poetic voice). Monika Shafi points out that Kolmar did not adhere to any set criteria in her understanding of justice.[16] Robespierre as the "executive authority" of a legislation without legitimacy is literally beyond the law. First, Kolmar conjures up the three revolutionaries Marat, Saint-Just, and Robespierre. The latter already stands out as the chosen one. Marat is the "ami du peuple" — the friend of the people — judging by the pious gesture of his hands, which are folded, holding the crumbs of the poor (375). Saint-Just is glorified as an almost celestial being. Robespierre, on the other hand, is the man who suffers, is ridiculed, and tortured. He is addressed as Christ would be addressed in a Christian prayer:

> Von Schmach durchstochen beide Hände:
> Sind deine Ostern jetzt? (376)

The poem answers this question affirmatively and calls upon the risen "saints" to use the righteousness that is theirs to bring justice into the world.

In the next poem, Kolmar invokes "Die großen Puritaner" ("The Great Puritans") and positions the "Stimmen des Thermidor" ("Voices of the Thermidor," 406) in the succession of the prophets: with Moses, Savanorola, and Milton. They are the conscience of humanity. The poet confesses to them: "euch ruf ich und liebe euch, ja, ich liebe euch sehr!" (406). In the introductory verse, her program is announced: This is the truth and the poet holds it in her hands (406). Her claim that she is heir to the commandments makes her the prophet who holds the claim to justice. It is a heavy burden, this inheritance, but she is ready to bear it. Robespierre, on the other hand, is characterized as the one who has the right to administer justice. The poem "... et pereat mundus" (" ... and May the World Perish") asks him in a series of invoking imperatives to ignite the fire of justice in us who are imperfect and weak. Moreover, Robespierre is chosen to administer justice because he is pure. In his purity lie all his virtues: his temperance, his incorruptibility, and his faith, the last being so important for Kolmar. Robespierre, a deist, promulgated the worship of the highest being along with the belief in the immortality of the soul through the law.

In the two crucial poems in which Kolmar's understanding of Robespierre and of herself as a poet is expressed most forcefully, she calls upon the Pure One. The metaphor of the candle was derived from revolutionary history. Kolmar uses it also as the motto for the first poem: "They called Mirabeau 'the torch of Provence' and they called Robespierre mockingly 'the candle of Arras'" (395). However, while this comparison served to devalue Robespierre in the first national assembly — he was a small, thin man and a poor orator vis-à-vis Mirabeau — the poet uses the candle metaphor to express his purity. She descends into the shattered vaults of the past, where she finds the candle without flame and the marble tablets of the law destroyed. Alone and without help, she seeks to reestablish the law.

> Will, du Kerze, dich inmitten setzen
> Als ein neues schauendes Gesicht,
> Meinen Mund mit deiner Flamme netzen,
> Daß sein Lied von ihrem reinen Licht
> Weilend töne. (396)

In the following poem, "Ein Gleiches" ("The Same"), Kolmar employs a cup as a metaphor for the poet. In it, the candle sacrifices itself, shedding its tears of wax. The poem also explains why the poet likens herself to the receptacle for the candle: She has been hardened like an earthen vessel by the fire of her memories of her own persecuted and murdered ancestors. She considers it a miracle that she is alive (397). This is the juncture at which Judaism and literary vocation meet, and it becomes clear once more that Gertrud Kolmar's understanding of her Jewishness was derived from her understanding of history, as has been noted by Dagmar Lorenz in her comparison of Kolmar and Else Lasker-Schüler.[17] The candle's flame, which the poetic voice saves from extinction and, as it were, passes on, provides the speaker with authority, as is evident in the poem "Gott" ("God"). The last sentence uttered by Saint-Just in Rolland's play about Danton becomes

Kolmar's motto: "People die, so God may live." The poem might also have been influenced by Büchner's play *Dantons Tod*, where in the first scene of the third act, Danton and those about to be executed with him discuss the nature of God.

This is the essence of the poem. However, it reaches far beyond the topic of the revolution itself and casts a harsh light upon men's idea of God, which often reflects their utilitarian needs and serves the purpose of a kind of insurance company. Opposite this "small God," Kolmar positions the incomprehensible and the perfect, a truly "supreme being." One other poem transcends the framework of "Robespierre," and is closely connected to Kolmar's cycle "Das Kind." It is entitled "Maximilian" and addressed to her unborn child, whom she would have named after Robespierre.

Kolmar's profound knowledge of the history of the French Revolution is evident from each poem. It ranges from Robespierre's biography to the many details about revolutionary events. An example of Kolmar's ability to include a plethora of historical facts in relatively few lines is the poem "Nacht" ("Night"). At the time in question, during the night from the 9th to the 10th Thermidor, only a handful of fighters of the commune were ready to counter the attack of the convent's troops. Among them were Robespierre and Saint-Just, whose defeat was thereby unavoidable. The poem "Rue Saint-Honoré" is an example of Kolmar's poetic technique of blending historical fact and expressive imagery: It describes the street in which Robespierre lived at the house of the cabinetmaker Duplay and through which he was taken to his execution on an executioner's cart. Half-dead already, he was dragged through the mob and past members of the *jeunesse dorée*. Not even the policeman's saber pointing at him so that his face would be recognized underneath his blood-drenched dressing is missing.

So many details — and still the picture is far from complete. Kolmar did not include in her depiction of Robespierre all that which could support a tradition of what in her eyes are unfair accounts of his reign of terror. She does not waste a single word on the thousands of executed people who were guilty of nothing but belonging to a certain class: "le crime de l'aristocratie" — the crime of the aristocracy. On the rare occasion when she alludes to the mass executions, such as in the poem "Marat," where she describes how Marat saw red, severed necks, heads and blood in tubs (394), the picture of horror is immediately converted into another vision of the future: his seeing bread in all hungry hands (394).

This interpretation can be traced back to Mathiez, who tries to prove in his many scrupulously researched articles that Robespierre rarely bore sole responsibility for arrests and executions. Mathiez argues that Robespierre tried to save, with occasional success, those sentenced, as was the case with seventy-three Girondists. In the case of Madame Elisabeth, the king's sister, he

did not succeed. Even the law of the 22nd Prairial, which made superfluous
both witnesses and defense attorneys for trials and which is attributed to
Robespierre, was, according to Mathiez, the decision of the entire committee.[18] Had he been the victim of an assassination attempt, says Mathiez,
Robespierre would have gone down in history as the greatest statesman of
the revolution.

Kolmar does not even touch upon these historical facts in her essay. Only
one comment on the fatal law can be found in the cycle, in one verse of the
poem "Nacht": "Und wissend, daß er selber sich entrechtet" (442), a verse
which, interestingly enough, appears before the image of Robespierre with
the broken scales and sword. Which readers who are not familiar with the
history of the French Revolution would understand this allusion? The readers
do not have to understand it, Kolmar might argue, because her intention is
to relate Robespierre's character. Shafi observes in her analysis of Kolmar's
essay, which she compares to Hannah Arendt's paper "On Revolution," that
Kolmar transfers the "historic actions" of the revolutionaries — she refers to
them as "saints" — into a "religious-transcendental dimension," which takes
away from them exactly that which characterizes their actions.[19] According to
Shafi, she successfully performs a "salto mortale" on several occasions. This is
supposedly necessary to justify Robespierre's cruelty. As a result, terror is
transformed into "a historical necessity"[20] so that the revolutionary can
achieve his goal: absolute justice.

From this vantage point, the failure of Robespierre's mission as well as his
end make him into a victim. The revolution is being turned into an account
of the passion that makes everyone, perpetrators included, a victim.[21] All the
characters in Kolmar's cycle are victims, from the anonymous Girondists to
the old Jacobins who, living in the Napoleonic era, deplore the end of the
revolution they brought about by betraying Robespierre. Even a humiliated
Louis XVI is included, who is forced to drink with others from a crude bot-
tle, the red prisoner's cap on his head (390); the murderess Charlotte Corday, Danton, Marat, and Saint-Just — all of them are depicted in the moment of their demise. Robespierre, however, is the preeminent victim and a
Messiah figure.

These figures are victims because of their suffering. History as a paradigm
of suffering is the epistemological precondition,[22] Shafi writes, subsuming
"Robespierre" under this paradigm. Indeed, the paradigm of suffering does
characterize each figure, but none as markedly as Robespierre. Even before
his birth, Robespierre was destined to suffer. In the poem "Grabschrift"
("Epitaph"), it says:

> Aber er, der Reine, der Gerechte,
> Ward gezeugt, als Opferlamm zu fallen. (453)

His childhood and adolescence are marked by suffering. Without friends, he spends his school years in Arras and accepts his "dark fate" (380). As an orphan, at the Collège Louis Le Grand, he is the recipient of a "meager" stipend (383). And when selected to recite "his Latin poem" to the king, the monarch pushes, "mit lässigem Schuh," the crumbs toward the shy boy (383). But his teachers push to the front and steal the king's praise and rewards from the youth.

Nature, too, put Robespierre at a disadvantage. His eyes are described as colorless and his forehead as pale (383). In addition, he is poor and therefore dependent on the king's charity. His shortcomings make him a laughing-stock, even in the poem "Die Nationalversammlung" ("The National Assembly"). But here, the poet turns Robespierre's weakness into his strength. When he intervenes in the chaos, he says:

> Zu der blinden, jammerwirren Schar,
> Die im Winkel sinnlos sich gerottet.
> Einer, den sie ausgelacht, verspottet,
> Weil er arm und trüb und linkisch war,
>
> Löste sich aus knisterndem Gefüge,
> Klein, nur wie der Rindenspan vom Stamm,
> Stand nicht größer unterm Feuerkamm,
> Schritt auf Scherben ihrer Wasserkrüge
>
> Tragend das unendliche Geflamm
> So, als ob er roten Mantel trüge. (387–88)

This is virtually the only mention made of Robespierre's triumphs. The most frequently used expression for the reactions shown Robespierre by his political opponents as well as by the people — which, by the way, appears exclusively as the mob on the streets of Paris — is scorn. This feeling runs through the entire cycle and is combined with hatred. Robespierre's image to this day has been surrounded by hatred, denounced by scorn (378). Therefore, he is a lonely figure, quite unlike Danton.

Not only political ideas separate Robespierre from other revolutionary groups, but also religion. Unlike the Hébertists, for example, Robespierre was religious. The poet alludes to this fact in "Am achten Thermidor," where she has Robespierre say:

> Ich weiß: ihr leugnet ein unsterblich Leben.
> Der Schöpfer wollte, daß es einst euch fehle,
> Und hat euch Bein und Fleisch und Nichts gegeben,
> Betrogne. Ich … Mir gab er eine Seele … (435)

It is here that Kolmar raises an objection to Mathiez. In her essay, she quotes his sentence: "Er [Robespierre] liebte minder Gott als das Volk, und er liebte Gott nur, weil er glaubte, daß ihn das Volk nicht entbehren könne." And she adds: "Mit aller Ehrfurcht, die ich dem Forscher schulde: Ist das die ganze Wahrheit?" (575). She counters Mathiez with the following confession by Robespierre: "Wie hätte ich, mit meiner Seele allen Kämpfen, die über Menschenkraft gehen, gewachsen sein können, wenn ich mein Herz nicht zu Gott erhoben hätte?" In her opinion, "Robespierre und die Seinen wollten die Kirche Gott entreißen, und Gott aus ihr reißen und sie zurücklassen als einen leeren, nutz- und sinnlosen Schrein" (575). In Kolmar's understanding of Robespierre, the religious aspect is more important than the political one. There is at least one indication of her intention: She wanted to subtitle the cycle "Religious poems."[23]

The poems in "Robespierre" are religious insofar as the great revolutionaries, just like the great Puritans, are characterized as saints and martyrs, and the main character is, of course, the one preeminent, godlike figure.

> Du mehr als Mensch. Du nichts als Schatten:
> Den eine Gottheit warf. (379)

"Der Unbestechliche" ("The Incorruptible") includes all the traits of the ascetic, who renounces

> Des Bechers Blinken, weiß und rot,
> Der Frauen sanfte Mirabelle,
> Das runde gelbe Honigbrot ... (422)

in order to "to dine with the hungry poor" and who, surrounded by lies, has been handed down to posterity in a distorted image. The Christian martyrs died knowing that they were to live on in the praise of their grandchildren:

> Sie griffen ihrer Nachwelt zu;
> Dem Lohn der Martertode: Du,
> Du hattest alles, alles hingegeben. (523)

This thought also lies at the heart of Gertrud Kolmar's unpublished drama "Cécile Renault." According to the author's handwritten notes in the typescript, this play in four acts was written between February 24, 1934, and March 14, 1935.[24] The period of its composition coincides with her essay and the cycle about Robespierre. The play is set in the circle surrounding the prophetess Cathérine Théot, whose sect had the reputation of worshiping Robespierre as the Messiah. In Act I, young Cécile Renault is accepted into the "Union" of Cathérine Théot, who sees God's finger point to the one who will extirpate all weeds and who goes by the name of "the Pure One," "the Untouchable One," and "the Incorruptible One." Act II introduces us to the petty bourgeois Renault family. Cécile's father, a stationer's store-keeper is overwhelmed by inflation and distress and sets all his hopes on the revolution. Her sixteen-year-old brother wants to join the Jacobins, but her Aunt Marie-Angélique, an old nun, does not expect any relief from them. She is the one who knows about "the Pure One," of whom Cécile talks after her initiation into the "Union." According to the nun, however, it is a child languishing in prison, Louis XVII, the Dauphin, and she suggests that some-one, a woman, should tell Robespierre about the incarcerated orphan child. A visitor, also a woman, describes Robespierre not only as the shy, quiet as-cetic who does not eat meat and does not drink wine; like a visionary, she uses most unusual images such as the lamb that tears wolves to pieces and as the anvil that flattens hammers. Both images are to be found almost identi-cally in the poem "Bildnis Robespierres" ("Robespierre's Picture") from the cycle "Das Wort der Stummen."

Having been introduced in this way, Robespierre appears on the scene in Act III, which takes place in his room in the Duplay house. Stage directions ask for a stern face bearing the expression of suffering. His conversation with his young pupil Julien reveals that he suffers because of his image, which is that of a tyrant who pays the executioner. He calls himself "die Rache der Waffenlosen" — the revenge of the defenseless. He admits to the terror of the revolution, but he justifies it — and himself — with the protection of a defenseless youth and his goal of establishing a "holy republic," where politi-cal and moral rejuvenation go hand in hand with scientific and technological progress. The scene with Eléonore Duplay is intended to show Robespierre as compassionate as possible. He is depicted as one who loves flowers and animals and who has saved seventy-three Girondists. When Eléonore asks him why he does not talk to other people as openly as he talks to her, he ex-plains that it is because of the "misery."

Upon Robespierre's learning about the arrest of "God's mother" Théot and her "shameless idolatry," which he downplays as irrelevant, Cécile Ren-ault appears on the scene. She complains to Robespierre about the people's plight: Sons are at war, inflation causes great hardship, and every day "those carts" are driving to the guillotine. Rather than suggesting the Dauphin as the future ruler, she proposes Robespierre. She kneels before him with Ju-lien, and they both worship him as the Messiah, using a language rich in quotations from the New Testament. Yet, when Robespierre rejects their adulation, Cécile draws a dagger.

There is an ongoing debate as to whether the historical Cécile intended to kill herself or Robespierre. Plenty of clues point toward murder, although in the play even Robespierre seems convinced that the dagger was not meant for him. However, in Act IV, he does not save Cécile from her arrest and en-suing death. When Julien begs for her life in the Security Council's Hall, he responds that he cannot save her, because she believed in him. It is the general opinion that Cécile made an attempt on his life — the second one within only a few days. If Robespierre were to pardon her, the world would regard him as a saint. The Incorruptible One, though, cannot do good "for the sake of higher interests." Thus, he loses even his friend Julien and in his final words admits to having sacrificed even his memory to posterity.

In her play, Kolmar intended to bring out Robespierre's messianic traits. The prophesies of Cathérine Théot in Act I are supported by quotations from the Book of Micah. They mark the beginning of such a characterization. In Act II, scene 4, he is worshipped with words from the New Testament as the Christian Messiah: "Lord, I am not worthy that thou shouldst come under my roof" (Matthew 8,8).

But it is the poet rather than the playwright who succeeds in tracing Robespierre's life of suffering. One reason for that is the short time frame in which the plot around Cécile Renault occurs — three days at the end of May 1774 — while the cycle spans three decades, including Robespierre's childhood and death. For the most part, though, it is the power of the poet's language that by far surpasses that of the playwright's. The didactic monologues lack the poetic force of the poems and, compared to poems such as "Eléonore Duplay," the corresponding scenes in the play appear sentimental. Toward the end of the cycle, the image of the misunderstood Messiah Robespierre becomes ever more prominent and so do the parallels with the Passion of Jesus. Like Christ, Robespierre is betrayed and executed. These events represent the climax of the entire cycle. The individual poems, too, are composed according to the principle of escalation. In German poetry, we rarely find poems with stronger conclusions than those in Kolmar's work.

The suffering of Robespierre is written with his gruesome end in mind, which overshadows his whole life story. Robespierre's stations of the cross lead him through the crowds first in an armchair, then on a cart. It takes him to his Golgatha, where the executioner tears the bloody bandage off his head:

> Bretter ... Pfähle ... eine Scharlachjacke.
> Fäuste griffen aus dem Knäul,
> Fetzen ihm das Linnen von der Backe;
> Sein Gesicht zerstürzte, rote Schlacke;
> Troff in grausigem Geheul. (452)

In order to express suffering with such power of language, one must have the ability to experience great suffering. Gertrud Kolmar seems predestined by the history of her people for suffering and compassion, which consequently helped her become a master in the depiction of suffering. Interestingly enough, the character of the old Jew Jom-Tob, who was accepted into the Union of Mère Cathérine, is one of the most convincing characters in the entire play, "Cécile Renault."

Clues for the composition in "Robespierre" are often clues pointing to the persecution of the Jews, most prominently in the poem "Ein Gleiches."

> Mag sein, daß wieder Erz und Feldstein schon bereit,
> Mich zu umschmieden, mich zu schlagen.
> Das feste Dach zerbirst im Ausbruch jäher Zeit,
> Von Karyatiden bröckeln Klagen, (397)

Of course, looking back on Kolmar's life and death, the final verse of the poem, "Ich aber werde schweigend sterben" (448), can only be read with great shock. Lawrence Langer is correct in reminding us that "her philosophical exertions to master present hardships and prepare for future anguish, admirable as they may be, echo for us with a mournful irony, since nothing in her prior experience, or in Jewish experience, or in human experience could possibly prepare her for the unprecedented cynical brutality of the Nazi final solution."[25]

The question as to how much in "Robespierre" must be understood in its contemporary context occupied all literary scholars interested in this cycle.[26] Kolmar's interest in the topic ranged over many years, during which time she was engaged in reading relevant literature. In addition, one needs to take into consideration the impact of the plays by Büchner and Rolland, which had been written long before Kolmar composed her cycle of poems. These facts lead to the assumption that even under different circumstances, she probably would not have written "Robespierre" in any other way. Nevertheless, the events around 1933, street fights and anti-Semitic violence, which Kolmar experienced firsthand in Berlin, are mirrored in her cycle. Her cousin, the physician Georg Benjamin — Walter Benjamin's brother — was committed to a concentration camp and released; then he was arrested again and finally killed. This experience gave her an understanding of the word *Schutzhaft* (protective custody).

It is particularly Kolmar's depiction of the mob that is marked by contemporary events. *Das Volk* — the people — which could conceivably be included in her paradigm of victimization and suffering and which is referred to with the term the "poor," never appears. However, the mob does, as a collection of drooling distorted grimaces. Shafi even believes that the people's constant degradation to the level of the mob constitutes the precondition for Kolmar's glorification of Robespierre.[27] Shafi goes as far as to say that Kolmar does not follow "the democratic demand for liberty, equality, and brotherhood. The juxtaposition of Robespierre and the masses reflects an elitist historical view."[28] If this were the case, Kolmar surely would not have recognized Mathiez as an authority and relied on his portrayal of Robespierre as the true democrat and friend of the people. Kolmar's depiction of the mob does not, however, suggest her putting Robespierre on the same level with Hitler.[29] To the contrary, the unappreciated Messiah could be seen also as the savior of the present time.

> Bau, du Türmer wieder Ewigkeit,
> Starke Himmel, die uns weisen,
> Da die Machtgestirne unsrer Zeit
> Wild in Untergängen kreisen. (431)

Robespierre's ability to suffer and feel compassion, as expressed in the poems, has led to the perception of him being a figure of identification and projection.[30] However, distinctions must be drawn. The poetic voice identifying with Robespierre through her own experience with suffering can do so only to a certain degree. Just as he is represented as being more than human (378–79), so his suffering assumes a superhuman quality as well. But the poetic voice lamenting his life of suffering is that of a human being, and the voice of a woman who asks herself if she might succeed in something that no woman has yet accomplished (396). As a poet, Kolmar positions herself as a servant. The beginning and the end of the final poem of "Robespierre" are to be understood this way, as a gesture of humility.

> Ich werde sterben, wie die Vielen sterben;
> Durch dieses Leben wird die Harke gehn
> Und meinen Namen in die Scholle kerben.
> Ich werde leicht und still und ohne Erben
> Mit müden Augen kahle Wolken sehn,
>
> . . . .
> Die weiche Krume Lehm, die ihr geknetet
> Und noch zur Form mit harten Händen zwingt.
> Ihr. Die ihr ernst aus euren Nischen tretet,
> Was wißt ihr von dem Herzen, das euch betet,
> Was von dem Mund, der eure Glorie singt? (456–57)

Notes

[1] Compare the poem "Wir Juden" ("We Jews"), *Frühe Gedichte* (1917–1922) in *Das Wort der Stummen*, ed. Johanna Woltmann-Zeitler (1933; reprint, Munich: Kösel, 1980), 224–26.

[2] Johanna Zeitler, ed., "Gertrud Kolmar. Das Bildnis Robespierres," *Jahrbuch der Deutschen Schillergesellschaft* 9 (1965): 553–80. In-text citations from this essay refer to this volume.

[3] See Johanna Woltmann, "Lebenslauf," in *Gertrud Kolmar, Leben und Werk* (Göttingen: Wallstein, 1995), 329.

[4] Albert Mathiez, "Pourquoi nous sommes des Robespierristes?" *Études sur Robespierre* (Paris: Messodor / Editions Sociales, 1988), 17–35.

[5] Günther Rühle, *Theater für die Republik 1917–1933 im Spiegel der Kritik* (Frankfurt am Main: S. Fischer, 1967), 207.

[6] Quoted in Rühle, 205.

[7] Hilde Wenzel, "Nachwort," in *Das lyrische Werk*, by Gertrud Kolmar (Munich: Kösel, 1960), 597.

[8] Mathiez, 22. Translation: "He did not limit himself to come to the defense of all the deprived, the Jews, the actors, the slaves."

[9] Ibid., 74.

[10] Friedrich Sieburg, *Robespierre. Napoleon. Chateaubriand.* (Stuttgart: Deutsche Verlagsanstalt, 1967), 128.

[11] Joachim Müller, "Das zyklische Prinzip der Lyrik," *Germanisch-Romanische Monatshefte* 20 (1932): 1–20.

[12] In the introductory stanzas of "Beschwörung" ("Incantation"), in "Rue Saint-Honoré," and in the last poem, "Nachruf" ("Obituary"), which concludes the cycle.

[13] Walther Wiegler, "Gertrud Kolmar. Rue St. Honoré," in *Wege zum Gedicht*, vol. 2, ed. Ruppert Hirschenauer and Albrecht Weber (Munich: Schnell und Steiner, 1963), 517–33.

[14] The cycle "Robespierre" can be found in Gertrud Kolmar, *Das lyrische Werk* (Munich: Kösel, 1960): 375–456. All in-text citations of the "Robespierre" poems are to this edition.

[15] Compare Inge Stephan, "Gewalt, Eros und Tod. Metamorphosen der Charlotte Corday-Figur vom 18. Jahrhundert bis in die Gegenwart," in *Die Marseillaise der Weiber*, ed. Inge Stephan and Sigrid Weigel (Hamburg: Argument, 1989), 128–45.

[16] Monika Shafi, *Gertrud Kolmar. Eine Einführung in das Werk* (Munich: iudicum, 1995), 150–51.

[17.] Dagmar C. G. Lorenz, "The Unspoken Bond. Else Lasker-Schüler and Gertrud Kolmar in Their Historical and Cultural Context," *Seminar* 4 (1993): 349–69.

[18.] Mathiez, 76.

[19.] Shafi, 145.

[20.] Ibid., 147.

[21.] Stephan, 142.

[22.] Shafi, 144.

[23.] Woltmann, 191.

[24.] Gertrud Kolmar, "Cecile Renault. Play in Four Acts by Gertrud [the name Kolmar is crossed out] Chodziesner," typescript (Marbach: Deutsches Literaturarchiv [93. 18. 1947]).

[25.] Lawrence Langer, "Survival through Art. The Career of Gertrud Kolmar," in *Yearbook 22. Publications of the Leo Baeck Institute* (London: Secker & Warburg, 1978), 252.

[26.] See Reinhard Döhl, "Gertrud Kolmar: Ludwig XVI., 1775," in *Geschichte im Gedicht. Texte und Interpretationen,* ed. Walter Hinck (Frankfurt am Main: Suhrkamp, 1979), 170–82.

[27.] Shafi, 151.

[28.] Ibid., 154.

[29.] See Shafi, 140.

[30.] Ibid., 152ff.

MONIKA SHAFI

Reconsidering Gertrud Kolmar
through the Cycle "German Sea"

> History is always based on a choice,
> and what enters the historical account
> is valorized by its inclusion.
>
> — Marie-Luise Gättens,
> *Women Writers and Fascism*

THE POET GERTRUD KOLMAR (1894–1943) has received a considerable
amount of scholarly attention during the past years. This renewed interest in a writer whose texts languished for many decades at the margin of the
canon can be explained by a number of factors. First, the commemoration of
her birth and her death helped in generating a certain publicity for the
author. The 1993 Kolmar exhibition organized by Johanna Woltmann in the
Marbacher Literaturarchiv as well as the exhibition *Orte*, which Marion
Brandt prepared and first showed in 1994 in Falkensee (near Berlin),
brought Kolmar and her work into the public forum.[1] The second, and more
important, reason for the ongoing rediscovery of Kolmar's works can be located in the emergence of a number of new theoretical approaches, most
notably feminist literary criticism, which enabled scholars to analyze her œuvre within the context of contemporary critical discourses. Finally, the debate
about Germany's legacy of National Socialism, which in the wake of the
German reunification has taken new directions,[2] perhaps also contributed to
the discussion of Kolmar as a German-Jewish poet to be examined in the
context of Jewish and Holocaust studies.

Yet, despite these numerous and varied efforts, Kolmar's work is by no
means fully analyzed, and many questions and queries await further investigation.[3] Another crucial lacuna in Kolmar scholarship is the lack of a critical
edition of her works. Not only do parts of her œuvre remain unpublished,
but the existing edition of her poems, to take just one example, is not consistent with Kolmar's original typescripts.[4] Hermann Kasack, the first editor
of Kolmar's lyrics, had rearranged her poetic cycles in order to present read-

ers with what he deemed to be a more coherent and effective organization. Despite this arbitrary procedure, Kasack and especially Johanna Woltmann, together with Kolmar's sister Hilde Wenzel and her brother-in-law Peter Wenzel, have to be credited for promoting and publishing Kolmar's poems in the years following the Second World War. Without their persistent efforts on behalf of Kolmar's œuvre, it might have been forgotten and lost forever.[5]

Gertrud Kolmar has aptly been called the poet of women and animals, suggested also by the title of her most important and last publication during her lifetime (*Die Frau und die Tiere*, 1938). In this as well as in other collections, the transformation of the lyric self into different personae, animals, or minerals plays a key role. These transformations often take place in exotic locales and landscapes, and Kolmar depicted numerous imaginary journeys.[6] Yet, she did not seem to be interested in the fictionalization of her own travels in Germany or of her 1927 journey to France. "German Sea," however, is the only cycle directly based on a trip Kolmar undertook, and it thus occupies a rather unique position in her œuvre. In the following, I would like to discuss this short cycle, consisting of only seven poems, both within the context of travel literature and of Kolmar's work and explore her thoughts on home and abroad, self and other as well as discuss the link she establishes between traveling and language. My argument is that "German Sea" constitutes not only an innovative contribution to the extremely diverse genre of travel literature, but that the poems also address Kolmar's relationship as a Jewish woman writer to the German "fatherland." Since this analysis is set within a reconsideration of Gertrud Kolmar, I furthermore wish to illustrate the divergent scholarly approaches to Kolmar and her texts that have emerged over the past years and explain what they have contributed to our understanding of this enigmatic author.

Not much is known about Gertrud Kolmar, who until the onset of Nazi dictatorship, led a rather protected and secluded life, which was quite removed from the urban modernity shaping the Weimar Republic.[7] One of Kolmar's decisive life experiences was an abortion she had to undergo in her early twenties and which appeared to have created a long-lasting trauma of self-doubt, self-accusations, guilt, and despair.[8] Since innumerous poems deal with motherhood, with the loss of a child as well as with mourning and death, biography and text seemed to be inextricably intertwined. An additional link between biographic experience and poetic realization can be seen in Kolmar's Jewishness, for the author devoted many poems to an exploration of (female) Jewish identity in past and present times. Kolmar's only autobiographical text, letters she wrote between fall 1938 and February 1943 to her sister Hilde,[9] provide further evidence that her writing was in many instances closely related to pivotal life experiences.

How to account for and interpret this liaison has, however, sharply divided critics of Kolmar's works. The scholars who after the war first paid attention to Kolmar hardly distinguished between the biographical and the poetic praxis. In Woltmann's publications, which can be taken as representative for this group,[10] basically no distinction was made between the person and the author, and interpretations subsequently focused on the poetic imagination, on the beauty of the images, or on the striking originality of metaphors through which personal pain and suffering were transformed into timeless art. In her 1995 biography, *Gertrud Kolmar — Leben und Werk* ("Gertrud Kolmar — Life and Work"), Woltmann continued to adhere to this mode. She directly juxtaposes, for example, her reading of Kolmar's œuvre as largely autobiographical with quotes from Kolmar poems, which are thus treated primarily as biographical documents, and not as literary texts.

Furthermore, inspired by the desire to keep Kolmar's memory alive as well as to promote her work, a classic *Dichterin* paradigm was created through which Woltmann and others hoped to do justice to Kolmar's œuvre, her poetic self-definition, and, perhaps most important, to account for the extraordinary heroism and courage Kolmar showed during her last years in Berlin. Elevating the author to this status required thus a devotional rather than a critical attitude, for the task of the critic was to present and highlight the exceptional qualities of her work. If her poetry was to be seen in the vein of the classic German literary tradition, then it had to be valued as immortal, beautiful art, which transcended any narrow social confines. Ironically, the norms and values of canon-formation were applied to an author who occupied at best a marginal position in the canon.[11]

Questioning and challenging the strategies of canon-formation and marginalization required, however, a different approach to Gertrud Kolmar as well as a different set of questions and goals. Since the early 1980s, a number of scholars have investigated Kolmar's work using a variety of feminist, historical, psychological, or deconstructionist theories.[12] The main difference between these works and the previously described scholarship is that the theory-inspired approaches situate Kolmar within an explicit sociohistorical context, examining her work as part of a tradition of, for example, women writers or as a Walter Benjamin–inspired critique of violence. Rather than celebrating Kolmar's poems and her two narratives as an expression of her personal and poetic accomplishments, Kolmar's texts were analyzed and critiqued as part of specific literary, historical, or theoretical traditions. Since a detailed explanation of these very distinct theoretical approaches is certainly beyond the scope of this article,[13] and since much of the criticism of the representatives of the older, *werkimmanente* method has been launched at feminist theories, I will focus on feminist literary criticism in order to explain the differences between two very diverse views of Kolmar's texts.

One of the main tenets of feminism is the argument that gender is to be understood as a social construction and not, as the patriarchal order has always claimed, as a "natural" distinction that separates the sexes according to their "given" abilities and functions.[14] Feminist literary criticism thus seeks to understand how the specific position women have occupied in society and culture is reflected and articulated in their texts. How do women writers deal, to give just one example, with the traditional gender concept? Do they accept, critique, or deconstruct it, and in which narrative or poetic forms do they express their views? Situating Kolmar and her work within a feminist context therefore does not mean to look for traces of Kolmar's participation in emancipatory issues and struggles, as Lorenz-Lindemann alleges.[15] Such an understanding mistakenly identifies the political struggle for women's emancipation with the much more broad-based critique of patriarchal power structures as they shape a writer's identity and texts. To inquire in which way Kolmar dealt with the prevailing gender definitions and the changes they underwent during the Weimar Republic or to analyze how her œuvre interacts with the notions of femininity, sexuality, and motherhood, after all major foci of her poetry, acknowledges the fact that "as it is impossible to step out of ideology, it is also impossible to step out of gender."[16]

In a feminist approach gender, class, religion, or ethnicity are used as analytic and historical categories that help explain how works reflect the prevalent social constructions of their times. Subsequently, this methodology can also account for the particular liaison between Kolmar's life and literature in a different manner. It recognizes that the equation of biographical elements and literary fiction is, in fact, a very common feature in assessing women authors, for it serves to solidify their status as lesser writers, who are "unable" to sever the connection between life and literature. Also, viewing texts as an expression of the authentic, biographical experience presupposes, as Toril Moi has argued, an inherently patriarchal perspective. The text has become "the transparent medium through which 'experience' can be seized. This view of texts as transmitting authentic 'human' experience is ... a traditional emphasis of Western patriarchal humanism."[17] Texts, however, neither reveal "true" experiences, nor are they able to shed the historical or ideological formations of the society in which they were produced. Instead, they either directly or indirectly reflect how authors respond to these conditions. In Kolmar's case, one could investigate, for example, how her novella *Susanna* addressed "the challenge of double-marginalization — sexist biases and antisemitism"[18] or, as Amy Colin did, one could inquire which gender and anti-Semitic stereotypes inform Kolmar's novel *Eine jüdische Mutter* (written 1930/31, "A Jewish Mother").[19]

In contrast to such studies, Woltmann and, more recently, Karin Lorenz-Lindemann continued to follow a decidedly atheoretical, *werkimmanente* methodology. Though outdated and naive in its refusal to take into account contemporary methodological developments, it is nevertheless a legitimate analytic tool. The trouble with these interpretations, however, is not their particular methodology, but rather their persistent refusal to acknowledge their own theoretical implications, that is, their dependence on Western humanism and essentialism. This blind spot becomes most obvious when the previously mentioned authors try to address analyses that situate Kolmar within a feminist theoretical framework.

Lorenz-Lindemann, to cite the most recent example, sets out to construct an opposition between a "biased" feminist and a "pure," or correct, approach to Kolmar's texts, and she concludes: "Nur unter Berücksichtigung der Tatsache, daß Kolmar sich dem Gesetz ihrer Dichtung bis zuletzt verantwortlich wußte, lassen sich ihre Werke im Wissen um ihre komplizierte Vieldeutigkeit und Komplexität angemessen entziffern."[20] Yet, concepts such as "law of literature" or "creative subject"[21] are never defined, presumably because they express universal "laws." Such arguments not only reiterate the ahistorical *Dichterin* paradigm, they also postulate it as absolute, supposedly containing an eternal meaning and validity. These paradigms and laws are, therefore, not recognized as manifestations of Western patriarchal humanism, as Moi aptly characterized the ideology of the white, male, bourgeois self. Pretending to be outside ideology, however, only serves to mask one's own ideological and epistemological assumptions. Since the humanist, or essentialist, argument is based on the "self-evidence" of its truths, it neither seeks to understand nor to respect different forms of knowledge. Not surprisingly, Lorenz-Lindemann's account of feminist interpretations of Kolmar is full of mistakes and misquotes, which reveal a very superficial, if not downright incompetent, grasp of its implications and goals.[22] At the same time, her own reading of Kolmar's cycle "Welten" ("Worlds"), claiming in the subtitle to address "Poetologie und Geschichtsverständnis" ("Poetology and View of History") is — depending on perspective — at best essayistic *Feuilleton* prose, at worst poor and inadequate scholarship, since she only paraphrases, but hardly analyzes Kolmar's poems. Though intent on clarifying Kolmar's work and opening it to a wider audience, essays such as Lorenz-Lindemann's, unfortunately, continue to perpetuate an ahistorical and uncritical image of the author that has an obscuring rather than an enlightening effect. The argument that a feminist analysis "disrespects" Kolmar's œuvre, for it inappropriately conflates theory and text fails to take into account the positionality of *any* critic and literary work. Given the subjectivity of both texts and interpretative processes, the goal of literary analysis, however, cannot be the contestations of "truths" or the uncritical adulation of an author, but rather the search to understand writer and œuvre in the most encompassing and refined way possible. This is by definition a dynamic process, and the following investigation of "German Sea" thus seeks to demonstrate how some of the questions and concerns raised by feminist and other critical theories have tried to expand the view of Kolmar beyond the narrow confines of an either purely biographical or *werkimmanente* perspective.

To start with, "German Sea" offers a prime example of Kasack's editorial policies.[23] In his 1955 edition of the poems, on which all subsequent editions were based, Kasack placed the first six poems of "German Sea" at the beginning of the third "realm" *(Raum)* of the cycle "Weibliches Bildnis" ("Image of Woman"). The seventh poem, entitled "Meerwunder" ("Sea Monster"), he inserted into the cycle "Kind" ("Child"). Kasack thus altered not only the sequence of poems, but also the cycle's status as a separate and independent unit. Without acknowledging its autonomy, which of course only became possible after the publication of the original typescripts in the *Marbacher Magazin*, one cannot do justice to the specific topic and message of "German Sea."[24]

The cycle owes its existence to Kolmar's brief trip through Germany's Hanseatic cities, which she undertook at the end of 1934 in the company of Karl Josef Keller. Keller, a chemist with poetic aspirations, had started to correspond with Kolmar after the publication of her poems in the *Insel-Almanach auf das Jahr 1930* ("Island-Almanac from 1930"), and it seems that Kolmar fell in love with him in the course of their correspondence.[25] "German Sea" was probably written shortly after Kolmar's journey to Hamburg, Travemünde, and Lübeck, locations which appear in some of the poems.

According to the title page of the typescript, the cycle appears like the German rendition of an original English text written by Helen Lodgers.[26] In view of the complete lack of information on "German Sea," which cannot even be dated accurately, one can only speculate why Kolmar chose to hide her authorship. It has been argued that the foreign language functioned as a kind of protective mechanism through which Kolmar hoped to facilitate a publication.[27] Though certainly a plausible explanation, it appears to me that the double masking of both language and authorship points toward an even more complex codification tactic, which touches deeply upon Kolmar's own status as a German Jew. For not only does she renounce her *patria* and pseudonym,[28] trading it for a more secure (British) citizenship, but instead of depicting a distinctly German landscape, she portrays a distinctly Kolmarian one. Although the title holds out the promise of a specific German maritime location, the cycle alludes to it only in a few poem titles ("On the Alster," "Travemuende"), thus undercutting its own premise. Instead of portraying and celebrating German geography and history, precisely what Nazi ideology propagated as valid art forms, the images, figures, and metaphors of "German Sea" reflect typical elements of Kolmar's poetry. The title seems to signal allegiance to the national cause, but in fact it serves to camouflage Kolmar's own poetic realm. This ironic play with nationality, which displays both affirmation and distance, can probably be linked to Kolmar's own, increasingly dangerous position in Germany. In "German Sea," which also seems to allude to Heinrich Heine's *Nordsee* ("North Sea") poems, Kolmar reflects on the concepts of home and origin and of her own artistic identity. While the author distances herself, as the language and author masks indicate, from a German origin as it is defined within a nationalistic and fascist *patria* discourse, she is at the same time reaffirming and reestablishing a home that originates within a poetic *matria* she seeks to establish through language, creativity, and love.

In *Das Prinzip Hoffnung* (1959, "The Principle of Hope"), Ernst Bloch describes love as a kind of travel, and he argues that the amorous journey merges traveler, route, and destination. But not only are eros and travel related in their utopian longing for renewal; according to Bloch, the same holds true for travel and artistic creativity. He concludes: "Das sind die Wirkungen der reisenden Verfremdung auf die Hoffnung; mit Eros in beiderlei Gestalt, der der Liebe und der der Schöpfung."[29] It is precisely this trinity of eros, travel, and creativity that characterizes "German Sea," for the cycle does not primarily focus on a different location, but on the lovers' experience and the artistic transformation of it. At the same time, the work adheres only partially to what Bloch calls hope for renewal.[30] The knowledge that both the journey and the love will soon be over lends the poems a somewhat melancholic mood, which could also indicate Kolmar's view of her own future in Germany.

In one of the last letters that Gertrud Kolmar wrote to her sister (dated January 21, 1943), she remembers both the trip and the poems based on it: "Meine letzte — und schönste — Reise ging nach Hamburg, nach Lübeck (auf Buddenbrooks Spuren) und Travemünde, und der unverwischbarste Eindruck war eine Winternacht am einsamen Meeresstrande. Mein Reisetagebuch bilden sieben Gedichte, von denen ein paar zu den besten gehören, die ich je fand. ... mehr Dichtung als Wahrheit — und doch auch Wahrheit."[31]

It is important to note that Kolmar characterizes these poems as *Reisetagebuch*, travel diary, thereby explicitly setting the cycle within the tradition of travel literature and emphasizing the prose character of these lyrics. The term *Reisetagebuch* stresses furthermore the subjective and autobiographical nature of these poems, that the double reference to Thomas Mann and Goethe[32] also places the work in a specific literary tradition, namely (auto)biographical prose. This merging of lyrical and narrative modes is a typical feature of Kolmar's poetic œuvre, which she also employed in such diverse cycles as "Weibliches Bildnis" and "Robespierre." Kolmar organized almost all of her poems in cycles, since a cycle's structural coherence and narrative quality allowed her not only to thematically link the individual poems but also to traverse genre boundaries, conceptual categories and distinctions. The genres Kolmar alludes to in her letter — biography, autobiography, and diary — all focus on subjectivity and expression of a self. This subjectivity certainly entails an autobiographical element, but it is not, as Kolmar herself points out, to be equated with the person.

The cycle emphasizes the visual impressions, moods, and feelings of a traveling and observing self. It is the self's inner realm, and not the outer world of the cities or landscapes, that dominates the seven poems. In contrast to both classical and modern travel literature, which relies on a self narrating different locations or experiences, in "German Sea," the new sights are mediated through introspection and self-reflection. The cycle neither portrays the Hanseatic cities, nor does it provide the readers with the adventures and surprises they have come to expect from travel literature. In this regard, "German Sea" seems to violate an important rule of the genre, which Michael Kowalewski has described as follows: "The most successful travel narratives generally blend outward, spatial aspects of travel ... with the inward, temporal forms of memory and recollection." In "German Sea," this outward sphere ceases to exist as an independent part, for it is being dissolved and integrated into the self's inner world. [33]

In his discussion of travel literature, Dennis Porter has identified "desire and transgression" as the main impulses that motivate travelers, for they seek to cross not only geographic and cultural, but also psychological borders. Karen Lawrence also examines the psychological drives underlying each journey, but she focuses on their implications for the woman traveler and examines the gender-specific elements of movement: "[T]he plot of the male journey depends on keeping woman in her place. Not only is her place at home, but she in effect is home itself, for the female body is traditionally associated with earth, shelter, enclosure.... This mapping of the female body underwrites not only travel literature per se, but the more general trope of the journey as well."[34] In "German Sea," Kolmar both subverts and confirms this traditional codification of the male hero and the female (body) topography. On the one hand, both the subject as well as the object of travel are female. It is indeed an exclusively female voice that describes the inner and outer worlds as well as her own body. Moreover, Kolmar depicts landscape and body not as entities to be conquered, but as fluid, dynamic spaces that merge the observer and the object observed. Yet, as "Leda," the first poem of the cycle, already indicates, Kolmar also remains committed to very traditional gender norms.

"Leda" describes a woman's wistful waiting for her lover, the swan. Her longing stands in stark contrast to the cold and still night that mirrors some of her lover's qualities. The woman's passionate desire violates not only social conventions, but — as the first stanza reveals — it also transforms and transcends physical boundaries:

> Mein Fenster ist im Dunkel aufgetan
> Und meine Seele aufgetan mit ihm.
> Ich seh den Sternenkranz der Cherubim
> Und warte auf den Schwan.[35]

In the highly erotic metaphor of the body as house, Kolmar develops some of the leitmotifs of this particular poem as well as of the cycle at large, namely, viewing the body as an open space waiting to be discovered and, second, the dual movement of aperture and closure. Although the theme of the woman waiting is rather conventional, the poem simultaneously subverts this traditional stance, as the last stanza shows:

> O komm. O komm. Mein Kelch ist aufgetan
> Und badet, schwer von Demut und von Duft,
> Sich blühend in der winterklaren Luft
> Und wartet auf den Schwan. (74)

The repetition of words, images, and movements mirrors the opening stanza, but by using the verb "to bloom" reflexively ("sich blühend"), the waiting acquires a more active and autoerotic component. Instead of being governed by natural laws, blooming appears to be under the control of a human being. That the laws of nature no longer function is also indicated by the contradiction between blooming and "winterclear air," which gives the impression of a magical figure and world.

In "Leda," Kolmar confirms, on the one hand, the female stasis that Lawrence identified as typical for the plot of the journey. Not only does she portray the woman and her body as waiting for the return of the hero, the use of a mythological paradigm gives this scenario moreover an archetypal quality. In this sense, the poem is reminiscent of Roland Barthes's thoughts in *A Lover's Discourse* (1978), in which he argues that historically it is the woman's task to wait for the absent lover. Barthes explains that in the "amorous absence, ... an always present *I* is constituted only by confrontation with an always absent *you*. To speak this absence is from the start to propose that the subject's place and the other's place cannot permute, it is to say, 'I am loved less than I love.'"[36] This perspective can certainly be detected in "Leda." The last stanza reveals, however, that this self is partly redefining her role and female identity, for she uses the waiting assigned to her in order to stage her own desire and sexuality. Through this *Selbstinszenierung*, she attempts to imaginatively transcend the boundaries of her role and space.

But how, one might ask, does this love poem fit within the context of travel literature, since it obviously lacks the description of a foreign place?

The poem does not follow a geographic travel path, but it is the prelude to an amorous journey. It also demonstrates the interplay of desire and transgression that refers, however, mostly to the exploration of sexual desire. In "Leda" as well as in the other six poems of the cycle, the external physical reality is of interest primarily as a reflection of the internal world. The journey thus focuses less on the exploration of new locations than on the amorous encounter in an unknown environment. The longing to be with the lover also indicates other forms of longing and transgression, as the second poem, "An der Alster" ("On the Alster"), demonstrates. "An der Alster," "Haus der Schiffergesellschaft" ("The Worshipful Company of Seafaring Men"), and "Travemünde" ("Travemuende") together form, as their titles already indicate, the core of the cycle's travel description, but they also participate in the erotic discovery.

In "An der Alster," a third-person narrator describes a couple's morning walk through a city. The only poem in which daylight reigns, it has a joyous, graceful tone, which stands in stark contrast to the melancholic mood of some of the other texts. Like the preceding poem, "Leda," "An der Alster," is structured by movements and transformations, of which the first stanza gives a particularly impressive example:

> Schüchterne Farben der Falterfrühen,
> Leiser perlmutterner Glanz,
> Wenn nun die Dächer, die Türme erblühen
> Und ihr gebundener Kranz,
> Summend umworben von schillernder Fliege,
> Rund um den Becher sich drängt,
> Schale mit süßer Fluten Geschmiege,
> Das, wie ein schwebender Schleier die Wiege,
> Milchiger Nebel verhängt. (75)

Kolmar not only naturalizes the city's architecture and buildings, but through her choice of verbs and verb forms, she also makes them dynamic. No longer heavy, static, and firmly anchored objects, they appear to be ephemeral beings, floating and dancing in space. The synaesthesis (timid colors, sweet floods), together with the numerous alliterations and assonances, create the impression of a motion suspended. In connection with the soothing, lulling sounds, this atmosphere provides the couple with both security and comfort.

"An der Alster" also exemplifies the multiple transformations and metaphorization that is a typical technique used in Kolmar's poetry. An object is described not only through a single metaphor, but the images continue to create new metaphors. The roofs and towers in this stanza, for example, are first referred to as wreath, then as cup or goblet, and in a final movement

Notes

I wish to acknowledge the help Bree Dahlmeyer provided in translating this article from the German original.

[1.] The catalogues accompanying each exhibition are important resources for information on Kolmar.

[2.] See Sigrid Weigel and Birgit Erdle, "Vorwort," in *Fünfzig Jahre danach: Zur Nachgeschichte des Nationalsozialismus,* ed. Sigrid Weigel and Birgit R. Erdle (Zurich: Hochschulverlag AG, ETH Zürich, 1996), ix–xii.

[3.] The influence of the Gnosis on Kolmar, for example, is discussed in Gabriele von Natzmer-Cooper, "Das süßere Obst der Erkenntnis: Gnosis und Widerstand in Gertrud Kolmars 'Lied der Schlange,'" *Seminar* 2 (1993): 138–51.

[4.] The existing typescripts were first published by Johanna Woltmann, "Gertrud Kolmar 1894–1943," *Marbacher Magazin* 63 (1993): 173–80.

[5.] See Johanna Woltmann, *Marbacher Magazin* 63 (1993): 154–59.

[6.] See also the interpretation of the poem "Die Fahrende" by Silvia Schlenstedt, "'Könnt' ich einen Zipfel dieser Welt erst packen.' Weltbeziehung in Gedichten Gertrud Kolmars," in *Orte,* ed. Marion Brandt (Berlin: Kontext, 1994), 51–60.

[7.] For a short but comprehensive overview of Kolmar's life, see Henry A. Smith, "Introduction," in *Dark Soliloquy: The Selected Poems of Gertrud Kolmar* (New York: Continuum, 1975), 3–52.

[8.] For a detailed discussion of the artistic impact of this event, see Monika Shafi, *Gertrud Kolmar: Eine Einführung in das Werk* (Munich: iudicium, 1995), 33–34.

[9.] The letters were edited by Johanna (Woltmann) Zeitler as *Briefe an die Schwester Hilde 1938–1943* (Munich: Kösel, 1970) and commented on in Zeitler's "Nachwort" (215–25).

[10.] Other authors include Bernhard G. Blumenthal, "Gertrud Kolmar: Love's Service to Earth," *The German Quarterly* 42 (1969): 485–88; Erika Langman, "The Poetry of Gertrud Kolmar," *Seminar* 2 (1978): 117–32; and Wolfdietrich Schnurre, "Gertrud Kolmar," in *Triffst du nur das Zauberwort: Stimmen von heute zur deutschen Lyrik,* ed. Jürgen Petersen (Frankfurt am Main: Ullstein, 1961), 168–87.

[11.] See Woltmann's introduction in the *Marbacher Magazin,* 2–4.

[12] Representatives of various feminist methods include Amy Colin, "Gertrud Kolmar. Das Dilemma einer deutsch-jüdischen Dichterin," in *Literatur in der Gesellschaft. Festschrift für Theo Buck zum 60. Geburtstag,* ed. Frank-Rutger Hausmann, Ludwig Jäger, and Bernd Witte (Tübingen: Narr, 1990), 247–57; Dagmar C. G. Lorenz, "The Unspoken Bond: Else Lasker-Schüler and Gertrud Kolmar in Their Historical and Cultural Context," *Seminar* 4 (1993): 349–69 and "Gertrud Kolmars Novelle *Susanna,*" in *Fide et Amore: A Festschrift for Hugo Bekker on his Sixty-Fifth Birthday,* ed. William C. McDonald and Winder McConnell (Göppingen:

Kümmerle, 1990), 185–205; and Monika Shafi, "'Mein Ruf ist dünn und leicht.'
Zur Weiblichkeitsdarstellung in Gertrud Kolmars Zyklus *Weibliches Bildnis*," *The
Germanic Review* 2 (1991): 81–88 and "'Niemals 'die Eine' immer 'die Andere'.'
Zur Künstlerproblematik in Gertrud Kolmars Prosa," in *Autoren damals und heute.
Literaturgeschichtliche Beispiele veränderter Wirkungshorizonte,* ed. Gerhard P.
Knapp, vols. 31–33 of *Amsterdamer Beiträge zur neueren Germanistik* (Amsterdam:
Rodopi, 1991), 689–711. For a more historical approach, see Marion Brandt, ed.,
Orte (Berlin: Kontext, 1994) and *Schweigen ist ein Ort der Antwort. Eine Analyse des
Gedichtzyklus 'Das Wort der Stummen' von Gertrud Kolmar* (Berlin: Christine
Hoffmann, 1993). Birgit R. Erdle, *Antlitz — Mord — Gesetz: Figuren des Anderen
bei Gertrud Kolmar und Emmanuel Lévinas* (Vienna: Passagen, 1994) uses a broad
spectrum of different contemporary theories in order to analyze the discourse of
violence in selected Kolmar texts.

[13.] For an overview of the various trends in and the main contributions to the scholarship on Kolmar, see Shafi, *Gertrud Kolmar: Eine Einführung,* 14–25.

[14.] It is important to bear in mind, however, that feminism is by no means a monolithic, unified theoretical construct, but rather a multi-faceted, varied approach
comprising theory and politics, which differs considerably according to the social location of its practitioners. For a short overview on the different branches of feminist
literary criticism, see Toril Moi, *Sexual / Textual Politics: Feminist Literary Theory*
(London: Methuen, 1985).

[15.] Karin Lorenz-Lindemann, "Einleitung," in *Widerstehen im Wort: Studien zu den
Dichtungen Gertrud Kolmars,* ed. Karin Lorenz-Lindemann (Göttingen: Wallstein,
1996), 10.

[16.] Gättens, 3.

[17.] Moi, 76.

[18.] Lorenz, 353.

[19.] Colin, 249.

[20.] Lorenz-Lindemann, "Einleitung," 11.

[21.] Ibid.

[22.] A case in point is her statement: "[E]ine im Rückblick vollzogene Übertragung
psychologischer Konzepte gegenwärtigen feministischen Diskurses [muß] im
Zusammenhang mit Kolmar fehlschlagen.... Ihr Denken setzt Maßstäbe voraus, die
vorrangig ihrer Dichtung verantwortlich sind und sich an anderen Momenten ori-
entieren als an der allgemeinen Emanzipationsgeschichte der Frauen." Lorenz-
Lindemann, "Einleitung," 10–11.

[23.] The following arguments were first briefly developed in Shafi, *Gertrud Kolmar:
Eine Einführung,* 96–101.

[24.] Gertrud Kolmar, *Weibliches Bildnis. Gedichte* (Munich: Deutscher Taschenbuch
Verlag, 1987). I am providing Kolmar's translations of the poem titles. See Woltmann, *Marbacher Magazin,* 98.

[25.] Woltmann, *Marbacher Magazin,* 99.

[26.] The title page reads:
SIEBEN GEDICHTE
aus
"'German Sea'" von Helen Lodgers
Nach dem Englischen
(*Marbacher Magazin*, 98)

[27.] Woltmann, *Marbacher Magazin*, 103.

[28.] Kolmar's family name was Chodziesner. For an extensive discussion of her pseudonym, see Shafi, *Gertrud Kolmar: Eine Einführung*, 33–34.

[29.] Ernst Bloch, *Das Prinzip Hoffnung*, vol. 1 (Frankfurt am Main: Suhrkamp, 1973), 433.

[30.] Ibid.

[31.] Gertrud Kolmar, *Briefe an die Schwester Hilde 1938–1943*, ed. Johanna Zeitler (Munich: Kösel, 1973), 196–97, 199.

[32.] The phrase *mehr Dichtung als Wahrheit* (more fiction than truth) clearly alludes to Goethe's autobiography, *Dichtung und Wahrheit*.

[33.] Michael Kowalewski, "Introduction: The Modern Literature of Travel," in *Temperamental Journeys: Essays on the Modern Literature of Travel*, ed. Michael Kowalewski (Athens: Georgia UP, 1992), 9.

[34.] Karen R. Lawrence, *Penelope Voyages: Women and Travel in the British-Literary Tradition* (Ithaca, NY: Cornell UP, 1994), 1; Dennis Porter, *Haunted Journeys: Desire and Transgression in European Travel Writing* (Princeton, NJ: Princeton UP, 1991).

[35.] Gertrud Kolmar, *Weibliches Bildnis. Gedichte* (Munich: dtv, 1987). The seven poems of the cycle "German Sea" are contained in this volume. In-text citations to these poems will be to this edition.

[36.] Roland Barthes, *A Lover's Discourse* (New York: Hill and Wang, 1978), 13.

[37.] This duality of absence and presence also characterizes the fourth poem, "Watching thy Sleep..." ("Wacht"), which describes a woman watching over the sleep of her lover, but the rather conventional poem does not add new images or ideas to the cycle.

BEATE SCHMEICHEL-FALKENBERG

Women in Exile

EXILE AS FALLING INTO EMPTINESS, exile as an incurable illness, exile once and for all — words like these you can read in many biographies of émigrés. Exile means loss, exile means fear, it means insecurity. Exile means changing your life completely, living from one day to another, means an uncertain future. Exile means crossing borders, living at the margin, losing your language and everything you could rely on, losing your friends and neighbors, being forced to change your habits, your identity, living in permanent danger. Exile means nightmares, humiliation, and misery — and a trauma for the rest of your life. At the same time, it could also mean new strength, new life force, new courage, energy, and creativity.

For women in Germany and Austria in the thirties, persecuted by Hitler, it was all that — and much more. For women, it involved not only their own losses, injuries, and anxieties, but also — feeling responsible for them — those of husbands, partners, children, parents, relatives, friends. Regarding the gender-specific aspects of exile, we see considerable differences between the exile of men and that of women.

Exile research began late and rather hesitantly in Germany after the war, and it largely neglected, even ignored, women and their part in the history of exile for a long time. The history of exile seemed to be the exile of men only, sometimes that of writers only, especially the prominent ones. Exile research was done by men about men.

This changed during the last few years. After some time of systematic studies and research, a great amount of material came to light, with the generous and open-minded help of survivors, women who had been in exile and camps themselves. Since 1990, there has been a yearly conference on "Women in Exile" and consequently new and interesting publications came out, films, TV interviews, and articles. We acquired more knowledge and understanding about the role of women in exile. We learned how they lived and worked, what they thought and felt, how they suffered, how they survived and helped others to do so, and how important their part in the fight and resistance against Hitler and fascism was.

A new handbook on female writers in exile now lists over 200 names, and many more could be added.[1] Much more research though still has to be done; it will have to be international, interdisciplinary, and multicultural, taking many more aspects into consideration.

The following statements try to present a few first results of exile research on women.

1. Women usually were the ones who urged husbands, families, and friends to leave Hitler Germany, later Austria. They were inclined to leave home and country earlier and easier than most men.

   They apparently understood the danger of life in Nazi Germany better and earlier than their partners. Even non-Jewish wives of Jewish husbands were the ones to urge their spouses to leave and decided it was high time to go. The male partner often still hesitated while women with energy and foresight prepared the escape from Hitler Germany.

As one example I quote from the private letter of an exile author. In it, Hans Keilson acknowledges that it was his wife who insisted on leaving Germany. It was she who saw the catastrophe coming much sooner than he did, and she was also more willing to leave everything behind: "Es waren doch die Frauen, die die lebenswichtigen Entscheidungen fällten."[2] There are a number of reasons for this attitude. Men found it on the whole more difficult to leave their jobs; they feared to be without prestige and importance and to lose their status symbols — women usually had none. In the case of writers, they did not want to lose their readers, their publishers, their influence, their income. It is well known that Thomas Mann, for instance, was reluctant to make a clear cut between himself and the Nazi government and to call his existence "exile." Even risking a break with her beloved "magician"-father, it was his daughter Erika who pressed and persuaded him to come to a decision in 1936 when he finally declared he would not return to Germany from a journey to Switzerland.[3]

Louise von Simson had to convince her husband, a famous art historian in Berlin, in a similar way.[4] Women showed considerably more foresight regarding the coming catastrophes. Nelly Sachs and Käte Hamburger both fled to Sweden, one to Stockholm, the other to Gothenburg. Each woman had to convince her aging mother to leave the country; both succeeded at the very last moment. They regarded it as the most important achievement in their entire lives to have saved their mothers from deportation and death in a gas chamber. The same applied to Grete Weil in Amsterdam. Others were not that fortunate: Anna Seghers, for instance, whose mother was deported to Lublin, suffered all her life from it. The poet Emma Kann, as a young woman of eighteen in Frankfurt, tried to convince her parents to leave with her. In the end, she fled alone, first to Cuba, later to New York. Her parents stayed behind and died in a concentration camp.

2. Women showed considerably more flexibility to adapt to new and strange conditions of life in exile.

As witnessed in numerous recollections, women could develop immense energies when it came to starting a new life, alone or with their partners or families in foreign surroundings in different countries. During one of the conferences on "Women in Exile," one speaker told the audience that she had lived in seventeen different countries since 1934, first with her parents, later alone. Women, it seems, thought and acted more realistically; they reflected and pondered not so much about what had been lost, but what had to be done, now, at this very moment — and they did it. Keeping this in mind, exile was not only a time of fright and misery, but also a time of a new beginning, new ideas, and creativity. In exile research about women, a paradigm change has taken place. The time in exile is regarded not only as purely negative, but also as a time of positive possibilities, a time where new chances were being offered, new aspects of life to be found. Friedrich Torberg, an Austrian writer and emigrant to the United States, talked to Adrienne Thomas about the "twelve wasted years," whereupon she answered: "It was a very rewarding time for me, a time of unexpected experiences, encounters, adventures. I could see chances everywhere."[5]

After their escape, women were inventive and resourceful when it came to finding jobs. They took on any odd job they could find to make a living for themselves and for their dependents: husbands, children, parents, relatives, and friends. Nearly no woman was able to continue the career she had started before Hitler was put into power. An exception was the dancer Lotte Goslar, who came to the United States with Erika Mann's "Peppermill." While other members of the cabaret team failed to establish themselves, resigned, and went back to Europe, Goslar could go on in America with her special way of dancing; she did not need a command of the language to be understood.[6]

The question of language was of utmost importance in exile. In this regard, women had fewer difficulties: They either already knew the foreign language — Jewish women in Germany usually had a very good education — or they learned the new language quickly. Immediately, they looked for a job, tried hard to find one. Others had creative ideas to start a business or remembered abilities they once had had. One woman started to color hair, another sewed gloves, another yet baked cookies or sold self-made sweets. Many women worked as maids or as secretaries; others worked as dog sitters, taking dogs out for walks, or they ran errands. No job was too odd or difficult not to be considered by them, regardless of their education or profession. Women who had had servants in Berlin now worked as servants themselves. One woman in Chicago who once possessed a magnificent art collection in her Grunewald villa in Berlin told me, not without sarcastic remarks about the strange course her life had taken, that she dusted the paintings of her American employer as a chambermaid. This leads to the next statement.

3. Women in most cases secured the necessary income for the family.

Due to gender differences and injustices, it was mostly the women who had to give up their own professions and careers. In those days, this was more or less a matter of course. They started in some other field to earn money, or they helped their husbands, who were on the whole less fit and less willing to take on odd jobs and do unskilled work.

A particularly sad story is that of Hertha Nathorff, who had been a leading gynecologist in Berlin. In New York, she first worked as a kitchen help and servant while her husband prepared himself with her support for the necessary examinations to become certified as a medical doctor. It was he who opened a medical practice after he received his American approbation. Only after her husband's death did she begin a new career as psychotherapist, in which she was successful again. From her diary, we learn about the deep wounds and humiliations in the life of an exiled woman in New York, of her longing to work again in her own field, and of the frustrations of being prevented to do so.[7]

Mascha Kaléko, a well-known writer in Berlin at the end of the twenties and beginning of the thirties, stopped writing nearly altogether to be able to assist her husband, a specialist for Jewish music, to organize concerts and tours for him and his choir. Although she would have preferred to stay in New York, which became her new home and where she felt she was growing new roots, she followed her husband to Hollywood and to Jerusalem. In New York, she had successfully invented a new language for her poems, an English-German-Yiddish mixture of emigrant "Yinglish," but she could not go on with it.[8]

Karola Bloch, the wife of Ernst Bloch, had been an architect in Europe. In America, she first worked as a maid to support her small family. Her husband refused to learn what he called "this dreadful language"; instead, he tried to continue his philosophical work, waiting for Hitler to disappear.[9]

4. Women authors had even less opportunities than men to write or to get published.

The conditions of writing and the possibilities to publish were bad for almost every writer in exile, but for women authors, because of gender conditions, the chances to write or to be published were worse. Only very few writers, such as Thomas Mann or Lion Feuchtwanger, could work in exile the same way as before; but even under relatively favorable conditions, life in exile was full of problems. Not a single woman though, whether she was a writer, a journalist, an artist, or a scientist, could continue as before 1933. To leave Germany meant a painful cut.

Even women who had been well known before 1933, such as Else Lasker-Schüler or Anna Seghers, found it very hard to write, to find a publisher and an audience. Lasker-Schüler's letters, just being published, show how desperately she tried to make her poems known from her exile in Zurich and Jerusalem. In one of her rare texts about private problems, "Frauen und Kinder in der Emigration" (1938), Seghers speaks about the many difficulties as a writer and a mother with two growing children.[10]

Women writers — and there were many of them — who had just begun to write and perhaps might have published their first book or had received good reviews and encouragement to go on — all these young authors had no chance to find a publisher abroad. Gabriele Tergit in London was one of them, the philosopher and literary historian Käte Hamburger in Gothenburg another; and so was Jenny Aloni in Jerusalem. They all had just started a promising career. When Hitler was given power, their lives and careers were interrupted for a long time or, in other cases, even finished for good before they had even begun. They were young girls like Anne Frank or Selma Meerbaum-Eisinger or the painter Charlotte Salomon — all of them highly gifted and certainly on the way to becoming masters in their fields.

Only very few women were able to contribute to exile papers and magazines. Although it was not possible for most of them to find a publisher, many tried, under immense difficulties, to continue their writing in exile. So did Nelly Sachs or Hermynia zur Mühlen. Others began to write during those terrible years in a completely insecure situation, like Stella Rotenberg in England or Klara Blum in the Soviet Union and in China. Some of them even started to write in a foreign language and developed a career in the new language, even for good, like Ilse Llosa in Portugal or Elisabeth Augustin in Holland. Both became well-known writers in the languages of their new homelands after the war. Others, Rose Ausländer or Emma Kann, for instance, changed back again from English to their mother tongue and then stayed with it for good. One great exception to the rule is Vicki Baum, who is always mentioned when it comes to perfect adaptation and acculturation to a new life abroad. It must be kept in mind that she left as early as 1931, before Hitler had come to power. Moreover, she had many excellent contacts in America and found favorable conditions there. She first continued to write in German but soon changed to English. In English, she wrote her many successful books, her film scripts, and her memoirs.

A last group of female writers to be mentioned is the one who always had the strong desire to write but could not do so or only secretly during the years of persecution. They began their literary production after 1945 like Ruth Weiss or Berta Waterstradt. Ruth Klüger became a famous author only in recent years, after her book *weiter leben* (1992, "living on") on her years in concentration camps appeared.[11] It is hard to imagine the conditions of writing — how difficult it was to find a quiet place for writing in the days of persecution and hiding. It is well known under which circumstances Anne Frank wrote her famous diary, hidden in an Amsterdam attic, or Gertrud Kolmar her poems in Berlin under the Nazis. Grete Weil, in exile in Holland, hidden by friends, living in a secret room behind book shelves, like the family of Anne Frank, describes the only place where she could be alone: It was under the staircase to the attic, where she wrote, in bad light, on her knees.[12]

Whoever saw it will never forget the tiny, narrow room where Nelly Sachs spent thirty years of her life, half of them with her mother. It is kept in its original state in Kungliga Biblioteket in Stockholm and shows the modest home of a great exiled author, the place where a Nobel Prize winner and one of this century's greatest German-speaking poets lived and worked until her death in 1972. Others such as Rose Ausländer and Emma Kann, because of their knowledge of foreign languages, worked as secretaries in import-export firms and for this reason could only write during their spare time in the evenings and at night. They were usually worn out and tired after a long day of boring work, as they both recall. They hoped through all the years the day would come when they would be able to give up the hated job and continue to work full-time writing poetry. Kann, now blind, continues her work with a tape recorder. Many important works by women were unknown for a long time and underrated before they finally could be published or were rediscovered.

The only socialist writer who in the 1930s wrote an antifascist and anti-Stalinist book in exile, showing both tyrannies as deeply inhuman systems, was a woman: Alice Rühle-Gerstel, author of the novel *Der Umbruch oder Hanna und die Freiheit* ("Change, or Hanna and Freedom"), written in 1938 in Mexico and published fifty years later in Germany, forty years after the author's death. If this fascinating book, full of politically explosive material, had been written by a man, it would certainly have become a celebrated milestone in exile writing.[13]

Ika Olden's book *Im tiefen Dunkel liegt Deutschland. Von Hitler vertrieben* (1996, "Germany Lies in Deep Darkness. Exiled by Hitler"), written together with her husband Rudolf Olden in 1934, tells about the situation of Hitler's opponents before 1933. This work, however, was not published until 1996 when two British exile experts edited and finally published it.[14] It is one of the few reports, detailed and realistic, about the thoughts and feelings of persons who were threatened by the prospect of exile. Thus, it is an important source of the history of the beginning of the experience of exile in the 1930s: a history of people feeling ignored, neglected, unknown, nearly forgotten. Ika Olden was killed with her husband while crossing the Atlantic when the *City of Benares* was sunk by the German navy in 1940.

A specially unfavorable exile situation was that of dramatists such as Christa Winsloe and Hilde Rubinstein. Both of them changed from writing plays to writing prose. Christa Winsloe, asked by a friendly publisher to write about her "milieu," wrote in a letter to a friend while being chased across France by the Nazi troops: "Aber was ist mein Milieu?"[15]

5. Generally speaking — there are always exceptions to the rules — writings by women about life in exile usually give a more realistic and more detailed impression of daily routines.

In the many documentary and autobiographical texts on living in exile, we find countless accounts of dealing with concrete situations of everyday life in exile — such a large amount indeed that its having been overlooked by exile researchers shows an obvious ignorance of daily life in exile, states Heike Klapdor in a fundamental essay on "Frauen in der Emigration" (1993).[16] Women tried to find and develop strategies for survival, in daily life and in writing, while men tried more to create life sketches, ideas, and theories. Most of the literature of women about exile, their memoirs and autobiographies, inform the reader of the conditions and survival strategies of life in exile.

One of the very first autobiographies written by a woman published after 1945 was that of Salka Viertel.[17] She is an excellent example of the characteristics of women in the fight for survival. In a fascinating, colorful, and often moving manner, she describes the life of German and Austrian exiles in California. Her house was a shelter for many of them. She was a great hostess, a good cook, and a generous friend, always willing to help, with good advice and with money. Many German-speaking refugees remember her with gratitude.

Alice Rühle-Gerstel and her novel *Der Umbruch oder Hanna und die Freiheit* has been mentioned earlier. There is also Erika Mann's book *Escape to Life* (1939), written together with her brother Klaus.[18] Hertha Nathorff's diaries belong into this category as well. Usually women prefer to write more personally, more about their private lives, their own experiences and feelings, and those of their families and friends. That is certainly one of the reasons for the immense number of autobiographies of women. Karola Bloch's fascinating autobiography, *Aus meinem Leben* (1995, "From My Life") is an important cultural-historical document and at the same time a self-critical report about her spiritual, political, and emotional development.

Margarete Buber-Neumann, Eva Busch, Elisabeth Castonier, Martha Feuchtwanger, Lisa Fittko, Lea Grundig, Gina Kaus, Ruth Klinger, Annette Kolb, Lola Landau, Ruth Landshoff-Yorck, Ruth Liepmann, Ruth von Mayenburg, Hertha Pauli, Lenka Reinerova, Trude Richter, Hilde Spiel, Steffi Spira, Gabriele Tergit, Inge von Wangenheim, Elsbeth Weichmann, Charlotte Wolff, Hedda Zinner, and many others help with their memoirs to keep the "common memory" alive and save it for generations to come. Motivation for writing them is often the plea not to forget the ones who did not survive.[19]

Regarding poetry, nearly all the important authors are women — with the exception of a few poets, most notably Paul Celan. Themes and topics of their poems are persecution, escape, loss, anxiety, and death. Many of their poems, mostly sad and often desperate, look out for hope and try to find an answer to the eternal question: Why? Speaking of the unspeakable, *"das Unsagbare sagen,"* seems to be a special gift of female poets.[20]

6. Women carried a multiple burden because of their responsibilities for others.

From every woman's autobiography, we learn about the many additional burdens all these women had to carry. Rarely they complained; the difficulties are often mentioned at random, in a matter-of-fact way, without lamentation. It is not new that women felt responsible for their families, that the others were their first concern, and that they had to carry the full burden of daily life, but at that time, sixty years ago, this was even more the case than nowadays.

Without questioning, women gave up their own interests, professions, plans, and ideas to provide for the daily needs of their families. Looking at these autobiographies or listening to some of these women, one has the impression that they did not even feel this injustice and did not or do not want to realize how disadvantaged they were.

In a poem entitled "Die Frauen" ("Women"), Berthold Viertel, theater producer and writer, says: "Und der Mann war oft eine schwere / Undankbare Last."[21] Ernest Bornemann, sociologist and writer, expresses his respect by saying that most of our great writers would have died miserably if the women hadn't somehow managed to pull them through during that time.[22] Although a rather dubious kind of gratitude, acknowledgments of this kind are rare.

The daily burden of working in the house, especially in the kitchen, worries about money, food, and housing, the running after documents, writing letters, asking for help, standing in line at embassies and consulates, talking to and charming officials, making friends and connections to help, playing tricks on the police: all this was done by women — and much more. Often we read, "I did not want to let him see my own misery," or "I tried to comfort him in his depression, how could I let him see mine." Some women even minimized their strength, for their partners' sake, as one of Irmgard Keun's women in exile says: "Ich muss mich schwächer zeigen, als ich bin, damit er sich stark fühlen und mich lieben kann."[23] They supported their husbands and friends in the political fight, they helped them to hide or tried to get them out of prison — like Else Rüthel, who helped to liberate Will

Schaber and fled with him in 1933. Henriette Hardenberg, an expressionist writer, worked in England for and together with the art historian Richard Offner to complete his thirty volumes on early Florentine painting. In her later years, she edited the works of her first husband, Alfred Wolfenstein, while her own writing was less important to her and always took second place.

7. Suicide of women during or after exile was extremely rare.

     Statistics show worldwide that women in general commit suicide less often than men. They attempt it more often, as a cry for help, not so much because they are determined to die. The number of men who committed suicide went up considerably during the years of exile. In this time of extreme stress and psychological and physical pressure, men felt much more inclined to resignation and gave up earlier.

Consider some of all the famous names we know, only among writers, whose lives ended in suicide during Hitler's regime. It began in 1935 with Tucholsky; other examples include Walter Benjamin, Alfred Wolkenstein, Walter Hasenclever, Ernst Weiss, Ernst Toller, and Stefan Zweig. We also remember the writers who died by their own hands even after the Second World War, such as Klaus Mann, Primo Levi, Paul Celan, Jean Améry, and Peter Szondi — to name just a few and only those best known. It is a remarkable fact that we find no women among them.[24] The greater ability of women to adapt to hard and strenuous conditions, the flexibility to change their way of life if necessary, and strong feelings of responsibility for others may be part of the explanation for this surprising fact. Many of the male writers in question lived alone and had no one at their side to help them, give them hope and strength — obvious in the cases of Tucholsky and Toller. They had lost all hope for a political change in Europe; they had no audience any more to talk to; and even the hard economic situation could have contributed to the decision to give up, once and for all.

8. Finally, it can be stated that women on the whole were less willing to return to Germany or Austria after Hitler was defeated.

     New roots in another country and with a different language grew slowly and carefully, hesitantly and anxiously, after they had been torn out so often. When the question of returning to Germany or Austria came up, usually because the husband received a rare offer for a tempting political or scientific position, it was the women who protested and found it extremely difficult to tear the new roots out again. Remigration was usually the intention of the male partner, seldom that of his wife and even less often the children. Women did not want to leave the newly won home, the children, sometimes grandchildren. If they left, again, they did it without enthusiasm and only because it was the wish of the partner. Some marriages that had held up throughout the long and bitter time of exile split up because of the question of remigration. I often heard from women who returned from exile: "It was my husband's wish."

I refer to Lili Faktor-Flechtheim's "Emigration und Remigration" (1987), in which she explains that usually individuals who were dependent on language in their work — scientists, writers, and actors — returned from exile. Many of them remigrated only due to their careers, in other words, for practical reasons. Men seemed more inclined to return to their countries of origin while women were less ready to remigrate. Faktor-Flechtheim believes they felt they had better career chances — in the United States at least — and that they did not want to impose another, unnecessary emigration on their children, who had found a new homeland.

> Vier glückliche Jahre von 1947–51 in Maine [where their daughter grew up] bis meinem Mann eine Gastprofessur an der FU [Freie Universität Berlin] angeboten wurde. Da wußte ich, die Stunde der endgültigen Rückkehr hatte geschlagen. Die vierte große Krise der Heimatlosigkeit, der Rückkehrschock war nun vorprogrammiert. Damals erwog ich eine Scheidung, aber der Horror vor der Familienlosigkeit, die Angst vor der mangelnden Selbständigkeit waren größer als die Angst vor der Rückkehr in die unwiederbringlich verlorene Heimat. Mir wurde eine Psychotherapie in Aussicht gestellt, die angeblich alle Wunden heilen konnte, auch schien der amerikanische Paß ein gewisser Schutz zu sein, zumindest eine Gewähr, daß man im Notfall zurückkehren konnte.[25]

In her book *Happy Exile* (1991) — a title no male author would have chosen — Louise von Simson reaches similar conclusions. She speaks about similar experiences. She, too, followed her husband back to Europe reluctantly, as Lili Flechtheim did, out of loyalty, and did not like life in Germany after the years in exile in America.[26] Yet, the problem of remigration of women is another chapter.

What women did during the time of exile and persecution is by far too little known. They themselves regard it as self-understood, as nothing spectacular to talk about. It is the duty of women and men of the following generations to keep it in mind, to write it down, and to preserve it for the future. The part of women in exile as a contribution to the fight for humanity must not be forgotten, because, as Jewish wisdom knows: "The secret of salvation is called remembrance."

Notes

1. Renate Wall, ed., *Lexikon deutschsprachiger Schriftstellerinnen im Exil 1933 bis 1945*, vols. 1 and 2 (Freiburg: Kore, 1995).

2. Hans Keilson, letter to the author, October 13, 1991.

3. Irmela von der Lühe, *Erika Mann. Eine Biographie* (Frankfurt am Main: Campus, 1993), 113–25.

4. Louise Alexandra von Simson, Prinzessin von Schönburg Hartenstein, *Happy Exile* (Darmstadt: private printing, 1991).

5. Quoted in Gabriele Kreis, *Frauen im Exil* (Düsseldorf: Claassen, 1984), 224.

6. Beate Schmeichel-Falkenberg, "Aufforderung zum Überleben. Lotte Goslar und das Exil," in *Frauen und Exil. Jahrbuch 11*, ed. C. D. Crohn et al. (Munich: edition text+kritik, 1993), 216–28.

7. Hertha Nathorff, *Berlin–New York Aufzeichnungen 1933–1945*, ed. and with an introduction by Wolfgang Benz (Frankfurt am Main: Fischer TB, 1988).

8. Beate Schmeichel-Falkenberg, "Hoere Teutschland. Mascha Kalékos Verse aus dem Exil," presentation in London, symposium "Deutschsprachige Exillyrik 1933–1945" (in print).

9. Karola Bloch, *Aus meinem Leben* (Mössingen: Talheimer, 1995).

10. Anna Seghers, "Frauen und Kinder in der Emigration," in *Anna Seghers — Wieland Herzfelde. Gewöhnliches und gefährliches Leben. Ein Briefwechsel aus der Zeit des Exils 1939–1946*, ed. Ursula Emmerich und Erika Pick (Darmstadt: Luchterhand, 1986), 128–45.

11. Ruth Klüger, *weiter leben* (Göttingen: Wallstein, 1992).

12. Grete Weil, *Spätfolgen* (Zurich: Nagel & Kimche, 1992).

13. Alice Rühle-Gerstel, *Der Umbruch oder Hanna und die Freiheit*, with an introduction by Ingrid Herbst and Bernd Klemm and an afterword by Stephen S. Kalmar (Frankfurt am Main: S. Fischer, 1984).

14. Ika Olden and Rudolf Olden, *Im tiefen Dunkel liegt Deutschland. Von Hitler vertrieben*, ed. Charmion Brinson and Marian Malet (Berlin: Metropol, 1996).

15. Quoted in Claudia Schoppman, ed., *Im Fluchtgepäck die Sprache. Deutschsprachige Schriftstellerinnen im Exil* (Berlin: Orlanda, 1991), 110.

16. Heike Klapdor, "Überlebensstrategie statt Lebensentwurf," in *Frauen und Exil Exilforschung. Ein internationales Jahrbuch*, vol. 11, ed. C. D. Crohn et al. (Munich: edition text+kritik, 1993), 17.

17. Salka Viertel, *Das unbelehrbare Herz* (original title: *The Kindness of Strangers*) *Ein Leben in der Welt des Theaters, der Literatur und des Films*, with a foreword by Carl Zuckmayer (Hamburg: Claassen, 1970).

18. Erika Mann and Klaus Mann, *Escape to Life. Deutsche Kultur im Exil* (Boston: Houghton Mifflin, 1939; German edition, Munich: edition spangenberg, 1991).

19. Ingrid Hannich-Bode collected 222 titles of exile autobiographies of women for the 1995 symposium "Women in Exile." Since then, many more have come out and many are yet to be published. See also her bibliography on exile research in *Ein internationales Jahrbuch,* vol. 14, ed. C. D. Crohn et al. (Munich: edition text+kritik, 1996).

20. Constanze Jaiser collected poems of 60 Jewish women writers in *Das Schweigen hütet die Schicksalsspur* (Berlin: private printing, 1994).

21. Berthold Viertel, *Das graue Tuch. Gedichte.* Studienausgabe, vol. 3, ed. Konstantin Kaiser (Vienna: Verlag für Gesellschaftskritik, 1994), 331.

22. Ernest Bornemann, "Vom freiwilligen Exil," in *Literatur des Exils. Eine P. E. N.– Dokumentation,* ed. Bernd Engelmann (Munich: Hauser, 1981), 34.

23. Irmgard Keun, *Nach Mitternacht* (Düsseldorf: Claassen, 1981), 129.

24. I can only think of Alice Rühle-Gerstel. She committed suicide after her husband, Otto Rühle, died from a heart attack.

25. Lili Faktor-Flechtheim, "Emigration und Remigration," in *Heimat und Heimatlosigkeit,* ed. Christa Dericum and Phillipp Warmboldt (Berlin: Karin Kramer, 1987), 38.

26. See von Simson (note 4).

RENATE S. POSTHOFEN

Claire Goll (1891–1977): Visionary Power and Creative Symbiosis — Fictionalized Identity as Survival Strategy

A T HOME IN A STATE OF DISPLACEMENT, the woman in exile fulfills several tasks. Her literary work achieves an existential function under the conditions of exile.[1] The process of writing as a literary task to deal with one's life experiences represents both an important and a necessary continuity in life, which helps the author to forget the loneliness and despair in exile — if only temporarily.[2] The literary reality becomes the author's imagined homeland; she herself in turn becomes a symbol of her homeland in exile.

According to Heike Klapdor-Kops, the situation of women in exile has only recently become the focus within the more broadly established field of exile research.[3] However, Anna Seghers already dealt with women and children in exile as early as 1939, calling it a highly topical issue.[4] In her essay "Frauen und Kinder in der Emigration" (1939), she writes that in keeping with the stated reason for emigration, the families were usually classified as political or economic emigrants. But reality did not always fit into such rigid categories. Regardless as to whether the initial reason for emigration had been political or economic, it was, according to Seghers, usually the woman who rose to the task of dealing with the burden of daily existence before and during exile. The decision to go into exile brought to life her whole being, and she discovered parts of her self that she probably would never even have shown in ordinary, everyday life: "In einem gegebenen Augenblick, wenn es nun wirklich fortgeht, dann überwiegt in diesem Umzug aus höchster Verantwortung, Entscheidung auf eigentümliche Weise das Technische, das Umzugsmäßige. Ob ein Möbelwagen gepackt werden soll oder ein Rucksack, ob ein paar Banknoten eingenäht werden müssen oder Butterbrote geschmiert, der letzte Laib Brot von daheim: denn Brot ist ja wie Sprache, einmalig."[5] The woman's participation in coping with exile is especially highlighted by Seghers[6] in her literary contributions dealing with that particular topic and has become central in establishing the literary reputation she has been assigned by her critics. Apart from that, it is becoming clear that the scholarly ignorance with regard to everyday life in exile has to be overcome. It is the biographical contributions — letters, memoirs, and autobiographies — that offer us an impression of the coping strategies for the living conditions in exile, essential for these women's well-being. Klapdor remarks that it was often the women who supported their families financially.[7] It is important to note the difference between finding a job and continuing one's career. It was often easier for the woman to find a job — although not necessarily in a field she had been trained in. Odd jobs were offered to women rather than men.[8]

The poet and journalist Claire Goll was among this group of working women, who during their years in exile in the United States continued to earn their living on account of their professional qualifications. With her extensive work experience in the fields of journalism and publishing, she followed a long line of female emigrants who used their knowledge, their professional experience, and their early acquired language skills to counteract the difficulties of life in exile by utilizing internal and external strategies and coping mechanisms of resistance. "Survival strategy" as a motto that was part of the "female blueprint of life"[9] was characteristic of the woman's experience in exile. Claire Goll's literary work falls somewhere in between autobiographical self-expression and lyricism.

After the divorce from her first husband, Heinrich Studer, in 1916, she got caught up in the pacifistic and expressionistic movement in Berlin during the First World War, where she met Kurt Wolff and Franz Werfel.[10] In 1917, Goll — a German Jew — left her homeland and begins her studies in Geneva. This is where she started her career as a journalist, essayist, and lyricist. It was between 1917 and 1919 that she published her first poems as well as short prose pieces and an essay in such publications as *Die Aktion* ("Action"), *Der Sturm* ("The Storm"), and *Die Neue Schaubühne* ("The New Stage").

In an essay entitled "Die Stunde der Frauen" (1917), which has been given little attention so far, she expresses her views on the situation of the woman during the war. She calls on all women to unite against the war on the basis of emotional, responsible, and conscious sisterly love and solidarity.[11] In 1918, her first volume of poetry is published under the title *Mitwelt* ("Contemporary World"). This and other collections of poetry, such as *Lyrische Films* ("Lyric Films"),[12] published in 1922, are written in the contemporary tradition of antiwar poetry and together with various expressionistic novellas and essays form the early body of her work.[13]

In Geneva, she met Yvan Goll, the bilingual lyricist from Alsace-Lorraine — "durch Schicksal Jude, durch Zufall in Frankreich geboren, durch ein Stempelpapier als Deutscher bezeichnet."[14] This marks the beginning of an ever changing, extraordinarily productive relationship rocked by

crises, separations, and reconciliations, which find their expression in the poems written by both individuals — in French and in German — about love,
jealousy, life, and death. Goll remembers in her controversial memoirs that in
Switzerland, she and Yvan survived by doing odd jobs. Yvan sold newspapers
and wrote argumentative articles, which, despite the war, were published in
Switzerland or in Germany. Claire worked for two antiwar papers herself.[15]

In 1919, Claire and Yvan Goll moved to Paris, where they got married in
1921. Her marriage underscores Claire Goll's continuation of her own career
as an author. Her commitment to writing becomes clear when one takes a
closer look at her literary œuvre. In the years following, she wrote her own
socially critical novels apart from the love poetry composed together with
Yvan.[16] She translated some of these novels either from German into French
or from French into German and published the translations throughout
Europe. Thus, her 1924 novel *Une Allemande à Paris*[17] was published in
Berlin in 1927 under the title *Eine Deutsche in Paris* ("A German Woman in
Paris"). The novel *Der Neger Jupiter raubt Europa* ("Black Man Jupiter
Steals Europe"), published in German in 1926, appeared in France in 1928
under the tile *Le nègre Jupiter enlève Europe*.[18] Her life and her literary work
is heavily influenced by her bilingualism. Indeed, Claire Goll exchanged her
German homeland for France, her home of choice. Similarly, she seems to
have favored French over German as her favorite medium of expression during the 1920s and 1930s.

In 1939, at the onset of the Second World War, Yvan and Claire Goll
fled to the United States. In 1945, they became naturalized U. S. citizens.
They both retained their acquired citizenship for the rest of their lives. The
now displaced couple had to deal with their American exile as best they could
until their return to France. The reason for literary researchers and scholars
to find only a sporadic interest in Claire Goll's literary work, while most research concentrates on her husband's work, lies in a prejudice of German literary criticism, which mentions her only as translator and publisher of her
husband's works.[19] However, Claire Goll wrote her own poetry and prose —
which generally appeared in two languages — until her death in 1977.

Following the literary tradition of the First World War, both Claire and
Yvan Goll wrote pacifistic articles in New York, which were to some extent
also published in France. With the takeover of the National Socialists in
Germany, Claire Goll no longer had the opportunity to publish her journalistic or literary works there. In New York, she worked as a journalist for the
journal *Aufbau — Reconstruction* as well as the monthly journal *Decision*.
She wrote film reviews for the journal *France-Amérique* ("France-America"),
and she reported the news from the New Yorker scene in the theater and
movie column of the Gaullistic journal *La Voix de France* ("The Voice of
France").[20] An important part of Claire Goll's literary work during this time

were her publications in the literary magazine *Hémisphère* ("Hemisphere"), founded by Yvan Goll. Various short stories were also published by the publishing house "Editions de la maison Française," which was cofounded by Yvan Goll and was mainly frequented by French-speaking emigrants.

What exactly does the specific life experience in exile look like for Claire Goll, and how does it manifest itself and the search for an identity in her literary works? First, it can be presupposed that for Claire Goll as for any publishing emigrant certain changes in her literary work are part of the new conditions of living in exile.[21] Claire Goll's œuvre produced in exile encompasses two novels, a new edition and translation of an already published novel,[22] and various novellas and revised editions[23] as well as an English translation of the well-known love poems she had written together with her husband, Yvan, and published in French in 1925. The novellas are typically set in France, the United States, or Italy. They are normally about people on the edge of society — "und doch im (steinernen) Herzen einer meist kleinbürgerlichen Gesellschaft."[24] As particular examples of exile as a specific topic in her writings from that time, I will discuss two of her stories in depth to demonstrate the extent to which the experience of being removed from a sheltered environment and homeland dominated Goll's search for a multicultural identity and functioned as a strategy for survival for herself.

The story of the Chinese laundry, the first one to be examined in greater detail, received a radio award in 1952.[25] Claire Goll recalls the true story that is the basis for this short story in her memoirs. She refers to the social realities and the level of poverty that she had experienced in New York City. She feels incapable of comparing this specifically American degree of being impoverished to anything that she had seen in Europe before. To illustrate her observation she cites the example of a Chinese man who had been washing lots of laundry for other people so he could support his family back home in China, whom he had not seen in a quarter of a century. This person inspired much of the following story, in which she writes about his life of poverty and self-denial: "Ein Leben lang in Armut und Verzicht, ohne sich je den einzigen Wunsch erfüllen zu können — welch eine Aufopferung!"[26]

Goll wrote "Chinesische Wäscherei" ("The Chinese Laundry") in 1940, initially in French although she lived in New York at the time. It is the story of a Chinese immigrant, the laundryman Lee Young Chum, who, sick with tuberculosis, ekes out a wretched existence during the last days of his life. While standing at the flat-iron ironing shirts, he dreams of his homeland. In his fever, during his TB fits, he fantasizes about the past. Seventeen years old, he began pulling rickshas in China. He married Su-Mei, the girl from next door. (Of the six children they had together, none of them lived at home any longer. Two died from hunger and misery, and the other four left home in different directions due to the war.) Su-Mei committed suicide a year ago because she apparently could wait no longer for the return of her husband, who preferred to send her his earnings rather than "waste" them on a return ticket for himself. In his hallucinations, he remembers his eldest son, Gun-poi, whom he had taken along on a Chinese freighter to earn money as a rower. During a storm, the boat turns over and Gun-poi, along with the entire crew, drowns and dies. Lee Young, who is part of the additional crew that pulls the freighter from the shore with heavy ropes, witnesses the events from the sidelines and is deeply traumatized by the fact that he was unable to save his son's life. Caught up in his memories, Lee Young dies from hemorrhaging. His death is shown as a positive experience: He enters Nirwana, where Su-Mei and Gun-poi await him.[27]

The Chinese man here symbolizes the experience of immigrants living in exile for economic reasons. As the emigrant, he becomes the voice for all the poor and those without rights in general when Goll uses him to highlight the miserable conditions he lives in: "Die Neue Welt, die alte Qual. Sechzehn Stunden Arbeit in der Wäscherei, um nach zwei Jahren dem Verwandten die Schuld abzubezahlen, und ist man endlich soweit, wieder von vorne anfangen für die Familie" (11). He is trapped within the walls of his laundry, where day-in and day-out he washes and irons the laundry of his customers. The small gas flames of his flat-iron, which Lee Young tries to keep under control, represent his vulnerability in a situation over which he has little control: "'Ho, ho, Lee! Aufgepaßt!' Der Kragen des Hemdes ist etwas versengt. Die Flammen haben Lees Unaufmerksamkeit ausgenutzt und sind größer geworden. Lee muß das Gas herunterschrauben. Damit glaubt er die Flammen gebändigt zu haben; in Wirklichkeit aber bändigen sie ihn. Wieder ist er ihr Gefangener; ihrer blauen Magie ausgeliefert" (11).

Lee Young's situation is characterized by his feeling of being at mercy due to his economic dependence, far from his homeland, lonely and sick. Typically, he is unable to communicate his situation, his misery to others, because his language and his culture separate him from them. "Unaufhörlich hämmert und echot der Gong des Wäschers in Lees Schläfen. Vielleicht hat er Hunger? Er vergißt seinen Hunger, wenn er arbeitet. Stets muß ihn die Schwarze ans Essen mahnen: 'C'mon, Mistah Lee, yuh gotta eat, c'mon, wash the lice!' Jeden Tag freut sie sich auf's neue über den alten Witz. Lee kann das Wort 'rice' nicht anders aussprechen. Die chinesische Zunge und das 'R' stehen miteinander auf dem Kriegsfuß" (13).

It becomes clear in this foreign world that exploitation in a class system is not unique to China. Goll's social criticism of the hardships of underprivileged people has to be seen globally. After leaving China for better opportunities, Lee Young finally dies from tuberculosis as a consequence of his miserable living conditions in the United States.

The artistic interweaving of Lee Young's American experiences in the present and the resultant memories of his former life in China show clearly that new beginnings, whether they are based on economic or political considerations, are impossible for any emigrant because one's past will always catch up with the present. This experience is also characteristic of Lee Young's life as he remembers his Chinese homeland: "'Damals fing es an, in Schanghai.' Er ist 17 Jahre alt und spannt sich vor die Rikscha. ... 'Rikscha, Sir! Rikscha, Sir!' Die Reichen schlemmen die ganze Nacht hindurch auf Banketten, in deren Verlauf 50 Gänge serviert werden" (14). The class distinctions Lee Young experienced in Chinese society now correspond with the poor life standards in his laundry and thus become universal elements, which have an immense influence on the common man and the common woman. Claire Goll's personal everyday experiences in exile are determined by sacrifices, which she remembers in her memoirs. She describes that in America, she and her husband lived like students. They had neither money nor rich friends on the Atlantic coast, but they profited from the generosity of the corned-beef billionaires and other benefactors who founded and financed whole colonies for artists."[28]

The other story central to my investigation here is entitled "Die Reise nach Italien" ("The Trip to Italy"),[29] which Goll wrote in 1942 while still in exile in the United States. Here, similar everyday experiences are expressed — and with the same orientation to detail. It is the story of an Italian family who had immigrated to Brooklyn. The focus is on Signora Maria, who as the family elder watches over her family's fate. "Eine alt gewordene italienische Madonna. Eine Statue, an der die Zeit einiges zerstört hatte. ... Nichts schien an der sitzenden Gestalt zu leben als die großen Augen, aus Alabaster und Onyx gemacht" (145). The first person narrator, who first discovers the old woman in a corner of her son's butcher shop, starts a conversation with her. Again, Goll points out the language barrier that has to be overcome initially. The narrator knows Italian and can therefore communicate with the old woman, who is delighted to be able to speak with somebody else in her mother tongue. After thirty-five years in the United States, she had never quit suffering from being homesick (146). Here, too, it becomes clear that the experience of an immigrant is characterized by cultural and linguistic isolation in a world that is experienced as "generous," but one that can never replace the warmth of the old home country. In both stories, Goll demonstrates that the status of an immigrant, even after decades of living in the foreign country, can never replace the missing feeling of a cultural and national identity, which is essentially the basis for a successful assimilation.

In this story, as in the one discussed previously, the experience of an economic exile leads to a larger, more comprehensive experience of missing one's homeland, which is expressed in the linguistic and cultural isolation of Signora Maria. As a consequence, she is just not integrated into the society that surrounds her. The generational difference — between Signora Maria and her sons — is not only a difference in age but also generally a difference in Weltanschauung and economics. The sons and their American wives, characterized as greedy, obviously feel at home in this American world, in which financial success comes before human warmth. "Seine etwas brutalen Züge verzogen sich jedesmal zu einem geschäftlichen Lächeln, wenn sich die Kasse öffnete und schloß, wenn er die Dollar der Kunden entgegennahm oder auf einen größeren Schein herausgab" (146). In contrast, Signora Maria stands for a part of her ever so beloved homeland. "All dieses und vieles andere Heimatliche war mit den Augen ausgewandert. Es war hier in dem kleinen Laden, in dem trostlosen Viertel von Brooklyn" (146). It might be interesting to note that Goll had used similar images in her 1930s Parisian novels, here in connection with Jews and Orientals.[30]

This story, too, makes clear that Claire Goll's own experience of living in exile finds its way into her literary texts. Both stories treat having no homeland and living in a foreign country as threatening aspects for the protagonist. The physical symptoms of deterioration, which in both Lee Young's and Signora Maria's case lead to their death, can be seen as a direct consequence of the immigrants' not having a homeland. Goll shows enormous empathy for those with whom she was able to identify the best in her own situation at the time: the poor and the despised, the border figures of society, those who even in exile cannot make it. The fact that both protagonists can only find their homeland again in death is just as important to note as is Claire Goll's instinct for the dead-end situations in which many of the emigrants find themselves. She elaborates on her own, personal, almost unreal, identification with those suffering through these almost nonhuman condition und which they have to exist. At the same time, she points to the lasting impression that the fate of these less privileged people made on her. Erhard Schwandt points out that it is precisely her bond with these disadvantaged and challenged individuals that enables her to focus on their destiny at large and by means of specific examples. "Anders als in allen früheren Texten wird hier die radikale Sensibilität und Verletzlichkeit der Autorin zu einer radikalen Kritik an der inhumanen Zivilisationsmaschinerie, die über Einzelschicksale teilnahmslos hinweggeht. Aus Mitleid wird Empörung, aus Anteilnahme Anklage."[31]

The power of her stories written during exile lies in her ability to observe casual little details or an unimportant occurrence, which later lead us to universal knowledge and therefore have a global power of expression. It is indeed her own experience in the strange and unusual everyday life in exile that sensitizes her to a closer observation of the living conditions of the Italian matron and the Chinese laundryman. Goll, however, does not develop a specifically female perspective in either one of these two texts as could have been expected in accordance with the initially mentioned theory by Klapdor regarding the situation of female writers in exile; instead, she just projects her own experiences into those of the Italian and the Chinese protagonists. Their behavior as exemplified in the literary formulation of the theme is not typically female or typically male but is portrayed as a universal lack of cultural and national identity resulting from no longer having a homeland to belong to. This experience ignores geographical boundaries as well, since Goll's writings represent Eastern as well as Western patterns of life, and their representatives react similarly upon the loss of identity.

Apart from her work in journalism for the French antiwar press, it is these little stories about everyday life in exile that — although not well known by German or American readers — comprise the literary work of Claire Goll as a writer in exile. It is to her credit that she points out the situation of emigrants in what we perceive to be a multicultural background in America, thus letting those emigrants know that their feelings of not belonging are shared by a multitude of sufferers.

Notes

[1.] "Dieses Bild bestimmt im übrigen die Frauenfiguren in Anna Seghers's Romanen und Erzählungen, vgl. hierzu neben *Transit* die Erzählungen *Post ins gelobte Land* (1943–44) und *Das Obdach* (1941), ein 'Denkmal der Dankbarkeit' für das Zufluchtsland Frankreich (zit. nach: Frank Wagner: *Anna Seghers*, a. a. O. [Leipzig, 1980], S. 44," cited in note 52 by Heike Klapdor, "Überlebensstrategie statt Lebensentwurf," *Frauen und Exil. Exilforschung. Ein Internationales Jahrbuch* 11 (Munich: Edition text+kritik, 1993): 29–30.

[2.] According to Anna Seghers, in a letter to Wieland Herzfelde, *Anna Seghers — Wieland Herzfelde. Gewöhnliches und gefährliches Leben. Ein Briefwechsel aus der Zeit des Exils 1939–1946* (Darmstadt: Luchterhand, 1986), 38: "Man ist manchmal schrecklich allein, aber wenn ich arbeite, wenn ich meine Erzählungen und meine Romane schreibe, bleibe ich ruhig und tapfer und fröhlich." This relationship between the experience and coming to terms with the experience produces a tension between myth and reality in the literary work, and especially the female characters tend to take on a mythological dimension: "Mythologische Tiefe haben die zeitgenössischen Erzählungen. ... Diese Verschmelzung ist das Zeichen ihrer Prosa" (Christa Wolf, "Zeitschichten," in *Ausgewählte Erzählungen*, by Anna Seghers [Darmstadt: Luchterhand, 1983], 363; cited here in Heike Klapdor, "Überlebensstrategie statt Lebensentwurf," *Frauen und Exil. Exilforschung. Ein Internationales Jahrbuch* 11 [Munich: Edition text+kritik, 1993]: 30 n. 52).

[3.] Klapdor, 13 n. 7. A preliminary bibliography referencing the first fundamental works on this topic are contained in note 7 on p. 27.

4. Klapdor, 13.

5. Anna Seghers, quoted in Klapdor, 14.

6. Seghers, "Frauen und Kinder in der Emigration," *Anna Seghers — Wieland Herzfelde,* 129–31.

7. Klapdor, 17.

8. Ibid., 25.

9. Ibid., 26.

10. Erhard Schwandt, "Postscript," in *Zirkus des Lebens,* by Claire Goll (Reinbek: Rowohlt TB, 1981), 186.

11. Claire Studer, "Die Stunde der Frauen," *Zeit-Echo* 3 (July 1017): 9–10.

12. Claire Goll, *Lyrische Films. Gedichte* (Basel: Rhein, 1922). In it also the poem "Tagebuch eines Pferdes," which was later published separately as Claire Goll, *Tagebuch eines Pferdes. Ein Gedicht in Prosa.* Series "Bibliothek des Expressionismus" (Nendeln, Liechtenstein: Kraus Reprint, 1973).

13. Claire Studer, *Mitwelt-Gedichte* (Berlin Wilmersdorf: Verlag der Wochenschrift *Die Aktion,* 1918). Reprint in *Der Rote Hahn,* vol. 20 (Nendeln, Liechtenstein: Kraus Reprint, 1973). Claire Studer, *Die Frauen erwachen. Novellen.* 3 editions (Frauenfeld, Switzerland: Huber, 1918). Claire Studer, *Der gläserne Garten. Zwei Novellen* (Munich: Roland, 1919). Also published in *Die neue Reihe 17* (Roland). Claire Studer, *Tendres impots à la France. Poèmes* (Paris: Editions Poésie, 1920).

14. Schwandt, 187.

15. Claire Goll, *Ich verzeihe keinem. Eine literarische Chronique Scandaleuse unserer Zeit* (Munich: Knaur, 1976), 33.

16. Examples of her own novels are *Der Neger Jupiter raubt Europa* (1st ed., Basel: Rhein, 1926; 2d ed., Berlin: Ullstein, 1926, 1929; 3d, 4th ed., paperback, Berlin, 1932 [?]); *Eine Deutsche in Paris* (Berlin: Wasservogel, 1927); *Une perle* (Paris: Les Editions Georges Crès, 1929), published in English as *The Jewel* (New York: Alfred Knopf, 1931); *Ein Mensch ertrinkt* (Leipzig: E. P. Thal, 1931); and *Arsenik* (Paris: Bergis, 1933).

17. Claire Goll, *Une Allemande à Paris* (Paris: Les Editions Georges Crès, 1924; 2d ed., 1929). Also published by Editions Rayot, Paris, 1928. Published in German as *Eine Deutsche in Paris* (Berlin: Wasservogel, 1972).

18. Claire Goll, *Le nègre Jupiter enlève Europe* (Paris: Les Editions Georges Crès, 1928). See note 16 for publication information of the German edition.

19. Schwandt, 186.

20. Goll, *Ich verzeihe keinem,* 171.

21. Klapdor, 24.

22. Claire Goll, *Le Tombeau des Amants Inconnus.* Series *La Voix de France* (New York: Editions de la maison Française, 1941); *Education Barbare* (New York: Editions de la maison Française, 1941). This is almost identical in text with *Le Ciel volé*

(Paris: Ed. Fayard, 1958) and *Der gestohlene Himmel* (Munich: List, 1962); *Arsenic (Un crime en Province)* (Canadian ed., Montreal: Les éditions variétés, 1944); first published in German under the title *Arsenik* (Paris: Bergis, 1933).

[23.] Claire Goll, *My Sentimental Zoo. Novellas* (Mount Vernon, NY: Peter Pauper, 1942).

[24.] Front inside cover, "Zu diesem Buch," in *Zirkus,* by Goll.

[25.] Schwandt, 186.

[26.] Goll, *Chronique Scandaleuse,* 177.

[27.] Claire Goll, "Chinesische Wäscherei," in *Zirkus des Lebens* (Reinbek: Rowohlt TB, 1981), 16. (Further references to this short story will be parenthetical in the text.) Originally published in French as *Ménagerie Sentimentale, Histoire des Bêtes, Nouvelles* (Paris: Les Editions Georges Crès, 1930); "Laverie Chinoise, Nouvelle," *Hémisphères* 1.2–3 (fall-winter 1943–44): 44–52. Reprint in French, Paris: Ed. Fayard, 1958; Paris: Ed. Emile-Paule, 1975. The first German version was published in Zurich, Switzerland: Pflugverlag, 1953. The first German edition of the collected novellas came out in 1976: Claire Goll, *Zirkus des Lebens, Novellen* (Berlin: edition der 2, 1976; rev. ed., Reinbek / Hamburg: Rowohlt, 1981). Prior to the German publication of the collected novellas, they were published in France under the title *Le cirque de la Vie, Nouvelles* (Paris: Ed. Emile-Paul, 1975).

[28.] Goll, *Chronique Scandaleuse,* 188.

[29.] Claire Goll, "Die Reise nach Italien," in *Zirkus des Lebens,* 145–55. (Further references to this short story will be parenthetical in the text.) Originally published in French in *Le cirque de la Vie, Nouvelles* (Paris: Ed. Emile-Paul, 1975).

[30.] Claire Goll, *Ein Mensch ertrinkt* (Berlin: Argon, 1988), 51.

[31.] Schwandt, 188–89.

ROBERT C. FUHRMANN

Masculine Form / Feminine Writing:
The Autobiography of Fanny Lewald

FANNY LEWALD (1811–1889) IS OFTEN placed along with the other great
women writers of the nineteenth century, among them George Sand and
George Eliot. Yet, outside the German-speaking world, and until very recently even within it, Lewald has played a meager role in the German literary
canon. Though she published a huge collection of novels, novellas, short stories, travel memoirs, essays, letters, and an autobiography, the years between
her death and the 1980s have tended to exclude her from most literary discussions. Clearly no dilettante in the world of writing, Lewald was not only
widely published, she was, unlike many writers, able to support not only herself through her work, but also, later in life, her husband and his children. As
was often the case with women writers of the time, Lewald's novels were often serialized in popular magazines. They were usually well regarded and, in
the case of *Clementine*, caused a great sensation. Her success as a novelist
also provided her with the financial means to leave her native Königsberg and
move to Berlin as well as to travel abroad, in particular to Rome, where she
met Adolf Stahr, whom she would later marry at the age of forty-three.

Lewald's early novels, *Clementine* (1842) and *Jenny* (1843), indicate a
close affinity with the writing of George Sand, and even more so, they reflect
the radical literary movement of the 1840s, commonly referred to as *Vor-
märz*. Regula Venske, writing in *German Women of the Eighteenth and Nineteenth Centuries* (1986), maintains that Lewald used her first novel to reveal
her secret love and sufferings to her cousin Heinrich Simon under the cover
of fiction.[1] At least one of her novels, "a biting satire on the excesses and
sentimentalities of the popular salon novel," *Diogena* (1847), is said to be
written in response to Ida von Hahn-Hahn, who was considered the George
Sand of Germany.[2]

As with most of Lewald's other publications, her autobiography, *Meine
Lebensgeschichte* (1862, "My Life Story"),[3] met with both popular and critical
acclaim. During the first half of the twentieth century, little attention was
paid to her works, and as with other Jewish writers, Lewald's work was

banned during Germany's fascist era (1933–1945). The 1980s and the feminist movement sparked a renewed interest in Lewald's work, but feminist scholars of the period viewed *Meine Lebensgeschichte* with mixed feelings. That attention was being paid once again to her works was certainly a positive sign for women's literature, yet some feminist scholars faulted Lewald for appropriating a male form of autobiography, thereby subverting the female narrative voice. Katherine Goodman points out that Lewald's autobiography is a utilization of Goethe's *Aus meinem Leben: Dichtung und Wahrheit* (published 1811–22, translated as *The Auto-Biography of Goethe. Truth and Poetry: From My Life,* 1849). Indeed, Goodman writes, "*Dichtung und Wahrheit* however epitomizes the ideally structured and focused autobiography. Like [Louise] Aston, Lewald wanted to convey the realities of women's lives. Where the former consciously rejected classical aesthetics as inappropriate for the task, however, the latter explicitly adopted Goethe as a model."[4]

There is little that can be argued against the contention that Lewald did, in fact, follow the structural lead of Goethe, yet her own comment in *Gefühltes und Gedachtes* (1871, "Emotions and Thoughts") seems to be a knowing nod to Goethe, hinting at the fictional qualities that seem to inherently infest the act of self-writing as well as a sly wink to her audience laying claim to an autobiography that is somehow less a victim of nostalgia and melancholia than that of Goethe's. She writes, "Meine Lebensgeschichte ist ebenso gut Dichtung und Wahrheit wie die von Goethe. Die Dichtung aber und ihre verklärende Darstellung habe ich den anderen zu gute kommen lassen, die Wahrheit ganz und voll dagegen von mir selbst gesagt."[5] The impact of Goethe's work was felt throughout the world of European letters, and the frequent mention of him throughout *Meine Lebensgeschichte* attests to the deep influence Goethe had on Lewald. But equally true is that she was also influenced by others, namely Henriette Herz, Rahel Varnhagen, and Heinrich Heine. Lewald employs narrative structures that are common throughout the autobiographical genre, and yet she resists in other ways the overarching paternal structure that would undermine her own goals and ideals as a feminist. Taking these accepted forms, Lewald faces the formidable task, as a woman and as a Jew, of writing her life as narrative. As Doris Maurer writes in *Die Zeit* on the hundredth anniversary of Lewald's death:

> Just because of her contradictions, her efforts to relax the dogmatic bourgeois rules for the behavior of women and in her own insecurity — "because I constantly listened for someone else's judgment, because I lacked that self-confidence which let men, who were far less significant than I, pursue their goals with calm concern" — Fanny Lewald is typical for the feminine dilemma and not only of her day. Limited by herself, by the considerations and concepts of a woman's role which were part of her upbringing, she nevertheless brought about significant changes. Her contradictions do not di-

minish her achievements, to which later generations of proponents for women's rights keep referring again and again.[6]

At the risk of oversimplifying, the autobiographical genre tends to employ distinct narrative patterns that have been long and substantially established in literature. One pattern, then, is to assume elements of the *Erziehungsroman*, that is, the novel of development that takes one from childhood innocence to experience. It relies on memory and may be controlled by nostalgia; it employs the myth of the Garden of Eden and was employed by one of the cornerstones of the autobiographical genre, Rousseau's *Confessions* (1783). A second pattern involves the metaphor of quest, or journey. The search may be for lost time, for identity, or simply to remember. Rousseau uses this, too, as does George Moore in *Hail and Farewell* (1925). Maturity provides the third narrative strategy; crisis is at the center, and in the case of St. Augustine's *Confessions* (1620), it is precisely crisis that brings the past and future together at once and creates conversion. For Augustine, the conversion is religious, but for the epic hero, it is a descent into the underworld and a reemergence, or rebirth, which brings knowledge and wisdom and the power to guide others. Finally, there is the confessional strategy in which the autobiographer simply tells his / her story and thus provides the very essence of "autobiography." In general, the autobiographer does not maintain one pattern but rather employs them all in recreating in literary form his / her life. Indeed, the examples of self-writing that we look to most often — Augustine, Rousseau, Goethe, Petrarch, and certainly Lewald — show that the authors were familiar with these. They blended various strategies in order to fully tell their stories. Lewald, too, narrates her life story in terms of certain distinct stages — childhood, youth, and maturity. And she describes these stages according to elaborate literary conventions not only in terms of summary titles, but also in terms of established narrative patterns.

Women have been telling the stories of their lives since at least the Middle Ages, but it was not until the 1980s that scholars faced with particular fortitude the difficult task of constructing a subgenre of women's autobiography. Mary Mason's "The Other Voice" (1980)[7] set an agenda for (re)discovering a tradition of women's self-writing. The agenda had very specific goals: the (re)discovery of lost or forgotten women's texts, the posing of literary questions about gender and genre, the posing of more general questions about women's self-representation, whether it has always been different from men's or whether women's writings show certain fundamental "human" patterns of development.[8] Following Mason, Estelle Jelinek's *The Tradition of Women's Autobiography* (1986), Sidonie Smith's *A Poetics of Women's Autobiography* (1987), and Carolyn Heilbrun's *Writing a Woman's Life* (1988)[9] provided a sturdy foundation for the continued evolution of the subgenre. All of these early critical studies of the feminist movement assumed a common argument: that women's autobiography represents a separate and distinct tradition, a genre or subgenre different from autobiographical writing produced by men. In Jelinek's words, "Women are writing out of and continuing to create a wholly different autobiographical tradition from that delineated in studies of male autobiography."[10]

But in *Institutionalizing Women's Autobiography*, Linda Peterson tries to issue a corrective to what she seems to understand as a heavy-handed attempt at creation of the subgenre. She writes, "That women's autobiography represents 'a wholly different autobiographical tradition' has been a practical, even necessary critical assumption. Prior to 1980 major critical studies of autobiography excluded serious consideration of women's texts."[11] While Peterson states that this exclusion demands "new approaches to, and new theories about, women's forms of self-representation," feminist studies of self-writing have tended to read women's texts as if gender were the sole determinant to authorial intention; "they have assumed that gender determines the form of women's autobiography or, at least, that it motivates women writers to seek a separate autobiographical tradition."[12] The possibility that gender may not be a crucial factor in some autobiographical writing, that some women writers may deliberately avoid a female literary tradition, or that a woman's autobiography may self-consciously invoke multiple literary traditions seems, to Peterson, to have been overlooked, as has the work of editors and critics in evaluating the tradition of women's autobiography. In tracing the history of women's self-writing, Peterson points out that "the desire to define a woman's tradition has, in other words, shaped the writing of literary history and practical criticism."[13]

Peterson undertakes a study of substantial scope and depth of the history of women's self-writing concentrating on spiritual autobiographies of eighteenth-century Quakers. A series called *The Friends' Library* includes both men's and women's memoirs and is meant to provide a model for the subsequent attempts at self-writing, pointing to the important idea that the Quaker editors believed that both men's and women's self-writing were suitable as seminal forms of autobiography. In terms of content, Peterson finds evidence to support the idea that Quaker women freely chose to follow a traditional model of spiritual autobiography. "They treated their lives as a struggle between opposing forces; they delineated a pattern of spiritual progress from bondage in sin to enlightenment and victory over the world, flesh, and devil; most importantly, they composed their lives without a sense that they were appropriating a 'male' tradition or that their experiences were radically different from men's."[14]

Lewald comes from a very different religion and culture — German and Jewish rather than Quaker and English, but Peterson's work provides us with a strong suggestion that women who set out to recreate their lives in narrative form approach the task similarly to men. Lewald's writings demonstrate that she was keenly aware of the role that women played in her own culture, and her life story reveals that she was equally aware of the choices available to her, even if these were difficult to obtain. Her decision, then, to employ what feminist critics would call a "male" form does not necessarily imply an inappropriate use of that form.

Whereas Goethe may have had an odd relationship to his work, as if each production were simply a layer of skin being shed off, Lewald appears to have attacked each new work with freshness and zeal. Goethe describes his own self- writing as his freshened-up or warmed-up life: "Hier kommt denn auch der zweite Teil meines wieder aufgefrischten oder aufgewärmten Lebens, wie man es nennen will. ... Wäre ich meiner abwesenden Freude nicht eingedenk, wo nähm ich den Humor her, solche Dinge zu schreiben?"[15] Clearly then, Goethe was not necessarily satisfied, nor at ease with the autobiographical form, which is part verifiable data and part interpretation of the data put through the filter of memory. His unease is not only evident in the previous quote, but also in the very title he chose for his autobiography: *Dichtung und Wahrheit.*

Over time, Goethe's conception of the relationship between truth and poetry changed. Three main stages may be traced in this development. As a young *Stürmer und Dränger* among like-minded raging individualists, his idea of the poet was of the creator *par excellence,* the Promethean genius, who, godlike, forms men and things after his own image.[16] His unfailing intuition, the divine spark within, strikes the truth and lights it up with the force of a revelation. So he lauds Erwin von Steinbach, the creator of Strasbourg's cathedral, in his early essay "Von deutscher Baukunst" (1772). It was the architect's feeling from the heart that had created a characteristic whole: "Eine Empfindung schuf sie [die Bildnerei] zum characteristischen Ganzen. Diese characteristische Kunst ist nun die einzige wahre. Wenn sie aus inniger, einiger, eigner, selbständiger Empfindung um sich wirkt, unbekümmert, ja unwissend alles Fremden, da mag sie aus rauher Wildheit oder aus gebildeter Empfindsamkeit geboren werden, sie ist ganz und lebendig."[17]

For Goethe, truth was the final goal, poetry the means of realizing it. In *Dichtung und Wahrheit,* he was dealing with hard facts — the verifiable data of his life — but in order to do them full justice, he had to bring his poetic gifts to bear, transfusing, combining, concentrating, giving them form. In the last resort, his criterion was the poetic eye of memory. *Erdichtung,* the fabrication of an incident, was not allowed. This latter process, which held full sway in his plays and novels, was not appropriate to the writing of autobiography. Nevertheless, the more the autobiography is a successfully realized work of art, the more the truth will shine out of it.

The philosopher that Goethe is, Lewald is not, and she has indeed been criticized for her "direct, didactic and hard-hitting" style.[18] Truth, however, was no less important to her than it was to Goethe, and it is in this regard that Lewald produces a work that precisely because of an emphasis on *reportage* allows the contemporary reader to have an unfiltered look at the life of a nineteenth-century Jewish woman. Unlike many European women's autobiographies of the period, Lewald describes in great detail her childhood, and includes kinds of information which allow the contemporary reader glimpses into her everyday life. During a period of illness, Lewald is prompted by her reading to keep a diary: "War es nun das eigene melancholische Zimmer, das mir solch ein Gefühl von Wichtigkeit gab, oder war es die Lektüre von *Rosaliens Nachlaß* von Friedrich Jacobs, die mich dazu begeisterte, genug, ich kam ganz plötzlich auf den Gedanken, ein Tagebuch zu führen. Bis dahin hatte ich mich begnügt, mir einzelne Stellen aus den Büchern, welche ich las, auszuschreiben, aber nun befriedigte mich das nicht mehr" (173). Lewald then describes the "advances" in orthopedics and the concern about the deformation of young women. Lewald was unfortunately entangled in this orthopedic craze, spending several months under the care of Dr. Ungher, director of the surgical clinic in Königsberg. She was forced to hang from a rack every day for several minutes, lie an hour on her back on the floor, and have four to six leeches applied to her shoulder every two weeks. During her therapy, Lewald chronicled her musings in two quarto books. One evening she decided to read what she had written. To her shock and dismay, she writes:

> Nicht ein Wort war wahr von alledem, was ich seit fünf Viertel Jahren zusammengeschrieben hatte. Ich hatte von Seelenleiden geredet, die ich gar nicht kannte, von einer Sehnsucht, die ich nie gehegt. Ich war ganz benommen, ganz verdutzt über mich selbst. Ich war mir widerwärtig und lächerlich zugleich. Ich kam mir wie ein Falschmünzer und im höchsten Grade malhonnette vor. Das war ein Wort, welches mein Vater für solche Unredlichkeiten brauchte, und ich hatte, nun ich mich einmal auf mich selbst besonnen, auch nicht eher Ruhe, bis das letzte Blatt dieser Lügenchronik im Ofenfeuer verkohlt war. (176)

Goodman writes that the "unfortunate result of this painful experience was that Lewald never kept a diary again."[19] But Goodman continues: "Herein lies a real strength of her autobiography. The particular irony in it all is that her very realism ultimately undermines her attempt at reading a teleology into her life. For her own precise observations and psychological perceptivity confront us with patterns of development radically different from that model. Her experience contradicts the 'dictionary' of accessible concepts in terms of which she would have been able to conventionally view her life."[20] Thus, whereas for Goethe poetry was the means of achieving truth, Lewald takes a more direct, unromantic approach with a journalistic eye.

This approach may be praised by a contemporary audience seeking historical information, for Lewald manages to situate her life against a very broad description of her times. Lewald, not unlike Goethe, introduces the reader to many different people. Certainly a major concern for any biographer or autobiographer is how to portray others, both those who are still alive and those who are not. It is a task that, particularly in the nineteenth century, required the utmost in scrupulosity. In *Dichtung und Wahrheit*, Goethe is never guilty of outright cattiness, but he does subtly manage to let the reader know to whom he is well disposed and to whom he is not. Even those acquaintances of Goethe's who we know, or at least suspect, were not in his good favor, Jakob Lenz and Heinrich Wagner, for example, are treated with great charity. Perhaps more important than portraiture itself is Goethe's method of portraiture. According to Derek Bowman, Goethe first provides a long, leisurely revelation of a person's character through numerous incidents, reported opinions, dramatic encounters — though these are used on the whole sparingly — repeated appearances at different turns of the story. From time to time, Goethe analyzes the person's character explicitly, explaining how, in Goethe's opinion, he or she came to act in a particular fashion. Such rational investigations are conducted with supreme confidence, as befits the omniscient chronicler. On the other hand, Goethe fully realizes how arbitrary a procedure it must necessarily be to reduce the way a person was to a formulation in words; what he writes of the depiction of incidents applies also to the delineation of people: "Bei Behandlung einer mannigfaltig vorschreitenden Lebensgeschichte, wie die ist, die wir zu unternehmen gewagt haben, kommen wir, um gewisse Ereignisse fasslich und lesbar zu machen, in den Fall, einiges, was in der Zeit sich verschlingt, notwendig zu trennen, anderes, was nur durch eine Folge begriffen werden kann, in sich selbst zusammenzuziehn und so das Ganze in Teile zusammenzustellen, die man sinnig überschauend beurteilen und sich davon manches zueignen mag."[21]

Lewald, however, dispenses with the rhetoric to which Goethe is so prone. Her descriptions of people are almost always positive to the point of pollyanna-ishness. One is sometimes led to believe that Lewald lives in a sugar-sweet world of enjoyable books, congenial people, cute friends, and pleasant outings: "Meine Eltern waren in den ersten Monaten nach meiner Geburt so glücklich, als ein schönes, junges, sorgenfreies Menschenpaar, das zärtlich liebt, es mit seinem ersten Kinde nur sein kann" (vol. 1, 16). Even when Lewald writes something less than generous about someone else, she still apparently feels the need to temper her observations. After meeting the famous Jewish hostess Sara Levy from Berlin, she writes about Levy: "Ebenso reich als die Hofrätin unbemittelt, ebenso unschön als diese schön gewesen und einander an Güte des Herzens und an Wohltätigkeit völlig gleich; nur daß bei der Hofrätin Herz alles was sie tat ein Gepräge hoher weiblicher Anmut an sich trug, während in Frau Levy überall ein gewisses männliches Wesen unverkennbar war" (vol. 3, 86).

Of course, we know that Lewald's life was not the mixture of sweetness and light that she sometimes portrays. Indeed, the evidence points clearly to the contrary: Young men were not forced to undergo the orthopedic therapy that she and other young women endured; Lewald's formal education ended early, whereas her brothers were encouraged to continue their studies; she was discouraged from reading and from becoming an educated woman, since her parents felt it would inhibit her development as a good wife and house-keeper; she was almost forced into an arranged marriage; and last but cer-tainly not least, her father was perfectly willing to have her brothers convert to Christianity but saw no point in letting his daughters do the same (al-though in the end, he did let Fanny convert).

Clearly, then, Lewald's life was not as sanguine as many of the descrip-tions in her autobiography might imply. Despite the generally blithe spirit in which Lewald recounts her life, the *Zeitgeist* was against her; the political climate allowed widespread anti-Semitism; women were generally regarded as chattel;[22] and war, along with famine and epidemic disease, was frequent. In keeping with her expressed intent, Lewald, and this is where her autobiogra-phy is at its most successful, traces the interrelation of public event and pri-vate experience, which often, for her and Goethe both, resulted in artistic creation. In *Dichtung und Wahrheit,* Goethe stresses at length the commerce between man, and especially the artist, and his / her environment. Both Goethe and Lewald use the time-honored device of the memoir writer — the eyewitness account of important events. Lewald, for instance, reports on the march of Napoleon's troops through East Prussia and reveals the Jewish am-bivalence toward the French invasion:

> Die französische Revolution hatte die staatliche Gleichberechtigung der ver-schiedenen Kulte in Frankreich festgestellt, und wenn Napoleon auch seinen Frieden mit der Katholischen Kirche gemacht hatte, so hatte er es doch nicht gewagt, die Glaubensfreiheit und die staatliche Gleichberechtigung der verschiedenen Religionsbekenntnisse anzutasten. In Frankreich, und wohin die französische Herrschaft sich ausbreitete, waren die Juden emanzipiert; in Preußen lasteten Unfreiheit und Verspottung auf ihnen. Es ist also natürlich, daß in jener Zeit sich in vielen Juden die Frage regte: ob Freiheit unter einem fremden Herrscher nicht der Knechtschaft unter einem heimischen Fürstenstamme vorzuziehen sei? (vol. 1, 22)

Lewald's writings — both her fiction and nonfiction — clearly reflect her commitment to a politically more liberal environment. Indeed, on the page, she is quite radical in her opinions. Yet, many of her actions off the page contradict her stated goals. In 1870, Lewald wrote *Für und wider die Frauen* ("For and against Women"), which advocates the emancipation of the middle-class woman by means of education to be able to work outside the home so that marriage will not be her only option. She wrote this as a reaction to her father's insistence that she get married. In her novel *Clementine*, however, Lewald's heroine writes a letter to her aunt heralding the splendor of marriage. In this letter, she advocates the idea of marriage based on love, commitment, and equality; she even goes so far as to champion the woman who is "carried away by momentary passion and sensual ecstasy." Going one step further, she writes: "The marriages I see being entered in to daily before my eyes are worse than prostitution. Don't avoid the word, since you want to persuade me to do the deed. Isn't this just what a wanton, morally debased girl does when she gives herself to a man for useless frippery or what parents do when they sacrifice their child for so many thousands of thalers?"[23]

Lewald eventually did get married — to Adolph Stahr, whom she met in Rome in 1845. While Lewald may have thought of Stahr as her equal, he quickly turned out to be a rather oppressive figure in her life. According to Venske, Stahr stepped in to take over Lewald's brother's position and functioned as her mentor. Stahr not only worked to change her affinity for Heine in favor of Goethe, he also oversaw her correspondence and attempted to moderate her opinions. Lewald appears to have no problem with Stahr's domination and even writes of him in glowing terms referring to him as "a teacher, an educator, and a model."[24]

Venske interprets Lewald's relationship with Stahr as typical of the masochistic way in which some women choose their partners: selecting intuitively the one who will most likely prevent them from reaching their real potential. Venske supports this thesis with Stahr's criticisms of Lewald's early novels, which he called "pathological novels," since she had used her writing as a catharsis of her feelings. Lewald, according to Venske, accepted this judgment and attempted to write in a more detached manner, at a distance from her own feelings and experiences.[25] To say the least, Venske's ideas are interesting, and they add a new dimension to any analysis of Lewald. Unfortunately, they also detract from the successful aspects of Lewald's *Meine Lebensgeschichte*. The autobiography is notable primarily because of the manner in which she reports the personal and historical events that shaped her life in nineteenth-century Germany. Not to have followed Goethe's lead, or Stahr's as the case may be, Lewald might very well have produced an autobiography not unlike her childhood diaries or Sand's *Histoire de ma vie* (1854, "History of My Life"), both of which she openly criticized. Venske observes another important factor in Lewald's life: that the biggest influences on Lewald's life and her writing were Stahr and her father, David Markus.[26] But Dagmar Lorenz points out in *Keepers of the Motherland* (1997), "The personal development of Fanny Lewald resembled that of earlier Jewish women writers; she was educated by her father, ... a man leery of traditional training for girls because of its emphasis on housework and needlework and its superficial exposure to languages, literature and music. He provided his daughter with a first-rate scientific and philosophical education but otherwise expected her to accept the established gender roles."[27]

In conclusion, Lewald's *Meine Lebensgeschichte* reflects the many and varied stimuli that influenced her life and her career. She exhibits diverse interests, which she explored both by the opportunities offered to her as well as by those she created for herself. Well-read and widely traveled, Lewald managed in the course of her life to face, if not overcome, the obstacles that confronted her as a woman and as a Jew. And unlike the woman to whom she is so often compared, George Sand, Lewald did not have the advantage of being born into a particularly privileged economic class. Her autobiography, like most others, is a mixture of fiction and truth, for this is the dilemma that faces all those engaged in self-writing. Autobiographers begin their task with a clear sense of themselves, but in the course of recreating their lives, they are forced to make use of the events, of the people, and of the ideas that have prevailed upon them.

Notes

1. Regula Venske, "Discipline and Daydreaming in the Works of a Nineteenth-Century Woman Author: Fanny Lewald," in *German Women in the Eighteenth and Nineteenth Centuries*, ed. Ruth-Ellen B. Joeres and Mary Jo Maynes (Bloomington: Indiana UP, 1986), 175.

2. Katherine Goodman, *Dis / Closures: Women's Autobiography in Germany Between 1790 and 1914* (New York: Peter Lang, 1986), 148.

3. Fanny Lewald, *Meine Lebensgeschichte* (1862; reprint, Frankfurt am Main: Ulrike Helmer, 1988) in three volumes. Further references will be cited parenthetically. English passages are taken from Fanny Lewald, *The Education of Fanny Lewald: An Autobiography*, ed. and trans. Hanna Ballin-Lewis (Albany: State U of New York P, 1992).

4. Goodman, 149.

5. Fanny Lewald, *Gefühltes and Gedachtes*, ed. Ludwig Geiger (Dresden: Minden, 1900), 148.

6. Doris Maurer, "Nähe nicht — lebe!" *Die Zeit* 32, Aug. 11, 1989, 19. As quoted in Ballin-Lewis, *The Education of Fanny Lewald*, xiv.

7. Mary G. Mason, "The Other Voice: Autobiographies of Women Writers," in *Autobiography: Essays Theoretical and Critical*, ed. James Olney (Princeton, NJ: Princeton UP, 1980).

8. Linda Peterson, "Institutionalizing Women's Autobiography: Nineteenth-Century Editors and the Shaping of an Autobiographical Tradition," in *The Culture of Autobiography: Constructions of Self-Representation*, ed. Robert Folkenflick (Stanford, CA: Stanford UP, 1993), 80.

9. Estelle C. Jelinek, *The Tradition of Women's Autobiography: From Antiquity to the Present* (Boston, MA: Twayne, 1986); Sidonie Smith, *A Poetics of Women's Autobiography: Marginality and the Fictions of Self-Representation* (Bloomington: Indiana UP, 1987); and Carolyn G. Heilbrun, *Writing a Woman's Life* (New York: Norton, 1988).

10. Jelinek, 8.

11. Peterson, 81.

12. Ibid.

13. Ibid.

14. Ibid., 83.

15. Johann Wolfgang von Goethe, *Gedenkausgabe der Werke, Briefe und Gespräche*, ed. E. Beutler (Zurich: Artemis, 1948), 355.

16. Goethe, vol. 1, 46.

17. Ernst Beutler, *Von deutscher Baukunst: Goethes Hymnus auf Erwin von Sternbach* (Munich: F. Bruckmann, 1943), 52.

18. Linda Rogols-Siegel, "Fanny Lewald's *Prinz Louis Ferdinand* and Theodore Fontane's *Vor dem Sturm* and Schach von Wuthenow," *The Modern Language Review* 88 (April 1993): 2.

19. Goodman, 158.

20. Ibid.

21. As quoted in Derek Bowman, *Life into Autobiography* (Bern: Peter Lang, 1971), 27.

22. This is equally true even within the community of Jewish intellectuals. The members of the Jewish Enlightenment (Mendelssohn, Auerbach, et al.) knew that since the destruction of the Jewish state, Judaism must let other nations, in this case Germany, decide political matters, including the position of women. But Mendelssohn, for example, never addressed the legal rights of women, except for putting down Jewish law in *Ritualgesetze der Juden* (1799, "Jewish Ritual Laws"). In *Jerusalem* (1783), Mendelssohn does treat the powers of church and state with respect to social contracts, maintaining that the state — here he means a state whose citizens are primarily of the Christian faith so that the laws may be biased on behalf of Christianity — has no power to legislate *Gesinnungen*. The specific example he uses is the case of a Jewish married couple, where the man converted to Christianity yet wanted to keep his wife. Marriage in Judaism, Mendelssohn points out, is a social contract. When both parties entered into the marriage, it was with the understanding that the household would be run under Jewish regulations. The wife could not be forced to remain in the marriage and live under conditions counter to her beliefs. Auerbach, on the other hand, would have argued that the laws of the state have to supersede religious law to bring about equality.

23. Fanny Lewald, *Clementine* (Berlin: O. Janke, 1872), 64.

24. Ballin-Lewis, 184.

25. Venske, 184.

26. Venske writes: "The most profound and the most subtle aspects of Lewald's autocensorship were of course a heritage from her father, a wine merchant and representative of the 'enlightened bourgeoisie.' The self-discipline which Fanny Lewald was forced to acquire had considerable impact on her writing. For example, her father was always strictly opposed to all expressions of imagination and sensibility, and as a writer she later found it difficult to overcome his perspective" (184–85).

27. Dagmar C. G. Lorenz, *Keepers of the Motherland: German Texts by Jewish Women Writers* (Lincoln: U of Nebraska P, 1997), 39.

NEVA ŠLIBAR

Traveling, Living, Writing from and at the Margins: Alma Maximiliana Karlin and Her Geobiographical Books

> Das Leben gibt uns fortwährend
> Bilder mit Sprüchen, aus denen wir,
> wenn wir nicht so auraversponnen
> wären, gar tiefe, helfende Weisheit
> schöpfen könnten, doch wir verstehen
> nur zu schauen, selten zu lesen.
>
> — Alma Karlin, *Einsame Weltreise*

"When you've gone, I'm never going to eat fish again," my aunt said. "Why not?"

"Because I'm not a cannibal. The *Scotland maru*'s returning empty to Japan. You'll be the only woman on board. The sailors will throw you into the sea. The fish will eat what's left of you."

I didn't want to upset her, so I decided to travel to Japan through South America.

I had actually begun preparing my journey round the world when I was studying in London. I spent hours in the library. I buried myself in books. I composed a dictionary of ten foreign languages. I thought, "My advantage will be my ability to understand everything everywhere I go."[1]

THE "I" SPEAKING HERE — AND, IN contrast to the feminists of a half-century later, not having any problems with the first person singular[2] — is that of Alma Maximiliana Karlin (1889–1950) in the opening scene of the one-person play *Alma*, a one-woman piece proper, written by the young Slovene playwright Ursula Cetinski.[3] The play was first performed in 1995 in two versions, a Slovene and an English one, by Polona Vetrih, a Slovene actress with British theater experience. It has since been invited to theater houses and festivals abroad, where it should also make known the protagonist of the play, Alma Karlin, and her more than adventurous and exciting life as a world traveler, journalist, and writer. The "rediscovery" and "resurrection" of Alma Maximiliana Karlin was overdue; she has always been known in Slovene ethnological and other insider circles but disappeared from the public and collective memory for several reasons: (1) she was a woman; (2) she wrote in German; (3) she was an outsider in the community of scientists and authors; and (4) there were many ambivalences contained in her life and in her work. The newly arisen interest in her, her books (also the many unpublished ones), and her vast legacy conforms with the boom of rediscovered, reprinted, and thoroughly analyzed travel descriptions by women,[4] including their development as a genre, and with the shifting of perspective in the last decade. This fascinating field of research became accessible through analytical instruments and critical patterns, of which many were constructed by feminist theory and discourse analysis, often combined with poststructuralist theory[5] as well as with the awareness of the imperialistic, colonial view toward the self and the other. Besides these general and theoretical reasons, the positive reaction to the attempts at integrating Alma Karlin into Slovene history agrees, last but not least, with the political self-consciousness of the young state of Slovenia and its interest in internationally representable figures. Bearing in mind the one-sided instrumentalization that goes hand in hand with such an officially mandated integration, it is the task of the scholar to counterbalance simplifications by pointing out ambivalences and by approaching the phenomenon from a critical perspective.

The fictitious first scene between aunt and niece, the aunt standing for the symbolic order and its notions of domesticated, petit-bourgeois womanhood — everything Alma Karlin tried to escape from — mentions cannibalism in both irony and true fear; since the era of the big discoveries and the development of the travel discourse, cannibalism has been considered as the utmost threat to the "conquerors of terra incognita" and as the last barrier between the barbarian and the civilized world.[6] Just like incest, promiscuity, nakedness, and wildness, cannibalism was a fascinating taboo for the white man. In fact, Alma Karlin's escape from the hands of cannibals and her experience with head hunters are the most frequently told and retold anecdotes of her eight-year-long journey around the world in her own presentations as well as in those about her. In the introductory chapter of her book *Einsame Weltreise. Die Tragödie einer Frau* (1929, translated as *The Odyssey of a Lonely Woman*, 1933),[7] she sums up her scariest adventures in a highly ironic, almost sardonic, way with a fling of resigned masochism. She reports how she offered her head to the head hunters of Formosa. However, they declined, because the heads of authors, Karlin jokes, are only considered valuable when they are made of marble and positioned in a hall of fame. She goes on to write that she hoped in vain to be eaten by a cannibal, because that would have put an end to everything. Yet, she claims that the most humble native considered her too bony — only the mosquitoes drank her blood with great enthusiasm (EW, 14).

In the following, I will sketch the life, travel, and works of this fearless woman by taking up the theme of transforming the center and eroding the margins. At least one dozen different manifest forms of marginality can be discerned in Alma Karlin's life, travel, and books: a national, geographical, social, gender-bound, physical, religious, professional, literary / aesthetic marginality, a scientific one, and her marginality in the travel tradition, the publication praxis, and the reception of her books.

Before entering into the discussion of each of these, it must be stressed that the revaluation of the marginal with its permeability and horizontal mobility is the opposite of the totalizing, power-absorbing, and power-attracting vertical structuring of the center. It is a useful pattern of cognition and analysis, especially when dealing with discourses constructed by an authorial voice whose vision and interpretation must / should — by unwritten contract — be relied upon, as it is the case with the discourses of discovery and travel. This being a recent paradigm, we must bear in mind that we generally evaluate mostly facts, actions, and texts conceived when the contrary was to be aspired. Moreover, a basic ambivalence in Karlin's writings needs to be stressed: on the one hand, her marginality; on the other hand, her conformity to mainstream expectations and her tendency to conform with the characteristics of women's travel discourse since the nineteenth century. Surprising is also the presence of colonial, racist, and sexist discourse characteristic of the 1920s and 1930s. This ambiguity is, as Gabriele Habinger points out, the dominant trait of Karlin's texts and constitutes their subversive potential. According to Habinger, other features include the complexity of the texts on many different levels, contradictions, and uncertainties as far as the evaluation of the unfamiliar is concerned. She speculates that these features may be connected to the problematic status of traveling and writing women both in their countries of origin and in the colonial environment. And she concludes by citing Sarah Mills that these women were "between the conflicting demands of the discourse of femininity and that of imperialism."[8]

Heterogeneity and multilayeredness seem to be basic to Karlin's texts insofar as in the evaluation of alien societies no universal truth is postulated. Rather, mutually contradicting statements stand side by side in contrast to "monovocal, totalizing forms of discursive authority."[9] It is a strange, but probably quite common phenomenon: Wherever Karlin, consciously or subconsciously, tried to conform to the mainstream, her writings turn against themselves. Regardless whether she conformed out of conviction, as was the case with her ideas on the pureness of the races, by cultural commitment, as was the case with her writing in German, or somewhat opportunistically, by adapting to an easily readable style and disregarding higher literary and scientific standards, her problematic discursive strategies become obvious. From today's point of view, her politically unacceptable ideological positions and rhetoric reveal themselves almost inadvertently. They deconstruct themselves openly, thus shifting the interest of the reader from the "objects" and the "facts" to their discursive "fictionalization" and "narrativization," focusing much more intensely on the narrator, her construction of otherness and foreign countries, and the futility of her endeavors.

Alma Karlin was born and grew up at the time of the crumbling Habsburg monarchy. She traveled shortly after the First World War and in the period of emerging Nazism in an atmosphere of the loss of values, chaos, upheaval, change, and insecurity. Like many of her educated contemporaries, she held on to the ideal of "enlightened" wisdom, to her love of the arts, to extreme self-discipline regarding her self-imposed task(s) — in short, her ego-ideal was to conquer the center(s). The possibility of eroding it or showing that it is in fact an empty sign did not occur to her on the conscious level; however, she seems to have had a sense of the relativity of notions such as center and margin, as is suggested by her highly (self)-ironic style in her travel books, the main element of which is understatement. She subverted and used three aspects of her marginalization: her physical petiteness, her gender, and her social status, although desire was not to have any of these characteristics. She is ambivalent and undecided as to her motives; therefore, contradictions arise. There are ruptures in her experiences and narrative textures as well as in her cognitive and verbal patterns, which set free the potential for subversion and exposure. The unmasking of her own carefully painted and upheld mask (despite her self-irony) leads her to the discovery that mirroring oneself in an opposite's otherness is an essential need for the white man's patriarchal cultures. Karlin recognizes the latent fear of emptiness in whatever is considered the "center."

Travel books, especially by women writers, are paradigmatic of the dialectic of crossing borders in the literal as well as the figurative sense. At the same time, they reinstate and emphasize the "transgressor's" personal and wider cultural identity, often by passing on stereotypes, prejudices, and racist views.[10] The intertwining of biography and travel descriptions is a tradition of the genre. According to the modern, Western, progress-oriented concept of self-perfection and self-fulfillment, a development toward more subtle cognitive structures and narrative strategies while en route would be expected. Karlin's sometimes irritating egocentrism, especially obvious in the first part of her travel accounts — ironically, she coins the expression of "the swollen head" — diminishes after her disconcerting experiences in South and Central America that let the wider geographical context fade out (several times, she escapes rape — or at least, that is what she tells the reader).[11] Karlin concentrates with growing differentiation on the various "objects" of her journey and thus creates a more balanced narrative of both elements, which could justifiably be called "geobiographical" texts. Annegret Pelz uses the term "autogeographical" in her enlightening book on women's travel writings, *Reisen durch die eigene Fremde* (1993, "Traveling through Your Own Foreignness"). The term implies theorems of the poststructuralist feminist discourse and integrates the notion of the "body landscape" and of "travels to get to know one's own geography."[12] My own term is, by contrast, explicit and straightforward: It emphasizes the interrelatedness of the traveler's search for self and the exploration of foreign territory; the drive of the traveler to the other, the unknown, is realized through concrete movement.

Alma Karlin explains her "Columbus-like spirit" as an inner urge with a fatalistic twist, and she stresses — a dominant trait of the women's travel discourse — that she was not driven by the desire for adventure,[13] but by the inner force that takes on the almost fateful appearance of an externally imposed task (EW, 21). Her firm belief in her "vocation" as a writer and (to a lesser extent) as a journalist — she began to write poems and stories at the age of eight — motivated her wish to experience and explore foreign cultures and countries. She writes that she wished to see strange continents, "denn ich hegte den sehnlichsten Wunsch, fremde Erdteile mit den Augen des Schriftstellers, des Malers, und vor allem mit *den Augen der Frau* zu schauen" (EW, 12, italics added). It helped her to endure unimaginable hardships day by day (BS, 329: "Mein einziges Heil war die Arbeit; ich segnete sie.") and to stick to her strict daily regime of working, reading, exploring, collecting plants and insects, interviewing, writing, drawing, and so forth, even when she was feverish. Her will to overcome difficulties (and solve problems, see EW, 12) and her defiance toward the "gods" who, she imagined, wanted to crush her (BS, 114) were probably formed by her early childhood experiences.

The child of an elderly couple, Karlin was born with several birth defects. She had a deformity of the left eye and was unable to walk properly, which had necessitated several complicated orthopedic surgeries. In order to forget her pain, she threw herself into reading and learning languages.[14] Her early experiences of being different, of not being able to conform to the norm, must have intensified her aloofness and need of loneliness, which, of course, proved a curse as well. Karlin's strong motivation for traveling, along with her fascination for mysticism, magic, and superstition, her exploratory interests represented an imaginary communication with her present and future reading public. In her self-imposed task, she transcended her self-exclusion from society. Her writings, including her fiction, were designed to provide her the gratifications she craved: appreciation as a writer, journalist, traveler, and explorer. She wanted to make these activities her vehicle to make a living, to overcome her overall marginalization, and to "penetrate" into the center. This very "masculine," phallic desire is also expressed in her choice of metaphorical figures: She sees herself as Columbus (EW, 31), as a warrior-king (BS, 363), and as a tradesman (BS, 345, 100).

Alma Karlin was born in 1889 in Celje, German Cilli, a small Slovene town, geographically, economically, and culturally peripheral to the Austrian-Hungarian monarchy. Karlin compensated for her off-center position by studying abroad and through frequent extensive journeys. However, when she returned home, she was again stuck in her native town for political, historical, and financial reasons. An additional drawback, which became increasingly significant in her later years, was her ambivalent national position: Both her parents came from Slovene families: Her mother, a teacher, was the daughter of a prominent solicitor, the first one in Celje. Her father was a son of peasants from the surroundings of Rogaska Slatina (now a famous spa). He had served as an officer in the Austrian-Hungarian army and was probably the descendent of an Italian family fleeing to the northeast, through Slovenia to France. At home, Karlin's parents conversed in German, both being Austrian state officials. Thus, Alma Karlin considered German her mother tongue (BS, 100). She speaks of her *inneres Deutschtum*, an inner sense of being German (EW, 76), and tries to educate the German-speaking minority in Celje and surroundings by sending one article of her journeys after another to the local newspaper free of charge, thus promoting their *Deutschtum* (BS, 100). How well Alma Karlin spoke Slovene is a matter of controversy:[15] On the one hand, it would be strange for somebody who mastered over a dozen languages — and learned them with ease (AP, 1) — not to be able to converse with her compatriots;[16] on the other hand, she never wrote or published in Slovene, which after her decision in 1937 to stop publishing in the German press was a matter of vital importance and led her into economic isolation. The marginalization of her nonexistent reception during and after the war are both due to this fact and her aloof and bizarre public appearances, which in the narrow-minded and unsophisticated environment of her hometown Celje inspired ridicule. The impression she made on the people around her is depicted by Janez Stanonik's observations before and after the Second World War. He was the first literary historian who tried to interest the wider public in her journey around the world and in her literary works. "During the thirties the inhabitants of Celje … could frequently see in the streets a middle aged lady, always rapidly walking, never stopping to have a talk with an acquaintance. She was of an average height, with a permanent smile on her face which, however, was rather polite than happy. She had a typical pageboy haircut and squinting eyes."[17] This haircut, of which she had been proud before it became fashionable (EW, 31), was one of her few external concessions to "masculinity": She maintained that it was the only masculine thing about her — except for her "'masculine soul' which had developed few feminine virtues (and my enemies would probably maintain no virtues at all)" (EW, 246).

In addition to this intermediate, ambiguous position of language, culture, and home country, there is yet another burning problem: Karlin's strange, again ambivalent "racism" in spite of her professed "cosmopolitanism": Karlin is a very strong propagator of the pureness of race, no matter where and in what culture. The Indian Parsis appealed to her because she believed them to be a pure race. She praises the fact that they outlawed intermarriage with members of other groups, and she attributes their strength and beauty to their exclusivity. Without hesitation, Karlin equates physical beauty with superiority in terms of character and mentality. "Kein Volk hat seine Rasse so rein erhalten, und Mischehen sind streng verboten, daher sind sie so stark, so tüchtig, so lebensfähig und so schön als Menschenschlag. Ihre Hautfarbe ist so licht, daß einige schon weiß wirken, aber nicht die Farbe, die ja nebensächlich ist, das ganze Gebahren ist sicher, fest, fortschrittlich. Ihre Feinde nennen sie die Juden des Ostens. Das ist an und für sich ein Lob, denn es beweist, daß sie fleißig und tüchtig sind" (BS, 361). Apart from recurrent contemptuous expressions and racist prejudices or prejudices toward indigenous populations, especially at times when she was in real danger or ill treated, Karlin shows a strong dislike for people of mixed background. She rejects most *Mischlinge* and attributes negative qualities to them as a result of her rigid notion of the superiority of a pure race. In her opinion, women had to uphold the purity of the race, for it was they who suffered the most from race-mixing and the immersion into a different racial environment. In her second book of travel, she states that she can understand a man's desire for women of color and exotic environments, which she envisions as a never ending sequence of singing, caressing, and daydreaming in the sunshine. Such a life might lead a man to forgetting his European origins, but a woman, according to Karlin, would feel a kind of racial nostalgia. She would feel unhappy in the tropical surroundings, even though it might be possible for a man to adjust (BS, 15; EW, 215).

Karlin's troubling objections to persons of mixed race, which she tries to corroborate with her own experiences of being treated arrogantly and being looked down upon by them. Having been abused by some individuals, she assumes that all of them have a propensity for abuse and arrogance. Moreover, she interprets their demeaning behavior as compensation for the feeling of inferiority she attributes to them (BS, 190). The unquestioned certainty of her convictions indicates, on the one hand, to what degree the atmosphere of her times was permeated with different kinds of racism, how easily these could lead to Nazism, and, on the other hand, how intimately her views were connected to the discourse of purity, cleanness, and hygiene — Karlin was oversensitive to odors and noise. Moreover, Karlin's asceticism and her conviction that deprivation would turn into spiritual good can be traced to her idealization of the *Bildungsbürgertum* as well as to her theosophic background, likewise part of the spirit of the times. In her first book, Alma Karlin goes as far as cautioning girls and young woman to be aware of the dangers of mixed relationships, marriages, and love affairs, pointing out primarily the incompatibility of the races and peoples (EW, 324). These attitudes are bewildering, considering that Karlin herself, although unambiguously white, was of uncertain nationality. She calls herself a Yugoslav by passport ("passportpolitisch," BS, 300) and is aware of Slavic cultures. Yet, she never speaks of the Slovene people, culture, or language, and her allegiance belongs to the Germans. During her journeys, she worked several times for German consuls (BS, 300). Nonetheless, she is highly critical of the "German character"; of all nations, she prefers the English for their politeness, their correctness, for not interfering and keeping to themselves.[18] Although her views have clearly emerged from European colonialism, she is a harsh critic of all kinds of "conquests" and questions the white man's cultural and religious superiority. Thus, she asks herself why white people feel obligated to impose their beliefs on indigenous peoples, who have their own laws, which are much more adequate to their environment (BS, 149). In the second part of her travel journal, she comments that for the most part, Christians are selfish in that they themselves lack the virtues that they want to force upon others (BS, 84–85).

It is this skepticism and her nonconformism from which results Alma Karlin's religious margin position. During her stay in London, where she supported herself by translating and tutoring (she writes that this experience taught her the "art of starvation," which proved very handy in her travels), she was introduced by her Asian acquaintances to oriental philosophy and theosophy. Buddhism appealed to her for its equal treatment of all beings and for its consistent reliance on the laws of cause and effect rather than divine being:

> Das war das Fest des Buddhismus, war das Heiligtum des stillen Glaubens, der im Gesetz ewiger Wiedervergeltung, in der Macht von Ursache und Wirkung wurzelt und von keiner Gnade weiß. Was ein Mensch getan hat, das muß er wieder abdienen, wie sehr er auch winseln oder beten mag. Es gab keine Barmherzigkeit. Es gab aber auch nicht, wie im Christentum, eine Bevorzugung. Kein Wesen war "Kind Gottes", sondern alle im gleichen Maße, und man konnte seine Taten nicht abbetteln, nicht abfasten, nicht "erlassen" erhalten. Man ertrug die Folgen — gut oder schlecht je nach der Tat — in der kaltgerechten Auslösung. Es schien mir die einzig faßbare Religion der Welt. Sie umfaßte alles — Mensch, Tier, Pflanze, Stein — und sie führte zum Urquell aller Schöpfung in sehend gewordener, verklärter und gereinigter Form zurück. (BS, 291)

Karlin was a member of the Theosophic Society, although she did not discuss such matters in any of her travel books[19] or in her later novels in keeping with the secrecy vows of its members. However, she seemed to have enjoyed significant support and practical help by other members (BS, 307). Her intense non-Christian interest in the occult, in white and black magic, rituals and rites, and different beliefs in the supernatural enabled Karlin to inquire with great passion and sensitivity about superstitions, spells and witchcraft, charms and potions, and to describe their preparation, not only in her travel books but in novels as well as in both parts of *Im Banne der Südsee* (1930, "Under the Spell of the South Sea"). The goal of her quest was to transcend all kinds of boundaries on the basis of her radical, untamable, in her words "Columbus-like," spirit of discovery and enterprise. She was persistent even when ill and feeble from disease, and she was convinced of the theosophic idea of gradual transition from one stage of awareness and enlightenment to the next, up until the realization of the unity of all life. These principles provide a bridge between science and religion, the material and the spiritual world. As Sonja Dular points out:

> Theosophy in its religious aspect communicates the meaning, the goal of all life; its philosophical aspect gives insight into causality, and its scientific part explains how Nature works. ... Exoterically theosophy aims to achieve three social goals: realisation of universal brotherhood without racial, religious, gender, or social discrimination, it wants to encourage a comparative study of religions, philosophies, and science, together with all the as yet unexplained laws of Nature and the hidden powers of Man.[20]

This explains the immersion into the material and spiritual manifestations of the different cultures Karlin encountered. With the ardor of the zealous and perfectionist dilettante — one of the many characteristics she shares with other women travelers before her — she collected every kind of information, which "was then carefully and systematically listed under appropriate headings of history, industry, minerals, flora and fauna, typical diseases, language, beliefs, rituals, symbolism, proverbs etc. She spent a few hours daily studying, writing, and painting, and she kept a herbarium, collected folklore, melodies, tales, legends, and a wide variety of objects — artistic, ritual and those for everyday use."[21] These she shipped to her agents and are partly kept in collections of the Museum of Celje.[22] Karlin was self-taught as far as her scientific knowledge was concerned: She read about and discussed her points of interest. Wherever there was a public library, she tried to deepen her knowledge of the specific culture — for example, she writes enthusiastically about the public library in San Francisco. However, her publications do not show any textual traces of her reading: There are no quotations. Except for oral explanations by the natives, settlers, and other local inhabitants, the external information has been absorbed into the text and submitted to the authorial voice. Karlin's work also lacks an overall theoretical structure; keeping in mind that Bronislaw Malinowski's change of paradigm began shortly before the First World War — but most of his important works were written and published during Karlin's travels and probably out of her reach — and that Lévi-Strauss's research began during the same period, the marginal position of a researcher without proper academic training becomes apparent once again. On the other hand, Karlin was certainly no "armchair ethnologist," and she tried to immerse herself in the foreign cultures and to proceed with scientific objectivity. There is no denying that the view of the perfectionist amateur unburdened by theory has the capacity of bridging different discourses. It possesses an uninhibited element that can produce unorthodox insights.

Although writing for more than two dozen papers, magazines, and journals in her life, Karlin was at the mercy of her German agent's allegedly questionable managing skills (BS, 70). Considering herself a writer and a journalist, she sometimes would demonstrate an irritating diligence in producing one article after another and had a remarkable instinct to present her adventures in a way that would appeal to the public. However, she clearly lacked commercial abilities and the right connections for a large distribution — she was an outsider at home and abroad. Again and again, she complained about lack of interest on the part of the press in her explorations and hazards (BS, 88, 155, 210, 282, 345). It has yet to be investigated if her agent's lack of initiative is in part to blame. Since Karlin was financially dependent on the small income from her articles, she found herself often in distressing financial situations.

Karlin's status as a writer changed, following the general rule that mainstream commercial literature becomes marginalized in due course. The great number of unpublished books in her estate suggests that she wrote with ease. She was excellent at storytelling and depicting exotic atmospheres; besides novels and short stories, set in the parts of the world she had explored herself, she took up several other genres, such as the so-called *Heimatroman,* the regional novel, of which her completely unknown, unpublished manuscript "Eine Blüte der Höhen" (probably written during the 1930s, "A Blossom of Heights") is an example. She also authored fantasy and science fiction books, set in Atlantis or in imaginary utopian pasts, and an epistolary novel about the life and fate of the anti-Nazi journalist Hans Joachim Bonsack, whom she sheltered for some time in Celje. In this still unpublished work, entitled "Fremde Frau" (probably written during the early 1940s, "Foreign Lady"), we see the author's skill in producing conventional semifiction; the manuscript consists mainly of the correspondence between herself and Bonsack. Literary and linguistic innovation are neither sought nor achieved; no apparent attempt is being made at an aesthetic shaping of the factual material. Karlin's literary ideal amounts to a popular version of *Geistesgeschichte* with a touch of positivism.

Yet, Karlin uses the traditional patterns of literatization and fictionalization with considerable skill — her books can still be read with pleasure. However, as Stanonik points out, "After long introductory chapters, the story in her novels suddenly begins to develop towards a deep tragedy, which frequently borders on sentimentality. Almost regularly her novels and short stories end in the death of the central character, frequently even in the death of a whole group of people."[23] Indeed, Karlin loves pathos and the workings of fate, sometimes subverted by a strange kind of irony.

Even in the traditions of women's journeys around the world and of travel books, Alma Karlin's position is marginal insofar as she belongs to the last generation of travelers before the systematic development of organized tourism, which set in after the Second World War. Karlin had a distinct preference for unexplored regions and took upon herself all possible hardships in order to have a firsthand experience. In contrast to earlier women travelers with whom she shares many characteristics, she hardly ever relied on the possibilities of traveling in company or of sharing parts of the journey. She was completely on her own in every sense, and it was a matter of her ingenuity to reach the remote and inaccessible parts of her route. From her complaints about the inflation of articles on exotic regions can be deduced that she ventured into the completely unknown and put her life at stake for journalistic and ethnographical reasons.

Probably quite inadvertently, Karlin's travel descriptions take up and develop several dominant features of the genre. They are, as Stephen Greenblatt points out in his studies on discovery writings, anecdotal in structure, held together by the vertical movement of the subject and his / her authorial voice.[24] Moreover, the diary-like impression of heterogeneous particles of time resulting in a "constant" present are syntagmatically held together by the narrative's illusion of the traveler's movement on her journey. The narrator, being the sole proof of the text's "truth," has to assert herself twice: in the real world, where she is in danger of being absorbed and disseminated by the otherness — of losing identity — and then in the semifictional world of her text, where again the chain of significants threatens to annihilate her. Therefore, even with the most empathetic of travelers — and Karlin tries hard to be one, but rarely with success — an often forceful and self-limited point of view emerges. The center of experience and of the narrative must be preserved or reinstalled, even if only as a cognitive and textual simulation. Karlin's ironic understatements toward herself, although a conventional feature of the genre, function as subversive and intensifying devices for the superlative of her "unique" experience.

Last but not least, there are the three elements of marginalization Alma Karlin was able to use in her favor, although they were also drawbacks from which she suffered at the same time: her disability, her sex, and her social status, including the fact that she had to work to earn her living, even during her travel around the world.

Ambivalence, albeit an explicit one, again is the striking feature of these three characteristics: While complaining about the disadvantages of being a *woman* traveler, Karlin knows exactly that it is a fact that will function to her advantage in the eyes of the readers. She often complains about not being a bachelor (BS, 103), but she repeatedly uses the fact of being a woman, combined with her physical petiteness, as protective mechanisms. Yet, Karlin thought of and generally presented herself as a sexless human being: "Please try to imagine a woman … No, 'woman' really is an immoderately feminine word, so I would prefer 'human being' which sounds more like something neuter (add the female article)" (AO, 1). The desexualization goes hand in hand with her fears of being mistaken for an adventuress (EW, 155). It may thus be interpreted as a reaction to a tradition whereby traveling women were taken for prostitutes,[25] on the one hand, and Karlin's negation of the body, resulting from her scarce means ("Die Mahlzeiten blieben skizzenhaft," EW, 291) and her longing for spiritualization: "Entledigen kann sie sich ihres Körpers nicht, obwohl sie ihn durch Hunger und Strapazen auf ein Minimum reduziert." Pelz points also at Karlin's ambivalent relationship to her body: "Auf der Reise erst beginnt ihr 'Frauenwert', die Aufwertung ihres Körpers aufgrund ihrer Hautfarbe. Sie sagt selbst, sie fühlt sich wie ein 'Dollar' unter 'Geldmist.'"[26] Karlin is aware of writing from a specialized position of double marginalization as a "desexed woman," which means, of course, that she at the same time conforms to patriarchal exclusion mechanisms,[27] but she also exposes how they operate. She writes: "My attitude to life has always been somewhat particular; I somehow swim beyond sex and love … and I therefore believe myself capable of fathoming things which escape other women" (AP, 1). Pelz draws attention to Karlin's special sensitivity manifest in her perceptions about the lives and occupations of women and her observations about human relationships. In a longer passage about Indian women, Karlin, although in favor of their marriage customs, reflects on the oppression women endure (BS, 307). In her attempts to reach an unbiased explanation of the inferior status of women, Karlin mixes traditional and modern views, reactionary biologism and unconventional insights. She ends up by telling a surprising anecdote about herself: "Aus der Botschaft kam ich oft sehr müde und abgehetzt in ein kaltes Zimmer, zu Rettig und Brot heim, und da ertappte ich mich einmal dabei, laut zu rufen: 'Nein, ich muß heiraten, damit jemand das Haus gemütlich macht!' Dann erinnerte ich mich, daß ich ein Weib war und keine Frau nehmen konnte, und zum Kochen und allen anderen Hausarbeiten taugen nur die Neuseeländer, die man nicht so leicht hierher bestellen kann" (BS, 309).

Although Karlin hated the hardships she had to endure, traveling as inexpensively as possible, she knew that she would get to know foreign cultures far better than first-class passengers. She points out: "It was above all the circumstance that I had always first to earn money in order to continue my journey ... brought me into closer contact with the people. They were not the kind of people one encounters when travelling first-class, ... they were ordinary people who do not pretend, who live and act instinctively, who do not hide their superstitions, like and dislikes behind masks and who, besides shortcomings, are also endowed with all the virtues of the poor and the oppressed" (AP, 1). She suffered and complained sometimes about the gap between the rights she felt to possess because of her breeding, education, and endeavors, and the way she was treated because of her limited means. She was aware of these contradictions and spoke of them in her highly ironic style. She calls herself "a capitalist" on land and a "socialist" or even "communist" on sea (EW, 222).

Karlin's intense and forceful self-assertion and, by contrast, the lacking rewards of her hardships, her deprivations, and at times foolhardy endeavors disclose under the fascinating surface of exoticism, adventure, and the undoubtedly exhilarating anecdotes a frightening lack of satisfaction and meaning. She seems incapable of grasping otherness and understanding foreign cultures on their own terms. And there is Karlin's discouraging self-absorption. All of these are typical of the auto-reflexive actions of Western civilization, even when "discovery" is involved. It is easy to see why this unusual, courageous, brilliant, and extremely lonely woman wished herself onto a lonely star:

> Ich ging in meinen Werken auf. Es war dies scheinbar das einzige Band, das mich an die Menschheit knüpfte. Sonst, wenn ich unter dem flimmernden, blauschwarzen Tropenhimmel stand und die Sterne beobachtete, wünschte ich mir zur Belohnung der irdischen Pein nur eins: Hinaufgenommen zu werden auf einen Stern, der ganz leer und ganz still war, der eine Bücherei in allen Sprachen und eine Erika [the trademark of her typewriter] hatte und auf dem ich allmählich vergessen dürfte, daß ich je so etwas wie die Erde gekannt. (BS, 136)

Notes

1. Ursula Cetinski, "Alma," manuscript, trans. Martin Creegan, 1.

2. See Tamara Felden, *Frauen Reisen. Zur literarischen Repräsentation weiblicher Geschlechterrollenerfahrung im 19. Jahrhundert* (New York: Lang, 1993), 14–22. Felden stresses the contrast between the necessity of the authorial "I" in travel books, a position guaranteeing the authenticity of the narrated, and the expectation, especially during the last century, for women to use a specific "womanly" language. She points out, "'Ich' zu sagen, bedeutet … in einem patriarchalischen, frauenfeindlichen Kontext bewußt als agierendes Individuum aufzutreten, trotz des Widerstandes und sozialen Stigmas, welches damit für eine Frau verbunden sein kann. … Um so beeindruckender ist es, daß Frauen in ihren Reiseliteraturwerken das eigene Ich, ob implizit oder explizit, in den Mittelpunkt stellen" (17). And she says, "Diese Frauen haben den Mut zu einem anderen Selbstverständnis, aber in Anbetracht der auch in der Sprache manifestierten gesellschaftlichen Normen sind sie ständig gezwungen, einen Balanceakt durchzuführen: sie haben sich einerseits von manchen der Beschränkungen weiblichen Lebens befreit, drücken sich aber sprachlich — bewußt oder unbewußt — meist so aus, als stünden sie mit gesellschaftlichen Konventionen in Einklang" (18). This is mostly the case with Alma Karlin's writing.

3. Ursula Cetinski, the remarkable young author, switched from a short and successful career as theater critic first to theater- and then to culture management. She is the founder and chief organizer of the "City of Women," a fascinating and unorthodox one-week festival of women's art in Ljubljana, the capital of Slovenia, an annual event since 1995.

4. The reprint of the first part of Karlin's world travel description in a German publishing house for women's literature is due to this fact as well as her being more or less extensively mentioned in some of the books or papers on women's travel books, i.e., Inge Buck, Helga Grubitzsch, Annegret Pelz, and Sabine Reinecke, "Frauenleben. Lebensmöglichkeiten und Schwierigkeiten von Frauen in der bürgerlichen Gesellschaft," *Weibliche Biographien Beiträge zur feministischen Theorie und Praxis* 7 (1982): 23–36. See also Gabriele Habinger, "Anpassung und Widerspruch. Reisende Europäerinnen des 19. und beginnenden 20. Jahrhunderts im Spannungsfeld zwischen Weiblichkeitsideal und kolonialer Ideologie," in *" … und tät das Reisen wählen!" Frauen — Reisen — Kultur,* ed. Doris Jedamski (Zurich: eFeF, 1994), 174–201; Annegret Pelz, *"…Von einer Fremde in die andere?* Reiseliteratur von Frauen," in *Deutsche Literatur von Frauen,* vol. 2, by Gisela Brinker-Gabler (Munich: Beck, 1988), 143–53.

5. Clement Murath, "Intertextualität und Selbstbezug — Literarische Fremderfahrung im Lichte der konstruktivistischen Systemtheorie," in *Reisen im Diskurs. Modelle der literarischen Fremderfahrung von den Pilgerberichten bis zur Postmoderne,* by Anne Fuchs and Theo Harden (Heidelberg: Winter, 1988), 3–18. Murath starts from a constructivist notion of "representation": "Repräsentation: Nicht eine

Außenwelt kann abgebildet werden, sondern sie wird durch den Rückgriff auf eigene kulturelle Erfahrungen je neu konstruiert, was offensichtlich von einiger Bedeutung für die Verarbeitung von Fremderfahrung ist" (3). Consequently, "'liest' der Reisende fremde Landschaften und unbekannte Bräuche, indem er auf eigene Intertexte zurückgreift und diese neu kombinierend appliziert, denn die Bedeutung einer Kultur ist die Bedeutung, die wir ihr verleihen. ... Unser Denken und Handeln bezieht sich reflexiv auf sich selbst im Rahmen unseres textuellen Universums, nicht aber auf eine äußere Realität. Und hier liegen die Wurzeln dessen, was als Zentrismus unhintergehbar ist und sich in kultureller Asymmetrie, in der Hegemonie eines kulturellen Systems über ein anderes ausprägt" (5).

6. "Dank einer machtvollen kulturellen Phantasie, die in beinahe allen frühen Begegnungen eine Rolle spielte, entzündete sich diese Furcht vor allem an einem: am Kannibalismus." Stephen Greenblatt, *Wunderbare Besitztümer. Die Erfindung des Fremden: Reisende und Entdecker* (Berlin: Wagenbach, 1994), 169.

7. Alma Maximiliana Karlin, *Einsame Weltreise. Die Tragödie einer Frau* (Minden: Köhler, 1929). The citations are taken from the recent publication Alma M. Karlin, *Einsame Weltreise. Erlebnisse und Abenteuer einer Frau im Reich der Inkas und im Fernen Osten* (Freiburg i. Br.: Kore, 1995). For in-text citations, the abbreviation EW will be used.

8. Quoted in Habinger, 175. An extensive bibliography (about 50 pages) is part of a recent publication on the subject: Stefanie Ohnesorg, *Mit Kompass, Kutsche und Kamel: (Rück-) Einbindung der Frau in die Geschichte des Reisens und der Reiseliteratur* (St. Igbert: Röhrig, 1996). Ohnesorg concentrates on the history of (German) women travelers and thus does not deal with Alma M. Karlin.

9. Mary Louise Pratt, *Imperial Eyes. Travel Writing and Transculturation* (London: Routledge, 1992), 162.

10. See Ulla Siebert, "Frauenreiseforschung als Kulturkritik," in Jedamski, 148–73. Siebert analyzes the contemporary reception of and research on women's travel writings in regards to their tension between the projection of an emancipatory discourse into the past and the problems of reproducing and representing racism. The responsibility for a racist view is shifted in most cases from the author to the racist atmosphere, the colonial Zeitgeist of the described period (163–64). She pleads for a differentiated analysis.

11. Alma M. Karlin, "How I Got to Sail Around the World (A Passage from Alma M. Karlin's Legacy)," in *Alma* (program of the one-person play by Ursula Cetinski), ed. Sonja Dular (Ljubljana, 1995), 1. Cited as AP in the text. "Now, try to imagine a human being who fancies that she is going to live like those wise men in the Himalayan caves, and who suddenly finds herself amidst people to whom life begins and ends with lust, who see nothing in a woman but a means to satisfy their wildest desires, whose blood runs through their veins as a red-hot river and, what is more, who are mad about white women. ... Though indeed men often tried to grab me and drag me away for their own personal (ab)use, in the way one would pick up a sack, found in the street those who have thought to have 'found' me, met

with disaster even if it cost me some hair or skin" (AP, 1). See also EW, 105–7, 124–27, 137–38, 204–6.

[12.] Annegret Pelz, *Reisen durch die eigene Fremde. Reiseliteratur von Frauen als autogeographische Schriften* (Vienna: Böhlau, 1993), 19.

[13.] Alma M. Karlin, *Im Banne der Südsee. Die Tragödie einer Frau* (Minden in Westfalen: Köhler, 1930), 77. For in-text citations, the abbreviation BS will be used.

[14.] Ursula Cetinski, Sonja Dular, Zenski Kolumb, "Alma Karlin, pisateljica, carovnica in popotnica," *Mladina*, Aug. 15, 1995, 43.

[15.] Janez Stanonik maintains, "Since her childhood, however, she could speak also Slovene and she had also some knowledge of Slovene literature." Janez Stanonik, "Alma Maximiliana Karlin," in *Australian Papers. Yugoslavia, Europe and Australia*, ed. Mirko Jurak (Ljubljana: Filozofska fakulteta, 1983), 41. On the other hand, various Slovenian Karlin scholars have questioned this optimistic view.

[16.] There are very few hints at her nationality or ethnicity: She seemed to consider herself as a relic of the German-speaking part of the former Habsburg Empire, and her Yugoslav citizenship to her meant merely an irritating political fact. She rarely refers to her origins. If so, she mentions the town Celje rather than Slovenia; the latter does not come up in her travel books. Once she mentions Slav peasants in a somewhat derogatory sense. However, she does not seem to have had any desire of being considered German, a *Reichsdeutsche* (BS, 300).

[17.] Stanonik, 41.

[18.] In the United States, Karlin visited only Los Angeles and San Francisco; she liked the latter but is very critical of Northern Americans, claiming that everything is pose for them (EW, 211–12).

[19.] There are sporadic hints, though, e.g., EW, 99, 365; BS, 348. This is occasionally the case in the somewhat longer paperback edition of her second travel book (it contains the report about her stay in Australia and New Zealand). Here, she mentions her theosophic friends and acquaintances, among others. Alma M. Karlin, *Im Banne der Südsee. Als Frau allein unter Pflanzern und Menschenfressern, Sträflingen, Matrosen und Missionaren* (Minden in Westfalen: Köhler, 1933).

[20.] Sonja Dular, "We Each Have Our Individual Destiny," in *Alma* (program of the one-person play, by Ursula Cetinski), ed. Sonja Dular (Ljubljana, 1995), 4.

[21.] Ibid.

[22.] Vlado Šlibar and Zmago Smitek, *Celjski muzej V — Zbirka Alme Karlinove*, no. 113 of the collection *Kulturni in naravni spomeniki Slovenije* (Maribor: Obzorja, 1982). This booklet presents and describes part of the formerly private Karlin collection of the Museum of Celje, most of which was donated by Thea Gamelin Schreiber after Karlin's death. The ethnologists Šlibar and Smitek assume that there are many other items scattered in Celje and surroundings, owned by former friends and their heirs; many have probably been already destroyed. The items sent to addressees in Germany and Austria (i.e., Karlin's agent etc.) have not yet surfaced and may be lost forever.

[23.] Stanonik, 47.

[24.] Greenblatt, 10–12.

[25.] Pelz, *"… Von einer Fremde in die andere?"* 146.

[26.] Buck, Grubitzsch, Pelz, and Reinecke, 35.

[27.] As pointed out before, Karlin seems not to be aware of the ambiguity connected with her often "male" choice of metaphors; Weigel points to the parallel between the conquest of the female body and the foreign country, which is often represented by a female figure. See Sigrid Weigel, "Die nahe Fremde — das Territorium des 'Weiblichen'. Zum Verhältnis von 'Wilden' und 'Frauen' im Diskurs der Aufklärung," in *Die andere Welt: Studien zum Exotismus,* by Thomas Koebner and Gerhart Pickerodt (Frankfurt am Main: Athenäum, 1987), 171–99, esp. 181.

ALAN LEVENSON

The Apostate as Philosemite:
Selig Paulus Cassel (1821–1892)
and Edith Stein (1891–1942)

GERMAN PHILOSEMITISM SOUNDS MORE LIKE an oxymoron than a subject for analysis. If philosemitism means a love of Jew qua Jew, without any hint of anti-Semitic prejudice, then oxymoron it is. But in a society whose general contours are hostile to Jews and Judaism *(Judentum)*, perhaps we should be more flexible in our understanding of what philosemitism might mean. Despite recent attempts to portray Germany as uniformly dominated by "revolutionary" anti-Semitism or "eliminationist" anti-Semitism,[1] there were groups that opposed anti-Semitism vociferously, championed the "Old Testament" as a foundation text of civilization, and expressed steadfast commitment to Enlightenment ideals of humanity and the rule of law. True, one can document deep ambivalence toward the Jews among political liberals, missionary Christians, and aristocratic supporters of Zionism. True, these groups defended Jews only in the context of defending Christianity, socialist doctrine, or the rule of law *(Rechtsstaat)*. True also, these groups would have preferred to ignore the Jewish question altogether. But the key role assigned Jewry in the rhetoric of reaction made this impossible, and a substantial body of defense material resulted.[2]

Dismissing the discourse about Jews produced by these groups has become a convenient way of making a case for a German national character and then using that "character" tautologically to explain German behavior from Luther to the Holocaust. How does one construct *Judentum*, or aspects of *Judentum*, ambivalently, or even positively, when the prevailing tendency is hostile? How far can this construction develop in a positive direction? What axioms of German society checked the development of philosemitic rhetoric? The following test case represents a small piece of this puzzle.

The apostate as defender of Jewish people seems as incongruous a construct as "German philosemitism." In Jacob Katz's classic portrayal of the late Middle Ages, European Jewry and Christianity were drawn up in opposing religious camps: Whatever the objective factors leading a medieval

Jew to the baptismal font, conversion was generally experienced in religious terms.[3] The apostate was anything but indifferent to his former faith and often played an important role in the forced disputations of the medieval world.[4] In modern times, another typology emerges; namely, the many Jews who opted out of Jewish identity for pragmatic or opportunistic reasons, and who far outnumbered the sincere converts.[5] The range of attitudes on both sides — toward those who apostatized and toward those who remained Jews — varied according to national and individual circumstances. Understandably, pragmatic converts in Germany tended not to call attention to their Jewish roots, nor expend much energy bringing other Jews over to their way of thinking. Yet, even in modernity "sincere" conversion persists. Contemporary examples such as the "Jews for Jesus" movement and the case of Oswald Rufeisen (a.k.a. Brother Daniel) illustrate the possibilities for dual loyalty that open up when ethnic descent and religious conviction are separated. "Jews for Jesus" and Brother Daniel represent two instances of retaining pride in Jewish descent while abandoning Jewish religion. In America and Israel, however, positive constructions of Jews and / or Judaism are either normative or easily achievable. In modern Germany, quite the opposite was true. The cases of Selig Cassel and Edith Stein, studies of the "apostate as philosemite," are fraught with the intensity and paradox so typical of the modern German-Jewish experience.

What led Selig Cassel to the baptismal font in 1855 remains unclear. Cassel makes only passing comments in his many writings.[6] Cassel's only preconversionary statement that sheds light on this decision, "The Prussian Citizen and Jewish Belief" (1850), analyzes the reversal in the Jewish progress toward emancipation between the edicts of 1812 and 1847. Taken together with the facts that Cassel served in the Royal Library in Erfurt and in the Prussian House of Deputies after becoming Paulus Stephanus, we encounter the sort of advancement suggesting pragmatic or opportunistic conversion.[7] With no other evidence, one would have assumed a minimum of religiosity led to his decision. And wrongly so. For in the summer of 1867, Cassel was persuaded by the Reverend W. Ayerst of the London Society for the Conversion of the Jews to take up the Ministry of Christ Church Königgrätzerstrasse in Berlin. On January 5, 1868, Cassel conducted his first service; for the next twenty-three years, Cassel preached, lectured, and wrote. He was a star at German missionary society meetings. He ran a flourishing church and Sunday school. At the Leipzig Messe, Cassel addressed an audience of one thousand. With evident pride, Cassel quoted the *Mainz Israelite:* "How strange that people passing for religious Jews should voluntarily come and listen to a sermon from a man who has turned his back upon the synagogue."[8] A sophisticated student of history who had studied with Leopold Ranke at Berlin, and a confident exponent of Judaica, Cassel's oratory was both impassioned and learned. In a letter published in Hermann Strack's missionary journal *Nathanael,* Cassel claimed to have converted 60 Jews to Evangelical Christianity between 1880 and 1885, a figure he placed at 100 in a letter to the home office in London in 1890.[9] These figures, dwarfed by the growth of Berlin's Jewish community, were impressive by the standards of the notoriously unsuccessful missionary movement.[10] Perhaps as many as 12,500 Jews converted to the dominant evangelical faith in Imperial Germany, but very few did so at the behest of missionaries.[11] Still, Cassel may have been Germany's most successful missionary.

Cassel's career came to an abrupt denouement in 1890 when the Berlin Police informed Christ Church that it must install an emergency exit. Cassel, as he was bound to do, informed the London office, which wired back a telegram instructing him to close the church at once. Despite his twenty-three years of service, Cassel had been terminated. The official reason given by the Society was, of course, financial. Yet, the mission was largely self-supporting, and missionary salaries were hardly munificent. In a bitter letter, Cassel took the closure as a sign of times: that the mission simply failed to interest Christians any longer. As England abandoned the conversion of the Jews as a national metaphor and the societies turned their attention to sub-Saharan Africa, many donors probably felt similarly to one of Cassel's allies in London, who told him: "The Jews have money enough to establish a mission for themselves."[12] Cassel never overestimated the commitment of others to the Jewish mission. As he wrote in a detailed report of missionary life: "That they [Christians] are Christian they find natural; that others can become Christians seems to them improbable."[13] Whether research into the London Society's records can disclose additional motives for his dismissal, Cassel was well aware that he had irritated German missionaries with his pro-Jewish attitudes.[14] Johann F. A. De Le Roi, the historian of nineteenth-century missionary efforts, derided Cassel's writings as "carried out absolutely on the Jews' behalf, dictated entirely by a party spirit."[15] Cassel never publicly charged that his vigorous polemics against anti-Semites contributed to his dismissal. But the possibility remains that Germany's most successful missionary lost his position for being a Semitic philosemite.[16]

Cassel earned his credentials as a defender of the Jews during the first great anti-Semitic debate of 1879–1880. Of the dozen or so pamphlets Cassel authored in opposition to anti-Semitism, the two most developed were responses to Heinrich von Treitschke and Richard Wagner. The latter's 1850 screed "Das Judenthum in der Musik," had been republished by the *Bayreuther Blaetter* during the anti-Semitic debate. Wagner wished "to destroy the old Jewish God who had slipped into a foreign Christian world" and remove the influence of that *Judenbuch,* the Old Testament, as a means of freeing the creative impulses of German Culture.[17] Wagner's Marcionist challenge to Jesus' Semitic ancestry and the severing of Old and New Testaments went to the heart of Cassel's faith and elicited a slew of arguments ad hominem and substantive. Accusing Wagner's "Das Judenthum in der Musik" as being inspired by jealousy toward Felix Mendelssohn, "because he came from Jewish stock and enjoyed many warm friendships in cultured Jewish circles as everywhere," Cassel exulted at how quickly the Jews had amalgamated the culture of the West and made significant contributions to the arts — especially to music.[18] Cassel rejected Wagner's Renan-inspired conjecture that Jesus the Galilean was a non-Jew. Not only did the evidence of the Gospels lead one to the opposite conclusion, but theologically, Jesus could not be the seed of David without this biological link. The revelation of Jesus, contained in the prophets, preceded the Christian Church. The *Judengott* of Wagner's essay was none other than the *Christengott* who came to fulfill, not destroy, the covenant begun with Abraham and legislated with Moses.[19]

Wagner claimed that contemporary German culture was not Christian, but a "barbaric-Judaic mix." Cassel objected on two grounds. First, the "civilization of the Nibelungen" was incompatible with Christianity, but the Old Testament was Christianity's necessary preparation. Second, Cassel also found contemporary Germany woefully un-Christian, but exactly where it betrayed the shared values of the two testaments. How could Wagner, ostensibly a Christian, deny in word and deed the promise of God to Abraham in Genesis 12 that "All the families of the earth / Shall bless themselves by you"? How could a Christian betray Abraham's practice of lobbying for those in need of spiritual rehabilitation, as he did for the inhabitants of Sodom and Gomorrah? Even if Wagner's view of German Jewry were just, berating them was no fit Christian response. Cassel's biblicist concept of Christianity is combined with his political conservatism in his departing shot at the Bayreuth bully: "Peace and quiet will be an ephemeral delusion without humanity and love toward one's enemy and toward the Jews."[20]

The willingness to praise the Jews' accomplishments and to criticize the un-Christian sentiments of their detractors is equally evident in Cassel's *Wider Heinrich von Treitschke und für die Juden* (1880, "Against Heinrich von Treitschke and for the Jews"). As the rhetorical norm of anti-anti-Semitic literature was to declare oneself neither an anti-Semite nor a philosemite, the second part of this title announced Cassel's aggressive approach. Rather than Treitschke's, the prominent Berlin historian's, slogan "Die Juden sind unser Unglück," Cassel contended that the Gospels' "Salvation comes from the Jews" (John 4:22) ought to be the guiding principle of the Prussian state's attitude toward the Jew.[21] As a politician in the thick of the 1848 debates, Cassel reminded Treitschke, who was fond of complaining about all that Germany had done for the Jews, that the logic of the liberal program, rather than Christian love, had led to Jewish emancipation.[22] Cassel had no sympathy for Treitschke's xenophobia, terming "pseudonational chauvinism the direst enemy of the Gospels."[23] To Treitschke's objection that the hard German head could not be easily Judaized, Cassel pointed to the French frivolity and English materialism that Germany had imbibed with little difficulty during the previous decade.

With this observation, Cassel believed that he had penetrated to the heart of the anti-Semitic movement: namely, scapegoating the Jews for the materialism that had overcome Germany since the mid-nineteenth century. What made this analysis unique, from a Christian perspective, was Cassel's interest in the deleterious effects of modernity on the Jews themselves. He wrote, "The Jews have lost their believing Semitic spirit among German heathenism."[24] The Jews, who, in prior ages, kept the Sabbath, the dietary laws, and studied the Talmud, had become legally free through the emancipation, but spiritually they had been cut adrift. Whereas anti-Semites considered emancipation a dangerous unleashing of the Jewish spirit in Germany, Cassel considered emancipation a dangerous unleashing of heathen materialism that claimed for its casualty all religious piety. Small wonder, in Cassel's opinion, that racialism, the real misfortune *(Unglück)* of the era, flourished and was entertained by the putative intellectual leaders of the nation. To be sure, Cassel did not let the Jews entirely off the hook. Since 1848, the Jews had deceived themselves in regarding civil equality as the Messiah, and they had erred in thinking that as these legal barriers fell, so too would prejudice against them. While many Christian voices regard anti-Semitism as primarily a Christian failing, Cassel's insistence that the Jews had been victimized by modernity in equal measure to Christians appears to be novel. Cassel's millenarian desire to convert Jews was driven by the fear of universal secularism, not by fears of Judaization.

Without dwelling on his Jewish roots, Cassel never tired of reminding Germans that at Christmas "we approach the crib of the Semitic child, whose Semitic parents shepherded him while the angels sung Semitic songs."[25] Unlike so many members of the Leipzig Circle — the conversionary movement centered around Franz Delitzsch — Cassel had no fears about the church becoming Judaized. Repeatedly, Cassel insisted that Christianity merely fulfilled Judaism, or more precisely, the potential inherent in the Semitic religion of the Old Testament. Cassel taught a variant of Christian supersessionism that did not turn on an assertion of Christianity's superior ethics, but only on its universal applicability. The opposition of the Jews to the truth of Jesus the Christ was the opposition of a national *Volk* to an all-encompassing humanity that knew neither heathen nor Jew.[26] The Jewish collective shared with Wagner and Treitschke the sin of chauvinism. Cassel explained the difference between Friday night *kiddush* and communion as expressing the difference between "the limited fleshly love of a people for one another and the love of God between all peoples, where not the flesh, but the spirit, not the children of a particular people, but rather [all] the children of God" participate.[27] To Cassel, the Jews' denial of Christ exhibited the same mistake as did their futile rebellions against Rome: Both emerged from the Jewish insistence on being different.

The Jews' lachrymose history testified to the penalties for their insistence on religious dissent. If their reintegration into Western civilization had enabled Jewry to produce a Giacomo Meyerbeer or a Mendelssohn, their denial of Christ had led to the overall passing of the scepter of spiritual accomplishment from the Jews to the Christianized Greco-Roman world. Cassel did not waste his time trying to prove that the rabbinic literature anticipated Jesus as the medieval scholastic Catholic tradition had, nor did he shed much ink defending the Talmud, as did Delitzsch and Strack.[28] The Jewish past offered the most glaring proof that they has cut themselves off from salvation. Cassel accepted the tenets of Christian political triumphalism. He catalogued every offense to Jesus and early Christianity and demonstrated that, tit for tat, Jews received punishment in return. One of these examples suggests the sort of Jewish self-conception that may have led Cassel to apostasy: "The Jews have abused Christ and his followers, and covered them with reproachful names — and their own honorable name Jude, which in the heroic time of the Maccabees deserved its glory, has become a name of reproach. *As a term of reproach one who bears this name is himself shamed*" (italics added).[29]

With Cassel, we are able to trace the theological residuum of a Jewish identity, although we are unable to specify the path that led him to baptism. Quite the opposite is the case with Edith Stein, the youngest of eleven children born to a Jewish merchant family in Breslau (now Wroclaw, Poland) in 1891, one year before Cassel's death. Both came to Christianity as mature adults: Cassel as a thirty-four-year-old, Stein as a promising philosopher in her late twenties. Both came to Christianity after years of study and speculation. Both came from Jewish families in Silesia — although Cassel's Grosglogau was a town, Stein's Breslau contained Germany's third largest Jewish population. Neither dwelt on the details of their conversionary experience, although with Stein, we know many of the relevant facts.[30] But the differences between the two cases are striking. Like most German-Jewish converts, Cassel joined the dominant Evangelical faith, while Stein became a Roman Catholic. Cassel's conversion, it seems, led to a severance of ties with his family. Stein continued to enjoy close if strained relations, especially with her mother. Whereas Cassel was a publicist, a battler for souls, and a scrappy polemicist in his missionary endeavors, Stein coaxed friends and relatives into the bosom of the church through letters and discussions.[31] Her interventions on behalf of Jewry, as we shall see, also tended to be behind the scenes, unlike Cassel's denunciation of Stoecker, Wagner, and Treitschke.

The greatest difference between these two philosemitic apostates, however, is certainly their respective posthumous reputations. Paulus Cassel has earned a few footnotes. Stein, on the contrary, made her mark in a variety of ways: as a noted expositor of Edmund Husserl's phenomenology, as a feminist, and, posthumously, as Saint Teresa Benedicta a Cruce. Indeed, Jewish-Catholic controversy over Stein's beatification has focused disproportionate scholarly attention on her death.[32] Rather than tread this well-worn path, and without any pretense of offering a comprehensive reading of her life and works,[33] I would like to focus on the context of Stein's childhood and her path to conversion. The youngest of eleven children, Edith grew up in the Imperial period in a distinctly Jewish family. The Steins sought relatives or acquaintances for marriage partners and shunned its one intermarried member — a severe sanction by the standards of the time. Although Auguste Stein's business brought her into contact with Gentiles, Jews predominated the Stein children's primary social circle. Stein's autobiographical *Aus dem Leben einer jüdischen Familie* (first published 1965, translated as *Life in a Jewish Family*, 1986) recalls Pesach and the Days of Awe (she was born on Yom Kippur) as the religious high points of the year. Nevertheless, Stein cannot be called an Orthodox Jew, as her biographers have insisted on doing, as this suggests a much higher level of observance and learning than her *Aus dem Leben einer jüdischen Familie* indicates.[34]

Siegfried Stein, Edith's father, died when she was only two, and Auguste Stein's energies were principally devoted to supporting the family's material needs. Auguste Stein's own formal Jewish education ended when she was a girl, and although her parents gave her lessons in German and French, neither she nor her children learned more than rudimentary Hebrew. Years later, Edith brought a Latin breviary to her mother's synagogue; one should not assume this choice was purely theological. A well-educated, turn-of-the-century German Jew would be very comfortable in Latin; Hebrew was a far rarer acquisition. Like many of her male contemporaries — she was five years younger than the renowned philosopher Franz Rosenzweig — Stein found Judaism very unsatisfactory by the time of her adolescence.[35] Auguste's simple piety has been offered as a reason that we should be surprised that Edith fell away from Judaism and announced her agnosticism while still a teenager. On the contrary, the lack of a sophisticated articulation to the question "Why be Jewish?" demanded by so many German Jewish youths in the postemancipation era, drove many to the baptismal font, albeit after a lengthy journey. Nothing in Edith's autobiography or letters indicates any involvement with Jewish learning.[36]

The one encounter relevant to evaluating Stein's relationship to the teachings of Judaism support this picture of a young woman well-acquainted with a Jewish lifestyle, but sharing the general fin-de-siècle disdain for Judaism as a religio-intellectual system. Having asked the journalist Eduard Metis, the only one of her relatives who would truly qualify as Orthodox,[37] whether he believed in a personal God, Stein recalls his answer and her response that God was spirit and nothing else could be said about it. "To me it was like receiving a stone instead of bread."[38] On another occasion, Edith and Eduard were walking together on a Friday afternoon. When Edith passed her house, she gave him her briefcase to hold while she went inside to fetch something. Realizing that the Sabbath had started, Edith apologized for making Eduard "carry," a violation of Sabbath law. Eduard dismissed her concern by noting that he had a foot in the entryway and replied that "carrying" was prohibited only outside. Stein remembers thinking that this was the sort of talmudic hair-splitting *(Spitzfindigkeit)* that repelled her, but she said nothing.[39] To belabor the point, her attitude represents a spiritual alienation from Judaism, not a sympathetic commitment to it.

Stein was hardly alone in being the child of German Jews whose loyalty to the ancestral faith obviated a concerted effort to pass it on to a younger, more secularized and better educated generation.[40] Under the spell of the Göttingen Circle, Stein was drawn to a reappraisal of religion in the midst of several who had recently found their faith. Husserl, the center of this circle, was born Jewish, converted to Protestantism, and later in life toyed with Catholicism. Anna Reinach, also a recent convert from Judaism to Protestantism, impressed Stein with her fortitude after the death of her husband Adolf Reinach (another philosopher-convert) at the front in 1917. Max Scheler, of partly Jewish descent, moved in and out of the church. Stein's pivotal moment came in the summer of 1921 while staying with Hedwig Conrad-Martius, yet another Göttingen philosopher. Looking for some bedtime reading, Stein picked up a book about the life of Saint Teresa of Avila, read it through until dawn, and declared herself ready to become a Christian.[41] Conrad-Martius indicates that Stein's conversionary moment — as was so often the case — was the product of a longer process that finally resolved itself.[42] In any event, like many others who took the plunge, and others (like Rosenzweig) who did not, Stein's conversion was long in preparation and took place in a social circle likely to be supportive of her choice.

From the day of her baptism, January 1, 1922, onward, Stein balanced her philosophical career, her increasingly intense religious life, and her family responsibilities. For Cassel, Christianity seems to have reconciled biblicism, millenarianism, and antisecularism. For Stein, Christianity represented ground zero from a faith perspective. Catholicism put her back in touch with all the components of her life — her connection to the Jewish people included. Nevertheless, despite her statement to her Jesuit confessor, Father Hirschmann, "You don't know what it means to me to be a daughter of the chosen people. To belong to Christ, not only spiritually but according to the flesh," I have been unable to isolate any distinctively Judaic components in Stein's theological and philosophical writings.[43] Stein's self-conception of belonging to Christ's fleshly lineage may have imparted a sense of Jewish belonging that transcended her close family connections, but I see no evidence that it prompted a working-through of religious tensions. Perhaps Stein felt the way another Jewish convert to Christianity put it when he recollected his Hanukkah conversion, "I believe that I was never a better Jew than today."[44]

Stein frequently alluded to her Jewish upbringing and Jewish family in letters to various church figures. As recounted in the English foreword to her *Aus dem Leben einer jüdischen Familie,* Stein had been previously approached by a priest to recount her life. While the churches prized these conversionary autobiographies, Stein's dwelt neither on Jewish blindness, nor her own spiritual transformation, the usual themes. Rather, she opposed the realities of Jewish existence against the realm of stereotype. Noting that there were many Germans who knew Jews personally and whose "sense of justice is outraged by the condemnation of this people to a pariah's existence," Stein decried the contemporary situation where a social wall was being built between Christian and Jewish existence and warned against the inevitable results: "[But] many others lack this kind of experience [of Jews]. The opportunity to attain it has been denied primarily to the young who, these days, are being reared in racial hatred from earliest childhood. To all who have been thus deprived, we who grew up in Judaism have an obligation to give our testimony."[45]

Stein, then, did not lack the courage to make a public profession of her Jewish descent. Her philosemitism, however, is best evidenced by the relationships she maintained with her mother and siblings, all but one of whom remained Jewish. Totally confident of the truth of her religious position, she was even less inclined than Cassel to be hostile toward her community of birth. Yet, Stein was not free from the convert's typical urge to convert others. Some of her closest friends reported that she had approached them to convert after she had become a nun. Kaufmann and Metis both severed their relationships with Stein for a number of years after her conversion. Stein also played a pivotal role in the conversion of her sister Rosa and a number of other Jewish-born "seekers." Despite her deep desire to see them brought into the church, Stein respected the loyalties of the rest of her family. Writing to the poet and novelist Gertrud von le Fort shortly after the Nazi seizure of power, Stein described her relationship with her mother's faith as follows:

I have never told my mother about you. It was not possible to give any of your writings to her because she declines anything that is beyond her Jewish faith. For that reason too, it was impossible at that time to say anything to her that might have somewhat explained the step I have taken. She particularly rejects conversions. Everyone ought to live and die in the faith in which they were born. She imagines atrocious things about Catholicism and life in a convent. At the moment it is difficult to know what is causing her more pain: whether it is the separation from her youngest child to whom she has ever been attached with a particular love, or her horror of the completely foreign and inaccessible world into which that child is disappearing, or the qualms of conscience that she herself is at fault because she was not strict enough in raising me as a Jew. The only point at which I believe you might make contact with her is the very strong and genuine love of God that my mother has, and her love for me that nothing can shake.[46]

The ascent of the Nazis opened a new chapter in the lives of all German Jews. In 1933, to the distress of her family, Stein entered the Carmelite Order. She also appealed to Pope Pius XI to issue an encyclical on the Jews' behalf. She was refused a direct audience, although, according to secondary accounts, she received a benediction for herself and her family.[47] For the next nine years, Stein kept up her academic work and her familial correspondence. With her sister Rosa, a fellow convert to Catholicism, Stein was deported from the Dutch Carmelite convent of Echt in the summer of 1942 and murdered on the morning of August 9. Her last words upon being deported from the convent were reportedly, "Come Rosa, let us go for our people."[48] In her own mind, Stein died a willing martyr for the Jewish people.

These case studies, on the surface, may seem very peripheral to the modern German-Jewish experience. Most German Jews remained loyal to their community; those who did not were motivated by the pragmatic benefits of joining the majority faith. I will conclude, therefore, with two observations aimed at dismissing these cases as marginal and unimportant. First, the modern separation of Jewishness into ethnic and religious components has widened the pathways in which the modern Jew can walk and still feel part of the Jewish experience. In Zionism and Reconstructionism, this is evident in a very positive sense. But the same bifurcation can work the other way too, enabling a sincere claim of Jewish identity while the betrayal of a key component of the Judaic legacy takes place. The apostate as philosemite is thus a case study in Jewish identity in the modern world. Cassel and Stein offer testimony to the divisibility, permeability, but also the tenacity, of Jewish identity in the most unlikely circumstances. Second, Germany was generally hostile toward *Judentum*, but not uniformly hostile. The existence of the missionary, evangelical Leipzig Circle and the religious-philosophical Göttingen school remained a magnet for Jewish "seekers," of whom Cassel and Stein were but two of several. Missionary Protestantism and Roman Catholicism alike rejected a racialist neopaganism that was growing in Cassel's day and came to fruition in Stein's lifetime. That neopaganism and racialist-Christianity proved to be a far greater danger than Judaism was a realization that came too late for the churches and too late for European Jewry. The anti-Judaic traditions of the churches militated against accommodating, either ideologically or personally, the philosemitism represented by the likes of Selig Cassel and Edith Stein, two devout Christians and proud Jews.[49]

Notes

I would like to thank Dr. Oliva M. Espin (San Diego State University) for providing me with a helpful bibliography of works by and about Stein.

[1.] Although Paul Lawrence Rose's *German Question / Jewish Question* (Princeton, NJ: Princeton UP, 1990) and Daniel Jonah Goldhagen's *Hitler's Willing Executioners* (New York: Vintage, 1996) make important contributions, they suffer from the same tendency: whatever its apparent complexities, German culture was about one thing only, hating Jews.

[2.] Frank Stern's *The Whitewashing of the Yellow Badge* (Oxford, NY: Pergamon, 1992) correctly treats the situation after the Second World War as entirely different.

[3.] "As medieval civilization was expressed almost entirely in religious terms, it is very likely that a Jew who was captivated by the values of Christian society experienced this process in the form of religious conversion." Jacob Katz, "Apostates and Proselytes," *Exclusiveness and Tolerance* (New York: Behrman House, 1961), 76.

[4.] Apostate translates into Hebrew as *meshumad* or *mumar*. As all conversions are fragile, the sincere convert typically attempts various means of verifying / solidifying the authenticity of his or her conversionary experience by trying to convert others.

[5.] I am skeptical about Endelman's useful, but overly neat division between "sincere" and "opportunistic" converts, as I have explained in "The Conversionary Impulse in Fin-de-Siècle Germany," *Leo Baeck Institute Yearbook* 50 (1995): 107–22.

[6.] Perhaps the papers of Selig's elder brother, David Cassel, a prolific historian and contributor to the *Wissenschaft des Judentums,* will yield some light on this matter. I have been unable to examine them.

[7.] Hermann Strack, a fellow missionary, confessed that it was unclear what induced Cassel to join the church. Strack contends, reasonably, that the reasons were obviously not mercenary.

[8.] Quoted in Cassel, "Wie ich über Judenmission denke," *Nathanael* 13, no. 5 (1897): 132–33.

[9.] Cassel's final "head count" of converts was placed at 262 by Reverend W. T. Gidney, *The History of the London Society for Promoting Christianity amongst the Jews, from 1809–1908* (London: Society for Promoting Christianity amongst the Jews, 1908).

[10.] Endelman, Clark, etc. (Often the converted were poor eastern European Jews looking for preferment, employment, or a one-time cash payment.)

[11.] Cassel, "Wie ich über Judenmission denke," tells us that he was brought to Christianity not by missionary activity, but by his own reading of history — Jewish history in particular.

[12.] Paulus Cassel, *The Martyrdom of Christ Church in Berlin by the London Society* (Berlin: Buchhandlung des Lesecabinets, 1891).

[13.] Cassel, "Wie ich über Judenmission denke," 131–32.

[14.] Paulus Cassel, *Die Antisemiten und die evangelische Kirche* (Berlin: J. A. Wohlgemut, 1881).

[15.] Johann F. A. De Le Roi, *Geschichte der Evangelischen Judenmission*, 2d ed. (Leipzig: Hinrich'sche Buchhandlung, 1899).

[16.] Cassel did complain about a trip to England: "I was hospitably received everywhere — but not by any members of the committee, not one of whom had the time to invite me to his house." Cassel, *The Martyrdom of Christ Church*, 14. Gidney, *The History of the London Society,* makes no mention of this event.

[17.] For differing views of Richard Wagner's developing anti-Semitism and for their disagreement about whether Wagner was initially philosemitic, see Jacob Katz, *The Darker Side of Genius* (Hanover, NH: UP of New England, 1986) and Paul Rose, *German Question / Jewish Question* (Princeton, NJ: Princeton UP, 1990).

[18.] Paulus Cassel, *Der Judengott und Richard Wagner* (Berlin: Wohlgemut, 1881), 32–34.

[19.] "Es ist kein anderer Gott, kein anderes Gesetz. Jesus ist nicht gekommen aufzuheben, sondern zu erfüllen." Cassel, *Der Judengott und Richard Wagner*, 42.

[20.] Cassel, *Der Judengott und Richard Wagner*, 44. Cassel's political quietism, his aggressive attack on anti-Semites, and his extreme biblicism no doubt were no doubt contributing reasons for the fact that many educated, well-off Jews were willing to attend the lectures of this apostate.

[21.] Christopher Clark, *The Politics of Conversion* (Oxford: Clarendon, 1995) shows that the Prussian government oscillated between expressing a considerable interest in converting Jews and practicing the tolerance of *Realpolitik*.

[22.] Paulus Cassel, *Wider Heinrich von Treitschke und für die Juden* (Berlin: Stahn, 1880), 8–9.

[23.] This quote comes from an article written against the Prussian Court Preacher Adolf Stoecker but is consistent as well with Cassel's attack on Treitschke.

[24.] Cassel, *Wider Heinrich von Treitschke und für die Juden*, 22–23. Cassel seems unaware, or unconcerned, that this could easily become an argument for Jewish Orthodoxy, which was beginning to regard the emancipation with ambivalence on exactly this point.

[25.] Ibid., 27–28.

[26.] Cassel's position is fairly close to that of the Tübingen school's F. C. Baur, who proclaimed that "Christianity developed within Jewish soil, grew out of Judaism, and wants nothing more than to be a spiritualized Judaism." Cited in Susannah Heschel, *Abraham Geiger* (Chicago: Univ. of Chicago, forthcoming), MS, 222. Cassel must have been disturbed by the ascent of Ritschlian influence with its "radical exclusion" (Heschel) of the Jewish background on Jesus' life and teachings.

[27.] Cassel, *Christus und das Judenthum*, 14.

[28.] Cassel's critique of Catholicism centered on its tendency to incorporate the Old Testament into practice (i.e., Judaizing). Cassel considered even Catholics too quick to equate Judaism with the Old Testament and inadequately aware of the Old Testament as a prophecy wholly fulfilled by the advent of Jesus. Paulus Cassel , *Israel in der Weltgeschichte* (Berlin: Beck, 1886), 8 pointed to the New Testament. In other words, its purpose was fulfilled and no Old Testament / New Testament integration was required.

[29.] Cassel, *Israel in der Weltgeschichte*, 8.

[30.] Michael Ragussis, *Figures of Conversion. "The Jewish Question" and English National Identity* (Durham, NC: Duke UP, 1995). Chapter 1 discusses the role that reading (although usually secret reading) played in the conversionary autobiographies. Here, we have an example from the German context.

[31.] Stein's rather closed nature is probably the salient reason for this difference, but it does raise the question of what role gender plays in the postconversionary careers of baptized Jews.

[32.] See Harry J. Cargas, *The Unnecessary Problem of Edith Stein* (Washington, DC: United States Holocaust Memorial Council, 1994).

[33.] Rachel Feldhay-Brenner, "Ethical Convergence in Religious Conversion," in *The Unnecessary Problem of Edith Stein* , by Cargas, 77–102; "Edith Stein, the Jew and the Christian: An Impossible Synthesis" in *What Have We Learned?* ed. Frank Littell and Alan Berger (Lewiston, Maine: Edwin Mellen, 1995) deserve mention as capable syntheses.

[34.] Edith Stein, *Aus dem Leben einer jüdischen Familie* (Louvain: E. Nauwelaerts-Verlag Herder, 1965).

[35.] As Rosenzweig wrote his mother on the occasion of his cousin's baptism: "In Germany today the Jewish religion cannot be 'accepted,' it has to be grafted on by circumcision, dietary observance, Bar Mitzvah. Christianity has a tremendous advantage over Judaism: it would have been entirely out of the question for Hans to become a Jew. ... A Christian, however, he can become." Quoted in Nahum Glatzer, *Franz Rosenzweig: His Life and Thought* (New York: Schocken, 1961), 19. Note that two-thirds of the items mentioned by Rosenzweig apply only to males. The Jewish home and family, important vehicles for transmitting Judaism, proved inadequate again and again in the case of intellectuals, male or female.

[36.] When Feldhay-Brenner writes that Stein "continued to fulfill" (78) the Mishnaic tenet "All Israel are responsible to one another," she implies this dictum would be recognizable to Stein. I see no evidence to support that; indeed, I doubt that Stein would even know the difference between Mishnah and Talmud.

[37.] Stein, by the way, was more careful than her biographers in distinguishing "traditional" from "Orthodox." She describes Metis as a "strenggläubiger and gesetzestreuer Jude" (*Aus dem Leben einer jüdischen Familie,* 142).

[38.] Stein, *Aus dem Leben einer jüdischen Familie,* 142.

[39.] Ibid.

[40.] Levenson, "The Conversionary Impulse." The locus classicus is Franz Kafka's *Brief an den Vater* (Frankfurt am Main: Fischer, 1995). Kafka wrote the letter to his father in 1919 but never sent it. The work was first published in 1953 by Max Brod.

[41.] Although Teresa of Avila had some Marrano roots, this common ancestry does not seem to have elicited any comment from Edith, an interesting contrast to Cassel's insistence on the Jewish roots of the first Christians.

[42.] Most writing about Stein tends toward the hagiographic and decontextualizes the conversionary moment. See, for instance, Freda Mary Oben, "Edith Stein the Woman," in *Carmelite Studies,* ed. John Sullivan (Washington, DC: ICS, 1987), 3–33. Oben, not surprisingly, is herself a Jewish-born Catholic.

[43.] Cited in Waltraud Herbstrith, *Edith Stein,* 5th ed. (San Francisco: Harper and Row, 1985), 63. As the Nazi assault mounted, Stein spoke often of her willingness to "bear the Cross" for the Jewish people. While this represents a desire for solidarity, the notion of expiatory human suffering is foreign to Judaism. The willingness to die for God's glory (in this case, Christ's glory) is akin to the idea of *kiddush ha-shem,* but differs in a critical way: *Kiddush ha-shem* is not something to be sought after, desired, or anticipated; it is only an appropriate response when faced with the choice of death or desecration of God's name through murder, incest, or idolatry.

[44.] Karl Jacob Hirsch, *Quintessenz meines Lebens* (Mainz: Haase & Koehler, 1990), 238–42.

[45.] Edith Stein, *Life of a Jewish Family,* ed. Josephine Koeppel (Washington, DC: ICS, 1986), 24.

[46.] Edith Stein to Gertrud von le Fort, Cologne, Oct. 17, 1933, in Josephine Koeppel, ed., *Edith Stein. Self Portrait in Letters, 1916–1942* (Washington, DC: ICS, 1993), 159–60. Stein, *Aus dem Leben einer jüdischen Familie,* foreword.

[47.] I have been unable to locate a copy of Stein's letter, or even a reasonable description of its contents. Setting described in Herbstrith, 64–65. As is well known, when the encyclical "Mit Brennender Sorge" was issued in 1937, the word "Jew" did not appear.

[48.] Quoted in Herbstrith, 103. Stein's self-perception as a "Jewish" martyr, obviously, is problematic from a Jewish perspective. That it represents Stein's self-perception is beyond doubt.

[49.] Cassel and Stein represent a nagging challenge to Judaism and a marker of failed opportunity to Christianity.

DAGMAR C. G. LORENZ

History, Identity, and the Body in Edgar Hilsenrath's
The Story of the Last Thought

A S THE SECOND MILLENNIUM DRAWS to a close and progress has failed to effect an improved quality of life for the majority of the world's population, human and nonhuman alike, Western cultural practices are coming under increasing scrutiny. The production of weapons and hazardous materials threaten global survival and genocide figures prominently on the balance sheet of history. Greater suffering than ever is caused by the extermination of nations, ethnic groups, and species for the benefit of a few privileged nations. The patterns of exclusion and destruction driving these processes are of particular interest to authors who experienced them firsthand, notably Holocaust survivors. One of the most uncompromising voices is that of Edgar Hilsenrath, whose novels explore the human proclivity to kill and to destroy, both inseparably entwined with European thought and reality.[1]

Hilsenrath's literary language and his conceptual framework constitute an attack on the concept of humanity and the boundaries between human and animal, showing their function to be the construction of difference. Hilsenrath's outlook is as radical as that of the Australian philosopher and animal rights advocate Peter Singer, who criticizes conventional language usage because it reproduces "the prejudices of its users." He notes that the term "'animal' lumps together beings as different as oysters and chimpanzees, while placing a gulf between chimpanzees and humans."[2]

By positioning his protagonists as other, as Jew, woman, or animal, Hilsenrath questions the Western hierarchy and assigns agency to those who have no voice. European thought has been criticized from anticolonial, feminist, and civil rights perspectives by the gay, lesbian, and animal rights movements, and by environmentalists. All of these movements call attention to the hegemony of white men. They denounce a value system that assigns the heterosexual Christian human male the most privileged position in the universe. Feminists have pointed to the oppression of women and nonwhite humans, animals, and nature, and have tried to identify the source of oppression as being one and the same in all cases.[3] Marjorie Spiegel, in *The Dreaded Comparison* (1988), reveals the correlation between the subjugation of animals and blacks, both rationalized by supposed evolutionary superiority.[4] According to her, for animals and disenfranchised humans, the same strategies of subjugation are used; they are dominated, shackled, punished, and destroyed.

Lawrence and Susan Finsen consider the polarization of spirit and body in Christian thought part of the problem. "The material world, including the earth, is thus devalued," they write. "In some strains of Judeo-Christian thought women are argued to be inferior on precisely the same grounds: they are closer to nature, less spiritual, less rational, and — like nature and animals — to be dominated by males."[5] According to the Finsens, early modern science supported an ideology of domination that victimized women and members of out-groups. Indeed, until the eighteenth century, gypsies could legally be hunted for sport. Otto Weininger's treatise *Geschlecht und Charakter* (1903, translated as *Sex and Character*, 1906), which inadvertently exposes entrenched strategies of codifying otherness in modern times, makes the interlinkage between misogyny and anti-Semitism transparent. Positioning himself as a white Christian male, the Jewish-born Weininger assigns Jews and women parallel positions of inferiority.[6] Some of the most striking culture critical texts in post-Shoah Germany and Austria have been written by Jewish authors, one of them Edgar Hilsenrath. In several works, he has examined prejudice and genocide from his dual perspective as German and Jew, thereby exposing patterns of domination. Certain aspects of his works call to mind the viewpoints of ecofeminists.

Few novels have been researched as meticulously as Hilsenrath's fantastic-historical novel *The Story of the Last Thought* (1990).[7] Yet, the overall impression of the work is surreal. Similar to other controversial works on the Holocaust, the novel conveys fact and fiction in the language and imagery of cruelty. One is reminded of Jerzy Kosinski's *The Painted Bird* (1976), Jakov Lind's *Eine Seele aus Holz* (1962, translated as *Soul of Wood*, 1966), and Peter Weiss's *Die Ermittlung* (1965, translated as *The Investigation*, 1966), texts which challenge traditional discourse, literary, historical, bureaucratic. They attempt to grasp absurdity as part of a post-Shoah consciousness.[8] Hilsenrath foregrounds the psychosexual aspects of genocide and warfare. He exposes greed and sadism in images of physical, often sexual, abuse. In a provocative language, he illustrates desires and activities commonly considered "inhumane." He associates them as belonging to the makeup of the human male. Hilsenrath's view of the human animal is diametrically opposed to that of the Enlightenment, which championed notions of man's goodness and perfectibility.[9]

Already in his first novel, *Nacht* (1964, translated as *Night*, 1966), set in a Romanian ghetto where Jewish civilians are starved to death, Hilsenrath foregrounds his character's physicalness.[10] Their sense of identity is directly linked to their survival instinct, which dictates how they respond to the plight. This body-centered concept of man is reminiscent of Nietzsche, who wrote: "The body is a great mind. ... Even your own small mind, my brother, which you call 'spirit' is merely your body's tool, a small tool and a toy of your great mind."[11] In Hilsenrath's work, the body is the true touchstone of humanity.

Singer likens the cruelty of the "Nazi concentration camp 'doctors'" toward those "they considered 'subhuman'" to that of the scientists performing experiments "on nonhumans in laboratories in America, Britain, and elsewhere."[12] He suggests that the opportunistic construction and manipulation of the category animal is something the Nazis and present-day scientists have in common. Singer dismisses any claims that the beings abused and tormented are non- or less-than-human, and he rejects any possible justification for inflicting gratuitous suffering and death upon them.

Hilsenrath, like Singer, gives priority to the body. He characterizes man's ability to speak and reason as secondary qualities. Thus, identity and character appear as random attributes. Anyone, regardless of racial or ethnic background, can access and cultivate them. This is the case in *Der Nazi und der Friseur* (1977, "The Nazi and the Barber"), Hilsenrath's satire about a German mass-murderer who takes on a Jewish identity. The protagonist of *The Story of the Last Thought* is another case in point. The story of the dying Thovma Khatisian cannot be verified, no matter how detailed his account — Khatisian's story may or may not be his own even though it pertains to contain information about his childhood and his ancestors and purports to trace the lineage of the Armenian people back to prehistoric times. There is no way to prove a biographical link between Hilsenrath's protagonist and Armenia beyond the fact that he identifies with the victimized nation.

It is left open whether Khatisian considers himself Armenian as a result of immersing himself into Armenian history.[13] "For 60 years I asked survivors to tell me stories from Hayastan, also called Turkish-Armenia or Anatolia — whichever you prefer — and from the many stories I patched together my own. And thus one day I had a genuine family history. ... I also had a name and a tradition, which I could procreate in my children and grandchildren" (21). Establishing identity was a matter of concern for Hilsenrath, who was born in Germany, spent his formative years in Romania, and lived in New York for almost twenty years. As a naturalized U. S. citizen, with his mother living in Israel, he could resume his German identity or assume an American or an Israeli one. He opted for the first.[14] The situation of his protagonist is similarly complex: It is possible that Thovma, a Swiss citizen, was born to

Armenian parents and raised by a Turkish couple. More important, he is deeply affected by the Armenian fate at the hands of the Turks during the First World War as well as by the Shoah. An academic can easily dismiss Khatisian's account as fantasy. Yet, it does reveal a truth that eludes the sanitized discourses of politicians and historians. The latter offer socially acceptable terms for war, mass-murder, and genocide, but they lack the words to describe the body, sexual organs and practices, female anatomy, and the processes of pregnancy, birth, and nursing. To write about them, Hilsenrath employs street slang and the language of legends and fairy tales.

Khatisian's view of himself with regard to his body, his language, his family, and his sense of belonging is a central issue as he embarks on an inner journey to his emotional homeland, Hayastan, the site of the extinguished Turkish Armenian culture, today's Eastern Anatolia. With nostalgic overtones, albeit not uncritically, Hayastan of the Ottoman era is portrayed as agrarian and patriarchal, replete with eccentric characters.[15] Obvious parallels between Armenian history and Ashkenazic Jewish history are revealed: Both nations suffered recurring aggression while interacting closely with neighboring cultures. The contacts between Armenians, Turks, Curds, and Arabs are manifest in the appended glossary (467–71). Like the Jews, the Armenians had networks extending across Europe to the Middle East and overseas.

The *Meddah* portrays the Armenians on the eve of the genocide, the "Great Tebk," as being almost completely assimilated into Turkish culture: The descriptions preclude clearly definable ethnic identities. In view of the imminent absorption of the Armenians into Turkish society, the massacres are tragically ironic.[16] However, the phenomenon of ethnocentric propaganda undermining integration is not unique. The attempt to exterminate the Cherokee nation, which was almost assimilated, the Holocaust, perpetrated at a time German Jewry had become indistinguishable from Gentile society, are other examples. Bypassing ongoing debates,[17] Hilsenrath explores mass-murder empirically. On the basis of his personal experience as a survivor, he examines two of this millennium's most recent and most violent episodes of mass-destruction. Foregrounding the body as the target of aggression allows Hilsenrath to identify patterns common to the atrocities of all ages, the crusades, the witch-hunts, pogroms, wars, colonization, and the enslavement and extermination of entire indigenous populations by Europeans, including the crimes against humanity committed during the world wars, the massacres of the Armenian people, and the Shoah. Hilsenrath's analysis intersects with ecofeminism, whose basic assumptions Lawrence and Susan Finsen characterize as follows: "In light of feminist — particularly ecofeminist — analysis the oppression of speciesism, racism, sexism, and environmental destruction are all aspects of a single worldview and methodology: each is part of a structure that cannot be dismantled without eliminating all of its manifestations."[18]

Hilsenrath dismisses ideological explanations for mass-murder as irrelevant. He deemphasizes political and religious issues, although they are mentioned, as they obscure the concrete acts and effects of physical violence.[19] *The Story of the Last Thought* highlights persecution, exile, and the loss of cultural identity in a relatively simple environment, the pretechnological setting of turn-of-the-century Turkey. The motives and individual acts of the perpetrators are, nonetheless, similar, and Hilsenrath draws parallels between National Socialism and Turkish nationalism. "They [the historians] will call the great massacre 'mass-murder,' and the scholars among them will say it's called 'genocide.' Not one smart alec among them will say it's called 'armenocide,' and in the end some crank will look up his dictionary and finally announce that it's called 'holocaust'!" (156)

By foregrounding birth, daily life, sexuality, aggression, and death, Hilsenrath suggests that once a population becomes the object of persecution, the only remaining point of reference is the body. The nakedness of the victims is juxtaposed to the costumes of the engineers of genocide; they are pampered and concealed from the public eye, as if they were exempt from the laws of nature. Despite the narrator's seeming refusal to compare the victim and the victimizer, he does acknowledge their essential sameness. "Your father has sensitive hands, but they are quite different from Enver Pasha's hands. ... But ought I to compare your father's hands with a hangman's? No, my little lamb, I won't do that" (*Story*, 67).

Perhaps the most uncomfortable aspect of *The Story of the Last Thought* is the invalidation of the established versions of the Turkish genocide and the German Holocaust. In Hilsenrath it is a matter of coincidence whether a person ends up a victim or perpetrator, not of conscious choice. None of the established social and political theories, conservative, liberal, or Marxist, offers a solution to the issue of genocide, because gratuitous violence, including genocidal acts, present a source of pleasure for the human animal, regardless of social status. Hilsenrath's supposition that male desire, cruelty, and aesthetics derive from the same source represents a challenge to the coming millennium.

Without dismissing spiritual and intellectual perspectives wholesale, Hilsenrath validates only those that arise from physical experience and sustain physical survival. Through his references to pre-Christian Armenian culture and the fertility goddess Anahit, he urges the abolishment of patriarchal values and male domination. Although the Armenian patriarchal culture at the turn of the century is configured as a counterpoint to Kemal Pasha's Young Turkish Regime and hence less destructive, it is flawed, as the forced disfig urement of a young woman to make her conform to male expectations and other incidents reveal.

In spite of the nostalgic overtones, Hilsenrath makes no attempt to condone this or any other transgression against the human body and consistently undermines the rhetoric of patriarchy, patriotism, and nationalism. His text admits no justification for the abuse of an individual for the sake of an ideology or in the name of cultural values. Similar to ecofeminism, Hilsenrath rejects notions of mutual exclusivity that reinforce hierarchy and demand that "we decide 'who will count more.'"[20] One of his examples is the failure of the protagonist's father's arranged marriage and the success of his unconventional later marriage to a social outsider, a disfigured woman.

Hilsenrath's novel constitutes an attempt to break through the barriers of misleading rhetoric and denial by uncovering the missing link between the body, memory, and history. Thovma Khatisian's statement "How will genocide be prevented in the future if everyone declares they knew nothing about it, and they did nothing to prevent it because they couldn't even imagine such a thing" (14) implies that merely more knowledge of past events is not enough. "Breaking the silence" (14) requires revealing every detail of the individual lives and deaths through acts of empathy and creative imaging similar to the processes elicited by the graphic descriptions of cruelty in the publications of animal rights activists.[21] Hilsenrath's narrative universe is divided into a sphere of violence and one of physical intimacy. The latter, the sphere of the oppressed, is associated with women and male members of oppressed groups excluded from power. In none of these spheres is there complete freedom from cruelty, but only in the latter does the possibility for intimacy and spontaneity exist at all.

The Story of the Last Thought links the issue of genocide to man's attitude toward his material existence and the body. The Nazi death factories being addressed only marginally, the novel highlights man's psychosexual obsessions, already present in a simpler era, which in conjunction with ideologically induced fanaticism lead to the kind of orgiastic wholesale slaughter that Klaus Theweleit terms "white terror" in his study on male fantasies.[22] In an era concerned with identity and ethnic, cultural, and gender diversity, Hilsenrath's work stands out because of its insistence on the universality of the human experience.

The Story of the Last Thought makes a case for a materialistic approach to reality as the only way to neutralize doctrines that create false group identities and foster wars, ethnic strife, and mass destruction, while systematically and willfully disregarding man's animal nature. As a result of its particular focus, Hilsenrath's work, inspired by the German-Jewish experience and rooted in the Holocaust experience, intersects with other critical perspective such as that of Peter Singer, Lawrence and Susan Finsen, and others. It is part of an expanding discourse that calls for the fundamental reexamination of the theories and assumptions that shape the human condition at the turn of the millennium.

Notes

[1.] Max Horkheimer and Theodor W. Adorno, *Dialektik der Aufklärung. Philosophische Fragmente* (Frankfurt am Main: Fischer, 1969).

[2.] Peter Singer, *Animal Liberation* (1975; reprint, New York: New York Review, Random House, 1990), vi.

[3.] Lawrence Finsen and Susan Finsen, *The Animal Rights Movement in America: From Compassion to Respect* (New York: Twayne, 1994), 246.

[4.] Marjorie Spiegel, *The Dreaded Comparison: Human and Animal Slavery* (New York: Mirror Books, 1988), 66, 72.

[5.] Finsen and Finsen, 249–50.

[6.] See Otto Weininger, *Geschlecht und Charakter* (Vienna: Braunmüller, 1903; reprint, Munich: Matthes & Seitz, 1980).

[7.] Edgar Hilsenrath, *The Story of the Last Thought* (London: Macdonald, 1991); originally published as *Das Märchen vom letzten Gedanken* (Munich: Piper, 1989).

[8.] Sem Dresden comments on Hilsenrath's earlier novel *Der Nazi und der Friseur* (1977) and similar works: "It is not a question of ambiguity but of polyinterpretability, having the disappearance of the historical reality as an inevitable consequence. Another, no less true reality, of a different order takes its place. This reality cannot be called documentary in the usual sense, yet it contains facts that can be tested for their reality and their general truth in a different way." Sem Dresden, *Persecution, Extermination, Literature,* trans. Henry G. Schogt (Toronto: U of Toronto P, 1995), 42.

[9.] Singer holds that the conceptions of the nature of nonhuman animals help buttress speciesist attitudes: "To say that people are 'humane' is to say that they are kind; to say that they are 'beastly,' 'brutal,' or simply that they behave 'like animals' is to suggest that they are cruel and nasty. We rarely stop to consider that the animal who kills with the least reason to do so is the human animal" (222). Singer emphasizes that wolves and lions must kill, but humans kill for sport and pleasure. "Moreover, human beings are not content with mere killing. Throughout history they have shown a tendency to torment and torture both their fellow human beings and their fellow animals before putting them to death. No other animal shows much interest in doing this. While we overlook our own savagery, we exaggerate that of other animals" (222).

[10.] This is the case in the novels *Nacht,* prompted by the author's imprisonment in the Nazi Concentration Camp Moghilev-Podolsk, *Der Nazi und der Friseur,* the dual biography of a German Jew and a Gentile before and after the Shoah and a satire on the anti-Semitic dual biographies by Freytag, Raabe, and Dinter, and *Jossel*

Wassermanns Heimkehr (1993, "The Return of Jossel Wassermann"), which commemorates the lost culture of Ashkenazic Jewry. Edgar Hilsenrath, *Jossel Wassermanns Heimkehr* (Munich: Piper, 1993).

[11.] Friedrich Nietzsche, *Also Sprach Zarathustra. Ein Buch für alle und Keinen*, vol. 6 of *Sämtliche Werke in zwölf Bänden* (Stuttgart: Alfred Kröner, 1964), 34.

[12.] Singer, iii.

[13.] Edgar Hilsenrath, *The Story of the Last Thought* (London: Macdonald, 1991), 1. All quotations are taken from this edition, later referred to as *Story*. "'It's simply extraordinary, Mr. Khatisian,' said the secretary-general, 'that you should remember everything so clearly. If I'm not mistaken, you never knew any of your family, nor even your own mother. For when you came into the world, Mr. Khatisian, in 1915, they were all either dead or had disappeared'" (*Story*, 15).

[14.] Susann Moeller, "Politics to Pulp a Novel: The Fate of the First Edition of Edgar Hilsenrath's Novel *Nacht*," in *Insiders and Outsiders: Jewish and Gentile Culture in Germany and Austria*, ed. Dagmar C. G. Lorenz and Gabriele Weinberger (Detroit: Wayne State UP, 1994), 224–34 discusses in detail some of the problems Hilsenrath encountered as a result of his decision.

[15.] It resembles Elias Canetti's autobiographical account of turn-of-the-century rural Bulgaria and Hilsenrath's account of his teenage years in rural Romania. Canetti describes Bulgaria as he remembers it in his autobiography, *Die gerettete Zunge* (Frankfurt am Main: Fischer, 1979), 7–44. See also Dagmar C. G. Lorenz, *Verfolgung bis zum Massenmord* (New York: Lang, 1992), 137. Edgar Hilsenrath, "Erfahrungsbericht," in *Literatur des Exils*, ed. Bernt Engelmann (Munich: Goldmann, 1981), 66–75.

[16.] Jeffrey Herf, *Reactionary Modernism: Technology, Culture, and Politics in Weimar and the Third Reich* (Cambridge: Cambridge UP, 1984) questions Adorno's and Horkheimer's assessment that Enlightenment, taken to its extreme, is also the source of reactionary irrationalism. Rather, he maintains that Enlightenment had never been taken to its full consequence.

[17.] Hilsenrath's conviction regarding war as murder corresponds to that of Elias Canetti. Canetti also reports on his mother's uncompromising attitude: "She referred to the war always as 'murder'" (*Zunge*, 178). Canetti characterizes his own thoughts as follows: "There are few negative things that I would not say about individual people and mankind in general. Nonetheless, I take so much pride in them that there is only one thing that I really hate: their enemy, death" (*Zunge*, 11).

[18.] Finsen and Finsen, 256.

[19.] As Hamid's pan-Islamic vision was replaced by virulent nationalism after the Young Turkish revolution in 1908, so did traditional German nationalism give way to Nazism in the interwar period.

[20.] Finsen and Finsen, 254.

21. Singer, chapters "Tools for Research ... your taxes at work," 25–94 and "Down on the Factory Farm ... or what happened to your dinner when it was still an animal," 95–158.

22. Klaus Theweleit, *Männerphantasien II: Zur Psychoanalyse des weißen Terrors* (Hamburg: Rowohlt, 1980).

DEBORAH VIËTOR-ENGLÄNDER

Alfred Kerr and Marcel Reich-Ranicki: Critics and Power in Germany in the Weimar Republic and the Federal Republic

ALFRED KERR WAS BORN IN BRESLAU, SILESIA, in 1867, completed his formal education at the University of Breslau, and went to Berlin as a student. He completed his Ph.D. at the University of Halle and then lived and worked in Berlin until 1933 when he was forced to flee from Germany. He lived in exile in Switzerland, France, and Great Britain and died while on a visit to Hamburg in 1948. Marcel Reich-Ranicki was born in Poland in 1920 and went to Berlin at the age of nine. He completed high school there in 1938 and was expelled from Germany and forced to leave for Poland in October of that year. He survived the Warsaw Ghetto, worked for the Polish government in London, and came to the Federal Republic of Germany in 1958. He is now regarded as the *Literaturpapst,* the eminent authority on literature, in Germany.

For Alfred Kerr, criticism was an art form in its own right. In the introduction to his book *Das neue Drama* ("The New Drama," published in 1904 when he was nearly thirty-seven and at the height of his powers and reprinted in 1917 as a foreword to the first volume of his *Collected Works*), he established a number of principles he considered essential for the critic. Not only was there a very strong personal element involved — he often wrote his theater criticism in verse or described what it was like getting to the theater — his criticism was impressionistic but based on very definite ideas of what he wished to achieve: "Immer wieder horchen, immer wieder feststellen, welche Gefühle hat man?"[1] In "Schauspielkunst" (1904) he adds: "Durch Eindruckslichter die Quintessenz der Gestalten spiegeln."[2] Criticism was, like that of King David, to be carried out with sling and harp, with hate and love. In the foreword quoted previously, he continues:

> Ich gebe hier Kritiken in deutscher Sprache. Sie suchen den Ewigkeitszug. Das Ziel ist: Lichter zu setzen; und durch herausgewählte Einzelzüge von der Kraft eines Beispiels Gattungen zu beleuchten. ... Die innere Form der Davidsbündlerkritik sei Zusammendrängung. Sie will lieber Extrakt sein als

Limonade; lieber mit Blitzlicht arbeiten als mit angereihten Petroleumfun-zen. Es reizt mich nicht, Strömungen zu verfolgen, sondern Seelen zu zer-gliedern. Den Kern eines Menschen auf eine bleibende Art festzuhalten.[3]

In Kerr's opinion, bad works were just as useful as good ones in order to demonstrate basic principles. A well-known contemporary of his, the critic Moritz Heimann said of him in 1897: "Er hat das schärfste Gehör für die Regungen der Gegenwart, ohne sich von ihnen betäuben zu lassen."[4] In "Schauspielkunst," he also describes the "principle of extract" regarding characters in a play: "Extrakt von Gestalten, welche dem Verfasser wesensvoll erscheinen."[5] The introduction to his *Collected Works*, written in 1917, was also divided into his characteristic short paragraphs, listing points and con-taining his credo as a critic: "35. Aus einem Gedanken macht der Stück-macher ein Stück. Der Schriftsteller einen Aufsatz. Ich einen Satz. ... 38. Dichter haben keine Sprachkraft. Sprachkraft ist in der Kritik."[6] This is what Kurt Tucholsky means in his poem for Kerr's sixtieth birthday:

> Doch einen, der die Sprache packt
> und nie Bolljong — und stets Extrakt
> des such dir man mit die Laterne
> Ick kann mir nicht helfen — ich hab Ihnen jerne.[7]

Forty-four years later, writing at the end of a long life and after fifteen years in exile from Germany, he still urges young drama critics to write what they specifically feel they should write, an expression of their own personalities. Thus, he concludes, "Redet deutsch. Redet greifbar."[8]

Reich-Ranicki, on the other hand, sees criticism as an auxiliary disci-pline, a Hilfsdisziplin. "Kein Herz-Rang. Alfred Kerr hat gesagt: Bis heute Epik, Dramatik, Lyrik; ab heute Epik, Dramatik, Lyrik und Kritik. Ich aber will nie die Kritik als gleichberechtigte Gattung. Wenn die Kritik der Lite-ratur dient — das genügt."[9] Criticism is not of necessity a genre of its own but is to serve literature. Kerr's criticism was in fact sufficiently popular for the S. Fischer Verlag to produce a major five-volume edition of it in 1917 and two more volumes in 1920. This was unusual for a critic at that time. Kerr also produced a Ph.D. dissertation on Romantic literature, travel books, librettos for operas and lyric poetry, in exile more film scripts and poems, short stories, a long novella, "Der Dichter und die Meerschweinchen" (written during the war, unpublished, "The Poet and the Guinea Pigs"), a biography of Walther Rathenau, and a number of lectures for the BBC. He wrote in numerous genres, although in his theoretical writings, he states that criticism was the essential one. Reich-Ranicki, on the other hand, who thinks that criticism should serve literature, has only written one short story to date, although he is said to be writing his autobiography.[10] Otherwise he has not, as far as I know, experimented with creative work in his own right. He currently has more than twenty books in print, but they are all of one genre: literary criticism.

Kerr began writing for newspapers as a student, but, as mentioned earlier, his first book was his Ph.D. thesis.[11] His early reviews contain paragraphs of normal length and few mannerisms. In later years, his style became somewhat manneristic (excessive addiction to a distinctive manner). He tended to write as people expected him to write, inventing his own words, concentrating on creating quotable sentences and overemphasizing his use of short sentences and short paragraphs under Roman numerals. He was probably also adjusting his style to the speed of life in the Berlin of the 1920s and also to the visual expectations of his readers. He frequently used dialect or expressions from other languages in his reviews. Reich-Ranicki's style is far simpler and more direct, sometimes rather sententious.

Kerr was forced to leave Germany at the height of his fame at the age of just over sixty-five; Reich-Ranicki has reached the peak of his fame at seventy after a checkered past. He now often tends to say what is expected of him, comparatively controversial expressions of either very strong approval or disapproval. However, this is less the case in his book publications. His essays are often remarkable for their lucidity. His style is not overintellectualized, but comprehensible and clear. He does not have fixed criteria of criticism. Unlike Kerr, he feels that the individual work deserves individual treatment and is not ashamed of being subjective.[12]

> Das ist aber die wichtigste Aufgabe der Kritik: zu zeigen, was die Literatur ist und was sie nicht sein darf, was sie leistet, was sie leisten könnte und was sie leisten sollte. Vermittelnd zwischen der Kunst und der Gesellschaft, zwischen der Dichtung und dem Alltag, der Vergangenheit und der Gegenwart, der Tradition und der Moderne, zwischen den Schriftstellern und den Lesern, will die Kritik die Existenz der Literatur verteidigen. Oder, um es noch kürzer auszudrücken: Kritik will Literatur ermöglichen — das ist alles. Und wann, frage ich, wäre dies nötiger und dringlicher als in unseren Tagen?[13]

Kerr, too, was of course exceedingly subjective but did try to establish principles. Reich-Ranicki's television appearances are geared to an audience who would frequently not read at all. In 1993, Reich-Ranicki remarks: "Der Kritiker, der im Fernsehen über Bücher spricht, muß an das breite Publikum denken und leider oft auf Nuancen verzichten."[14] It has frequently been said that he gets his standards from the nineteenth and early twentieth centuries,[15] whereas Kerr was in fact very innovative at the turn of the century. Gerhart Hauptmann was only one of his discoveries. He indulged in harsh polemics against Hermann Sudermann's plays and many disagreed with him at the time, but basically his judgments of what was good in the theater of that period have held up, and Sudermann and others whom he condemned are hardly ever performed.

Kerr was distinctly vain: He emphasized his characteristic appearance, immediately recognizable. (His daughter Judith noted his special pose for press photographers on many occasions.) Many people also found him insufferably arrogant. Wilhelm Herzog comments: "Seine Sucht, aufzufallen, zu glänzen, von sich reden zu machen, koste es was es wolle, war ebenso groß wie seine Begabung als Künstler."[16] (It is notable that Herzog's formulation agrees with Kerr's own estimation of the critic as an artist in his own right.) Kerr was extremely sure of himself and insisted that people accept him as he was and agree or disagree with him. In *Empfindsame Flucht* (1933, "Sentimental Flight"), the first thing he wrote after his flight from Germany, he comments: "Was sollen die Theater in Berlin ohne mich anfangen?"[17] Kerr featured in advertisements for Adler typewriters. Reich-Ranicki also features in numerous advertisements. He deliberately uses his voice and his mannerisms and cultivates his lisp and his own PR. In November 1994, the American toy chain Toys "R" Us used a radio advertisement for their Christmas toy catalog on a popular radio station (Hessen III) featuring Reich-Ranicki's voice. The significance of this was that the advertisement did not say who the speaker was. This is the first time in the history of the Federal Republic that the characteristic voice of a literary critic has been so much in the minds of the general public that it was not necessary to give his name. This indicates his current popularity and power. Reich-Ranicki, in fact, comments on the vanity of critics: "Ein Kritiker muß eitel sein. ... Keinem der bedeutenderen Kritiker ist der Vorwurf der Eitelkeit erspart geblieben. ... Die Eitelkeit gehört seit eh und je zum Berufsbild des Kritikers. Ja, mir will es sogar scheinen, daß die Eitelkeit nicht nur eine unumgängliche Folge der Arbeit des Kritikers ist, sondern eine unbedingt notwendige Voraussetzung. Wer nicht eitel ist, der sollte sich hüten, Kritiker zu werden."[18] He also feels that the critic is essentially lonely: "Er steht im Mittelpunkt und ist trotzdem einsam."[19]

Reich-Ranicki is an excellent speaker who can make a tremendous impression on television. Kerr made radio broadcasts on Radio Berlin from 1929 onward, but for political reasons. He tried to warn his audience against National Socialism and against the *Entrepublikanisierung der Republik*. Consequently, he had to have police protection in order to get to the radio station safely. He was not trying to further the interests of any particular party, but to alert to dangers. Both Kerr and Reich-Ranicki enjoyed / enjoy feuds and arguments. Kerr admitted this freely. In an autobiographical sketch for a book celebrating his sixtieth birthday in 1927, published in 1928, he writes: "Ein Almanach wollte neulich meine Lieblingsbeschäftigung wissen. Ich schrieb: 'Seefahren. Musikmachen. Kindern Gutnachtsagen. Atmen. Sätze meistern. Und Krach.'"[20] And Volker Hage comments to Reich-Ranicki: "Sie zanken sich eben gerne. Und in der Vereinfachung waren Sie schon immer ein Weltmeister."[21] Kerr was a fanatic who was rarely able to forgive. This is illustrated by his revenge against Gerhart Hauptmann in exile. They had been friends for many years, but Kerr could not forgive Hauptmann for consorting with the National Socialists and concluded his attack entitled "Gerhart Hauptmanns Schande" (1933) with the words: "Sein Andenken soll verscharrt sein unter Disteln; sein Bild begraben in Staub."[22]

As a schoolboy, Alfred Kerr was extremely patriotic and was, therefore, selected to give the speech for the Kaiser's birthday during his last year at school. At the beginning of the First World War, he wrote some ultrapatriotic poems, which he was never ashamed of, and, in fact, included in a book of poems he published in 1926, admitting that his opinions had since undergone changes. He felt that he was German until the Third Reich, although he always felt at home in France. He comments: "Chaque homme a deux pays, le sien et puis la France."[23] But in the latter years of his exile, he referred to Germany as his *Sprachland,* the land of his language. He was always acutely aware of his Jewish identity but was obviously more preoccupied by it in exile than before and wrote a good deal on Jewish subjects during that period. Reich-Ranicki is, in his own opinion, a typically German critic,[24] but he does not necessarily feel German. Nor does he feel particularly Polish or Jewish. He does not feel that any country is his home, but German literature and music are.[25]

Is it possible in Germany today to be "ein deutscher Staatsbürger jüdischen Glaubens," a German citizen of Jewish faith, as Ignaz Bubis called it, after the Holocaust? In the Weimar Republic, anti-Semitism could be quite open — in the Federal Republic after the Shoah, the situation has changed. Kerr was not a religious Jew but was well aware of his Jewish identity; however, he never hesitated to attack other Jews if he disagreed with them, as was the case with Maximilian Harden, Karl Kraus, and others. In Reich-Ranicki's case, one feels that many attacks on him are not made because the possible attackers think they might be accused of anti-Semitism; people did not have these inhibitions in the Weimar Republic. Both critics published works on Jewish topics.[26] The title page of the *Spiegel* magazine when the Reich-Ranicki lead story was published in 1993 was rightly considered by many to be a caricature with anti-Semitic tendencies.[27] Reich-Ranicki claims he learned a great deal from Kerr, but he also makes clear that he has no single model among critics, although he acknowledges the influence of a number of Jewish critics of the nineteenth and twentieth centuries.

In an article for Kerr's one hundredth birthday in 1967, George Salmony writes in the *Süddeutsche Zeitung,* "Er war Zar, Papst, Diktator, Harfenist und Henker in einmaliger Personalunion."[28] Kerr was fully aware of the power he had to make or break a play. An extract from Carl Zuckmayer's autobiography about Kerr and about the premiere of his play *Der fröhliche Weinberg* (1925, "The Joyous Vineyard") is perhaps the best-known description of this: "Ganz rechts, mit undurchdringlicher Maske und ironisch geschürztem Schnäuzchen, saß Kerr, der gefährlichste Scharfschütze, dessen Daumen auf- oder abwärts über Tod und Leben des neuen Dramatikers entscheiden konnte."[29] And he goes on to say, "Gleich neben meiner Mutter saß der grimmige Kerr, der mich bisher so entsetzlich verrissen hatte. ... Auch meine Mutter, als ich sie in der Pause für eine Minute hinter der Bühne traf, war starr und bleich, und sie flüsterte nur mit verkrampften Lippen vor sich hin: 'Kerr hat zweimal gelächelt.' Es klang wie: der Scharfrichter ist erkrankt. Die Hinrichtung ist aufgeschoben."[30]

In the Weimar Republic, critics like Kerr (who was the *Berliner Tageblatt*'s theater critic from 1919 onward) and Herbert Jhering had a very considerable influence on the decisions of theaters on whether or not to stage particular plays. This was vital for authors trying to get their plays performed. The theaters in the provinces would have hesitated to accept a play that had been badly reviewed in the most important papers. The "feuilletons" of the major papers had a vitally important function as multipliers. They were the main means of popularizing plays. Hence a very real financial power emanated from their reviews. The critics who wrote for the major papers were possessed of real media power.[31] Kerr, too, was conscious of his own power and of the power of the press medium. The high priests of criticism operated essentially through the written word, and full-page essays or reviews in the major papers could influence opinions throughout Germany.

Reich-Ranicki is well aware that in his case, literary criticism has an auxiliary function, but the power is there nevertheless. He has simply adapted it to current media culture in the Federal Republic, which uses television to reach a different audience. The fact that *Der Spiegel* has devoted two cover stories to him (Oct. 4, 1993 and Aug. 21, 1995) is a most unusual phenomenon and the first time in the history of the Federal Republic that this has ever been done for a literary critic. The first of the two articles concludes: "Gott schwieg. Und sein für Literatur und literarisches Leben zuständiger Stellvertreter auf Erden lächelte triumphierend."[32] None of the incidents and revelations about his past have affected Reich-Ranicki's power much. He is nationally known in the field of literature. The television program "Das literarische Quartett" ("The Literary Quartet") can have a decisive effect on the sales of a book and the attention devoted to it by the media. It has always been a question of money, but one cannot compare the amounts between then and today. A play could only reach so many people. They had to be on the spot to fill the theater. It did, of course, help plays to be accepted by other theaters if Kerr approved. But he wrote for a major newspaper and certainly affected the popularity of authors and in particular of playwrights. As mentioned earlier, his judgment has proved right in most cases. But the money publishers can make on a book popularized on "Das literarische Quartett" is in quite a different category. It can also affect printed media coverage, translation rights, and more. It is not merely a question of a good or a bad review. Many people buy and read the book before the program is broadcast. However, if Reich-Ranicki condemns a book (as in the case of Grass's *Ein weites Feld* [1995, "A Wide-Open Field"]), many people will buy it because of its controversy. In this sense, the program can make or break the sales of a book. Bookshops order only after the books to be discussed are announced. Kerr discovered radio as a medium, and Reich-Ranicki was the first critic to make major use of television. One can only speculate as to what Kerr's influence could have been given the media of today. Instead, he was forced to leave Germany and to face exile and poverty at the height of his fame. To date, nearly fifty years after his death, the new edition of his works is still incomplete, and there is no biography available.

Notes

1. Alfred Kerr, "Die Sucher und die Seligen," in *Gesammelte Schriften. Erste Reihe, Die Welt im Drama,* vol. 3 (Berlin: S. Fischer, 1917), 304.

2. Alfred Kerr, "Schauspielkunst," in *Die Literatur. Sammlung illustrierter Einzeldarstellungen,* vol. 9, ed. Georg Brandes (Berlin: Bard, Marquard, 1904). Quoted here from the new edition, Alfred Kerr, *Essays. Theater. Film,* vol. 3 of *Werke in Einzelbänden* (Berlin: Argon, 1991), 241.

3. In the foreword, written in 1904 as an introduction to his book *Das neue Drama* and reprinted in 1917 as a foreword to the first volume of his *Das neue Drama,* vol. 1 of *Gesammelte Schriften in zwei Reihen, Die Welt im Drama* (Berlin: S. Fischer, 1917), 8–9.

4. Moritz Heimann, *Die Wahrheit liegt in der Mitte* (Frankfurt am Main: Fischer, 1966), 122–23.

5. Kerr, *Essays. Theater. Film,* 241.

6. Kerr, "Einleitung," *Gesammelte Schriften,* vol. 1, xviii.

7. Kurt Tucholsky, *Die Weltbühne* , Dec. 20, 1927, 936.

8. Alfred Kerr, "Die junge Theaterkritik," in *Essays. Theater. Film,* 340.

9. Marcel Reich-Ranicki, "Der Verreißer," interview, *Der Spiegel,* Oct. 4, 1993. Rpt. in Volker Hage and Matthias Schreiber, *Marcel Reich-Ranicki* (Cologne: Kiepenheuer & Witsch, 1995), 187.

10. Marcel Reich-Ranicki, "Eine sehr sentimentale Geschichte" (1958), reprinted in Hage and Schreiber, 207–22.

11. Alfred Kerr, *Godwi* (Berlin: Bondi, 1898).

12. Hage and Schreiber, 115.

13. "Ein Kritiker muß eitel sein," Dankesrede 1983, printed in Marcel Reich-Ranicki, *Nichts als Literatur. Aufsätze und Anmerkungen* (Stuttgart: dtv, 1985), 134.

14. Reich-Ranicki, "Der Verreißer," 279. A slightly different version appears in Hage and Schreiber, 166.

15. Marcel Reich-Ranicki, *Zwischen Diktatur und Literatur. Ein Gespräch mit Joachim Fest* (Frankfurt am Main: Fischer, 1993), 104.

16. Wilhelm Herzog, *Menschen, denen ich begegnete* (Bern: Francke, 1959), 397.

17. Alfred Kerr, *Die Diktatur des Hausknechts* (1934; reprint, Hamburg: Konkret Literatur, 1983), 29.

18. Reich-Ranicki, "Ein Kritiker muß eitel sein," 130.

19. Reich-Ranicki, "Der Verreißer," 284 or Hage and Schreiber, 180.

20. Alfred Kerr, *Lesebuch zu Leben und Werk* (Berlin: Argon, 1987), 33.

21. Hage and Schreiber, 166.

22. Kerr, *Die Diktatur des Hausknechts,* 27.

23. Alfred Kerr, *Ich kam nach England* (Bonn: Bouvier Verlag Herbert Grundmann, 1979), 181. Translation: "Everybody has two countries, one's own and France."

24. Hage and Schreiber, 180.

25. Reich-Ranicki, *Zwischen Diktatur und Literatur,* 104.

26. Marcel Reich-Ranicki, *Über Ruhestörer. Juden in der deutschen Literatur* (Stuttgart: dtv, 1989). Kerr planned a book in exile that was to be entitled "Ein Jude spricht zu Juden." It has never been published.

27. Hage and Schreiber, 148–49.

28. George Salmony, "Ein Epikureer des Theaters," *Süddeutsche Zeitung,* Dec. 23, 1967, 27.

29. Carl Zuckmayer, *Als wär's ein Stück von mir* (Frankfurt am Main: Fischer, 1966), 321.

30. Ibid., 410.

31. See Siegfried Jacobsohn, *Der Fall Jacobsohn* (Berlin-Charlottenburg: Verlag der Schaubühne, 1913).

32. Reich-Ranicki, "Der Verreißer," 279.

BERND FISCHER

The Memory of Multiculturalism
and the Politics of Identity

IN THE INTRODUCTION TO THEIR 1995 conference volume on identities,
Henry Gates and Kwame Appiah offer the following periodization of the
recent discourse on multiplying identities:

> A literary historian might very well characterize the eighties as the period
> when race, class, and gender became the holy trinity of literary criticism. ...
> In the 1990s, however, "race," "class," and "gender," threaten to become
> the regnant clichés of our critical discourse. ... Scholars in a variety of disci-
> plines have begun to address what we might call the politics of identity.
> Their work expands on the evolving anti-essentialist critiques of ethnic, sex-
> ual, national, and racial identities ... . The powerful resurgence of national-
> isms in Eastern Europe provides just one example of the catalysts for such
> theorizing.[1]

While this is one of the strongest critiques of essentialist ideologies of
ethnicity and race[2] that have permeated the multiculturalist debates for more
than two decades, Appiah and Gates, somewhat surprisingly, do not include
culture in their list — although culture tends to be situated at the theoretical
center of many aspects of "the cliché-ridden discourse of identity."[3] Another
contributor to the volume, however, Walter Benn Michaels, describes the
dominance of culture with regard to race. He concludes his analysis as follows:

> Our sense of culture is characteristically meant to replace race, but part of
> the argument of this essay has been that culture has turned out to be a way
> of continuing rather than repudiating racial thought. It is only the appeal to
> race that makes culture an object of affect and that gives notions like losing
> our culture, preserving it, stealing someone else's culture, restoring people's
> culture to them, and so on, their pathos. ... Without race, losing our culture
> can mean no more than doing things differently from the way we now do
> them and preserving our culture can mean no more than doing things the
> same — the melodrama of assimilation disappears.[4]

One might want to add that, depending on specific ideologies of identity in concrete societies, it is not only race, but, for instance, also nation that can potentially inflate questions of cultural development and change into melodramas of life and death.

In his critical polemic of 1992, *The Great Migration*, Hans Magnus Enzensberger criticizes multiculturalist identity politics as follows: "The multicultural society remains a confusing slogan as long as the difficulties which it throws up, and fails to clarify, remain taboo. The wearisome dispute will never be resolved if no one knows, or wants to know, what culture means — 'Everything that humans do and do not do' seems the most precise definition. For this reason alone, the debate is condemned to reproduce the contradiction between deliberate underestimation and denunciation, idyll and panic."[5]

More often than not, the U. S. debate on multiculturalism and cultural identity has circumvented this most crucial problem to its theoretical validity by implicitly, and for all practical purposes, equating culture with ethnicity and, furthermore, by defining ethnicity along the lines of some rather crude racial categories that were imposed by the history and presence of racism and in that sense remain "racist." The debate on cultural diversity and identity was for many years dominated by literary critics whose political roots could be found somewhere on the left. On the one hand, the debate provided new conceptualizations for the aging and faltering idea of a pluralist society, and, on the other hand, it provided an ideological justification for traditionally leftist political programs like political recognition, affirmative action, minority rights, or subsidization of subcultural enterprises. It did not take long, however, before ideas of a separatist African American nation or of Native American nations (for instance, designed around casinos on tribal reservations) and an infinite number of smaller independence movements began to show a structural resemblance to classical nationalisms that were and are equally based on imaginations of ethnicity, race, religion, and history.[6] The classical meaning of culture was thus slowly contaminated and ultimately inverted from cultivated or cultured to natural; that is, to the idea of supposedly natural belongings to historical or imagined communities[7] characterized by ethnic, religious, or ideological sameness. Consequently, ideas that claimed to be in favor of rejuvenating the old Enlightenment project of an open and pluralist society actually tended to preach the opposite: the compartmentalization of constitutional democracies into ideologically closed, monolithic, and emotionally charged identity camps. Paradoxically, all this was and is possible at a time when central nationalist categories like history, cultural conformity, ethnicity, and race have been seriously undermined by recent scholarship in genetics, ethnography, archeology, regional history, and so forth.[8] Gates puts his finger on this paradox when he reminds us of the ethnologist Jean-Loup Amselles's objection to the politicization of ethnicity.

According to Gates, Amselles contends that the very notion of discrete ethnicities is an artifact of his discipline. Warning against what he dubs ethnic or cultural fundamentalism, Amselles maintains that the notion of a multicultural society, "far from being an instrument of tolerance and of liberation of minorities, as its partisans affirm, manifests, to the contrary, all the hallmarks of ethnological reason, and that is why it has been taken up in France by the New Right.... Cultures aren't situated one by the other like Leibniz's windowless monads," he argues. Rather, "the very definition of a given culture is in fact the result of intercultural relations of forces."[9]

Gates draws the following important conclusion:

> While the discourses of identity politics and of liberation are often conflated, they may be in mortal combat on a more fundamental level. Identity politics, in its purest form, must be concerned with the survival of an identity. By contrast, the utopian agenda of liberation pursues what it takes to be the objective interests of its subjects, but it may be little concerned with its cultural continuity or integrity. More than that, the discourse of liberation often looks forward to the birth of a transformed subject, the creation of a new identity, which is, by definition, the surcease of the old.[10]

In my view, there is an important lesson to be learned from the North American debate: namely, that multiculturalism cannot succeed as a theoretical model for a pluralist and open society if it refuses to inherit the old Enlightenment and, yes, modernist concept of the multicultural individual, the cosmopolitan citizen, and with it an understanding of culture that retains notions of cultivation, of intercultural communication, of integration and acculturation, of a dynamic and open-ended history that is characterized by creativity and change — progress, if you wish.

From the eighteenth century to the present, such a multi- or intercultural individual has been at the center of constitutionalism, that is, of a state whose idea of nationhood is defined by citizenship, and not by heritage, ethnicity, culture, or religion. Serving as a building block and stepping stone for an ultimate world republic, a republic of republics (Kant), the constitutional republic is one of the central political projects of the Enlightenment and of what I would call Western modernism as opposed to its Central and East European counterpart — which, in one way or another, refers back to German Idealism.[11] Within the framework of the civic society, interculturalism (along the lines of some universalist concepts like human rights and democratic representation) describes the process of civilization — which, in this sense, is indeed, as Gates states, in "mortal combat" with the politics of cultural identity.

A word of caution might, however, be in order. We are, of course, not dealing with absolute opposites when we employ our structurally shaky and theoretically questionable concepts of ethnicity, culture, and acculturation — a complication that might, in part, be responsible for the political confusion and ideological potential of the multicultural debate. Ethnicity and acculturation are neither independent entities nor oppositional concepts; they are at best regulative ideas. Every sociogenesis we know of takes place in a space that is not fully marked by either one of these two poles in spite of their implicit ideological claims to totality. From a historical point of view, ethnicity and acculturation are closely intertwined. Not only does one not exist without the other, more often than not, they describe the very same phenomenon or process. Historically speaking, ethnicity comes about by way of acculturation, that is, acculturation can be defined as the forming of ethnicity.

Ethnicity must be described as process, a complex and ever shifting interplay of numerous formations, such as family, class, custom, mentality, generation, language, religion, region, state. The only permanence of ethnicity is its state of consistent fluctuation. The ideology of ethnicity, on the other hand, lies in its claim to be or become the opposite of the never ending interplay of acculturation and differentiation that it is. Enzensberger cites a number of observations that support this thesis. "The normal state of the atmosphere is turbulence. The same is true of the settlement of the earth by human beings. ... Stationary populations form again and again over the millennia. On the whole, however, they remain the exception. ... A considerable proportion of humanity has always been in motion, migrating or in flight for the most diverse reasons, in violent or peaceful manner."[12]

The differences between competing concepts of identity that are significant for our discussion regard their intellectual outlook. Most important, the constitutional nation views itself, in a more radical sense, as a political and intellectual project, as a revolutionary idea pursuing a political formation that has not existed before, but should, for it seems reasonable (within the framework of what one might call humanism). The identity project of this type of nation (in theory) relies on the integrational force and potential of its constitution. We must not fail to understand that political integration — i.e., a politically defined identity — is not a mere side effect of constitutionalism, but rather one of its most essential concerns. Therefore and strictly speaking, the constitutional project cannot be reconciled with the notion of displacement that has recently gained much notoriety, if not ideological primacy, in postmodern thought. According to Enlightenment theories of constitutionalism, the place of humans depends to a lesser extent on where they come from than on where they ought to go in order to become individual selves and sovereigns of their political affairs. In this context, displacement or foreignness can be seen as emancipatory: It describes the individual's escape from a state of existence and mind that only seemed natural (for instance, the family, region, culture, class one is born into by mere chance) but now appears as political or cultural and, therefore, can be analyzed, and its *self-inhibiting* aspects can be criticized. In other words, foreignness is one prerequisite of political and cultural enlightenment. To a certain degree, one has to become foreign to one's own origin, heritage, and familial culture in order to enter the open-ended project of becoming an individual self for whom little can remain unquestioned and untested. This is, by the way, not only true for the Enlightenment, but indeed for many spiritual and intellectual movements that build upon the centrality of the individual self, including many religions. Civic societies (nations of politically represented citizens) are the product of Western Enlightenment thought and constitutional revolutions, and not of any kind of cultural nationalism that attempted to emulate the successes of Western modernism by such means as the identity politics of fictitious ethnicity or mythological historicity.

Notes

1. Kwame Anthony Appiah and Henry Louis Gates, eds., *Identities* (Chicago: U of Chicago P, 1995), 1.

2. See also Henry Louis Gates and Cornel West, eds., *The Future of the Race* (New York: Alfred Knopf, 1996).

3. Appiah and Gates, 1.

4. Walter Benn Michaels, "Race into Culture: A Critical Genealogy of Cultural Identity," in *Identities,* ed. Appiah and Gates, 61–62.

5. Hans Magnus Enzensberger, *Civil Wars: From L. A. to Bosnia* (New York: New Press, 1994), 134–35.

6. Some better-known recent examples are the politics of Louis Farrakhan, leader of the Nation of Islam, the warfare of different factions of the 200-member tribe of the Lake County Pomo Indians over the management of the Pomo Palace Casino, and, of course, the numerous right-wing movements like the Aryan Nation.

7. The term was coined by Max Weber and is discussed extensively in Benedict Anderson's *Imagined Communities: Reflections on the Origin and Spread of Nationalism* (London: Verso, 1983).

8. See Werner Sollors, ed., *The Invention of Ethnicity* (New York: Oxford UP, 1989); Luigi Luca Cavalli-Sforza, "Alle aus demselben Holz," *Die Zeit* 7 (1992): 17–20; Mark B. Shchukin, *Rome and the Barbarians in Central and Eastern Europe: 1st Century B.C.–1st Century A.D.* (Oxford: B. A. R., 1989).

9. Henry Louis Gates, "Beyond the Culture Wars: Identities in Dialogue," *Profession* (1993): 8.

10. Ibid.

11. See Bernd Fischer, *Das Eigene und das Eigentliche: Klopstock, Herder, Fichte, Kleist. Episoden aus der Konstruktionsgeschichte nationaler Intentionalitäten* (Berlin: Schmidt, 1995).

12. Enzensberger, 103–4.

MATTI BUNZL

Counter-Memory and Modes of Resistance: The Uses of Fin-de-Siècle Vienna for Present-Day Austrian Jews

S INCE THE MID-1980S, STUDIES CONDUCTED under the conceptual heading of "History and Memory" have provided ample evidence for the inherently social processes by which politically sanctioned narratives project and construct the "past" as a seemingly unproblematic domain of knowledge and experience.[1] This collective effort has given the postmodern academy the epistemological realization that a previously reified dichotomy between history and memory only obfuscates the contestatory nature by which these socially structured categories constitute each other in the shifting terrains demarcated by the monumentalization and musealization of the past, its public commemoration, and its sociodiscursive delineation.[2] In this manner, we now tend to conceive history and memory not as separate entities (the former designating that which objectively happened, the latter referring to its selective and inherently subjective representation), but as the constitutive elements of a dialectic process through which understandings of the past are structured and mediated at the intersection of "historical reality" and the social contingencies of its more or less strategic recollection. It is in the dialectic of this (often mass-mediated) process that history is fashioned and refashioned in light of the social realities of memory, while memory is (re)constituted vis-à-vis the socially sanctioned narratives of objectified history.

While deeply indebted to the analytic orientation developed under the heading "History and Memory," the present study — itself part of a larger ethnographic project seeking to elucidate the conundrums of Jewish existence in post–Second World War Austria[3] — attempts to augment the literature by performing an interrelated, two-fold corrective to the theoretical apparatus underlying the majority of investigations of the representational dimensions of the past: (1) Over the last years, many scholars have been concerned with the critical elucidation of the variously articulated, socially dominant narratives, which construct history as an extension of politically sanctioned knowledges.[4] In contrast to this analytic approach (which has given us vital insights into the historico-mythical dimensions of the foundation and sustenance of "national histories" and similarly privileged narratives), I seek to highlight the functions and uses of oppositional modes of memory — forms of memory, in other words, that derive their salience from their deployment in contested sociopolitical fields. (2) Related to this investigative shift from hegemonizing to resistive constructions of history and memory is an analytic reconceptualization of the domains in which such constructions occur. Whereas most studies of "History and Memory" emphasize the critical interpretation of such official(ized) texts as public monuments, museums, large-scale commemorations, textbooks, and politicians' speeches,[5] I employ a more anthropological approach, centered on a conception of memory as narrative practice. In this manner, I locate the construction and reconstruction of histories and memories less in the complexly mediated domains of high culture and official politics, but in the sociodiscursive dimensions of everyday life. There, the dialectic of history and memory constitutes a continuous process demarcated by the ongoing negotiation and appropriation of socially available narratives through which individualized subjects can ground their "personal" histories / memories in collectively figured experiential tropes.

The Foucauldian term "counter-memory" — purposefully defamiliarized and invoked in the title of this article — gestures to this analytic approach. As an integral part of the "archaeological" project of the "early" Foucault, the notion of counter-memory alludes to an antihistoricist historiography centered on the critical retrieval and decoding of the discursive practices that are lost in the continual resignification of the symbolically coded spaces of cultural landscapes. In this manner, Foucault reads the emergence of the modern insane asylum in the eighteenth century in conjunction with the physical remains of the medieval lazar house where those stricken with leprosy were consigned to temper the anxieties of the population at large. In the wake of the retreat of leprosy, the strategic social exclusion of the leper was superseded by the Enlightenment construction of the "insane" — a new kind of social pariah, who, in analogy to the former, needed to be separated from the public at large (a process for which the vacated medieval lazar house provided the ready-made physical and conceptual structures). As Foucault argues, the crucial link between these enduring spaces of symbolic exclusion, however, has been virtually erased. This situation calls forth the archaeologist's critical excavation of the previously repressed, ancient counter-memory of the modern insane asylum, which reveals this symbol of Enlightenment spirit as a continued locus for the social need to demarcate and contain the undesirable.[6]

While my conception of counter-memory is related to Foucault's notion of the socially strategic construction and exclusion of selective others, it ultimately owes more to the "late" Foucault's understanding of power / knowledge and resistance. Developed primarily in his studies of the prison and his research into the history of sexuality, Foucault poses a new conception of power as a generative (rather than merely restrictive) force in human relations. In this framework, power is omnipresent; it is "always already there," affording no opportunity to move outside of it.[7] Neither the product of individual wills, nor the result of particular ideologies, power is generated at the intersection of institutional structures, the production of knowledges, and the self-subjectifications derived from complex sociodiscursive matrices. At the same time, this socially amorphous conception of power suggests a radical reconceptualization of the notion of resistance. Since any conception of freedom is contained within the structures of power itself, resistance can never be articulated from a position of complete social and epistemological autonomy. Rather than pointing to revolutionary overthrow, Foucault's notion of resistance thus intimates the strategic deployment of disruptive modes of signification (and by implication memory), which not only allow the temporary exposure of the internal contradictions and inconsistencies of dominant discourses and practices, but enable the imagination of alternative sites of subjectification and identity formation.[8]

Derived from a reading of Foucault's early archaeology in light of his later "genealogy," my conception of counter-memory unites the concern with the abject construction of social deviance with modes of resistance developed in the strategic disruption of the workings of power / knowledge. In this manner, my focus rests on the retrieval of communal counter-memory, tactically deployed as a socially veiled and culturally articulated narrative practice. Specifically, I intend to show how present-day Austrian Jews — abjectly defined as an other in Austria's anti-Semitic sociocultural field — can construct and deploy counter-memory of (or perhaps better, through recourse to) Vienna's fin de siècle as a resistive strategy of affirmative identification. It is ultimately my argument that the ensuing, narratively fixed (counter-)memorial topography constitutes the "alternative geographies" and "phantasmic histories," which structure the *Lebenswelt*, the environment, of contemporary Austrian Jews as a concrete mode of resistance against an anti-Semitic social field. In doing so, contemporary Austrian Jews not only actively interrogate, but effectively reverse a historically underwritten cultural logic, which places them in constitutive marginality vis-à-vis a seemingly unmarked Austrian "self." For, in the end, it is the deployment of counter-memorial narratives of affirmative Jewish identification that exposes and challenges, on the level of everyday practice, the operative fictions of a hegemonizing Austrianness.

Jews and Austrians after 1945:
A Brief History of Difference

Situated in the context of Central Europe's genocidal contingencies and Austria's lackluster *Vergangenheitsbewältigung* (the coming to terms with the past),[9] contemporary Jewish practices of narrative counter-memory can only be read in view of the inherent difficulties and complexities of post–Second World War Austrian-Jewish existence. In this manner, postwar Jewry's experiential tropes need to be understood, first and foremost, as the socially structured manifestations of a cultural field marked by the failed normalization of Austrian-Jewish relations in the wake of 1945's proverbial *Stunde Null* (point zero, the notion of a new beginning after 1945). For even though the social marginalization of Austria's Jews had just been taken to its most catastrophic extreme, anti-Semitic power structures remained effectively unchallenged in the wake of Austria's liberation. Continuing to enact an anti-Semitic cultural logic — derived in no small part from such fin-de-siècle spearheads of political anti-Semitism as Georg von Schönerer and Karl Lueger[10] — the Austrian state greeted Jewish survivors with sheer contempt, often denying returnees their Austrian citizenship. Faced with a plethora of administrative harassments, Jews not only had to struggle for entitlements under the *Opferfürsorgegesetz* (the law regulating support for war victims) but had to contend with a social field where — following earlier models that figured the Jew in constitutive opposition to a normative and unmarked in-group — they were once again placed in antithesis to a now reconstituted Austrian self.[11] Especially in light of Austria's official postwar historiography — which construed the country and its citizens as the first victim of Nazi aggression, thereby absolving it from any responsibility for the Holocaust — the position of Jews in postwar Vienna was rather precarious. Signifying in their role as victims to Austrians' contributions to the Nazi genocide, they were a constant reminder of the inherent instability of Austria's postwar "founding myth."[12] In consequence, the implementation and maintenance of the Second Republic's historical master narrative required the ongoing vilification of the Jews and their inherent difference. Clearly reflecting the widespread practice of defining postwar Austrian identity in opposition to a threatening Jewish other, Austria's first postwar chancellor, Karl Renner, took ready recourse to persistent stereotypes when noting rather tellingly that in its "present mood," the country would not stand for the restoration of "Jewish monopolies."[13] In the course of this effective reversal of the roles of victim and perpetrator, Jewish demands for restoration were not only denounced as greedy and unjust but were met for decades with various stalling tactics.[14]

How pervasively postwar Austrian national identity was (and is) constructed in constitutive opposition to a Jewish other is suggested by a number of quantitative studies conducted over the past few decades. Setting aside for the moment the inherent problems of "representative sampling," it seems clear that the overwhelming majority of Austria's population has adopted the postwar master narrative of Austrian victimization and its concomitant anti-Semitism. Surveys conducted in the 1970s and early 1980s have shown that roughly 80 percent of the populace reject Jewish claims for restitution, a stance rationalized by the notion — voiced by the same percentage of respondents — that Jews are at least partially responsible for their repeated persecutions.[15] At the same time as non-Jewish Austrians sought to purge the Holocaust from their collective history, they continued to feel uneasy vis-à-vis an imaginary, yet threatening Jewish presence.[16] In 1976, nearly 90 percent of Austrians overestimated the number of Jews living in Austria by a factor of 50 (with 50 percent missing the actual mark of roughly 7,000 by more than a factor of 100). If these numbers hint at the significance of Jewish difference in the constitution of non-Jewish Austrian selves, its centrality is only confirmed by the responses to a range of classic survey questions. In this vein, studies in the late 1960s and 1970s indicated that only 23 percent of Austrians regarded Jews who had converted to Christianity as true Christians, while fewer than 50 percent entertained the notion that Jews could be considered genuine Austrians. None of this should be very surprising given that nearly half of those sampled in a particular national survey readily located Jewish difference on the level of the body, reporting that it was possible to detect Jews on sight.[17] The infamous Waldheim affair of 1986 (with its ready political recourse to anti-Semitic stereotypes) merely confirmed the social valence of such anti-Jewish sentiments.[18] And in this context, it should surprise little that to this day, Jews continue to be referred to in official discourse as mere *Mitbürger* (fellow citizens) — the term *Bürger* (citizen) being reserved for more "genuine" Austrians.[19]

Aside from the continued threat of anti-Semitism, Austrian-Jewish existence is further complicated by the inherent fragmentations of Austria's Jewish community. On the eve of the *Anschluß* of Austria to Germany in 1938, almost 200,000 Jews lived in Austria, the overwhelming majority in Vienna. Following the Holocaust — in which 65,000 Austrian Jews perished — Vienna's Jewish community counted less than 7,000 members.[20] To the present day, this number has remained relatively steady in spite of significant demographic shifts. Many survivors left Austria in the decades after the war, as did some emigrants who had returned, but found postwar Austria a hostile and inhospitable place. While the number of Jews of German-Austrian background continued to dwindle, Polish, Romanian, and Hungarian Jews settled in Vienna. In conjunction with a recent surge of immigrants from the former Soviet Union, Jews of Eastern European background now make up the overwhelming majority of Vienna's Jewish community.[21] It is ultimately in this context of ruptured historical continuities that the deployment of counter-memory of fin-de-siècle Vienna by present-day Austrian Jews assumes its strategic significance. As the following analysis of the narrative practice of Jewish counter-memory will demonstrate, the creative construction of the memorial topography of an imagined moment of Jewish cultural efflorescence affords contemporary Austrian Jews the resistive potential required to sustain an affirmative sense of ethnic self in a persistently anti-Semitic sociocultural field.

Narratives of Counter-Memory

In light of Jews' abject figuration in Austria's social environment, the narrative construction of Jewish counter-memory usually occurs in a discursive context marked by a willed demarcation from a "normative" Austrian self. Indeed, most Austrian Jews readily disavow an Austrian identity, seeking instead to differentiate themselves from (imagined) Austrian traits. In so doing, Jews often use the term "Austrian" in constitutive opposition to a Jewish self, a linguistic practice that is not without subversive potential. For example, when Ilana — a thirtyish restaurateur and homemaker of Hungarian descent — ventured to describe Jewish life in Vienna, she noted with some irony, "In my eyes, there are few contacts with *actual* Austrians," evoking the dichotomous social fabric through which Jews are figured as different, while simultaneously suggesting her deliberate nonmembership in the category of "actual Austrians." Later, she elaborated on some of the favorable distinctions she perceives between "Jews" and "actual Austrians," which she locates both "historically and culturally":

> For example, I see great differences in the way children are raised; it's there where it all starts. I believe that most Jews raise their children like I do. I don't think that the majority of Austrians think as much about the education of their children as we do. Regarding my children, it would be my dream that they would spend some time studying abroad. That is almost a must for me. It is very important to me that my children won't attend university here after the *Matura*,[22] like the average Austrian child, but leave the country.

In the context of an explicitly anti-Semitic social field, such narratives constitute active forms of resistance. While they ultimately reify — and thereby reproduce — the structured dichotomy between "Jews" and "Austrians" from which they emerge, they do so by destabilizing the constitutive valuations underlying the nationalizing fiction of genuine Austrianness.

In this manner, such constitutive narratives of self — whose crucial function in the (re)production of Jewish *communitas* is documented through their salience in the everyday interactions of Austrian Jews — underwrite an elaborate social schema by which Jewish counter-memory is transported through the construction of alternative cultural geographies. In this sense, Ilana's wish for her children to "leave the country" and "study abroad" following their high school graduation is a case in point, suggesting in very concrete terms how the cultural geographies constructed by Austrian Jews transcend the political and symbolic confinements of (a Jewish-imagined) "Austrianness." Explicating the distinction she perceives in cognitive geographies, Ilana comments that "in contrast to average Austrians, Jews *can* imagine living in Paris, Tel Aviv, or Moscow." Indeed, that Austrian Jews live in a conceptual world extending far beyond the borders of the Austrian state is readily apparent. In this regard, Arie — a writer of Romanian background in his early thirties — suggested to me that the spatialized sense of self among Jews in Austria incorporates at least two alternative sites of identity: Israel and America — a conceptual scheme, whose complexity is only underscored by the many other points of reference Austrian Jews regularly evoke when discussing geographical locations of identity, ranging from London and Brussels (symbolically coded as the "home" of the "New Europe") to Boston (often invoked as a "haven" of higher learning) and Prague (occasionally figured as the best a newly accessible Eastern Europe has to offer).

But if Austrian Jews evade identification with an imagined Austrianness through a plethora of spatial identifications, the main topographical locus for Austrian-Jewish counter-memory is Vienna — home to the overwhelming majority of Austria's Jewish community. In the narratives of Jewish Austrians, "Vienna" is habitually figured in self-evident opposition to "Austria." In this respect, Vienna's urban space is often seen as synonymous with the possibility of living as a Jew within the social framework of contemporary Austria. As such, many Jews appreciate the fact that the city is home to an at least moderately sized Jewish community. As Jakov — a business student of Romanian descent in his early twenties — put it, "This affords the possibility to join Jewish organizations — to partake in Jewish life in general." But if Vienna thus emerges as the one social space in Austria's cultural landscape that can sustain Jewish life (in terms of its size and the presence of a Jewish community), most Viennese Jews find genuine pleasure in their urban environment. As these urban sentiments are constituted in typical opposition to an imagined Austrian other, this urban environment is in turn figured along very particular lines of difference, which at once reflect and reproduce a specific Austrian-Jewish experience and the strategic deployment of Jewish counter-memory. In this respect, Vienna is often figured as a metropolis and a cosmopolitan city, a genuine *Weltstadt*,[23] whose distinct atmosphere and character not only set it apart from Graz or Linz but put it in a league with other European megalopolises such as London, Paris, or Berlin. Citing reference points ranging from the world-renowned *Staatsoper*, state opera, and the many theaters to the magnificent architecture and the wide-spread prosperity, Austrian Jews recognize in Vienna the model of an idealized urban space. For Peter — an economics student in his late teens — Vienna's topography is synonymous with the "great cultural attractions it has to offer," central among them the University of Vienna. Echoing the importance of Vienna's diverse cultural scene, Jenny — a translator in her late forties — also offers the numerous *Kaffeehäuser*, coffeehouses, sprinkled across the city as a fundamental element in the constitution of a distinct metropolitan space, while Arie evokes the city's lively nightlife alongside its spectacular gardens and parks as distinctive features of its urban geography.

But despite the genocidal ruptures, which left very few Viennese Jews with personal links to pre–Second World War Austria, the Vienna imagined as an idealized contemporary metropolis does not exist in a memorial vacuum. Rather, in Austrian-Jewish narratives of spatial belonging, the city is frequently embedded in complexly layered historical references, which — almost invariably — situate its present-day urban topography in relation to a counter-memory of Vienna's fin de siècle. It is through this process of historico-temporal structuration that Vienna's urban space can become intelligible as a specifically Jewish space bearing in its social geography the counter-memorial imprints of a venerable Jewish-Viennese tradition.

In this constitution of historically located sociospatial meanings of Vienna, the mediated (counter-)memory of the Habsburg monarchy plays a crucial role. Specifically, it is the ethnic pluralism embodied in the supranational semblance of the crown that continues to serve as a reference point for contemporary Jews. As such, a vision of the House Habsburg (itself a metaphoric term for the diversity of its constituency) stands at the core of an urban Viennese topography that promises the possibility of Jewish immigration and integration following and approximating late-nineteenth- and early-twentieth-century models of Jewish emancipation and assimilation. Especially in light of the large-scale postwar Jewish immigration from East-Central and Eastern Europe, the metonymic link between the imperial capital and the Habsburg lands defined in relation to it proves a lasting cultural trope. For Jews placed within the borders of an enduring imperial geography, the recognition of an affirmatively figured Habsburg legacy in the symbolic landscape of contemporary Vienna ultimately creates a powerful nexus in the constitution of a viable Viennese-Jewish identity. As Arie puts it succinctly, the "forging of links with Habsburg elements" allows many Jews "whose families came from the East" to feel at home in Vienna.

How this linkage between contemporary Vienna and the symbolic reality
of a pluralist Habsburgian entity (and its specifically Jewish connotations) is
enacted in the narrative practices of counter-memory becomes evident in the
following passage, in which Ilana attempts to locate herself in the complex
historical layers serving as reference points for the constitution of present-day
Viennese-Jewish identity.

> Vienna is certainly — at least in terms of geography — the Western-most
> edge of Eastern Europe. And historically speaking, Vienna has always been
> the destination for, and melting pot of, all these East-Central European ways
> of life. For centuries, Vienna was very welcoming. A hundred years ago, it
> was neither chauvinistic nor nationalistic, but identified through the figure
> of the *Kaiser* rather than the nation. But this mixture of various peoples has
> lived on. Every group has brought its culture, its particular foods, its way of
> life, and so on; and I can still feel that, even today when I walk through the
> second district or parts of the third district. It remains a mixture of these
> elements.

Ilana's statement is particularly illustrative of how contemporary Jews are able
to locate the urban geography they inhabit in relation to an imagined historical moment of Habsburg pluralism.[24] By going back to Vienna's fin de siècle,
Ilana not only seeks to invoke a privileged moment of Jewish immigration
and assimilation but effectively constitutes her own world in conscious continuation of a Habsburgian topography figured through the ideals of tolerance and integration. In this manner, she emerges as a flaneuse, reveling in
the (imperial) diversity of the contemporary Vienna she encounters when
strolling around certain districts.

If present-day Vienna (in its abstract entirety) can thus stand in metonymic relation to the inclusivist cultural geography of the turn of the century, late-twentieth-century Austrian Jews also locate specific institutions of
Vienna's contemporary, urban topography in explicit relation to a Jewish-
coded moment in late imperial Vienna. Perhaps stereotypically — but for
that fact no less significantly in terms of the strategic deployment of counter-
memory — it is the *Kaffeehaus* that occupies a privileged position in this discursive fixing of Jewish cultural continuities between the fin de siècles. As
such, the abstract institution of the *Kaffeehaus,* the intellectual or literary
coffeehouse, is seen as the embodiment of explicitly Jewish cultural meanings
that could survive *die Stadt ohne Juden,* the city without Jews, thereby serving as a bridge between pre- and postwar Jewish Vienna. Ilana, for example,
invokes the *Kaffeehaus* when she asserts that "there are Jewish continuities in
Vienna; even though Vienna was almost *judenrein,* there still is a continuity."
Sarah — a writer and filmmaker in her forties, whose parents immigrated to
postwar Vienna from present-day Ukraine — echoes this sentiment when she
constructs and locates an explicit link between specifically Jewish contribu-

tions and Austria's cultural scene in the urban space of the *Kaffeehaus*. To her, the history and tradition of Vienna's metropolitan geography both reflect and reproduce a Jewish element: "Jews have played a pivotal role [in Vienna], because they were the ones, who introduced the element of urbanity to this city. The remnants [of this urbanity] are preserved in a few *Kaffeehäuser* and some other spaces that are even more rudimentary."

In order to figure the institution of the *Kaffeehaus* as a transhistorical fixture of Viennese-Jewish existence, such narratives of Jewish counter-memory ultimately recur to a tropological field in which the *Kaffeehaus* occupies the focal point in a discourse of Jewish cultural achievement. In this sense, the *Kaffeehaus* becomes the embodied site of a glorious Jewish cultural tradition, constructed by present-day Viennese Jews not only as the space where Jews exercised the privileges accorded them in the course of emancipation, but also as the very locale that propelled (Jewish) Vienna to the pinnacle of modernity. In evoking the counter-memory of a liberal, humanistic tradition circumscribed by such pillars of respectability as *Kultur* and *Bildung*, the *Kaffeehaus* can thus signify to the cultural capital associated with the Jews' successful transformation to European burghers. How this complex articulation of Jewish distinction *qua Kaffeehaus* is at once constituted historically as a fin-de-siècle phenomenon and located / preserved in contemporary Vienna by way of narrative praxis can be gleaned from this fascinating account offered to me by Ilana:

> Recently, I went to the south of Moravia with a friend, and it was incredible. For political reasons, it is very backwards economically, of course, but what fascinated me immensely was that I saw the same culture, the same food, the same faces, and the same language as in Vienna — and the same goes for Hungary. I have a lot of relatives in Hungary, and when I go there, or when they come to Vienna, I can sense something that makes me incredibly fond of [East-Central Europe] and its way of life. I am not sure whether this is specifically Jewish, but the Jews have certainly brought it to perfection. The Jews have not only adopted this way of life but have cultivated it — cultivated this way of life and made it into a culture. You can see this in literature, in music, some of it even in painting — not only did they work in the *Kaffeehaus*, but this played a major role. And even today, when you go to the smaller *Kaffeehäuser*, where "Chaimowitsch"[25] and company sit, you can see that. That is a form of culture that is manifested there at its most genuine, even if this sounds like a cliché. It is the cliché, but in this case the cliché is the truth. And I don't find any of that in Paris, for example, or London. For me, it is and was a wonderful cultivation of this way of life.

Ultimately, this passage illustrates how present-day Jews can find the continuities of a distinctly Jewish tradition in Vienna's contemporary, urban landscape. At once predicated on the significance of the East-Central European culture areas encompassed by the Habsburg monarchy and the specific ways of life they are supposed to engender, Ilana imagines the Jewish achievement in this sociocultural context as that of a productive and climactic synthesis. Significantly, the cultural work of this synthesis occurred (and occurs) in the distinct urban space of the *Kaffeehaus*, which thus figures as a unique microcosm, embodying and transporting the (Jewish) cultural sensibility that, according to her, remains recognizable in such fields as literature, music, and art. If Ilana specifically excludes such metropolitan spaces as Paris and London from the cultural geography of Jewish *Kaffeehauskultur*, coffeehouse culture, she ultimately suggests how Austrian Jews can locate a unique conception of present-day Vienna within the symbolic landscape demarcated by the counter-memory of the Habsburg monarchy and late imperial Vienna.

If the evocation of historical continuities in Jewish-Viennese existence serves the resistive possibility of positioning affirmative Jewish selves vis-à-vis Austria's anti-Semitic social field, the important narratives of "actual" linkage (centered around such "transhistorical" Jewish tropes as the *Kaffeehaus*) are complemented by even more powerful associations of fantasmatic counter-memory. Enabling the formation of empowering subject positions through a mode of historically embedded transhistorical identification, the fantasmatic ties constructed by present-day Austrian Jews thus function as yet another antidote against a social field that positions Jews on the margins of the cultural order. In the case of Bettina — a fortyish physician of Romanian background — for example, the affirmative relation between the fin de siècle and her Viennese-Jewish identity is imagined and articulated in reference to a counter-memory of literature: "To me, Vienna's Jewish connotation exists primarily in the realm of fantasy. This is how we grew up, with the literature of the turn of the century, and that has stayed with me. It is a part of Vienna and it is a part of me, even though in reality, there might not exist much of it." Such fantasmatic links remain of particular relevance for Austrian Jews of Eastern European background. As Bettina's narrative suggests, in such a familial context, recourse to the fin de siècle and its vision of *Bildung* and cultural efflorescence offered a culturally desirable means of assimilation by vicarious emancipation within the counter-memory of an actively imagined glorious Jewish past. In the conclusion of her account, Bettina examines this process of Jewish-Viennese identity formation by way of fantasmatic association in critical retrospection:

> As a child [in 1950s Vienna], I was enamored by these great stories of turn-of-the-century Vienna, and I believe that it was that seemingly perfect, Jewish, intellectual, pristine world of bourgeois and artistic bliss that was so attractive. This was in contrast to my parents, who seemed Eastern European and un-Austrian. Even though my mother's native language is German, I did not perceive her as Austrian. And my father was even more Eastern

European. He always refused to learn German, and I believe that I had a slight feeling of contempt because of this. Strangely, it was my parents who paid for the books and the theater. It's always the same.

For Sarah — like Bettina, the child of Eastern European immigrants — Jewish counter-memory of the fin de siècle figured similarly in the constitution of a specifically Jewish-Viennese sensitivity. As she puts it, "My entire history" is caught up in "those books that I feel I truly understand — that is Schnitzler or Joseph Roth." In turn, these texts were constitutive of a fantasmatic field, in which Sarah could actively envision a viable Jewish subject position at a historical moment when Austrian hegemonies seemed to preclude its affirmative articulation:

> I believe I started reading these things [in the late 1950s] when I was around ten. In my girlish fantasies, I wanted to live at the turn of the century. I so longed to sit in the *Kaffeehaus* with Schnitzler and all these other people, to have a salon — all these things greatly excited me. I would have loved to have the clothes of the time. I wanted to be surrounded by all these smart men — the fantasies of a young girl. I imagined that this city was a fascinating place and that I played an important role in it.

If Sarah imagined her role in fin-de-siècle Vienna in conjunction with the counter-memorialized cultural efflorescence associated with the historical moment, her successful career as a writer and filmmaker (whose work often addresses specifically Jewish issues) suggests how Austrian Jews could (and can) capitalize on the alternative spatio-temporal modes of identification they are culturally positioned to adopt.

In this manner, Viennese-identified Jews continuously take recourse to the resistive potential of intervening in the ways Jews are figured in present-day Austria — a process that comes to the fore in their narrative practices of counter-memory. While these narratives and the experiences they reflect and (re)constitute are structured within Austria's variously configured social and cultural fields (and thus shaped in relation to deeply rooted and complexly articulated anti-Semitisms), they reveal the crucial dimension of Jews' agency in the cultural constitution of Viennese-Jewish identity in contemporary Austria. Disrupting a seemingly hegemonic field that positions Jews on the margins of the social fabric in order to preserve the semblance of Austria's founding myth, Jews negotiate and affirm their lives through the construction and sustenance of a store of counter-memory that draws its visceral rootedness from alternative geographies and fantasmatic histories.

It is in that sense that contemporary Jews succeed in laying claim to the symbolic capital of fin-de-siècle Vienna, effectively challenging its often cynical instrumentalization at the hands of Austria's nationalized culture industry.[26] Against official constructions of (late-)twentieth-century Viennese and Austrian history and identity as an emanation of an ethnically unmarked cultural efflorescence at the turn of the century, Jewish counter-memory figures late imperial Vienna's high cultural field, along with its contemporary remnants, as a highly localized phenomenon. In this manner, present-day Austrian Jews' constitutive narratives of nationally marginalized identification strategically disrupt the iconic representation of fin-de-siècle Vienna as the cradle of genuine Austrianness, deploying it instead as the privileged site of resistive Jewish identity formation. It is through such subversive practices of Jewish selfhood that present-day Vienna can be sustained as the site of a vibrant (albeit small) Jewish community — a community that lives in the presence of its past, for good.

Notes

This article is an extended and revised version of a piece published under the same title in the *Proceedings of the Fifth Conference of the International Society for the Study of European Ideas (ISSEI)* — CD-ROM (Cambridge: MIT Press). The original analysis was written in the spring of 1996 during a three-month tenure as Junior Fellow at the Internationales Forschungszentrum Kulturwissenschaften (IFK) in Vienna. There, the institute's director, Gotthart Wunberg, and its senior academic secretary, Lutz Musner, enabled me to pursue my work in a most stimulating intellectual environment. For their critical input at various stages of this project, I would like to thank Ruth Wodak, Susan Gal, George Stocking, Jack Kugelmass, Robert Rotenberg, Alaina Lemon, Daphne Berdahl, John Bunzl, and Billy Vaughn. As is common ethnographic practice, all names used in this article are fictitious. This leads to the odd situation that a few rather well-known persons are not explicitly identified. I trust, however, that those who have traveled in Viennese-Jewish circles will recognize them quite readily.

[1.] The original impetus for the reconceptualization of memory as an inherently social phenomenon can, of course, be traced to Maurice Halbwachs's investigations. Maurice Halbwachs, *On Collective Memory*, trans. Lewis Coser (Chicago: U of Chicago P, 1992) and *The Collective Memory* (New York: Harper & Row, 1980).

[2.] The seminal theoretical formulation of contemporary research into history and memory is Pierre Nora's introduction to the three-volume project *Les Lieux de mémoire*. It is reprinted and translated as "Between Memory and History: *Les Lieux de Mémoire*," *Representations* 26 (spring 1989): 7–25; see also Natalie Zemon Davis and Randolph Starn, "Introduction" to the special issue on "Memory and Counter-Memory," *Representations* 26 (spring 1989): 1–6. For two historiographically conservative accounts that preserve the traditional separation of history and memory (albeit in innovative and productive ways), see Jacques Le Goff, *History and Memory*

(New York: Columbia UP, 1992) and Patrick Hutton, *History as an Art of Memory* (Hanover: UP of New England, 1993).

3. Matti Bunzl, "On the Politics and Semantics of Austrian Memory: Vienna's Monument against War and Fascism," *History & Memory* 7, no. 2 (1995): 7–40 and "The City and the Self: Narratives of Spatial Belonging among Austrian Jews," *City & Society* (1996): 50–81, which analyzes some of the empirical material presented in this article in an anthropological context.

4. John Gillis, ed., *Commemorations: The Politics of National Identity* (Princeton, NJ: Princeton UP, 1994); Yael Zerubavel, *Recovered Roots: Collective Memory and the Making of the Israeli Nation* (Chicago: U of Chicago P, 1995); John Bodnar, *Remaking America: Public Memory, Commemoration, and Patriotism in the Twentieth Century* (Princeton, NJ: Princeton UP, 1994); Henry Rousso, *The Vichy Syndrome: History and Memory in France since 1944* (Cambridge, MA: Harvard UP, 1991); Charles Maier, *The Unmasterable Past: History, Holocaust, and German National Identity* (Cambridge, MA: Harvard UP, 1988); Kurt Piehler, *Remembering War the American Way* (Washington, DC: Smithsonian Institution Press, 1995); Richard Handler, *Nationalism and the Politics of Culture* (Madison: U of Wisconsin P, 1988); Ruth Wodak, Florian Menz, Richard Mitten, and Frank Stern, *Die Sprachen der Vergangenheiten: Öffentliches Gedenken in österreichischen und deutschen Medien* (Frankfurt am Main: Suhrkamp, 1994); Meinrad Ziegler and Waltraud Kannonier-Finster, *Österreichisches Gedächtnis: Über Erinnern und Vergessen der NS-Vergangenheit* (Vienna: Böhlau, 1993); Katharina von Ankum, "Victims, Memory, History: Antifascism and the Question of National Identity in East German Narratives after 1990," *History & Memory* 7, no. 2 (1995): 41–69; Israel Gershoni, "Imagining and Reimagining the Past: The Use of History by Egyptian Nationalist Writers," *History & Memory* 4, no. 2 (1992): 5–37.

5. See many of the works cited in footnote 4 as well as James E. Young, *The Texture of Memory: Holocaust Memorials and Meaning* (New Haven, CT: Yale UP, 1993); James E. Young, ed., *The Art of Memory: Holocaust Memorials in History* (New York: Prestel, 1994); Jay Winter, *Sites of Memory, Sites of Mourning: The Great War in European Cultural History* (Cambridge: Cambridge UP, 1995); Andreas Huyssen, *Twilight Memories: Marking Time in a Culture of Amnesia* (New York: Routledge, 1995); Rudy Koshar, *Revisioning History: Film and the Construction of a new Past* (Princeton, NJ: Princeton UP, 1995); Daniel Sherman, *Worthy Monuments: Art Museums and the Politics of Culture in Nineteenth-Century France* (Cambridge, MA: Harvard UP, 1989); Daniel Sherman, ed., *Museum Culture: Histories, Discourses, Spectacles* (New York: Routledge, 1994); Daphne Berdahl, "Voices at the Wall: Discourses of Self, History, and National Identity at the Vietnam Veterans Memorial," *History & Memory* 6, no. 2 (1994): 88–124.

6. Michel Foucault, *Madness and Civilization: A History of Insanity in the Age of Reason*, trans. Richard Howard (New York: Random House, 1973) and *Language, Counter-Memory, Practice: Selected Essays and Interviews*, ed. Donald Bouchard, trans. Donald Bouchard and Sherry Simon (Ithaca, NY: Cornell UP, 1977); see also

Patrick Hutton, *History as an Art of Memory* (Hanover: UP of New England, 1993), ch. 6.

7. Michel Foucault, *Power / Knowledge: Selected Interviews & Other Writings, 1972–1977* (New York: Pantheon, 1980), 141.

8. Michel Foucault, *Discipline & Punish: The Birth of the Prison*, trans. Alan Sheridan (New York: Vintage Books, 1976) and *The History of Sexuality: An Introduction*, trans. Robert Hurley (New York: Vintage Books, 1978). On Foucault's notion of resistance, see David Halperin, *Saint Foucault: Towards a Gay Hagiography* (Oxford: Oxford UP, 1995), esp. 48–56; see also Paul Morrison, "Coffee Table Sex: Robert Mapplethorpe and the Sadomasochism of Everyday Life," *Genders* 11 (fall 1991): 17–36.

9. See Sebastian Meissl, Klaus-Dieter Mulley, and Oliver Rathkolb, eds., *Verdrängte Schuld, verfehlte Sühne: Entnazifizierung in Österreich 1945–1955* (Vienna: Verlag für Geschichte und Politik, 1986); Robert Knight, *"Ich bin dafür die Sache in die Länge zu ziehen": Wortprotokolle der österreichischen Bundesregierung über die Entschädigung der Juden 1945–1952* (Frankfurt am Main: Athenäum, 1988); Brigitte Galanda-Bailer, *"Wiedergutmachung kein Thema: Österreich und die Opfer des Nationalsozialismus* (Vienna: Löcker, 1993).

10. On Schönerer, see Andrew Whiteside, *The Socialism of Fools: Georg von Schönerer and Austrian Pan-Germanism* (Berkeley: U of California P, 1975). On Lueger, see John Boyer, *Political Radicalism in Late Imperial Vienna: Origins of the Christian Social Movement 1848–1897* (Chicago: U of Chicago P, 1981) and *Culture and Political Crisis in Vienna: Christian Socialism in Power, 1897–1918* (Chicago: U of Chicago P, 1995); see also Peter Pulzer, *The Rise of Political Antisemitism in Germany and Austria* (Cambridge, MA: Harvard UP, 1988).

11. See Ruth Beckermann, *Unzugehörig: Österreicher und Juden nach 1945* (Vienna: Löcker, 1989), 71–84; see also Helga Embacher, *Neubeginn ohne Illusionen: Juden in Österreich nach 1945* (Vienna: Picus, 1995).

12. John Bunzl, "Austrian Identity and Antisemitism," *Patterns of Prejudice* 21 (spring 1987): 4.

13. Robert Knight, "'Neutrality' not Sympathy: Jews in Post-War Austria," in *Austrians and Jews in the Twentieth Century*, ed. Robert Wistrich (New York: St. Martin's, 1992), 222.

14. Beckermann, 85–96; see also Knight; see also Embacher.

15. John Bunzl and Bernd Marin, *Antisemitismus in Österreich* (Innsbruck: Inn-Verlag, 1983), 227ff.

16. See Ziegler and Kannonier-Finster.

17. Bunzl and Marin, 227ff.

18. See Richard Mitten, *The Politics of Antisemitism: The Waldheim Phenomenon in Austria* (Boulder, Colo.: Westview, 1992) and "Reflections on the Waldheim Affair," in *Austrians and Jews in the Twentieth Century*; Ruth Wodak, Peter Nowak, Johanna Pelikan, Helmut Gruber, Rudolf de Cillia, and Richard Mitten, *Wir sind*

alle unschuldige Täter: Diskurshistorische Studien zum Nachkriegsantisemitismus (Frankfurt am Main: Suhrkamp, 1990); Ruth Wodak, "The Waldheim Affair and Antisemitic Prejudice in Austrian Public Discourse," *Patterns of Prejudice* 24 (summer-winter 1990): 18–33.

[19.] See Bunzl, "The City and the Self."

[20.] On the national-socialist reign in Austria and the fate of Austrian Jewry, see Gerhard Botz, *Wien, vom "Anschluß" zum Krieg: Nationalsozialistische Machtübernahme und politisch-soziale Umgestaltung am Beispiel der Stadt Wien, 1938/39* (Vienna: Jugend und Volk, 1980) and *Nationalsozialismus in Wien: Machtübernahme und Herrschaftssicherung* (Buchloe: DVO, 1988); see also Herbert Rosenkranz, *Verfolgung und Selbstbehauptung: Die Juden in Österreich 1938–1945* (Vienna: Herold, 1978).

[21.] See Beckermann, 97–106; see also Embacher.

[22.] The passing of the *Matura*, the high school graduation examination taken at age eighteen after twelve years of schooling, is the prerequisite for attending university in Austria.

[23.] Often used to designate Vienna, the term *Weltstadt* not only evokes connotations of worldliness and internationalism but suggests that the city functions as a nexus for transnational concerns. In this regard, Vienna's UN headquarters is a critical reference point, signifying the city's ongoing role as a globally relevant meeting point.

[24.] On the "reality" of Jewish life in fin-de-siècle Vienna from a deliberately anti-nostalgic perspective, see esp. Steven Beller, "The World of Yesterday Revisited: Nostalgia, Memory, and the Jews of Fin-de-siècle Vienna," *Jewish Social Studies* 2 (1996): 37–53.

[25.] In Ilana's narrative, "Chaimowitsch" functions as a generic (Eastern-European) Jewish name.

[26.] For decades, the state of Austria has instrumentalized the cultural luminaries of turn-of-the-century Vienna for the purposes of internal and external propaganda. In such instances, the Jewish backgrounds of many of the figureheads of fin-de-siècle Vienna's cultural efflorescence have either been discounted or downplayed in favor of their identification as exemplars of Austrian cultural excellence. See for example *Austria: Fin de Siècle — First Republic, 1880–1938* (Vienna: Federal Press Service, 1986), part of the series *Austria Documentation*.

NEIL G. JACOBS AND DAGMAR C. G. LORENZ

If I Were King of the Jews:
Germanistik and the *Judaistikfrage*

> Sollten wir beide die Menschheit regieren,
> der Primas die Christen und ich die Juden,
> wir wollten sehen, wer besser fertig würde.
>
> — Bettina von Arnim, "Die Klosterbeere"

T HIS ARTICLE DEALS WITH THE REPRESENTATION of Jewish studies within the field of German literary, cultural, and linguistic studies. Much work in the field of German studies has dealt with, and continues to deal with, Jewish themes. Approximately one millennium of contact and interaction between Germans and Ashkenazic Jews has led to significant areas of mutual influence and overlap in language, literature, culture, and national experience. German studies has an intellectual stake in addressing Jewish concerns. However, the latter are typically appropriated and marginalized within the German context; they are seen in terms of how Ashkenazic Jews and Ashkenazic Jewish civilization do or do not "fit" within German paradigms. There is little that recognizes the internal dynamic of Ashkenazic Jewry, possessing its own centers and margins, which may or may not interact with German centers and margins. The field of Yiddish and Ashkenazic studies, on the other hand, has traditionally addressed that Jewish-internal dynamic. However, the insights from this field have remained largely ignored or misunderstood in German studies. The current article addresses this problem. The study at hand explores manifestations of this "Jewish question" within German Studies, the *Judaistikfrage,* in the realm of textual representation and scholarship and suggests ways of addressing the problems it poses.

Bettina von Arnim, the Romantic poet, positions herself in the short text "Die Klosterbeere" (1808) in a way seemingly sympathetic to the plight of the Jews, illustrated by the example of the Frankfurt ghetto.[1] Von Arnim's persona traverses the Jewish lane, marveling at the children wearing rags, the dark narrow houses, the heat, and the squalor in which the brothers of Nathan the Wise are forced to live. On her way back, she distributes flowers among the Jewish children, since they are the ones to whom Christ says: "Let them come unto me." She hands flowers to the pale young girls in the ghetto so that they can enjoy the smell of the Orient, which emanates from their petals (267). Von Arnim casts herself as the ruler of the Jews and engages in an imaginary controversy with the Christian leadership to demand greater humanity and better treatment for the Jews. Her fantasy as the benefactor and defender of the oppressed stands in stark contrast to the anti-Jewish position proclaimed openly by her husband, Achim von Arnim, at the *Christliche Tischgesellschaft*, an association formed after the demise of the Holy Roman Empire of German Nation *(Heiliges Römisches Reich deutscher Nation)* in opposition to the Napoleonic occupation. However, a comparison between texts on the same subject by German-Jewish authors such as Rahel Varnhagen, Heinrich Heine, or Fanny Lewald shows the problematic aspects of Bettina's philosemitism. A different kind of concern and knowledge is obvious from the works of authors who were raised in a Jewish context and who, regardless of whether they converted or not, remained identified with the fate of their ancestral community. Lewald's description of the Frankfurt ghetto suffices as an illustration:

> Zuletzt dann die Judengasse! Und wären alle Machthabenden der Welt durch die Revolutionen dieses Jahres in Leid und Schmerz versenkt worden, so würden sie mit ihren Tränen noch lange nicht die Schmerzentränen aufwiegen, welche jenes unglückliche Volk in zweitausendjähriger Knechtschaft, in schmachvoller Unterdrückung vergossen hat. Als wir durch die lange, schmale Judengasse gingen, als ich Gehöfte dieser turmhohen Häuser sah, welche aneinander- und ineinandergeklebt sind wie die Zellen eines Bienenstockes, und als ich mir dachte, hier hat Börne seine Jugend verlebt, hier hat man ihn allabendlich wie einen Verbrecher eingesperrt, und hier hat man sich geweigert, das Tor zu öffnen, selbst bei Feuersbrünsten, schauderte ich vor dem unmenschlichen Treiben der oft gepriesenen Vorzeit. ... Ja, es waren Börne und Heine, welche seit der Julirevolution und schon früher den Deutschen zuriefen: "Wir sind Knechte und Ihr mit uns!"[2]

Lewald's commitment and identification, no less than the mixture of familiarity and embarrassed detachment with which Heinrich Heine in *Der Rabbi von Bacherach* (written 1824/25, published 1840, "The Rabbi of Bacherach") portrays the ghetto, make for different reading than the descriptions of ghetto life by Gentile authors.

Rather than attempting yet another analysis of anti-Semitism, the following discusses the representation of Jewish culture from the point of view of Gentile literature and scholarship by ostensibly neutral or even well-intentioned authors. As the previously mentioned example suggests, German literary writers use Jewish themes and characters to their own ends, whereas *Germanistik,* or German studies, as a discipline deals with Jewish or Jewish studies topics for the sake of its own agenda, thereby disallowing for the discussion of Jewish concerns in their own right. Martin Luther's assertion in "Von den Juden und ihren Lügen" (1890),[3] claiming that Jewish religious practices serve the sole purpose of offending Jesus Christ, is a blatant example of the blind spots that prevent a supposed expert knowledgeable in Hebrew from properly interpreting Judaism and Jewish tradition. Biases and misunderstandings have traditionally skewed the description of Jewish phenomena in Gentile texts. The attempt to analyze Yiddish, a Jewish language, with paradigms and tools appropriate to German, with German as the norm against which Yiddish characteristics are measured as deviations, is no less limited in its scope than the discussion of Jewish phenomena by way of theories, cultural and literary, that claim for Christian German culture, religious and secular, a position at the cutting edge of world history. Thus, Hegel's and Fichte's philosophy of history provided decisive concepts for nineteenth-century German thought, including the fledgling field of Germanistik, a product of Romanticism and newly awakened patriotism.[4] "Der in der preußischen Staatseinheit lebende und wirkende Deutsche wird nur wollen und wirken, daß in dieser Staatseinheit zunächst und am allervollendetsten der deutsche Nationalcharacter hervortrete, daß derselbe von hier aus sich verbreite über die verwandten deutschen Stämme und von diesen aus erst, wie dies denn auch ohne alles sein Wollen von selbst also erfolgen wird, allmählich über die ganze Menschheit,"[5] writes Fichte, an opponent of Enlightenment cosmopolitanism.

Germanistik and German philology, rooted in German Idealism and Romanticism, have set paradigms and developed tools that subordinate European Jewish culture and the European Jewish language, Yiddish, to the German culture and language. The German-centered discourses, which have traditionally provided the basis within Germanistik for the study of Ashkenazic culture, deny by their very structure and objectives the autonomy of Ashkenazic phenomena and overlook their distinct cultural and linguistic codes and processes.[6] The same is true for the representation of Jewish life and characters in German literature and scholarship. With the tacit assumption of German agency and the implied Jewish object status, it is not surprising that authors introducing Jewish characters provided glimpses of a Jewish world constructed to fit their own goals and agendas (as is the case with Lessing's *Nathan* [1779], Stifter's *Abdias* [1843], Freytag's *Soll und Haben* [1855, "Debit and Credit"]), or they dispensed with the representation of a larger Jewish cultural context altogether (Grillparzer's *Die Jüdin von Toledo* [1872, "The Jewess of Toledo"] Fontane's *Unwiederbringlich* [1891, "Beyond Recall"]). Similarly, the attitudes toward Jews and Jewish culture, anti-Semitism, and the Holocaust that encourage the casting of non-Jews as agents /

perpetrators and that of Jews as objects / victims also dominate the field of Judaica in German-speaking countries.

The following examples of Jewish literary figures illustrate the problematic representation of Jews in German discourse. These texts must be interpreted both as historical documents and cultural paradigms. One recurring pattern is the impossibility of a sustained Jewish and Gentile coexistence, signaled by the barrenness of Jewish male characters: Lessing's Nathan, Stifter's Abdias, and Freytag's "noble Jew" Bernhard die childless. So do young Jewish women, including Grillparzer's Rahel, Stifter's Ditha, and Hebbel's Mariamne. Judging by the character of Fontane's *femme fatale* Ebba, her becoming a mother also seems unlikely. Another pattern is that of passivity and helplessness, most eloquently expressed by the figure of the only Jew in Bruno Apitz's Buchenwald novel *Nackt unter Wölfen* (1958, "Naked among Wolves"), a boy small enough to be handed from one heroic Gentile protector to the next.[7] The tendency to configure Jews as women and children in post-Shoah literature, the tremendous popularity of Anne Frank as opposed to the general ignorance about Jewish resistance fighters such as the Auschwitz prisoner Mala Zimmetbaum,[8] and the continued negative stereotyping of Jewish males in the works of Günter Grass, Albrecht Goes, and Gerhard Zwerenz are indicative of the difficulty of reconsidering and reshaping cognitive and discursive practices even when presented with the reality of the Shoah.

In contrast, in the postwar works by Jewish and Jewish-identified authors (e.g., Ilse Aichinger, Irene Dische), similar fates and characters are represented in such a way as to expose not only the Nazi crimes and the widespread popularity of the Nazi movement and the Nazi legacy (Peter Weiss, Edgar Hilsenrath, Elfriede Jelinek, Jurek Becker), but also to show resistance and survival strategies on the part of the Jewish community and persecuted individuals (Ilse Aichinger, Anna Seghers, Cordelia Edvardson, Kitty Hart). They also write about the situation of Jews living in Germany and Austria today (Robert Schindel, Nadia Seelich, Ruth Beckermann, Jurek Becker, Ester Dischereit, Irene Dische). These examples reveal a Jewish reality that is inaccessible when approached with the representational tools and the ideological assumptions generally made by Gentile writers.

The "deep moat" that, according to Hans Thalberg, separates Gentile and Jewish perceptions and discourses[9] is noticeable already in the emancipation debate of the Enlightenment, conducted in the spirit of secular progress. It is important to note that the concepts of *Aufklärung* and *Haskole* are by no means synonymous; the former term refers to a broad-based philosophical and social movement in Christian Europe, which spread from England and France to the German-speaking sphere. The term *Haskole* signifies a specifically Jewish reaction to a reality impossible to avoid. In that sense, the

Haskole must be interpreted as a strategy designed to ensure the survival of the Ashkenazic world in the modern era while preserving its internal structures as much as possible. Moses Mendelssohn, its most prominent exponent, is paradigmatic of what *Haskole* was designed to achieve. He participated fully in German-speaking culture and expected educated Jews to do likewise. At the same time, he did not convert and adhered to Jewish traditions. His translation of the Bible into German transcribed in Hebrew letters so as to facilitate Yiddish speakers' transition into the majority language preserves the content and spirit of Judaism while transposing it into a new medium, which Mendelssohn considered the language of the future. Mendelssohn's translation prepares Ashkenazic Jews for coexistence with the coterritorial German-speaking Christians, for an era of tolerance rather than toleration. Joshua Fishman differentiates between *Haskole* in Western and Eastern Europe.[10] It was a strategy for adaptation and integration in the West and for national consolidation in the East.

Christian von Dohm's treatise *Über die bürgerliche Verbesserung der Juden* (1783, "Concerning the Amelioration of the Civil Status of the Jews"), on the other hand, has as its ultimate goal the elimination of Jewish culture by peaceful means. Portraying life in the ghettos in the bleakest terms possible, as a social and spiritual deformity, he explains Jewish culture as a social problem caused by Gentile oppression. He supports the idea of Jewish emancipation because in his mind, it will eventually bring about the assimilation and absorption of the minority into the German majority. By characterizing Jewish culture this way, von Dohm turns a blind eye to Jewish religious life, the national aspects of Ashkenazic Jewry, and European Jewish history which, as Heine illustrates in *Der Rabbi von Bacherach*, began during the Roman Empire prior to any manifestation of a German nation. He also ignores the structures and institutions of the existing Jewish communities and the collective will of their constituents.

Rather than being the exception, von Dohm represents a trend among even the best-intentioned German writers — even in Lessing the absence of a specific Jewish cultural code both in *Die Juden* (1749, "The Jews") and in *Nathan* (1779) is striking. The same tendencies observed in von Dohm are apparent in Emperor Joseph II's "Moravian Toleration Edict" (1782), which does increase the civilian rights of Jews while cautioning: "Our Highest Intention is in no way to increase the number of Jewish believers in Our Patrimonial Margravate through this new ordinance, or to attract foreigners without important reasons and special merit."[11]

Contrary to the objectifying Gentile perspective on Jewish society, the portrayal of the Ashkenazic world in the memoirs of Glikl Hamil, written between 1690/91 and 1719[12] reveals the inner consistency of pre-*Haskole* Jewish culture. Glikl's geography is that of a seventeenth-century Jew who considers the supranationality of the Ashkenazic sphere to be the norm. She did not view the Jews as a minority; rather, she identified with an internal homeland that stretched from Russia to the Netherlands, with Yiddish as its indigenous language. Within this domain, families and communities shared a common religion, lifestyle, and culture. For Hamil, the boundaries of Christian countries were mere trade and tax barriers. Her notion of history is also exclusively Jewish. She takes notice of Gentile history and activities only as they affect Jewish life — pogroms and wars — but does not even mention the Thirty Years' War, the most devastating Christian religious war, whose aftermath overshadowed Europe for many decades. Instead, she discusses the exodus of the Vilna Jews from Poland in 1648, the Cossack rebellions, and the settlement of a group of survivors in Hamburg.[13] Hamil meets Gentiles with the attitude of a foreigner: secure in her own identity, but with caution, aware of her vulnerability as a Jew. Each time an encounter with Christians ends without her or her family being mistreated, she is relieved. Topics such as intermarriage and integration are not even an issue. Hamil does not imagine herself to be German, nor does she want to be. She writes in the languages of Ashkenazic Jewry: Yiddish with Hebrew prayers and benedictions interspersed;[14] and she considers her language to be the linguistic standard rather than a deviation from German. This point of view prevailed among Jews well into the eighteenth century. Crises of identity such as the ones experienced by Jewish intellectuals in the post-Enlightenment era reflect a dilemma caused by the conflicting paradigms arising from the emancipation debates and the transition from the Yiddish realm into the German-speaking sphere, undertaken by Jews in Central Europe, individually and as communities. Note, however, that a large segment of the Jewish population did not aspire to assimilation into the surrounding German-speaking cultures. Indeed, the late eighteenth and early to mid-nineteenth century represents a decisive turning point in Jewish cultural and linguistic identity, in which we see both the shift of most German Jews from Yiddish to German and the emergence of a modern Standard Yiddish national language in Eastern Europe.

As mentioned earlier, Mendelssohn's translation of the Bible into German (1783), not Yiddish, was nevertheless German, albeit printed in the Jewish alphabet, the only script the Jewish masses could read. However, it is not only a matter of alphabets. Mendelssohn's translation of the Psalms[15] — again German in Jewish letters — includes a word list explaining the meanings of difficult German words for the still Yiddish-speaking readership.[16] One Maskil — a Jewish adherent of the Enlightenment — of the times criticizes a rival for giving sermons in German, a language inaccessible to the majority of the Jewish congregants.[17]

The first association devoted to the study of Jewish culture and science *(Verein für Cultur und Wissenschaft der Juden)* was formed in 1819 in the wake of the violent anti-Jewish "Hep-Hep" riots, instigated by German intellectuals, professors, and students. The Jewish attempts to assess and represent Jewish culture to German-speaking Jews and the Gentile public, the expansion of the reform movement, and the founding of temples such as the Vienna *Stadttempel* (1826), as well as texts such as Heine's fragmentary historical Jewish Bildungsroman, the educational novel, *Der Rabbi von Bacherach* and Leopold Zunz's publication of *Die Gottesdienstlichen Vorträge der Juden* (1832, "The Sermons of the Jews during Religious Service") have both a Jewish-internal and an externally directed function.

The following section traces the development of a coherent Ashkenazic-internal perspective in Yiddish scholarship. This perspective is largely ignored in Germanistik, yet the insights are crucial and fundamental. The section outlines the history of Yiddish studies and the evolution of Yiddish studies from an exocentric to an endocentric enterprise,[18] and places the Ashkenazic perspective in its European modern context.

As discussed in Ber Borokhov (1913)[19] and Max Weinreich (1993 [1923]),[20] and outlined in Dovid Katz (1986),[21] the main contours of the history of scholarly interest in Yiddish can be drawn as follows:

1. Christian Semitists of the sixteenth and seventeenth centuries who wrote grammars of Hebrew (written in Latin) and included appendices on Yiddish. These authors saw Yiddish as a "sideline to Hebrew studies" or "a bridge to Hebrew."[22]

2. Christian authors of self-instructional handbooks of Yiddish (written in German). These handbooks served business purposes and contained practical information on specialized terms used, for example, in the horse and cattle trade, the numerical value of Hebrew letters, and so forth.

3. Missionaries and their teachers. Here, the goal was the learning of Yiddish as a means of converting Jews to Christianity.

4. Anti-Semitic works of the eighteenth and nineteenth centuries.

5. Criminological research, a by-product of the description of thieves' cant and other marginal speech varieties; these speech varieties often contained significant Hebrew / Aramaic-origin lexical components.

6. Beginnings of Yiddish studies for its own sake.

Yiddish studies evolved from an exocentric to an endocentric enterprise. Initially, the interest is not in Yiddish, but in Hebrew; Yiddish comes into the picture only secondarily. Then, there arose a utilitarian interest in Yiddish itself, in which the German sought something from the Jew. Then, Yiddish was used as a tool to achieve other desired ends, namely, the abstract representation of groups / the "other." Eventually, Yiddish came to be a focus of study for its own sake. However, even this last point can be subdivided. The first substage involved establishing the value of Yiddish linguistic research as having intrinsic merit. Katz discusses the work of Philipp Mansch (1888–1890) as the missing link. Mansch set the stage for looking at Yiddish as a self-contained linguistic system. Shortly thereafter, we see the work of Saineanu and Landau.[23] Saineanu showed that the German component of Yiddish traces back to Middle High German sources. Thus, Yiddish was no longer to be evaluated in terms of New High German. Landau moved discussion of Yiddish even further away from normative German, showing that the German component in Yiddish traces back to Middle High German dialect sources, and not to canonic or normative Middle High German.

Modern Yiddish linguistics evolved further from an enterprise dependent on German philology as a point of departure to one which uses Yiddish as the point of departure, with German only as an external reference point. Gabriele Strauch compares two works (written in German) dealing with Yiddish: Jacob Gerzon's *Die jüdisch-deutsche Sprache* (1902, "The Jewish-German Language") and Jechiel Bin-Nun's *Jiddisch und die deutschen Mundarten* (1936, translated as "Yiddish and the German Dialects," 1973).[24] In Gerzon's work, the rationale for dealing with Yiddish is that Yiddish is seen as constituting an authentic German dialect. Thirty-four years later, the rationale had changed: Bin-Nun sees Yiddish as an autonomous language. In between lies much development of a national model for Ashkenazic Jewry. This Yiddish-based nationalism had begun in the nineteenth century; for instance, with Sholem Aleykhem's call for a national literature in 1889.[25] However, the early twentieth century marked the blossoming of the Yiddishist national model on several fronts: the pre–First World War An-ski ethnographic expedition, the development in the 1920s of normative and research academies (the YIVO in Vilne and the academies in Minsk and Kiev), the canonization of a Yiddish-based school curriculum in the 1920s by the Central Jewish School Organization of Poland was adopted as normative for the Yiddishists in Lithuania and Latvia as well. German-speaking Jewish authors rediscovered and reassessed East European Jewish culture and the Yiddish language at approximately the same time. Works such as Martin Buber's *The Legend of the Baal Shem* (1907), Arnold Zweig's *Das ostjüdische Antlitz* (1919, "The East European Jewish Face") with lithographs by Hermann Struck, Alfred Döblin's *Reise in Polen* (1926, "A Journey in Poland"), and Joseph Roth's *Juden auf Wanderschaft* (1927, "Jews en Route") represent different ways in which assimilated Jews position themselves vis-à-vis European Jewish history and the Yiddish language, and how they use them as a background for configuring their own identity in religious, spiritual, socio-logical, cultural, and historical terms.[26]

Generally, the linguistic atlas serves a nationalist agenda; it shows clearly that the folk language possesses a natural linguistic topography and is thus an organic, rooted part of the land. The French and German versions of nine-teenth-century nationalism spurred production of their respective linguistic atlases. As the national model spread to Eastern Europe, and as peoples in Eastern Europe were concerned with demonstrating their autonomous and distinct peoplehood, linguistic-atlas projects were undertaken there as well. The first linguistic atlas produced among all the nationalities of the newly formed Soviet Union was the Yiddish one.[27]

Furthermore, several language standardization movements took place during the period of the late nineteenth and early twentieth centuries. The formation of a canonized standard language was part of a national concern. Indeed, the 1908 Tshernovits conference was convened to address the issue of what is the national language of the Jews. Borokhov calls Yiddish philol-ogy a national responsibility.[28] The Ashkenazic / Yiddishist agenda was Jew-ish-internal rather than an agenda of a minority or the subset of coterritorial nation-states (e.g., Poles, Lithuanians, etc.).[29]

The question of perspective or approach to the phenomena under inves-tigation is crucial. In his discussion of changes in written Yiddish during the modern period (approximately the last 150 years), as well as the rise of a standard literary spoken language, Fishman makes an important distinction between external (exocentric) and internal (endocentric) causation of change: "The usual explanatory assumption with respect to changes in Yid-dish as with respect to change in other politically unprotected fusion lan-guages is an exocentric one."[30] Fishman shows that the changes in Yiddish resulted from endocentric causations according to Ashkenazic-internal social and sociolinguistic dynamics.

Standard literary spoken Yiddish arose in the context of the emergence of a secular sector in Jewish life. Fishman's distinction between exocentric and endocentric continues the basic line of reasoning of Max Weinreich's paper "The reality of Jewishness vs. the Ghetto Myth: The Sociolinguistic Roots of Yiddish."[31] Weinreich debunks the ghetto myth, which sees Yiddish as having arisen out of externally imposed factors. In Yiddish, we find present a combi-nation of features not found in any single German dialect. In the exocentric view, this is attributed to an externally imposed ghettoization of Jews in Germany. This ghettoization forced together Jews from various German re-gions, supposedly speaking the respective German dialects. Only then did Yiddish arise as the result of externally imposed circumstances. Once again, the German is the agent, the Jew is the object.

Weinreich argues, rather, that Yiddish origins are to be seen as the result of Ashkenazic-Jewish internal processes. He shows that early on, Jews sought the right to live in collective, connected communities, where they could continue a communal life with autonomous structures. The paths of linguistic development in Yiddish were shaped primarily by internal factors in the Jewish speech community and only secondarily by contact with the external German speech community. In Weinreich's terms, Jewish culture is to be seen on Jewish terms, not in terms of general culture plus a Jewish additive. Much of Weinreich's Yiddishist agenda can be seen on this background; he sought to position Yiddish culture generally, and Yiddish language particularly, as distinct and autonomous. While acknowledging the connections to Middle High German, Weinreich develops the fusion model, which sees Yiddish grammar as an internally coherent dynamic.

Neil Jacobs distinguishes between germanocentric and yiddocentric views of Yiddish, and claims for Yiddish studies not only a center, but the margins as well.[32] Crucial to the discussion is the consideration of Jewish ethnolects of German. Traditionally, the germanocentric view saw both Yiddish and Jewish German as marginal variations of German and failed to systematically differentiate between the two. Thus, Florian Coulmas, in an otherwise excellent discussion of German nationalism and language, refers to the Jewish targets of Nazi genocide as German speakers rather than as speakers of Yiddish.[33] In the yiddocentric view, German-Jewish speech arose via a language shift from Yiddish to German and is evaluated along a continuum whose end points are both Yiddish and German. Using Yiddish as the point of departure, Jewish ethnolects of German are viewed from the context of Yiddish.

Max Weinreich, perhaps the pivotal figure in the Yiddishist national model in academe, received his doctoral training (Ph.D. 1923) in Marburg, the seat (to this day) of the German linguistic atlas project.[34] Thus, he was trained in a philological tradition intimately linked to the nineteenth-century German national agenda. Seeing clearly the German attempts at self-definition, Weinreich endeavored to articulate and define the distinctness of Yiddish language and Ashkenazic culture. Thus, for example, he was actively concerned with defining the boundaries of "authentic" Yiddish vis-à-vis the heavy usage of New High German loan words current in popular speech of the nineteenth and early twentieth centuries.[35]

The Ashkenazic / Yiddish national model was autonomous, but it did not arise in a vacuum. Many of the markers of Yiddishist nationalism reflect similar or identical developments among coterritorial peoples: normative academies, standardized orthography, linguistic atlases, the development of a national literature, and so forth. The Yiddish national model arose in the context of a European Zeitgeist in which the other peoples of Europe sought to define themselves as nations.

Endeavors to forge cohesive national identities produced a general concern about authenticity and legitimization. In the German-speaking sphere, this was the case after the collapse of the Holy Roman Empire of German Nation (1806/7), which necessitated a redefinition of Germanness. Achim v. Arnim's and Clemens Brentano's collection of folk songs, *Des Knaben Wunderhorn* (1806–8, "The Youth's Magic Horn"), the Grimm Brothers' *Kinder- und Hausmärchen* (1812–15, translated as *The Complete Fairy Tales of the Brothers Grimm*, 1987) as well as their *Deutsches Wörterbuch* (1852–1961, "German Lexicon"), as in fact the formation of Germanistik as a discipline are understood in this context as a quest for linguistic, cultural, and ethnic cohesion. The sense of Germanness taking shape in the nineteenth century was elicited by artifacts, architecture, and the arts, just to mention the construction of statues and monuments, the presentation of original, but artfully reshaped literary documents such as the *Nibelungenlied (Song of the Nibelungs)*, medieval courtly poetry and epics, the reconstruction of historical languages, including Old and Middle High German, Wagner's operas, as well as a growing museum culture demonstrating the superiority of European, particularly German, culture. In short, German cultural identity in the modern sense was based on the reconstruction and construction of linguistic and cultural traditions extending from Arminius the Cheruscan, better-known as Hermann the German, to Bismarck. Jewishness as conceived by German discourses is an integral part of this construction: representing the other, the contrast and enemy image, it was and, to a certain extent, continues to be a necessary foil for German national identity and an added factor in its consolidation. The German discourse on Jewish phenomena is itself an artifact. No less that the Orientalist fantasies examined by Edward Said, it is used for specific cultural and ideological purposes. Within the German agenda, the use of Jewish phenomena can be a German garnish on a German plate. This is not in itself invalid; however, it must be recognized for what it is.

As discussed here, within Yiddish and Ashkenazic studies, an autonomous scholarly tradition has established itself over the last several centuries. Clearly, it is time for Germanistik to avail itself of and profit from the insights and perspectives of its sister discipline. What we are calling for is a reasoned approach that recognizes multiple causations where internal and external factors interact regularly and crucially.

Notes

[1] Bettina von Arnim, "Die Klosterbeere. Zum Andenken an die Frankfurter Judengasse," in *Werke und Briefe*, vol. 3 (Cologne: Bartmann, 1959), 263–407. Page references to this work are contained parenthetically in the text.

[2] Fanny Lewald, *Erinnerungen aus dem Jahre 1848*, ed. Dietrich Schaefer (Frankfurt am Main: Insel, 1969), 128–29.

[3] Martin Luther, "Von den Juden und ihren Lügen," in *Luthers Sämtliche Schriften*, ed. Johann Georg Walch (St. Louis, MO: Lutherischer Concordia-Verlag, 1890), 1989.

[4] "Weil in der europäischen Natur ein vereinzelter Typus nicht so hervortritt wie in den andern Weltteilen, so ist hier auch der allgemeinere Mensch. ... Der europäische Staat kann wahrhaft europäischer Staat nur sein, wenn er mit dem Meere zusammenhängt. Im Meere liegt das ganz eigentümliche Hinaus, das dem asiatischen Leben fehlt, das Hinaus des Lebens über sich selbst. Das Prinzip der Freiheit der einzelnen Person ist dadurch dem europäischen Staatsleben geworden." Georg Friedrich Wilhelm Hegel, "Die philosophische Weltgeschichte," in *Sämtliche Werke. Neue kritische Ausgabe*, vol. 18A, ed. Johannes Hoffmeister (Hamburg: Felix Meiner, 1952), 240.

[5] Johann Gottlieb Fichte, *Über patriotische Erziehung. Pädagogische Schriften und Reden*, ed. Heinz Schuffenhauer (Berlin: Volk und Wissen Volkseigener Verlag, 1960), 61.

[6] See Max Weinreich, "The Reality of Jewishness vs. the Ghetto Myth: The Sociolinguistic Roots of Yiddish," in *To Honor Roman Jakobson*, vol. 3 (The Hague: Mouton, 1967), 2199–2211.

[7] See Ruth Klüger, "Gibt es ein 'Judenproblem' in der deutschen Nachkriegsliteratur?" in *Katastrophen. Über deutsche Literatur* (Göttingen: Wallstein, 1994), 9–39.

[8] Ingrid Strobl, "Vergessene Heldinnen. Jüdische Frauen im Widerstand," in *Das Feld des Vergessens. Jüdischer Widerstand und deutsche "Vergangenheitsbewältigung"* (Berlin: Edition ID-Archiv, 1994), 45.

[9] Hans J. Thalberg, *Von der Kunst, Österreicher zu sein* (Vienna: Böhlau, 1984).

[10] Joshua Fishman, "'Nothing New under the Sun': A Case Study of Alternatives in Language and Ethnocultural Identity," in *Yiddish: Turning to Life*, ed. Joshua Fishman (Amsterdam: John Benjamins, 1991), 40.

[11] Emperor Joseph II, "The Moravian Toleration Edict," in *The Jews of Bohemia and Moravia. A Historical Reader*, ed. Wilma Abeles Iggers (Detroit: Wayne State UP, 1992), 48–49.

[12] Glickel von Hameln, *Denkwürdigkeiten*, trans. Konrad Feilchenfeldt (Berlin: Jüdischer Verlag, 1913). Glückl von Hameln, *Die Memoiren der Glückl von*

Hameln, ed. Viola Roggenkamp (Weinheim: Belz / Athenäum, 1994). Dorothy Bilik, "The Memoirs of Glikl of Hameln: The Archeology of the Test," *Yiddish* 8 (1992): 5–21.

13. Glückel von Hameln, *Denkwürdigkeiten* (Darmstadt: Darmstädter Blätter, 1979), 30.

14. Alfred Landau, "Die Sprache der Memoiren Glückels von Hameln," *Mitteilungen zur jüdischen Volkskunde* 7 (1901): 20–68.

15. Moses Mendelssohn, *Sefer zemirot yisrael* (Offenbach: Tsevi Hirsh u-veno Avraham Shpits, 1804–5).

16. Steven Lowenstein, "The Yiddish Written Word in Nineteenth-Century Germany," *Leo Baeck Institute Yearbook* 24 (1979): 179–92.

17. David Sorkin, *The Transformation of German Jewry, 1780–1840* (New York: Oxford UP, 1987).

18. Fishman, 203.

19 Ber Borokhov, "Di oyfgabn fun der yidisher filologye," in *Der pinkes,* ed. Sh. Niger (Vilna, 1913), 1–22.

20 Max Weinreich, *Geschichte der jiddischen Sprachforschung,* ed. Jerold C. Frakes (Atlanta, GA: Scholar's Press, 1993 [=*South Florida Studies in the History of Judaism* 27. This is the critical edition of Weinreich's Marburg dissertation, *Studien zur Geschichte und dialektischen Gliederung der jiddischen Sprache. Erster Teil: Geschichte und gegenwärtiger Stand der jiddischen Sprachforschung.*])

21. Dovid Katz, "On Yiddish, in Yiddish, and for Yiddish: 500 Years of Yiddish Scholarship," in *Identity and Ethos: A Festschrift for Sol Liptzin on the Occasion of his 85th Birthday,* ed. Mark H. Gelber (New York: Peter Lang, 1986), 23–36.

22. Ibid., 23–24.

23. M. Lazar Saineanu, *Studiu dialectologic asupra graiului evreo-german* (Bucharest: E. Wiegand, 1889); see also Alfred Landau, "Das Deminitivum der galizisch-jüdischen Mundart: Ein Capitel aus der jüdisch-deutschen Grammatik," in *Deutsche Mundarten,* vol. 1 (Wiesbaden: Dr. Martin Sandig, 1895), 46–58.

24. Gabriele Strauch, "Methodologies and Ideologies: The Historical Relationship of German Studies to Yiddish," in *Studies in Yiddish Linguistics,* ed. Paul Wexler (Tübingern: Niemeyer, 1990), 83–100; see also Jechiel Bin-Nun, *Jiddisch und die deutschen Mundarten* (Tübingen: Max Niemeyer, 1973); see also Jacob Gerzon, *Die jüdisch-deutsche Sprache. Eine grammatisch-lexikalische Untersuchung ihres deutschen Grundbestandes* (Cologne: Salm, 1902).

25. Sholem-Aleykhem [Sh. Rabinovitsh], "A briv tsu a gutn fraynd," in *Di yidishe folk-biblyotek,* vol. 2 (Kiev: Druk fun Yankev Sheftil, 1889), 304–10; see also Sholem-Aleykhem [Sh. Rabinovitsh], *Shomers mishpet* (Barditshev: Druk fun Yankev Sheftil, 1888).

26. Martin Buber, *Die Chassidischen Bücher* (Berlin: Schocken, 1927); Alfred Döblin, *Reise in Polen* (Freiburg: Walter, 1968); Martin Buber, *Die Legende des Baalschem,*

trans. *The Legend of Baal-Shem* (New York: Schocken, 1969); Joseph Roth, *Juden auf Wanderschaft* (Cologne: Kiepenheuer & Witsch, 1976); Arnold Zweig, *Das ostjüdische Antlitz* (Wiesbaden: Fourier, 1988).

[27.] L. Vilenkin, *Yidisher sprakhatles fun sovetn-farband* (Minsk: Vaysrusishe visnshaft-akademye-Yidisher sektor, 1931).

[28.] Borokhov, 1–22.

[29.] So was the Jewish criticism directed against the European *galut*. Examining the Zionist debate about Hebrew in the early 1900s, Berkowitz describes the role of the German language as crucial, because it "provided a cultural tie to the largely Yiddish-speaking Jewish masses" (109), but even from a Zionist point of view critical of the Ashkenazic history associated with Yiddish, it had to be admitted that Yiddish represented the reality as opposed to Hebrew, which was interpreted as a reflection of the "ancient spirit" (111). Michael Berkowitz, "The Debate about Hebrew, in German: The *Kulturfrage* in the Zionist Congresses, 1897–1914," in *Insiders and Outsiders. Jewish and Gentile Culture in Germany and Austria,* ed. Dagmar C. G. Lorenz and Gabriele Weinberger (Detroit: Wayne State UP, 1994), 109–15.

[30.] Fishman, 203.

[31.] See Weinreich, "The Reality of Jewishness vs. the Ghetto Myth."

[32.] Neil Jacobs, "Zentrum und Peripherie im Jiddischen," paper delivered at the Ninth World Congress of the Internationale Vereinigung für Germanische Sprach- und Literaturwissenschaft, Univ. of Vancouver, British Columbia, Aug. 13–19, 1995.

[33.] Florian Coulmas, "Germanness: Language and Nation," in *The German Language and the Real World: Sociolinguistic, Cultural, and Pragmatic Perspectives on Contemporary German,* ed. Patrick Stevenson (Oxford: Clarendon, 1995), 55–68.

[34.] Ferdinand Wrede, *Deutscher Sprachatlas, auf Grund des von Georg Wenker begründeten Sprachatlas des Deutschen Reiches, und mit Einschluß von Luxemburg … unter Leitung von Ferdinand Wrede* (Marburt: Elwert, 1926–56).

[35.] Max Weinreich, "Daytshmerish toyg nit," *Yidish far ale* 1 (1938): 97–106.

RENATE S. POSTHOFEN

Of Inclusions and Exclusions:
Austrian Identity Reconsidered

THIS ARTICLE WILL TOUCH UPON A VARIETY of concepts and ideas that are part of the shifting paradigms so characteristic of the formation of a "New Europe" at the turn of yet another century, with a specific focus on Austria. As Jacques Le Rider points out in his analysis of the last Viennese fin de siècle,[1] the artistic questioning of traditional principles and the reasoning about the position of modern art between democratizing principles and elitist ideas appear now as the critical consciousness of those crises that were caused by the process of modernization itself.[2] The representational function of the present fin de siècle — in transition from the twentieth to the twenty-first century — within its European context then would be to critique "modernity" and to prepare and possibly rewrite its reconstruction in a variety of multidisciplinary layers. Hence, Austrian cultural politics could act as an emerging catalyst and integral element in redesigning its cultural heritage for the future by inviting and consciously including more multicultural and progressive voices to participate in the reconfiguration of its national self-representation.[3] Attempts in this direction have been made since the end of the war in otherwise conservative journals such as *Literatur und Kritik* ("Literature and Criticism") and *Wort in der Zeit* ("Word in Time"). Authors from Eastern Europe, that is, from the former Habsburg territories, were regularly included. Yet, the public impact was not significant.

One structural distinction that is central to the process of change and transition as such is the notion of a public and private sphere. It is here that every member of a community, every person crosses the boundaries between identifying her- / himself as an individual and a member of a group.[4] It is the threshold between the two categories and the margin between the individual as a private or public representative of any given group — these overlapping elements — that are of interest. In my analysis, I will first look at public representations of the Austrian nation in its historical and current contexts as they reflect their own changing cultural self-understanding and promotion thereof. Second, I will introduce a fictional text, Robert Menasse's novel

Schubumkehr (1995, "Inversion of Power") as an additional source that constitutes for me the individual testimony of one writer's private sphere. In a final analysis, I will demonstrate how the private and the public, as categories, are very much interdependent and form a powerful alliance to constitute such concepts as identity and self, the known and the unknown, home and abroad.

The German promotion of a national identity based on the Prussian version of the new foundation of the German Empire in 1871, the "'kleindeutsche' Lösung," excluded Austria from the "German Federation" in 1866. The result of this political decision prompted the writer Franz Grillparzer, one of Austria's national icons, to lament: "Ihr glaubt, Ihr habt ein Reich geboren, und habt doch nur ein Volk zerstört."[5] According to Rudolf Burger, it is the inversion of this "trauma of exclusion," the "Ausschluß," dating back to 1866–1871 that constitutes the dialectic tension between what was to be termed the "annexation of Austria by the Nazis" in 1938, also called the "Anschluß."[6]

Austria's integration into the European Union in 1995 seems to have ended the psychological trauma of exclusion as well as the fear of annexation[7] within its European context and has, according to Burger, conclusively neutralized any feelings of anxiety regarding either possibility.[8] Thus, the process of Austria's own understanding as a European nation with Western, liberal tendencies can now universally continue to develop and seek to find more stabilizing elements for a revised concept of national identity that will no longer have to be based exclusively upon the ideologically useful myth of the small, neutral country, which had been the victim of Hitler's will to power. (Not to be confused with Switzerland at any rate.)[9]

In the fall of 1995, Austria spent about 70 million Austrian schillings (the equivalent of 10 million German marks) to stage its national presence at the forty-seventh, annual Frankfurt book fair, "the world's biggest and most important market-place for the international book trade."[10] The focal theme "Austria" was dedicated to Austrian literature and culture of the twentieth century, including a large "cross-section of its cultural life today."[11] As the project coordinator for the focal theme "Austria," Rüdiger Wischenbart, put it: "A picture of Austria will be presented that reaches far beyond the popular cliché of a nation characterized either by waltzing, skiing or ugly remnants of a totalitarian past."[12]

It is the long-standing tradition of such pluralistic contradictions to question and to critique that the political scientist Anton Pelinka points out in his essay entitled "Die Erfindung Österreichs — Zur dialektischen Entdeckung von Wirklichkeit": "Daß alle ihr Österreich haben, und daß das eine Österreich dem anderen widerspricht, mag die Geschichtswissenschaft stören. Doch die politische Wirklichkeit ist nicht um der Wissenschaft willen da.

Aber weil eben Österreich immer wieder neu und im Widerspruch erfunden wird, gibt es keinen Stillstand — Österreich ist nicht zu Ende. Die Widersprüchlichkeit der verschiedenen Österreiche garantiert die Zukunft Österreichs."[13] In light of this relatively optimistic self-prognosis regarding Austria's future, it is necessary to look at the present situation once more and to examine also how the public discourse in Austria has positioned itself vis-à-vis the critical remembrance of two anniversaries in 1995, which marked the rise of other critical voices of national importance that focused on Austria's most recent history: In April 1995, the fiftieth anniversary of the liberation from national socialist rule was commemorated, and on May 15, the country celebrated the signing of the Austrian state treaty forty years ago in 1955.

These events concurred with the broadcast of a series of lectures and discussions — the "Ringturmgespräche,"[14] subtitled "Inventur 45/55." Wolfgang Kos,[15] cultural historian and moderator, organized the forum and speakers such as Robert Menasse, Ruth Beckermann, Rudolf Burger, Anton Pelinka, and Günter Bischof to share their ideas pertaining to the interpretation of facts and myths that took part in shaping the ideological foundation of the Second Republic. The result was a multidisciplinary analysis of the strategies and ideologies that have influenced and shaped the process of constructing a postwar Austrian identity since 1945/55.[16]

With a critical focus on the founding myths that shaped Austria after the war, the participants analyzed and explained how the myth of the small and vulnerable country that fell victim to the powerful Nazis, but was otherwise pronounced innocent of its war crimes, had been successfully created. Austria's newly assigned status of neutrality, in combination with the theory of Austria's victim status, was instrumentalized and emerged as the official doctrine of the newly founded republic. This played a central role in externalizing any guilt for the national socialist crimes.[17] The official doctrine of the state was very effective for Austria's reemerging identity in the 1950s, since it could project a historical connection to the old restorative imperial myths that were prevalent well into the 1920s and 1930s. This projected continuity used the revitalization of the pre- and post–First World War cultural and historical heritage as something that could be reclaimed and could serve as the foundation for rebuilding not only old architectural structures,[18] but also for resurrecting many well-known Austrian writers, such as Adalbert Stifter and Franz Grillparzer, who represented the traditional monarchical values associated with the Old Empire.[19] The concept of Austria as a newly founded nation, for many a story of success,[20] projected a political and cultural consensus that focused primarily on capping those sentiments of the Austrian continuity that were closely related to the grand imperial tradition of the Austro-Hungarian Empire. Thus, *die Insel der Seligen,* as Austria was once called, could continue to be reinvented as the quintessential revival of cultural and imperial myths that were embedded in old monarchical traditions. The "Habsburg Myth," as Claudio Magris terms it, was projected and revitalized in order to stabilize the newly founded community as "the cultural power at large" that it once proclaimed to have been.

Since the Waldheim scandal in the late 1980s and as recent as in 1996, with Austria officially celebrating its millennium, it has become public knowledge and receives the attention of the media that the type of immediate postwar identification propaganda operated under questionable premises and as a consequence evoked a fragile national identity. Images based on isolationism were connected to the idea of cultural supremacy and an overall neutrality, while numerous taboos were reinforced simultaneously, incongruent with the historical facts and resulting in Austria's ambivalent relationship with its own past.[21]

The celebration of the Austrian millennium in 1996[22] reminds us that fifty years of history of the republic do not seem to suffice for Austria's progressing and redefined understanding of its own national history in the eyes of the governing cultural politicians and the national tourist bureau.[23] With the 1,000-year celebration of Austria's first mention in the year 996, a different type of nationalism and identity than that of a young European republic seems to be invoked for yet another time: Here again, we can perceive the tremendous difference between a projected restorative, traditional ideal and wish versus a reality that decisively has pointed toward a more progressive Austrian mentality. The Austrian critic Sigrid Löffler comments on the obsessive need to celebrate and remember events as a means for self-legitimization and a yearning for self-representation and an expression of self-ascertainment.[24] The same holds true for the public presentation at the 1995 Frankfurt book fair, as she concurs with Robert Menasse: The country needs the money that is generated by tourists and publishers, and the government needs the revenue that can be drawn from the profits as well to assure the continued support for Austrian culture and its export.[25]

Robert Menasse, an Austrian author of Jewish descent born 1954 in Vienna, is one of Austria's most prominent critics and analysts of current cultural affairs. He advocates a more open and inclusive representation of issues that deal with Austrian cultural politics at large. At the same time, he distinguishes publicly[26] between his official statements as a writer, such as his opening address for the 1995 Frankfurt book fair,[27] and his critical essays written after 1990. These essays represent, from an interdisciplinary perspective, a critical and political analysis of Austrian institutions, politics, and identity at large in their practices, as they manifest themselves in the public cultural sphere and in their literary expressions.[28] In his discussion entitled *Die sozialpartnerschaftliche Ästhetik. Essays zum österreichischen Geist* (1990, "The Aesthetics of Social Partnership: Essays on the Austrian Intellect"), he attempts to distinguish the most important elements of Austrian literature for the period from 1955 until 1980.

His critique entitled *Das Land ohne Eigenschaften — Essay zur österreichischen Identität* (1992, "The Land without Qualities — Essay Concerning Austrian Identity") deals with today's mentality in Austria and analyzes it to be a sum of a variety of factors and constellations. Menasse analyzes the mental continuities between the Austro-Hungarian monarchy and the Second Republic and builds his argument around his definition of the *Entweder-und-oder-Republik*, a polarized sum of — not only — historical contradictions, no clear self-definition in political terms and thus the overall absence of a clear definition of identity at large. But this seems understandable to Menasse when one considers that Austria's founding generation already had to take on four identities until the present. He mentions them as the Habsburg Monarchy, the First Republic, the "caste system" *(der Ständestaat)*, and then Nazi Germany. Thus, there has been a deep-rooted distrust against any clear and positive self-definition in Austria, which led to the state of the "Either-and-or-Republic." According to Menasse, Austria is a nation, but no "homeland" *(Heimat)*. "The feeling of being a nation" *(das Nationalgefühl)* is historically too young and too weak in substance to have instilled an identity, a feeling of belonging and of being at home. He asserts that the continuous decision of Austria to become and remain a country for tourism has destroyed the identity of those who live in the beautiful landscape. *Heimat* was replaced by ideological transvestitism, the exchange of stages, and the folkloristic theater / spectacle of a people of proprietors and hosts.[29]

Menasse's fictional texts deal with the aforementioned issues on a more sublime level, that is, with more indirect and symbolic allusions, yet with a direct reference to the place he tries to claim as his *Heimat*.[30] The distinction between the private and the public sphere of Menasse's works is not a simple one: It crosses and bridges a number of borders and mixes common knowledge with individual interpretations, convictions, and confrontations.[31] The focus of *Schubumkehr*, Menasse's most recent novel, published in 1995, is the periphery of the "homeland" *(die Heimat)* as a personal and individual construct versus an omnipresent "foreign, alien territory" *(die Fremde)*. The main topic is the interconnection between the mental and cultural realities and their psychological impact on the protagonist, Roman Gilanian, who is confronted with recognizing and treating his dissolving identity in the face of those seemingly neutralizing agents.[32]

The potentially apocalyptic location where the novel *Schubumkehr* takes place is a small village called Komprechts, located in the *Waldviertel* (the Forest Quarter) in Bohemia, adjacent to the still closed Austrian-Czech border, near a small lake, called Braunsee. Roman Gilanian, a 35-year-old Austrian with strong autobiographical features resembles Menasse in more than one way. Roman is an intellectual approaching the coming fin de siècle with fear and ambivalence. The feeling of encountering borders and limitations plays itself out in a variety of ways for him: At present in Brazil, he is looking to find home back in Austria, the place that he had left a number of years ago.[33]

The lack of a reaction on the part of his disinterested girlfriend, and his personal notion of being an alienated and useless intellectual, prompt his sudden return to Austria while realizing the uncertainty that is associated with this move. "Nun ging es heim. Heim, das gab es nicht mehr. Was wird dort sein? Ich weiß es nicht."[34] There too, his ability and wish to read books as an ongoing dialogue with the exterior world are not being realized, since his ultimate desire is really of a different nature: "Er wollte, vor dem Regal stehend, von den Buchrücken Signale empfangen, die ihm sagten, was er möglicherweise in seinem Kopf hatte" (41). While still in Brazil, he had closed his books, since it is not conventional knowledge that he seeks to acquire any more, but something far more personal for him: his home and individual identity. The overall description of Roman as having a dysfunctional and fragmented personality crosses private and public boundaries as a result.

Being the outsider that he perceives himself to be, he is able to feel from geographical and individual margins what it is like for him to live in two worlds. At the same time, his physical border-crossing from Brazil to Austria he resumes with ease. The continuity of his personal crisis, however, continues to haunt him.[35] While he almost personifies the typical Austrian, and furthermore Western European intellectual at the wake of the twenty-first century, one we could easily encounter in reality, his disposition becomes more clear now that he returned to the place of his origin. Here, Menasse features the perspective of the Austrian exile vis-à-vis the returned exile and amalgamates both perspectives into a hybrid to be something typically Jewish-Austrian. His border-crossing and relocating to the rural village of Komprechts, "inmitten einer tiefschwarzen Region" (13), from an urban center in Brazil presents a distinct geographic and thematic break, yet it does not change his individual malaise, but rather intensifies it. Here, Menasse features the perspective of the Austrian exile vis-à-vis the returned exile, and amalgamates both perspectives into a hybrid to be something typically Jewish-Austrian.

It is Roman who embodies one of the quintessential questions that Menasse raises with his text: How do individual memory and recollection correlate with the individual formation of identity, and how does a person deal with one's own past in light of the actual collective presence of prolonged history and memory? The protagonist serves as the illustration of the postmodern perplexity to affirm and implement the authoritative, psychological conviction that the process of individuation, a concept of a singularly centralized, self-governed individual existence, was traditionally based upon, within the pertinent dogmatic Weltanschauung since the Age of Enlightenment. Within the broader context of contemporary Austrian society and as a complementary concept to the traditional notion amounting to its negation, Austria and its citizens are implicitly being thought of as an entity that is in continuous need to redefine and rewrite historiographical representations in order to accommodate change and to include decentralized, marginal perspectives.[36] Roman's arrival in Komprechts is consequently marked by continued alienation, which he reflects upon in his mind: "Komprechts. Tiefste Provinz eines ohnehin schon zutiefst provinziellen Landes. ... Zum ersten Mal nach all den Jahren empfand er Heimweh: Entwurzelung. Als wäre er erst jetzt, nach sieben Jahren Wegsein, in der Fremde angekommen. Weil das, was hinter ihm lag, nun nicht mehr hinter ihm lag, sondern fort war, verschwunden, das was so war, wie es war" (46). It is a void and vacuum that Roman is presented with despite his premonition of his own memory and recollection of his childhood in Austria in light of many obvious signs in his mother's renovated farmhouse. She had taken Roman's childhood toys and rearranged his whole bedroom from earlier years in a rather small closet in the new farm. Roman does not feel at ease with these signs of his own past. He does not want to be reminded and is haunted by his past, a theme that presents itself throughout the novel via a constant denial and suppression of personal memory. The collapse of the present in the past and of the past in the present serves as a vehicle to illustrate and symbolize the fear of coming to terms with one's own past and thus laying the foundation to build a more oscillating identity. This reduces the need to either include or exclude contradictory behavioristic patterns instead of simply accepting them for their inherent worth.[37] Roman does realize that the only mechanism that had assured him of a certain balance in life was the fact that he had such a hard time remembering. "Er hatte nie etwas vermißt, wenn er vergaß, auch nie etwas Vergessenes für etwas anderes verantwortlich gemacht" (77).

The traumatic microcosm of his own family and the experiences that make up for his childhood bring to light even more powerful images of the past that deal with his Jewish father, who died when Roman was a young boy. It is the anguish related to his father's death and the process of massive internalization of his fear that he himself was to blame for his death that Roman recognizes now. He still deals with this guilt in the image of an overwhelming darkness, which surfaces now in the psyche of the adult. An indirect result of his father's death is his mother's decision to send him to a boarding school. His father, an assimilated Jew, who once said to Roman, "Ich bin kein Jude. Ich wurde nur als Jude verfolgt" (95) must have conveyed to him a sense of being other, of being different. Roman is able to evaluate his stay at the boarding school as a measure of bringing him up differently: "Er wurde umerzogen, so empfand er es, umerzogen wegen einer nie aufgedeckten Schuld" (114).

Here, too, the process of his reemerging thoughts brings to light segments of his past, vis-à-vis a historical framework, but he is seemingly unable to put these sketches together so that they would provide the basis of a beginning of coming to terms with the past. It is this struggle and anxiety of coming to terms with *his* past that dominates his present existence and prevents him from developing an adult identity that embraces and includes his otherness by means of acknowledging him as being different. These differences manifest themselves within the microcosm of his family and the macrocosm of the Austrian society, as Roman envisions becoming functionally integrated, and throughout this dialectic process, to reemerge as the person he is trying to claim from the debris that marks his past. His private dilemma — being of Austrian-Jewish descent — combines with his dysfunctional presence and existence as a marginalized intellectual in 1989[38] and shows that the dominance of private and public spheres can form a powerful alliance to include or exclude concepts of an individual existence — however peripheral they are perceived or perceive themselves to be — from finding and expressing self-esteem in Menasse's fictional Austrian society as a whole, while being entangled in the upheld taboos that restrict and mark the limited access to a bigger group-based identity for marginalized individuals.[39]

What Roman claims to know and recognizes pertaining to the external and public environment that surrounds him can also not be digested and processed in a conclusive way, even with the help of a video camera, which he uses to film the new historical phase in Komprechts. The new program is called "Komprechts 2000" (101) and deals with a reform in image and structure of the economically weak community that needs to orient itself toward the demands of a free market economy in order to compete more globally. The old village of Komprechts, reminiscent of nineteenth-century industrialism, with an old glass factory, the Braunsee, and a defunct quarry as well as a good number of working-class dwellings will change its outward appearance and image to attract tourists by undergoing a transformation of its presupposed identity.

This determination to rebuild and recreate an already existing landscape and village is not entirely new within the Austrian context: Kos points out that renovating, remodeling, and rebuilding per se have been instrumentalized already in the 1950s as a unifying ideology and strategy to create an optimistic spirit of moving forward to project progress and continuity.[40] While such ideological design plays out differently in a fictional text, when compared to the historical postwar reality in Austria, it still bears similarity from a thematic perspective: the will to redesign but leave old structures underneath, to use existing principles while reusing their façade is not without its

own problems, as one can observe when looking at the people in Komprechts and some of their presumptions regarding the potential result of the
changes.

The idea of a conscious will to redesign the town and its surrounding environment to appeal to strangers points to the problematic nature of tourism
overall: Komprechts' motto — "Wir haben Ihnen nichts zu bieten. Was wir
haben ist unverkäuflich" (133) — shows the paradoxical nature of tourist advertisement, but also the lack of specific qualities and features when dealing
with the definition of its own demographic and sociocultural composition.
Now that Komprechts has rebuilt its past and reorganized its planning and
beautified the borders of its "brown lake" *(Braunsee)*, it does not even have
time to ask critically about the next step, since these changes blended right in
with the nonviolent revolution during which the Austrian-Czech border was
opened. At the end of the novel, we see the Austrian and the Czech foreign
ministers applaud the exciting event at the newly opened borders while symbolically cutting big holes into the barbed wire fences that once detained the
Easterners within their borders. The question as to potential success of rec-
reation in Komprechts' new image is not conclusively answered in the novel,
since we do not read about the tourists swarming in. Here, Menasse has illustrated yet another transition that could lead to the idea of a new identity if
the anticipated tourist trade indeed will bear fruit.

It is this potential for an anticipated change and outward aggression and
how it occurs and the questions if the apparent signs are recognized and if
they are met with openness or resistance that Menasse continuously examines
in its many facets within the borders of this text, within the public and the
private dimensions of the microcosm that he calls Komprechts.

Komprechts also functions as the paradigm for contempt and recognition, inherent in any form of tourism that continues to dominate relationships such as that of the Austrian host and the German tourist in particular,
and Menasse incorporated yet another chapter of partial illustration of this
same mechanism. Since he does not write more extensively about the tourist
trade in Komprechts but connects it to a phenomenon that is linked to this
contempt and fear of something seemingly more foreign to an Austrian than
a German tourist, he stirs the reader's attention into most recent monstrosi-
ties. He alludes to acts of xenophobia: the killings of Oberwart, where four
Roma were found murdered in the early spring of 1994.

In the novel, Bruno Maria König, the son of Adolf König, the mayor of
Komprechts, is approximately eight years old and rather shy and lonesome.[41]
His interaction with an eight-year-old girl of presumably Czech origin is
Menasse's way of touching on Austrian xenophobia in this novel and expos-
ing it in the fictitious context.[42] The narrator tells us about the boy playing
with a girl named Maria at the shore of the lake. The girl, whose name is

partially identical to that of her playmate, emphasizing the resemblance of the two children, speaks very little German. To the boy, she seems mysterious, possibly coming from the other side, beyond the barbed wire. A play with the letters of her name in the mud on the shore, where Bruno writes her name to be Mary, makes her tense, and she runs away. While the two children share their secret play, Bruno Maria is aware that his female playmate is different from him, since she speaks a different language and he is not quite able to get to know her. At the same time, he is preoccupied to hide his new acquaintance from his parents, in fear of being ridiculed by them.

It is Roman who witnesses the two playing together another time. The children change clothes, and as a result, the boy now wears the girl's red dress and the girl wears the boy's green shirt and his pants. The children, void of prejudice and racism, change roles and playfully exchange the trademarks of their gendered identity and individuality. The dialectic between the negation of the foreign and the affirmation of the known proves to be paradoxical and absurd. Once the girl wears the boy's outfit, she runs into the open and public sphere of the newly designated bathing beach, but the boy, wearing her red dress, is not comfortable with being out in the open. When a group of men from the village see them, they run after the child in the red dress, who is later found dead and identified as Bruno Maria König.

The tragic murder in its catastrophic dimension manifests itself as ignorance and the desire to exclude by annihilation. Again the dialectic between those borders that are seemingly opening up between East and West and those that are being preserved and erected by murder and aggression is only marginally predictable: The act of hatred fails to hit its supposedly implied proper target and thus functions as the symbolic materialization of subversiveness within its own presumably destructive center. The death of the child is a clear sign of the real dangers that are not only latent but apparently exist in reality. As they are symbolized in the text, one may conclude that potentially they are present in Austria today. It serves as a clear illustration that the adherence to a construct such as historical justice and progress can never even be thought of to achieve anything in the wake of such blatant aggression.

Thus, the dialectic of the Enlightenment manifests its omnipresence here as well while the unpredictable dynamics and the state of total flux are the background to the absurd chain of events that lead to the death of a child. At the same time, the main protagonist withdraws into a sphere where his feelings of inadequacy and not belonging can be better compensated in a more open environment than that of the paralysis on the native soil ideology and the craziness of the "mistgabelschwingenden Alltagsfaschisten" (49) of Komprechts.

The child's death also shows in its coincidence and the complete unpre-
dictability of the victim's ultimate identity that the categories of "known"
and "knowing" versus the "foreign" and its exclusion by annihilation are extremely subversive when applied within a political agenda of integration versus segregation. It is here, too, that Menasse suggests to leave behind inherent monocausal determinations in favor of more global and inclusive gestures.

In conclusion, one might ask the following question: Is the specific search
for a latently modern identity linked to the modern subject in transition in its
particular space and place, thus an admitted illusion that Menasse convinc-
ingly deconstructs within his text? For Roman, who returns to Brazil in the
end, after having witnessed the murder of the boy, it is eventually true that
"home" *(die Heimat)* and the "foreign" *(die Fremde)* are no longer mutually exclusive, but that they in essence become one, thus proving that those
traditional concepts indeed remain no longer valid for and applicable to himself. He is prompted to interrupt and postpone the search for his "identity,"
his "home," and the "foreign," and carries his project on elsewhere, presumably in Brazil, after recognizing that his idea of finding home in Austria is
ultimately not possible for him, at least not at the very moment when the
concepts of *Heimat* and *Fremde* have neutralized and dissolved each other.

Menasse's textual strategy leads the reader to think that any conventional
understanding of a set of principles regarding the idea of a singular personal
identity and individual self-assessment as they relate to an optimistic concept
of historical progress and continuation can no longer be validated and applied in their known and conventional structure. It is overall not the total
lack of an identity that proves to be the challenge for the protagonist, but the
constant impulses for a changing one, within and around himself, in his family and village, and just how that process and those dynamics can be dealt
with constructively, in order to feel integrated and included in the outer
world of change, one quite familiar to Austria in general and Komprechts in
particular.

Thus, we will have to speculate for the moment about what will become
of Komprechts, now that its borders are open to the East, and what would
happen to Roman should he decide to return to Austria for yet another
time.[43] It is here that the private discourse and its public reception intersect,
and in the case of Menasse and his novel *Schubumkehr,* the same holds true
for Austria per se.

Austrians today find themselves at the threshold of a new consciousness
and time, and need to continuously deal with the questions and issues that
are arising as a result of the new political alliance within and beyond their
borders. Only with unanimous commitment on the part of those who, like
Menasse, contribute openly to the forum[44] for expressing and negotiating

constructive ways to increase the awareness and interest of the public, to continuously reevaluate their progress toward the goal of a more open / inclusive and multicultural society[45] will Austria in its cosmopolitan facets be distinguished as one of Europe's smaller, but no less intellectually and culturally influential nations traversing into the twenty-first century.

Notes

1. Here names such as Felix Salten, Hermann Bahr, Hugo von Hofmannsthal, Richard Beer-Hofmann, Arthur Schnitzler, and Karl Kraus come to mind as literary figures and critics. Sigmund Freud and Otto Weininger as well as Ernst Mach contributed much to the psychosocial discussion and the philosophical ideas. In the arts, names such as Gustav Klimt and Egon Schiele need to be mentioned. The musicians Arnold Schönberg, Alban Berg, and Gustav Mahler were pioneers in composing modern symphonies. For a more detailed analysis of the last fin de siècle in Vienna as it bears characteristic similarities to the present fin de siècle, see Jacques Le Rider, *Das Ende der Illusion: Zur Kritik der Moderne* (Vienna: Österreichischer Bundesverlag, 1990).

2. See especially Le Rider, chapter 1, "Überlegungen zur Wiener Moderne," 36–37.

3. Ibid., 38. See here footnote n. 70 with its reference to Jean-François Lyotard, "Réécrire la modernité," *Cahiers de philosophie*, nos. 5 and 6 (Lille, 1988).

4. See also Jürgen Habermas, *Strukturwandel der Öffentlichkeit* (Darmstadt: Luchterhand, 1983) and his latest collection of essays, *Die Normalität einer Berliner Republik* (Frankfurt am Main: Suhrkamp, 1995).

5. Quoted in Rudolf Burger, "Die Zeit der Reife: Zum Abschluß der österreichischen Nationsbildung," *Falter* 43 (Vienna), October 27, 1995, 16. Also in *Transit: Europäische Revue* 10 (Vienna / Frankfurt, fall 1995): 59–67.

6. The main thesis of his essay ascertains that what many analysts term to be the crisis of a national as well as public identity is in reality what he calls more conciliatory a crisis of maturation of the Austrian nationality as a whole.

7. Gabriele Holzer, *Verfreundete Nachbarn. Österreich-Deutschland: Ein Verhältnis* (Vienna: Kremayr&Scheriau, 1995).

8. Burger, "Die Zeit der Reife," 16.

9. Ibid. Here Burger criticizes the conventional journalism in Germany that mostly refers to Austria as the *Alpenrepublik,* thus demonstrating complete ignorance for the country's history and culture, and in error reducing it to a mere mountaneous republic, an image rather invoked by Switzerland.

10. Rüdiger Wischenbart, "47th Frankfurt Book Fair 1995: Austria Focus," *Austria Kultur* 5, no. 2 (New York, 1995), 7.

11. Ibid.

[12.] Ibid.

[13.] Anton Pelinka, "Die Erfindung Österreichs — Zur dialektischen Entdeckung von Wirklichkeit," in *Reden über Österreich*, ed. Manfred Jochum (Salzburg: Residenz, 1995), 21.

[14.] The *Ringturm*, located in the first district in Vienna, houses city hall and was built in the 1950s. It functions as a symbolic building, attesting to the newly found optimism that was architecturally constructed as an integral part of the Second Republic.

[15.] Wolfgang Kos is the author of *Eigenheim Österreich. Zu Politik, Kultur und Alltag nach 1945* (Vienna: Sonderzahl, 1994).

[16.] Kos's main thesis, a result from his own research, postulates that for the immediate postwar era, the image of communal building of new structures on top of the old ruins in Austria proved to be very powerful to reach a consensus regarding the importance of a future-oriented "model Austria." Thus, the past and the question of the specific national-socialist guilt in Austria, connected with a conclusive analysis of the phenomenon "Austro-fascism," could easily be buried with the old rubble as well and as such become part of what was to be ultimately left behind very quickly. Most of the restructuring efforts happened in order to promote the myth of consensus that was reached and implemented with the political and economic measure of a "social partnership" as well.

[17.] Anton Pelinka and Erika Weinzierl, eds., *Das große Tabu: Österreichs Umgang mit seiner Vergangenheit* (Vienna: Verlag der Österreichischen Staatsdruckerei, Edition S, 1987); see also F. Parkinson, ed. *Conquering the Past: Austrian Nazism Yesterday and Today* (Detroit: Wayne State UP, 1989).

[18.] See Kos, *Eigenheim Österreich*.

[19.] See Dagmar C. G. Lorenz, *Grillparzer, Dichter des sozialen Konflikts* (Vienna: Böhlau, 1986) and "Franz Grillparzer und die alten und neuen Ordnungen," *Modern Austrian Literature* 28, nos. 3 and 4 (Riverside, 1995): 29–41.

[20.] As recent as 1995 has the critic Walter Klier established a more positive tone in placing the cultural and national achievements of the Second Republic in a rather multicultural context, thus connecting past and present achievements to render a potentially optimistic prognosis for the future. Walter Klier, *Es ist ein gutes Land: Österreich in den neunziger Jahren* (Vienna: Deuticke, 1995).

[21.] For a more detailed and recent discussion about concrete and theoretical issues that constitute nationalism, see Walter Klier, *Es ist ein gutes Land*, especially chapter 3, entitled "Belebung des Nationalismus im Westen schwach, im Osten heftig," 28–34; see also Tony Judt, "Europa am Ende des Jahrhunderts," in *Transit: Europäische Revue* 10 (Vienna / Frankfurt, fall 1995): 5–28. For a more theoretical discussion, see Ernest Gellner, *Nationalismus und Moderne* (Berlin: Rotbuch-Verlag, 1995), translated from its original English published in 1983 by Meino Büning; see also William Pfaff, *The Wrath of Nations: Civilization and the Furies of Nationalism* (New York: Simon & Schuster, 1993).

22. The year 996 marks the first written mention of Austria in Latin as "in regione vulgari vocabulo Ostarrichi" in an official document "in the tiny hamlet of Niuvanhova (Neuhofen an der Ybbs)." The author was the Emperor Otto the Third, "the subject was the granting of some 2,500 acres of land to the bishopric of Freising." Susan Schwarz, "Celebrate the Millenium! 996–1996," *Austria Kultur* 6, no. 1 (New York, 1996): 4.

23. A critical analysis and summary of the celebrations can be found in Michaela Ecklbauer, "Die Kunst, Feste zu feiern," *Akademia, Zeitschrift für Politik und Kunst* 46, no. 1 (Vienna, March 1995): 12–14.

24. Sigrid Löffler, "Tausend Jahre Österreich Oder Wie Die Republik Vom Feiern Nicht Lassen Kann," *Art* 11 (Hamburg, 1995): 28.

25. "Österreichbilder: Zum Länderschwerpunkt der diesjährigen Buchmesse in Frankfurt am Main," *Freie Presse* (Chemnitz), October 6, 1995. Critical commentaries regarding the use value of the forty-seventh Frankfurt Book Fair 1995 with its Austria focus.

26. Ulli Springer, "Frankfurter Blätterrauschen, Interview mit Robert Menasse," in *City, Stadtzeitschrift für Wien* (Guntramsdorf, October 1995); Hubert Patterer und Berndt Rieger, "Apolitisch wird's nicht: Ein Interview mit Robert Menasse," *Kleine Zeitung* (Graz), September 1, 1995; Barbara Zwiefelhofer, "Einer, der die Wirkung der Buchmesse skeptisch sieht," Autoren im Gespräch, *Berliner Morgenpost*, September 24, 1995; dpa Pressemeldung, "Robert Menasse: Schreiben ist die Gestaltung der Wahrheit," *Vorarlberger Nachrichten*, September 23/24, 1995.

27. Robert Menasse, "'Geschichte' — der größte historische Irrtum," *Die Zeit* 42 (Hamburg), October 20, 1995, Feuilleton, p. 15. This essay, together with several of Menasse's most recent critical essays, was published under the title "'Geschichte' war der größte historische Irrtum" in Robert Menasse, *Hysterien und andere historische Irrtümer* (Vienna: Sonderzahl, 1996), 23–36.

28. Robert Menasse, *Die sozialpartnerschaftliche Ästhetik. Essays zum österreichischen Geist* (Vienna: Sonderzahl, 1990); *Das Land ohne Eigenschaften — Essay zur österreichischen Identität* (Vienna: Sonderzahl, 1992); "Nation ohne Nationalliteratur? Einige Anmerkungen zur österreichischen Literatur und ihrer Rezeption," *manuskripte* 199 (Graz, 1993): 113–23; *Phänomenologie der Entgeisterung. Geschichte des verschwindenden Wissens* (Frankfurt am Main: Suhrkamp, 1995); *Hysterien und andere historische Irrtümer* (Vienna: Sonderzahl, 1996).

29. See Menasse, *Das Land ohne Eigenschaften.*

30. Menasse himself is of roman-mosaic belief. His personal relationship with his own understanding of *Heimat* is expressed in an interview. Robert Menasse states: "Meine Sehnsucht nach Familie, Heimat und Seßhaftigkeit steht im totalen Widerspruch zu meiner Ratlosigkeit. Kaum angekommen, fahre ich wieder weg. Ich fühle mich immer im Exil. Manchmal sogar dann, wenn ich von einem Zimmer ins andere gehe." From "Gespräch mit Robert Menasse: Sehnsucht nach Heimat — aber immer im Exil," *Die Furche* 15 (Vienna), April 13, 1995, 2. See also Eva Menasse, "Die Koffer stehen im Hinterkopf," *Profil* 16 (Vienna, 1995). More information

regarding his biography can be found in numerous interviews and articles in "Österreich Schwerpunkt zur Frankfurter Buchmesse 1995," *Pressespiegel* (selections); final date of inclusion for *Pressespiegel* was December 5, 1995.

[31.] Ilse Aichinger, "Das Vergessen der Geschichte im staatlichen (Literatur-) Betrieb," offener Brief von Ilse Aichinger, *Der Standard* (Vienna), June 29, 1995; Horst Christoph, "Zählen nur Promis?" *Profil* (Vienna), August 28, 1995; Egyd Gstättner, "Vom Reden über das Schreiben," *Die Furche* 35 (Vienna), August 31, 1995, 3ff; Walter Titz, "Zielsein kostet Kraft: Ein Interview mit Gerhard Roth," *Kleine Zeitung* (Klagenfurt), September 3, 1995; Thomas Trenkler, "Im eigenen Garten in die Nesseln gesetzt," *Sonntags Zeitung* (Zurich), October 8, 1995.

[32.] "Home," "known," and "foreign" neutralize each other in the novel. As such, everything and everybody is foreign or at home, as Roman demonstrates. In this context, the traditional categories of a personalized identity and individuality, connected to a specific geographical and historical reality, can no longer be upheld in favor of a more universal concept of an individual and a national identity. This is the mechanism with which Menasse exposes the concept of relativity that governs constructs such as "home," "known," and "foreign."

[33.] The explicit reference to the fusion of different genres, especially of autobiography and novel, does not reach the reader. The first sentence of Menasse's manuscript — "Der Roman is autobiographisch, es war wirklich ich, der das alles nicht erlebt hat." — was left out of the final text. It still attests to Menasse's proximity to postmodern narrative strategies by distancing himself from modernist concepts and an omniscient narrator as a representative of such visions. See Ute Hermanns, "Selige Zeiten, brüchige Welt," *Der Tagesspiegel* (Berlin), August 15, 1994. For a more general discussion of postmodern tendencies within the literatures written in German, see Paul Michael Lützeler "Von der Präsenz der Geschichte — Postmoderne Konstellationen in der Erzählliteratur der Gegenwart," *Neue Rundschau* 104 (1993): 91–106; see also Paul Michael Lützeler, ed., *Schreiben zwischen den Kulturen: Beiträge zur deutschsprachigen Gegenwartsliteratur* (Frankfurt am Main: Fischer Tb Verlag, 1996), especially his introduction for this critical edition, 7–18.

[34.] Robert Menasse, *Schubumkehr* (Salzburg: Residenz, 1995), 61. In-text citations refer to this edition.

[35.] See Tony Judt's most recent and compelling analysis of the crisis of the intellectuals within the overall changing European context: "Europa am Ende des Jahrhunderts," *Transit: Europäische Revue* 10 (Vienna / Frankfurt, 1995): 3–28, especially the chapter entitled "Die Krise der Intellektuellen," 19–22.

[36.] The fact that Roman had a Jewish father and that Menasse himself is of Jewish descent, and the effect of this on the text as a multicultural element with a specific Jewish theme, that of the "eternal wanderer," is one that deserves more attention and recognition than can be accorded to in this context. While it appears that Menasse is reaffirming old Western stereotypes and prejudices harbored against Jews, in essence reminiscent of Robert Schindel's narrative *Gebürtig* (1992, translated as *Born-Where*, 1995), it becomes increasingly clear that this stereotype seems to continuously apply itself successfully within a larger global context.

[37.] The question as to how Roman as a narrative figure fits into Sander Gilman's notion of Jewish self-hatred needs to be addressed more extensively than can be done here. See Sander Gilman, *Jewish Self-Hatred: Anti-Semitism and the Hidden Language of the Jews* (Baltimore: Johns Hopkins UP, 1986).

[38.] The only specific reference to time in the novel is January 29, 1989, which expresses a concrete scenario for the anticipated and induced changes (*Schubumkehr*, 9).

[39.] Amy Colin explores the transnational elements and implications of Leo Singer's search for identity in Menasse's previous novel, *Selige Zeiten, brüchige Welt* (1991). Leo Singer is like Roman Gilanian of Jewish descent and spends part of his time in Brazil. Amy Colin, "Multikulturalismus und das Prinzip der Anerkennung in der zeitgenössischen deutsch-jüdischen Literatur," in *Schreiben zwischen den Kulturen: Beiträge zur deutschsprachigen Gegenwartsliteratur*, ed. Paul Michael Lützeler, 165–95.

[40.] See Kos, *Eigenheim Österreich*.

[41.] As a typological description, one is reminded of Alice Miller's classification as it relates to her analysis *The Drama of the Gifted Child — The Search for True Self* (New York: Basic Books / Harper Collins, 1994).

[42.] See also Reinhold Gärtner and Anton Pelinka, "Die Politik der Universalisierung der Fremdheit," *manuskripte* 33, no. 121 (Graz, September 1993): 68–75; see also Franziska Lamott, "Monsterbilder-Spiegelbilder," *manuskripte* 33, no. 121 (Graz, September 1993): 27–37.

[43.] The titles and topics of Menasse's other books do suggest a continuity in their plots and in their development. Amy Colin's essay provides first valuable insights into this aspect of Menasse's œuvre.

[44.] See Wendelin Schmidt-Dengler's most recent analysis regarding the broad potential of literary magazines and cultural journals as an instructive vehicle of this publicized dialogue in its historical development, in *Bruchlinien, Vorlesungen zur österreichischen Literatur 1945–1990* (Salzburg: Residenz, 1995). (He discusses specifically the literary journals *Der Plan, das silberboot, Stimmen der Gegenwart, Wort in der Zeit, Forum Stadtpark / manuskripte*). An analysis of the potential impact of such journals as *Wespennest, Transit, Gegenwart, Die Rampe, Profil, News,* and *Falter* on the public forum of opinions could shed much light on their critical potential and place them in the proper context of contemporary discourse and the formation of popular public opinion.

[45.] Most recently, Menasse has been offering a more future-oriented and conciliatory analysis regarding the process of normalization in Austria, as expressed on the occasion of his lecture at the Symposium "Österreich und Deutschland in Europa," Frankfurt am Main, May 6, 1995. Robert Menasse, "Ein verrücktes Land," in *Hysterien und andere historische Irrtümer* (Vienna: Sonderzahl, 1996), 9–19; see also in this volume, "'Nützlicher Idiot Haider?' Robert Menasse im Gespräch mit Armin Thurner," 39–50.

PETER ARNDS

The Fragmentation of Totality
in Robert Menasse's
Selige Zeiten, brüchige Welt

"'ÖSTERREICHISCHE IDENTITÄT' — DIESER BEGRIFF hat etwas von einem dunklen und muffigen Zimmer, in dem man, wenn man aus irgendeinem Grund eintritt, sofort die Vorhänge beiseite schieben und das Fenster öffnen möchte, um etwas Luft und Licht hereinzulassen. Doch wenn das Fenster keine Aussicht hat und sich der Raum daher nur wenig erhellen will?" With these lines, the Viennese author and critic Robert Menasse opens his essay on Austria, *Das Land ohne Eigenschaften* (1995, "The Land without Qualities").[1] Throughout his work, Menasse has made it his main concern to provide Austria with such a room with a view, by which he hopes to achieve a double effect: The people inside will be able to enjoy the view of the world and will profit from the light and air that comes in, and, inversely, the world outside will be able to look into the room and, thanks to the light now inside, discern more clearly what is within.

Texts as culturally self-contained entities do not exist. The concept of intertextuality as the intentional reference of one text to another had been employed by writers like James Joyce, T. S. Eliot, and Arno Schmidt long before Julia Kristeva introduced the term in 1967. Since then it has been used and abused by numerous theoreticians.[2] Intertextuality most often implies the idea of interculturalness. Although it generally originates within one culture, the text in varying degrees opens its own cultural boundaries to incorporate more of the world. Particularly the literatures of smaller countries seem to feel an urge to transcend their own cultural boundaries. What is Swiss about Max Frisch's *Homo Faber* (1957, translated as *Homo Faber*, 1989), what is Dutch about Cees Nooteboom's *Philip en de anderen* (1955, "Philip and the Others"), we may ask. The will to establish a national literature coincides with a pull away from the national, that is, it is the author's instinct to be national as well as worldly. Another example of the extent to which a literary text wants to transcend its culturally determined boundaries is Menasse's novel *Selige Zeiten, brüchige Welt* (1991, "Blissful Times, Fragmentary World").

It is a text about the gestation of a philosophical text, Menasse's *Phänomenologie der Entgeisterung* (1995, "Phenomenlogy of Despiritualization"). The novel's protagonist, Leo Singer, a Viennese Jew who is at home both in Austria and Brazil, unsuccessfully attempts throughout his life to write this sequel to Hegel's *Phänomenologie des Geistes* (1807, translated as *Phenomenology of Spirit*, 1977). Leo falls in love with Judith Katz, herself a Jewish Brazilian of Austrian origin. After being students in Vienna, both end up in São Paulo, where Leo can live comfortably thanks to the property his parents have bequeathed to him and where Judith finally writes the text that Leo has always wanted to write. To make himself its author, he first eliminates her voice from it and then kills her.

With this novel, Menasse attempts to open his country's windows primarily in two ways. On the one hand, the author widens the ethnic boundaries of his text by giving it multicultural characters and by locating the plot both in Vienna and São Paulo. On the other hand, the text transcends strictly delineated cultural and chronological barriers through its intertextuality. Menasse's novel contains a great variety of intertextual references, which, in order to obtain a deeper understanding of the novel, future research will have to look at more closely than has so far been done in a number of reviews. These discuss in a rather limited way the novel's subtexts, which can be broadly categorized as follows:

1. Historical biographies: A few reviewers mention the parallels between the love relationship of Leo and Judith and that of the critic Georg Lukács and Irma Seidler.[3]

2. Literary texts: We find an abundance of allusions to the literatures of other cultures. The list includes such texts as Lawrence Sterne's *Tristram Shandy* (1760–69), Lewis Carroll's *Through the Looking-Glass* (1871), Goethe's *Faust* (1808, translated as *Faust*, 1866), Gottfried Keller's *Der grüne Heinrich* (1854–55, "Green Henry"), the novels of the Brazilian writer Jorge Amado, and Heimito von Doderer's *Die Dämonen* (1956, translated as *The Demons*, 1961).[4]

3. Philosophical texts: Subtexts can be either partially determining factors, or they can pervade a whole text. As has been recognized, albeit not extensively analyzed by most reviewers, Hegel's *Phänomenologie des Geistes*, one of the most difficult texts of Western philosophy,[5] is such a structure-forming subtext in Menasse's novel.

4. Film: Robert Greuling mentions Woody Allen as a model for the *Aschengag*, the scene in which Leo with great relief at his mother's death throws her ashes into the wind only to have them blown back into his face and hair.[6]

5. Art: Giorgione's presentation of Giuditta decapitating a man, an art postcard that Judith gives Leo after their trip to Venice.

6. Generic: As Erich Hackl has pointed out, Menasse's novel is "many things in one."[7] As a love story and a Jewish family saga, it unites the literary generic traditions of the Bildungsroman, the picaresque novel, and the detective story.

A detailed analysis of all of the aforementioned subtexts would go beyond the scope of this essay. I have listed them, however, in order to show the extent to which Menasse erodes the margins of his literature. His novel is an example of the kind of recent Austrian literature[8] that lets in the world and, therefore, contributes to what the author himself called "Erosion der versteinerten Verhältnisse," an erosion of his petrified surroundings.[9] In this study, I will elaborate only on those subtexts that illustrate my argument.

By creating a transcultural and densely intertextual text, Menasse aims at a totalization of the world in his novel, an objective he shares with many of the realist writers in the nineteenth century. At the same time, however, he also fragments his fictional world. Hegel's principle of totality is the motivating force behind his attempt to transcend cultural boundaries. When asked for the links between Hegel and Brazil, Leo Singer answers that in his view, Hegel's central category of totality implies that no country as only a small part within a whole can shut itself away from the world, which is that whole ("Ein Ort wäre nur ein kleiner Teil vom Ganzen").[10] With the help of Hegel, the central character tries to annul qualitative differences that people make between the so-called First and Third Worlds. Menasse does the same on a narratological level by juxtaposing Vienna and São Paulo. Hegel's notion of totality corresponds to that final stage in the development of the history of the mind, of *Geistesgeschichte,* which he calls the absolute spirit. Hegel places his own philosophy at this peak of history, where in his eyes reason reigns supreme. Fredric Jameson has eloquently summarized what can be understood by this notion of the absolute spirit: It is "a space in which all contradictions are presumably annulled, the gap between subject and object abolished, and some ultimate and manifestly idealistic form of Identity is established."[11] The *selige Zeiten* in Menasse's title echoes this concept in all its idealism. It heralds the possibility of a world in which the gap between subject and object has been largely obliterated, in which the subject recognizes (Hegel's term *anerkennt*) the "other" and forms with it a synthesis, in which monocultural subjectivity is replaced by multicultural objectivity. The impossibility of such a world is suggested by the second half of the novel's title, *brüchige Welt,* and especially by its sequel, which describes the mind's development from Hegel's absolute spirit back to its disjunct beginnings. On a pragmatic level, the novel attempts to achieve some degree of objectification in that it exposes the reader to two cultures. In all attempts at totalization and consequent objectification on a textual level, however, the novel fails, whether as a synthesis of the two places or of Leo and Judith. In the following pages, I will show how Menasse systematically deconstructs the blissful times of the traditional Bildungsroman utopia of the nineteenth century. The realist novel in particular, with its aim of the character's successful integration into society, was an attempt to realize Hegel's concept of totality. By making use of a number of narrative categories typical of the Bildungsroman of the last century, Menasse tells us of the potentialities of the *selige Zeiten,* were these not continuously thwarted by a world out of joint. That the world is indeed fragmented and that the individual's objectification is an illusion is his novel's sinister conclusion.

In his *Vorlesungen über die Ästhetik* (1835–38, translated as *Aesthetics, the Science,* 1962), Hegel employs the concept of totality in connection with narrative art. What he sees represented in epic poetry, a "unified totality," he also prescribes for the novel.[12] For the Bildungsroman, this means that it is to aspire to a balance at the end of the hero's formation between his personal egotistical aims and society's expectations of him, a resolution of what Hegel calls the conflict of the hero's poetry of the heart and its antagonistic prose of external conditions.[13] Various novels that were influenced by the genre's prototype, Goethe's Wilhelm Meister novels, have in equal manner tried to resolve this central conflict. The hero and his world form a unity at the end of these novels. After a number of formative experiences, the protagonist was finally expected to lose part of his subjectivity; he was being objectified. Of great importance to this process of totalization were such harmony-inducing factors as a home, a wife, and a profession. These are the *selige Zeiten* of some of the nineteenth-century Bildungsromane[14] to which Menasse's title makes reference and which he deconstructs.

One formative step in the traditional Bildungsroman was the hero's journey away from home. At some point in his life, he would usually return home, whether to stay or not, and understand how much he has changed. Menasse uses this concept but transforms it. Being in the privileged position of having lived in both Austria and Brazil, he succeeds in describing two vastly different cultures. Their description fulfills two purposes, one for the reader and one for the hero. For the reader, who is catapulted from one place to the next in a matter of a few lines (144–45), he attempts an objectification of these two places, that is, a recognition of their equal status within the totality of the world. In Hegelian terms, the subject Austria, the thesis, meets its antithesis, the object Brazil. The idealistic goal is their synthesis, the subject's redefinition of its own identity through an encounter with the object. The reader's reassessment of his / her own culture through contact with another culture is, however, not shared by the main characters. For Leo and

Judith, their two homes stay drastically different, and their personalities are
divided between the two cultures, although they move with ease in both of
them. Due to their common background, both are vigorously opposed to
the Vienna of the sixties, which is described as fascist (46), rigidly immobile
(16), and cold (36). Leo's parents never cease to give him warm clothes from
his father's textile company. In leaving Vienna, Leo primarily recognizes a
way of escaping his mother, whom the novel identifies with the Austrian
capital. She is described as equally rigid and incapable of understanding cultural differences, as Amy Colin has recently shown.[15] On the other hand,
Brazil is initially presented as open to Leo's ideas on Hegel (159–60), although his public lectures on the German philosopher are later prevented by
the Brazilian fascists (205). While to Leo Brazil is primarily the romantic
home of his youth, to Judith it is the place where she sees a chance for com-
munism. In this light, it is no wonder that she, and not Leo, eventually
comes to grips with the Hegel project.

Leo's jump from Vienna to Brazil is foreshadowed by his fall into a canal
in Venice. As so often, he plays with the Hegelian terminology of subject and
object also in connection with this accident. He contends that subjectively,
he may have fallen, while objectively he has jumped into the canal ("Subjektiv gefallen, objektiv gesprungen" [98]). Leo views the dark surface of the
water as a mirror through which he has entered another world. Throughout
the novel, the mirror image becomes a persistent leitmotif. In this early phase
of his development, Leo already understands that he must go through the
mirror to obtain a glimpse of objectivity. Getting submerged in the object
world necessitates such stepping onto the other side of the mirror, because
merely looking at it would only produce the reflection of the subjective self.
Austria's closed windows, of which Menasse speaks in the quotation at the
beginning, are therefore the equivalent of a mirror not transgressed. One is
reminded of Alice's experiences in the Looking-Glass World. Entering
through the mirror into another world, the subject Alice merges temporarily
with the other, the object. Thus submerged in the object world, she returns
from the wonderland with an altered self-understanding; her journey leads to
what Hegel calls *Selbstbewußtsein*.[16] Going through a mirror implies the act of
looking at it, twice that is, on departing and on coming back. Reflecting oneself in the mirror means that one also reflects upon oneself, and if this happens twice, then the reflection before the journey through the mirror differs
from the reflection after this journey. The gain of such a journey to the object world, becoming conscious of oneself, does not come about if the subject never leaves the sphere of its own subjectivity, that is, only looks at its
own reflection in the mirror, but never at a reflection of itself after it has
given up its original identity through contact with the object by which it en-
riches itself. Brazil functions as the land behind the mirror, and the reader

follows Leo on his journey. Through this journey, the reader's self-understanding changes as did Alice's; the result is *Bildung*, the education of the reader. Consequently, Menasse erodes the narrow cultural margins of his readers by exposing them to Brazil. They leave their subjective sphere, Austria, to reemerge from the land behind the mirror enriched by this process of objectification, *gebildet*. Altered through the experience of this journey the subject / reader then also transforms the subjective sphere to which he / she returns. The erosion of Austria's margins has led to its transformation. The more Austrian readers Menasse's novel receives, the more Austria changes. This kind of transcultural literature, therefore, results in Austria's gradual depetrification.

As far as the reader's *Bildung* is concerned, Menasse's novel fulfills one of the traditional aims of the Bildungsroman, with regard to the *Bildung* of the protagonist, however, it fails. This is where the Alice subtext collapses into irony. While Alice returns from her wonderland and is changed through her experience, Leo has no return ticket for his trip through the mirror. The process of his formation takes a plunge as soon as he arrives in Brazil: His initial romantic vision of his lost home is destroyed through an unfulfilling love affair with a prostitute; reality displaces his illusions about his Uncle Löwinger; and above all, he does not succeed in completing the book about Hegel, his main concern in life. He ends up drinking more and more heavily (251), his flatulence increases (351), and he ages prematurely (251). The *selige Zeiten*, the ideal vision that he had of Brazil as long as he still lived in Vienna, vanish, and reality reveals itself to him as a *brüchige Welt*.

Another category of the realist Bildungsroman that Menasse deconstructs is the hero's socialization through love and marriage. While Charles Dickens's David Copperfield and Hans Unwirrsch in Wilhelm Raabe's *Der Hungerpastor* (1864, "The Hungerpastor") — to use two representative examples — are happily married at the end, Leo unites with Judith merely in authoring the short sequel. The novel shares this frustrated love relationship with *Der grüne Heinrich*, on which Leo writes an essay (125–26). Leo achieves as little objectivity through exposure to two cultures as he does through love. Instead, he repeatedly comes to stand in front of mirrors (e.g., 97–98), an activity that reveals his infantile admiration for his own image, reflected but not recognized. In an evaluation of Freudian theories, Jacques Lacan has argued that the infant goes through a narcissistic mirror phase before it starts objectifying itself in the dialectic of an identification with the other, which is the beginning of the subject's socialization.[17] Leo shares his mirror neurosis with Judith, who is constantly surrounded by mirrors (35). Their love is largely thwarted because, according to Hegel, love is a dialectic process that entails giving oneself up for the sake of the partner. The loving subject loses itself in the beloved object, the thesis thus merging with an antithesis. The thesis finds its original identity obliterated but gains an altered and enriched identity through the experience of love. This new identity is the synthesis, which, much like in Hegel's dialectics of history, is located on a higher rung.[18] Hegel understood this synthesis as an act of socialization, its product being the child. In the child, the parents recognize that they are one.[19] Whether the subject (Leo) has the possibility of being unified with the object as a foreign culture (Brazil) or as a lover (Judith), the success of such a unification would in both cases be a step toward the Hegelian ideal of totality. Yet, in his fixation with himself, with his own reflection in the mirror, Leo never unites with any other, neither Vienna, nor Brazil, nor Judith. None of these manages to alienate him from himself and his self-involved intellectual pursuit. The unbridgeable distance between Leo and Judith may be best rendered by an image the protagonist describes in one of his early attempts at coming to grips with Hegel: He imagines himself in front of one mirror and Judith in front of another, with the two mirrors facing each other. The result of such positioning of mirrors is that both characters disappear in the infinitude of their own reflections, forever distancing themselves from one another (79–80).

The synthesis between Leo and Judith in the sense of an act of socialization does not come about. Yet, in a perverted sense, the sequel to this novel, Menasse's *Phänomenologie der Entgeisterung,* can be considered a synthesis, as it is the product of Leo's and Judith's warped relationship, their child as it were. On the one hand, this book engendered within the book can be interpreted as the product of their battle of intellects, which Judith wins. Giorgione's painting of Giuditta, who has the decapitated head of a man at her feet, an art postcard that Judith gave Leo after their trip to Venice in the early days of their courtship, already indicates her ultimate intellectual superiority over him. She "decapitates" him by authoring the text on which he has been working for so long. As a consequence he "decapitates" her by extinguishing her intellect, thus putting his own head back on. By killing her, he installs himself as the author of the sequel. On the other hand, in writing the Hegel text for Leo, Judith shows more love for him than he has ever shown her. In light of Hegel's dialectic of love, it is not surprising that Judith writes the book on Hegel before Leo does. In thus reaching out to Leo, she does what Hegel prescribes, whereas Leo commits the ultimate act of self-love and infantile mirroring by killing her. He resembles a canary in love with its own reflection in the mirror that, therefore, manages to live happily alone in its golden cage of subjectivity.

The novel's title gains its meaning not only from the two places but also from the relationship between Leo and Judith. The *selige Zeiten* represent what Leo calls *Sittlichkeit* (194), the ethical order, which, following Hegel, he attributes to the Age of Antiquity. Hegel, however, distinguishes between two ages of *Sittlichkeit:* According to him, the Greek times were naturally ethical, *sittlich,*[20] whereas in the bourgeois age of the nineteenth century and today, *Sittlichkeit* is a synthesis emerging from the dialectic union of the *Rechtszustand,* the legal status, and *Moralität,* morality. At the beginning of the novel, when Leo and Judith are still in Vienna, Leo considers her a "congenial woman" (65) and dreams of a "symbiosis" with her. Menasse thus toys with the possibility of bestowing *selige Zeiten* upon them, the totality of their love. Their relationship, however, increasingly moves toward its fragmentation, the notion of a *brüchige Welt.* As one critic puts it, it shows all the signs of the typically hypernervous relationships of our age. The product of such a relationship, an opus on the *brüchige Welt,* the story of the fragmentation of the mind, comes as no surprise.[21]

Other customary categories of the nineteenth-century Bildungsroman deconstructed by Menasse include the hero's search of a profession, his relationship to his parents, and his vacillation between passivity and activity. Leo never gets a profession. From being an eternal student who cannot finish his dissertation, he rises to financial independence after his parents die and his Uncle Löwinger, a banker in São Paulo, has helped him invest his inheritance. A major divergence from the traditional Bildungsroman is the hero's relationship with his mother. There, the hero's love for his mother often determined the choice of his wife. The oedipal connection that existed between such heroes as David Copperfield and his first "child"-wife Dora Spenlow or between Hans Unwirrsch and Franziska Götz in Wilhelm Raabe's *Der Hungerpastor,* in a perverted way also occurs in the Menasse novel. The nineteenth-century Bildungsroman often removed the father first in order to allow the hero to develop more freely. In Menasse's text, the father likewise dies first, only to be replaced, however, by Löwinger as another father figure whom Leo increasingly resembles (238–39). Leo hates his mother and wants to kill her, a wish that is partly fulfilled when he kills Judith, in whom he largely sees his mother. Menasse does not try to conceal Freud's theories on the Oedipus complex when he describes Leo's aggressive lovemaking (117), and the poem he writes afterward (119). It becomes obvious how antique times, the *Sittlichkeit* or *selige Zeiten* of which Leo speaks (194), are turned upside down: Instead of wanting to sleep with his mother and to kill his father, like Oedipus, Leo wants to kill his mother, and he becomes identical with the father figure under whose tutelage he lives.

Yet, Menasse's novel cannot only be read as discordant with the Bildungsromane of the last century. With *Der grüne Heinrich,* for example, to which it also refers openly (125–26), the novel shares the irreconcilability of the hero's personal aims — the poetry of his heart — and the prose of circumstances. An obvious parallel between both novels is Judith, with whom neither hero is united at the end. Moreover, like Leo, Heinrich Lee is removed from the objective world through his art. He is so self-involved that he does not return in time for his mother's death. The hero's presence at his mother's deathbed is another stock element in the nineteenth-century Bildungsroman that Menasse subverts. Leo deliberately avoids returning to his dying mother. What Leo also shares with the heroes of earlier centuries is his passivity. Menasse discusses in particular the parallels between Leo and Tristram Shandy (63), who are both forever procrastinating. In this context, it is interesting to note that the modernity of Lawrence Sterne's picaresque novel lies in its deliberate rejection of any attempt to depict the world's totality as did his contemporary Henry Fielding in *Tom Jones* (1749) and as was done later in the nineteenth-century Bildungsroman. Sterne's novel discards the traditional notion of chronology; its hero shows almost no change or development. It plays with the notion of competing authorship between the actual author and the hero, and it largely builds on a philosophical subtext: John Locke's *Essay Concerning Human Understanding* (1690). For all these reasons, *Tristram Shandy* must have had a great appeal to Menasse. While in the picaresque novel of the eighteenth century the hero's recognition of his faults was not ordinarily needed to make him happy at the end *(Tom Jones)*, this became a requirement for the nineteenth-century *Bildungsroman*. In novels like *David Copperfield* (1848–50) and *Der Hungerpastor*, the hero, like his cousin of the picaresque novel, drifts rather passively through life and finally succeeds in finding love and happiness. Unlike the picaresque hero, however, he has, at some point, to recognize himself. This moment of objectivity about his character then usually entails some activity on his part in order to set him on the right track for a happy ending. The opposite happens to Leo in that he regresses from initial activity to a long phase of passivity during the years in Brazil. His apathy does not end until the moment he murders Judith, the end of the novel. This *Antibildung* can best be demonstrated by the two passages in which Leo falls into water. After sinking into the canal in Venice, at a time when with youthful self-confidence he still likes to compare himself with Hegel, he insists that he has jumped, and not fallen, into the water. This urge to merge with an object world later gives way to an understanding of his own passivity, to which he admits at the moment of falling into a swimming pool in the Brazilian interior. There he gives up the initial thought of "subjektiv gefallen, objektiv gesprungen" (98) and concedes that subjectively, it may have looked as if he had jumped into the pool, but objectively he has *fallen* (227). Leo regresses from an active youth full of ideals about other people and aspirations for his Hegel opus to a phlegmatic old man, who in his self-encapsulation ruins the life of Judith (354). He never gives up believing, however, that the book on Hegel will one day be written (350), his one hope that at the expense of everything else comes true. In the nineteenth-century Bildungsroman, it was primarily the hero's disillusionment about his personal aspirations that made his socialization possible. The hero enjoyed love and happiness in return for forsaking some of his goals. With Leo, it is precisely the other way around. The product of his selfishness, Menasse's *Phänomenologie der Entgeisterung*, then mimics for the development of history from Hegel until today the same concept of *Antibildung* that is at work in the life of Leo Singer.

In my discussion of Robert Menasse's *Selige Zeiten, brüchige Welt*, I have shown how, as the novel's title indicates, the author toys with the notion of a totality of the world, which he then goes on to fragment.[22] By opening his text to a variety of subtexts and by exposing his readership to two cultures, he demonstrates how nowadays there is a renewed need for Hegel's concept of totalization, the world's objectification. Particularly in view of rising fascism in Austria and this country's fragile identity, opening windows becomes important in order to rid it of its ethnocentricity and to shape its self-understanding, since according to Hegel's dialectic, one gets to know oneself better by getting to know the other.[23] This optimistic trend on the pragmatic level of the novel is, however, in stark contrast to the author's deep pessimism concerning human and historical development. Leo Singer's *Bildung* is a permanent deconstruction of Hegel's aesthetic view of totality as it applied to the individual and his world in the nineteenth century and as it was primarily reflected in the Bildungsroman of that century. In our age of egotistical interests, in which the individual is no longer willing to give up his / her subjectivity (hence the rise of fascism), the reconciliation between the poetry of the heart and the prose of circumstances to which the nineteenth-century Bildungsroman aspired has become a utopian ideal. This difficulty of an objectification between individuals as well as between individuals and their own cultural surroundings repeats itself between cultures. In his recently published inaugural speech for the 1995 book fair in Frankfurt, Menasse expresses his disillusionment: "Es hat keinen Sinn zu klagen oder zu verurteilen, wie es auch keinen Sinn hat, schön zu reden und auf etwas zu hoffen — eine schöne Utopie, wie zum Beispiel die, daß weltweit wirklich werden möge, was wir in dieser Woche auf dieser Messe erleben: ein friedliches und produktives Zusammensein von Menschen aller Nationen, Sprachen und Kulturen."[24] For Menasse, writing is like a loud chant in dark forests.[25] This chant carries with it the possibility of a depetrification of the conditions in Austria, yet how can he be heard from the middle of these dark forests? Windows can be opened, but what if they have no view and therefore not much light can enter?

Notes

1. Robert Menasse, *Das Land ohne Eigenschaften* (Frankfurt am Main: Suhrkamp, 1995), 7.

2. I hesitate to add another definition at this point. For the purpose of this study, "intertextuality" ought to be seen within much narrower confines than Kristeva's "universe of texts." Where Menasse makes use of subtexts, he does so consciously to add meaning to his text. For further information about the theory of intertextuality, refer to Ulrich Broich and Manfred Pfister, ed., *Intertextualität. Formen, Funktionen, anglistische Fallstudien* (Tübingen: Niemeyer, 1985), esp. 1–31; see also Heinrich F. Plett, ed., *Intertextuality* (Berlin: De Gruyter, 1991).

3. See, e.g., Karl-Markus Gauß, "Ein großer österreichischer Roman," *Literatur und Kritik* 259/260 (1991): 107 or Konrad Paul Liessmann, "Donquichotterie des Geistes," *Der Standard* (Vienna), Aug. 30, 1991, supplement A9.

4. See Robert Greuling, "Komische Katastrophen," *Lesezirkel*, Nov. 1991, 18.

5. Bertrand Russell, *A History of Western Philosophy* (New York: Simon & Schuster, 1972), 730.

6. Robert Greuling, "Begeisterung — Entgeisterung — Zeitgeist," *Gegenwart* 12 (1992): 38.

7. Erich Hackl, "Weltgeist zu Besuch," in *Die Zeit* (Hamburg), Oct. 11, 1991, 7.

8. The œuvre of Barbara Frischmuth is another example.

9. Menasse, *Land ohne Eigenschaften*, 13.

10. Robert Menasse, *Selige Zeiten, brüchige Welt* (Frankfurt: Suhrkamp, 1994), 160. All following quotations from this text are marked merely as page numbers in parentheses.

11. Fredric Jameson, *The Political Unconscious: Narrative as a Socially Symbolic Act* (Ithaca, NY: Cornell UP, 1981), 50.

12. See Georg Wilhelm Friedrich Hegel, "Die Poesie," part 3 of *Vorlesungen über die Ästhetik* (Stuttgart: Reclam, 1971), 178.

13. Ibid., 177.

14. For a concise, but very critical discussion of these nineteenth-century Bildungsromane, see Jeffrey L. Sammons, "The Mystery of the Missing *Bildungsroman*, or: What happened to Wilhelm Meister's Legacy?" *Genre* 14 (summer 1981): 229–46.

15. Amy Colin, "Multikulturalismus und das Prinzip der Anerkennung in der zeitgenössischen deutsch-jüdischen Literatur," in: *Schreiben zwischen den Kulturen*, ed. Paul Michael Lützeler (Frankfurt am Main: Fischer, 1996), 180–81.

16. It is interesting to note in this context that the German term *Selbstbewußtsein* has two meanings, consciousness of oneself as well as self-confidence. Consequently, in German-speaking countries, immersion in another world leaves one stronger,

whereas to the English speaker, the result of self-consciousness is a feeling of diffidence.

[17.] See Jacques Lacan, *Écrits* (Paris: Éditions du Seuil, 1966), 94.

[18.] This process is described very intelligibly in Wilhelm Weischedel, *Die philosophische Hintertreppe* (Munich: dtv, 1973), 213–14.

[19.] See Gunnar Skirbekk and Nils Gilje, *Geschichte der Philosophie* (Frankfurt am Main: Suhrkamp, 1993), 596.

[20.] See Samuel Assefa, "Commentary on 'From Jena to Heidelberg: Two Views of Recognition,'" in *Hegel's Philosophy of Spirit*, ed. Peter G. Stillman (Albany: State U of New York P, 1987), 64.

[21.] Gerald Schmickl, "Leo säuft, Judith schnupft Koks," *Die Weltwoche* 41 (Zurich), Oct. 10, 1991, 94.

[22.] Linda Hutcheon identifies this postmodern tendency for a number of novels. She calls it "the postmodern paradox of anti-totalizing totalization in … novels which structurally both install and subvert the teleology, closure, and causality of narrative, both historical and fictive." Linda Hutcheon, *The Politics of Postmodernism* (London: Routledge, 1989), 63.

[23.] "Österreich droht neuerlich im Faschismus zu versinken." Robert Menasse, "Nützlicher Idiot Haider?" in *Hysterien und andere historische Irrtümer* (Vienna: Sonderzahl, 1996), 39.

[24.] Robert Menasse, "'Geschichte' war der größte historische Irrtum: Rede zur Eröffnung der 47. Frankfurter Buchmesse 1995," in *Hysterien und andere historische Irrtümer*, 33.

[25.] Ibid., 36.

IMAN O. KHALIL

From the Margins to the Center:
Arab-German Authors and Issues

MIGRANT AUTHORS IN GERMANY ARE the voices of minorities speaking to the majority in their host country. Like their non-Western counterparts living in other Western countries, they are positioned between cultures and languages and can mediate the current discourse on multiculturalism and ethnocentrism in societies at crossroads. In this analysis I focus on Arab writers in Germany, particularly on the Syrian author Rafik Schami who has lived in the Federal Republic since 1971.

Emerging from the margins of literary production in German-speaking countries, Arab-German authors challenge the center's misconceptions concerning the Arab world. Whether intentionally or not, they react in their writings to clichés they face in the West regarding their stigmatized cultural heritage and ethnic background. Their texts confront negative images that often obscure Middle-Eastern realities, images that build walls between the Arab-Muslim world and the West. By making the unfamiliar familiar, they seek to engage the reader in questioning the division between the Orient and the Occident perpetuated by Western media. Arab authors reveal many Western descriptions of the "Arab mind"[1] as stereotypical. Thus, they challenge Arab-phobia in the West.

Arab-German authors originate from a number of Arab countries and portray different regions of the Arab Orient. They confirm, at least with regard to their culture, Edward Said's argument that partly because of imperialism, "all cultures are involved in one another; … all are hybrid, heterogeneous, extraordinarily differentiated, and unmonolithic."[2] Salim Alafenisch,[3] a Bedouin, depicts the customs and mores of the nomadic tribes in his native Negev desert. Ghazi Abdel-Qadir[4] and Wadi Soudah[5] focus on life in Palestinian villages. Hassouna Mosbahi[6] deals with Tunisian rural patterns of living, and the female writer Huda Al-Hilali[7] explores Iraqi women's everyday life, particularly after the Iran-Iraq war. The Western reader encounters in the works of these writers a diversity of local cultures and subcultures, including many types of people within diverse geographical environments and their historical and sociocultural contexts. This variety calls attention to the complexities and the heterogeneity of an area that encompasses more than twenty countries.

Texts with Arab settings evoke a Middle Eastern atmosphere from the viewpoint of Oriental protagonists. The characters appear as individuals,[8] not as "objects of the Western viewer's gaze,"[9] to use Nicholas Thomas's term about the colonial view in the Pacific region. The texts depict Arabs within their respective cultural settings. This differentiated portrayal defies Western perceptions that attribute to Arabs an "overall national character"[10] measured by Western criteria.[11] Rafik Schami's novel *Damascus Nights* (1995, *Erzähler der Nacht* 1989)[12] stresses the individual character of the Syrian capital and its inhabitants, and makes it clear that the Arab peoples are not a "collective entity."[13] The contents of books by Arab-German authors spark skepticism in the minds of readers in regard to one-sided Western views about the Arabs. They also address characteristics of Arabs unknown to the West; for example, the appreciation of poetry and music, and the sense of humor. Such features are not irrelevant, because they display humane dimensions of a people often associated in the Western public opinion with brutality and barbarism.

These writers also address religious issues in the Middle East. Arab authors target a Western audience conditioned to a set of preconceived ideas about animosity and hatred between Islam and Christianity, Arabs and Jews. In their writings, contrary to common Western approaches, Arab-German authors discuss the Middle East conflicts not in terms of race, but politics. Arabs and Jews are never portrayed as eternal foes. In contrast to the Arab view, the German journalists Peter Scholl-Latour and Gerhard Konzelmann — considered German experts on the Middle East — serve as a poignant example of Western propagation of ambiguous notions about Muslim and Arab issues in their widely read publications[14] and in TV documentaries. Only recently, after years of popularity, have they encountered criticism from German scholars.[15]

The literary choices of Arab authors, both Christian and Muslim, also show clearly that there is no inherent or genetic racial hatred between Arabs and Jews. The Iraqi poet Khalid Al-Maaly translates Paul Celan, the hermetic Jewish poet, into Arabic to familiarize Arab readers with his work. Al-Maaly, whose poetry is hermetic, considers Celan his mentor.[16] Adel Karasholi, from Syria, wrote a poem in memory of the Jewish-German author Louis Fürnberg, who found refuge in Palestine during the Holocaust.[17] In an essay, the Moroccan writer Abdellatif Belfellah describes his odyssey to the United States to meet Isaac Singer in Miami.[18] His favorite book is Elias Canetti's *Die Stimmen von Marrakesch* (1967, translated as *The Voices of Marrakesh*, 1978). Schami and Al-Hilali praise Heinrich Heine's sense of humor and irony. When Schami received a literary prize in 1985, his Jewish friend Dan

Diner, the Israeli history professor at the Universities of Essen and Tel-Aviv, gave the encomium at the award ceremony held in Munich at the Bavarian Academy of Arts.[19]

In his novels, Schami deals parenthetically with human relations between Arabs and Jews in the Orient. He portrays the situation of Jews in an Arab country, such as Syria. From an Arab perspective, he illustrates to the Western reader that Jews reside in small numbers and are not satisfied with local conditions but have never been exposed to isolation in ghettos. Even though some individuals were persecuted, Schami points out in a novel[20] and in an audio recording[21] that Jewish communities were never threatened with extinction in Arab countries that lost wars against the Jewish state. Jews and Christians are, as Schami's novels *Damascus Nights* (1995) and *Der ehrliche Lügner* (1992, "The Honest Liar") show, part of the multireligious society of large Arab cities. In the latter novel, the clever Damascus beggar Salman develops a tactic of observing a cycle of religious holidays. He is a Christian on Sundays, during Easter, and during Christmas holidays, a Muslim on Fridays, during Ramadan, and on other Islamic occasions, and a Jew on Saturdays and on Rosh Hashanah, Yom Kippur, and Passover.[22] Schami demonstrates the multireligious foundation of the region as a centuries-old tradition.[23] Furthermore, Schami sees in the history of premodern Andalusia[24] a successful model for peaceful coexistence.[25] Based upon the Andalusian experience, he derives his optimism for the future and advocates a cosmopolitan outlook and a multicultural identity suitable for the "global village." Schami and other Arab authors regret that in the West, public opinion is unaware of historical interaction between Jews and Arabs, Muslims and Christians in the Orient as well as in Andalusia. They criticize the fact that many Western commentators diagnose the current political conflicts in the Middle East mainly from an ethnic and religious point of view.

The Palestinian author Ghazi Abdel-Qadir addresses the Arab-Jewish issue in the children's book *Die sprechenden Steine* (1992, "The Talking Stones") through the eyes of a Palestinian child who lives in a Westbank village. The protagonist is a Muslim with a Jewish grandmother who immigrated from Russia some sixty years ago. Because of a curfew by the Israeli military, they find themselves locked with a Muslim family in the store of a Christian merchant. They realize that common people can coexist peacefully, but not politicians, nor religious fanatics.[26] Abdel-Qadir, a Muslim, and Schami, a Christian, prompt the reader to make a distinction between individual human interaction and the world of politics and ideologies. Thus, their texts, like those by Karasholi, a Muslim, and Jusuf Naoum, a Christian, offer alternative readings of the Arab-Jewish and Christian-Muslim relationships.

Another topic addressed by Arab authors concerns the notion of Western supremacy. Some texts directly take up the issue of Western cultural hegemony. In a satire set in Damascus, Schami portrays a clash between American tourists and a Syrian butcher who is the owner of a kabob shop. Mahmud, in a gesture of hospitality toward the "civilized" guests from abroad, serves them his best kabob. He is outraged when they spice it with ketchup that they had brought along. Mahmud comments, "They are rich, but have no culture."[27] The satirical juxtaposition of cultures in the form of eating habits contrasts kabob with ketchup. The butcher's view is prefigured in the title, "Kebab ist Kultur." Kabob defies the imposed flavor of ketchup. Similarly, the Orient resists Western cultural hegemony, which is now shaped largely by the United States and to which Schami and the Italian-German writer Franco Biondi refer in an essay as the "North-American Ketchup culture."[28] The epigraph of "Kebab ist Kultur" anticipates the result of the clash: "pro Mahmud contra McDonald [sic]."[29] Mahmud symbolizes the identity of the Orient, particularly that of common people, who have not been influenced by Western ways of life. Their lifestyles are in conflict with the materialism produced by Western conglomerates that are rapidly taking over in the Middle East. This takeover by Western economies is associated with neocolonialism. Another trait, on a cultural scale, affects indigenous literary traditions. Television and imported soap operas from Europe and the United States have gradually replaced the oriental storytellers of the coffeehouses and marketplaces. Naoum describes the television as the "Western monster" that threatens the oriental art of oral narration.[30]

In a theoretical essay coauthored by Schami and Biondi, they criticize the growth of "the monolithic culture of the metropolis and the ruling classes in each country." They attack the impact of a potential American-style "transcontinental cultural conformity," epitomized in the TV series "Dallas."[31] Both migrant authors present the idea of multiculturalism as a countermodel.

Ideals of the Enlightenment and the French Revolution with the claim of universal validity led — according to Verena Klemm — to an ideology that regards Western thought and civilization as the measure of human development. Like other migrants, Arab-German authors question this Eurocentric hierarchy[32] that judges non-Western societies according to the degree of their adaptation to Western models. In postcolonial discourse, this concept explains the colonial or imperialist ideology of cultural and racial superiority and inferiority.

From such a non-Western perspective, the economic, technical, and military power of industrial nations does not justify Western cultural supremacy. Arab-German authors familiarize the Western reader with Arab priorities in human relations and in ethical values. These authors introduce cultural codes, local customs, popular beliefs, and superstitions that shape everyday life in Arab societies. They present rural and urban traditions as constituting lifestyles and communal systems appropriate to specific societies and educational levels. The texts point out diversities and nuances within Arab cultures. They compel readers to think in terms of cultural plurality and require mutual respect of difference.

Other works by Arab authors address patterns of behavior, mainly in response to what they perceive as lacking in the West. Schami and Abdel-Qadir, for example, touch upon a problem they perceive as typical of Western industrial societies that measure people by success and productiveness.[33] Instead, Arab authors illustrate aspects of communal life in non-Western societies, characteristic of the Middle East as well as other cultures. Such features include the high esteem enjoyed by the elderly, strong family ties and vivid social interaction among neighbors. The Swiss social scientist Jean Ziegler considers the maintenance of these features as essential for the survival of impoverished nations worldwide.[34]

Addressing Western education in an Arab country, Schami plays on stereotypes about appearances and mentalities in order to depict their absurdity. In a French-oriented, Christian elementary school in Damascus, Josef — a pupil in the religion class — asks, "'Why does Jesus have blond hair and blue eyes in all the pictures?' … The priest jabbered something about Jesus radiating peace. But cheeky Josef would not buy this explanation. 'Was Jesus born in Palestine or wasn't he? Palestinians and Jews have dark eyes and hair, and they look peaceful, too.'"[35] Schami here addresses the Western concept of Palestinians, which associates them with violence. Other stories by Arab-German authors depict Palestinians as ordinary people or as victims, contradicting the prevalent misconception that equates Palestinians with terrorism.

Karasholi likewise questions the Western perception of a backward Arab world in his poem "The Old Turban." The title of another poem — "So wollen sie uns sehen" — suggests that the world of camels, sand, and turbans constitutes "the way they want to see us."[36] Karasholi opposes the Western belief in the inability of the East to change that ignores the achievements of modernization in the Arab world. On the other hand, Schami remarks on the negative side effects accompanying modernization, that is, Westernization of the Orient that, according to Said, led to a "vast standardization of taste in the region."[37]

Non-Western writers are not the only ones who represent alternatives to Eurocentrism in viewing global issues. Some Western authors, through their experiences abroad, have also acquired a "postcolonial view."[38] Paul Michael Lützeler addresses this perspective in his analysis of works by contemporary German authors. However, Lützeler's study also reveals that such involvement with the Third World mainly focuses on Latin America and the Far

East. Thus, except for a few notable writers,[39] the Arab world is portrayed primarily in media reports and by poorly informed and / or biased commentators regarded in the German public arena as experts in the field. In addition, Western movies and television portray Arabs in a negative fashion. Jack Shaheen's *The TV Arab* deals with this anti-Arab sentiment in the U. S. media.[40] Schami, along with other authors I have interviewed, regrets from his Arab perspective the Western attitude that rejects discrimination but reacts indifferently when verbal injuries target Arab integrity. Questioning this attitude raises the awareness of the Western reader to inconsistencies in "political correctness" when Arabs are involved.

To illustrate how the views of German and Arab authors on Arab issues differ, it is helpful to compare two literary works revolving around the Lebanese Civil War. The late Nikolas Born is one of the few German authors who focus on the Middle East with justice. His 1979 novel *Die Fälschung* ("The Deception")[41] deals with the same time and place as the collection of short stories entitled *Der Scharfschütze* (1988, "The Marksman")[42] by the Lebanese author Jusuf Naoum. Born portrays a German journalist's dissatisfaction with his life. He treats a Western theme, set against a background of political turmoil, while Naoum analyzes the underlying causes of the war. In Born's novel, the main characters are Germans and other Europeans torn between the fighting parties. In Naoum's accounts, the protagonists are Lebanese victims of the war. Thus in Born's novel, the setting in a Middle Eastern trouble spot is not crucial to the plot, but Lebanon is essential to Naoum's stories.

Another difference in perspective derives from a postcolonial view of issues not necessarily confined to the Arab world. A good example is Schami's literary response[43] to Michael Ende's novel *Momo* (1973),[44] which deals with the problem of time. Ende's heroine, Momo, is a poor child. She defeats the gray men who steal time from human beings. She returns the stolen hours to the human race so that people again have time for each other. Schami rewrites Michael Ende's happy ending, adding a continuation that he introduces as the second and untold part of Momo's story. A shift in perspective is evident. Schami's Momo is now a married woman. She falls in love with the notorious J. R., who arrives from Dallas in a helicopter on a business trip. She shares his luxurious lifestyle and becomes an essential part of his American methods of mass production, specifically tourism as an industry. Her former friends in Ende's novel lose their jobs in Schami's parody. Struck with poverty, they protest. The police side with the rich, dynamic, and charming businessman and fire on the masses. From a non-Western perspective, the short text criticizes Western, particularly American, capitalism, profit-making, and mass production at the expense of the underclass and Third World peoples. While Michael Ende addresses the lack of time as the problem for industrialized nations, Schami dwells on the concerns of the "Wretched of the

Earth," including underprivileged groups in the West. Schami's focus is on economic needs and social injustice in a world governed by materialism and consumerism. In his parody, he alludes to Ende's Eurocentric concern, pointing out that in the southern part of the world, people have time, but they are lacking essentials such as bread.[45] Schami's rewriting of Ende's story aims at altering the reader's perspective and at promoting a broader view than the purely Western interpretation of Momo's concerns.

German writings by Arab authors not only address stereotypes and question Western ideology, they also incorporate motifs, metaphors, and elements of style from Arab narrative traditions. Schami and three contemporary authors — Alafenisch, Naoum, and the woman writer Huda Al-Hilali — successfully introduced in their public readings strategies of Arab oral narration to their German audience. Especially Schami's publication record indicates that the German reader has found continuing appeal in his literary work.

The debate on inclusion and exclusion of marginalized literatures is, however, fairly new in Germany. Unlike Francophone writings in France, Commonwealth literature in the United Kingdom, and U. S.-Latino and African American literatures in the United States, which have found wide recognition, migrant authors in Germany have far to go to establish themselves as a visible part of the center's literary scene. Nevertheless, several foreign authors, including some of Arab origin, have been successful in terms of book sales and the readership in Germany. Schami, for instance, is now a bestseller and has advanced to prominent publishing houses. Lack of acknowledgment, as most Arab authors state, comes from the literary critics and the academics in German studies, who pay little or no attention to migrant literature as a whole. In addition, Arab authors face a major obstacle in Germany with regard to the attitude of some literary critics who treat them as a collective group — and often reminiscent of *The Arabian Nights* and of Arab folklore — relegate their literary efforts to the realm of the exotic. Exoticism is a label that diminishes the significance of non-Western literary patterns to Western mainstream literature. Suleman Taufiq, from Syria, questions the criteria that dominate German literary criticism, which Leslie Adelson rejects as "fixed categories."[46] Taufiq sees "ethnocentrism" in the phenomenon where everything alien to the European is considered in a derogatory way, praised as "exotic specialty" or rigidly set apart in such a way that "otherness" in the society becomes unrecognizable.[47]

An expansion of the canon of German studies to include works written by migrants in Germany is necessary to display the heterogeneous reality of German society today. Such changes in the field of *Germanistik* have been suggested.[48] They would involve the revision of concepts of inclusion and exclusion,[49] which are based on aesthetic norms and expectations of genres that do not always apply to non-Western literary devices.

The import of oriental literary models and — what is more important — new perspectives of Arab-German writings offer an alternative narrative to Western "master narratives."[50] Like Jewish, Afro-German, and other minority literatures, the addition of the "Arab accent" is an expansion of the literary scene in German-speaking countries. Expanding the canon by including cultural diversity, as Leroy Hopkins[51] suggests, implies a growth of consciousness, that is, to use Hans Robert Jauss's term, a change of the horizon of expectations.[52] The inclusion of previously marginalized literature such as women's writings[53] and non-Western literary contributions can ultimately transform the center by redefining boundaries such as ethnocentricity in Western literary discourse.

Notes

I would like to thank the University of Missouri — Kansas City and the University of Missouri Research Board for supporting my research project on migrant authors.

[1.] Raphael Patai, *The Arab Mind,* 3d ed. (New York: Charles Scribner's Sons, 1983).

[2.] Edward W. Said, *Culture and Imperialism* (New York: Alfred A. Knopf, 1993), xxv.

[3.] Salim Alafenisch, *Das versteinerte Zelt* (Zurich: Unionsverlag, 1993).

[4.] Ghazi Abdel-Qadir, *Sulaiman* (Weinheim: Beltz & Gelberg, 1995).

[5.] Wadi Soudah, *Kafka und andere palästinensische Geschichten* (Frankfurt am Main: Brandes & Apsel, 1991).

[6.] Hassouna Mosbahi, *So heiss. So kalt. So hart. Tunesische Erzählungen,* trans. Erdmute Heller and Mohamed Zrouki (Frankfurt am Main: Eichhorn, 1991).

[7.] Huda Al-Hilali, *Von Bagdad nach Basra. Geschichten aus dem Irak* (Heidelberg: Palmyra, 1992).

[8.] Edward W. Said, *Orientalism* (New York: Vintage Books, 1979), 154–55.

[9.] Nicholas Thomas, *Colonialism's Culture. Anthropology, Travel, and Government* (Princeton, NJ: Princeton UP, 1994), 36.

[10.] Patai, 19.

[11.] Patai even proposes that Arabic grammar be transformed and modernized according to "Standard Average European" (Patai, 72).

[12.] Rafik Schami, *Damascus Nights,* trans. Philip Boehm (New York: Simon & Schuster, 1995); the German original is *Erzähler der Nacht* (Weinheim: Beltz, 1989).

[13.] Said, *Orientalism*, 230.

[14.] Peter Scholl-Latour, *Das Schwert des Islam* (Munich: Heyne, 1990); Gerhard Konzelmann, *Die islamische Herausforderung* (Hamburg: Hoffmann und Campe, 1980).

[15.] Verena Klemm and Karin Hörner, eds., *Das Schwert des "Experten"— Peter Scholl-Latours verzerrtes Araber- und Islambild* (Heidelberg: Palmyra, 1993). Gernot Rotter, *Allahs Plagiator. Die publizistischen Raubzüge des "Nahostexperten" Gerhard Konzelmann* (Heidelberg: Palmyra, 1992).

[16.] Khalid Al-Maaly, personal interview, Aug. 9, 1994.

[17.] Adel Karasholi, "Louis Fürnberg in arabischer Tracht," in *Daheim in der Fremde* (Halle: Mitteldeutscher Verlag, 1984), 91.

[18.] Abdellatif Belfellah, "Auf den Spuren Isaac Bashevis Singers," *Am Erker: Zeitschrift für Literatur* 30 (1995): 33–46.

[19.] Dan Diner, "Über Rafik Schami," in *Chamissos Enkel: Zur Literatur von Ausländern in Deutschland*, ed. Friedrich Heinz (Munich: dtv, 1986), 63–67.

[20.] Rafik Schami, *Der ehrliche Lügner* (Weinheim: Beltz & Gelberg, 1992).

[21.] Rafik Schami, *Murmeln meiner Kindheit — Geschichten aus Damaskus* (Network Medien, MC 2, 1996).

[22.] Schami, *Der ehrliche Lügner*, 255.

[23.] Schami, *Damascus Nights*, 145–46.

[24.] Rafik Schami, "Foreword," in *Auf-Bruch. Lyrik*, by José F. A. Oliver (Berlin: Das Arabische Buch, 1987), 7–10.

[25.] Rafik Schami, personal interview, July 26, 1993.

[26.] Ghazi Abdel-Qadir, *Die sprechenden Steine* (Weinheim: Beltz und Gelberg, 1992), 85–86.

[27.] Rafik Schami, "Kebab ist Kultur," in *Der Fliegenmelker und andere Erzählungen* (Munich: dtv, 1989), 16.

[28.] Franco Biondi and Rafik Schami, "Ein Gastarbeiter ist ein Türke," *Kürbiskern* 1 (1983): 98.

[29.] Shami, "Kebab ist Kultur," 9.

[30.] Jusuf Naoum, *Die Kaffeehausgeschichten des Abu al Abed* (Munich: dtv, 1993), 8.

[31.] Biondi and Schami, "Ein Gastarbeiter ist ein Türke," 98.

[32.] Verena Klemm, "Das Feindbild Islam und Peter Scholl-Latour," in *Das Schwert des "Experten,"* 16–17.

[33.] Rafik Schami, "Das Schwein, das unter die Hühner ging," in *Der erste Ritt durchs Nadelöhr* (Kiel: Neuer Malik, 1985), 14–20; see also Abdel-Qadir, *Sulaiman*.

[34.] Jean Ziegler, *Der Sieg der Besiegten. Unterdrückung und kultureller Widerstand*, trans. Elke Hammer (Wuppertal: Hammer, 1989), 9.

[35.] The story continues, "Josef had only asked the first question so he could push on to the real issue: 'And why haven't we had a Palestinian Pope yet? ... Or an African Pope?'" Rafik Schami, *A Hand Full of Stars,* trans. Rika Lesser (New York: Puffin Books, 1992), 74.

[36.] Adel Karasholi, "So wollen sie uns sehen," in *Wenn Damaskus nicht wäre* (Munich: A1, 1992), 20.

[37.] Said, *Orientalism,* 324.

[38.] Paul Michael Lützeler, "The Postcolonial View: Writers from the German-Speaking Countries Report from the Third World," *World Literature Today. Multiculturalism in Contemporary German Literature* (special issue, 1995): 539–46.

[39.] On Walter Vogt in Morocco, see Lützeler, 543.

[40.] Jack J. Shaheen, *The TV Arab* (Bowling Green, Ohio: Bowling Green UP, 1984). On anti-Islam sentiments, see Edward W. Said, *Covering Islam. How the Media and the Experts Determine How We See the Rest of the World* (New York: Pantheon Books, 1981).

[41.] Nikolas Born, *Die Fälschung* (Reinbek bei Hamburg: Rowohlt, 1979).

[42.] Jusuf Naoum, *Der Scharfschütze: Erzählungen aus dem libanesischen Bürgerkrieg* (Frankfurt am Main.: Brandes & Apsel, 1988); see also Iman Khalil, "Writing Civil War. The Lebanese Experience in Jusuf Naoum's German Short Stories," *German Quarterly* 67, no. 4 (1994): 549–60.

[43.] Rafik Schami, "Warum Momo sich in J. R. verliebte," in *Das letzte Wort der Wanderratte. Märchen, Fabeln und phantastische Geschichten,* 6th ed. (Munich: dtv, 1994), 94–108.

[44.] Michael Ende, *Momo* (Stuttgart: Thienemann, 1973).

[45.] Schami, "Warum Momo sich in J. R. verliebte," 98.

[46.] Leslie A. Adelson, "Migrants' Literature or German Literature?" *German Quarterly* 63 (1990): 384.

[47.] Suleman Taufiq, "Sehnsucht als Identität," *Neue Generation — Neues Erzählen. Deutsche Prosa-Literatur der achtziger Jahre,* ed. Walter Delabar et al. (Opladen: Westdeutscher Verlag, 1993), 244.

[48.] Robert Bledsoe et al., eds., *Rethinking "Germanistik," Canon and Culture,* vol. 6 of *Berkeley Insights in Linguistics and Semiotics,* ed. Irmengard Rauch (New York: Peter Lang, 1991), xiii.

[49.] Georg Gugelberger, "Rethinking *Germanisitk: Germanistik,* the Canon, and Third World Literature," *Monatshefte* 83, no. 1 (1991): 52–56.

[50.] Ellen G. Friedman and Miriam Fuchs, eds., *Breaking the Sequence: Women's Experimental Fiction* (Princeton, NJ: Princeton UP, 1989).

[51.] Leroy T. Hopkins, "Expanding the Canon: Afro-German Studies," *Die Unterrichtspraxis* 25, no. 2 (1992): 121–26.

52. Hans Robert Jauss, *Literaturgeschichte als Provokation* (Frankfurt am Main: Suhrkamp, 1970), 177.

53. Ellen G. Friedman, "Where Are the Missing Contents? (Post)Modernism, Gender, and the Canon," *PMLA* 108, no. 2 (1993): 242.

PETER WERRES

National Identity under Siege:
Postwall Writing in Germany

W HEN ONE ANALYZES THE RICH BODY of contemporary German literature and explores the complex cultural matrix informing present-day
literary production, a critically balanced perception is, of course, impossible at
this point — in the aftermath of truly disorienting changes and in a time of
crisis for even the most long-standing cultural paradigms. Contemporary
German literature is generated by a culture that in the course of this century
has undergone extraordinary historical experiences, although most contemporary writers have personally experienced only postwar German life. With
the end of the millennium in sight, some may wonder whether history will
repeat itself. The ends of centuries traditionally have generated a flurry of
disquieting writing that questioned concepts of national identity. At the end
of a millennium, one can expect to see the reemergence of cyclical views of
history,[1] proclamations of the end of history altogether,[2] or even apocalyptic
notions of impending Armageddon.[3]

The sequence of events known as German history has over time seen
various attempts at national identity formation. Contemporary German literary discourse about issues of national consciousness and identity has moved
toward the end of any preestablished consensus, even in dissent.[4] German reunification did not come to be a unifying theme, rather it seems to have precipitated a loss of consensus.[5] It remains to be seen whether German intellectuals, in the tradition of *hommes de lettres*, will be capable of reconstruct-
ing — out of competing notions of identity in a multicultural society — a
German collective or cultural identity, a supposedly irreducible positionality
of individuals considered German (as happened earlier, albeit under different
premises, in German Romanticism, along the lines of German "cultural nation"[6] versus French "national state").[7] It also remains to be seen whether an
identity, and what kind, will emerge in a hybrid culture or whether it will
simply be superimposed by the dictates of political and economic reality.

The emerging trends to be discussed in this article did not necessarily
start with the fall of the wall; for the most part, they constitute trends that

have, for some time now, been reflecting a changing social fabric, yet they intensified or changed direction after 1989. In some cases, there is no causal link to the fall of the wall and the ensuing dismantling of Real Socialism; in others, not the literary production itself underwent changes, but rather its public recognition or its forum. General recognition of an emerging media pluralism, including literary fringe genre artists such as *Liedermacher* (songwriters), had markedly increased in numbers and visibility over a decade prior to 1989. Yet, it was only after the fall of the wall that some fringe genre artists, guitar poets, for example, who played a key role in the political earthquake of 1989, received official recognition in the form of major literary prizes. Such honors have been previously denied to such *Kleinkunst* (minimal art). Also, prior to reunification, German authors had primarily become known through their books; now writers increasingly write (and talk) in and for the media. Broadcast as well as print media have turned into multimedia battlegrounds for literary discourse. Instead of the media discussing literary developments, many writers have become their own literary agents in any public forum, from literary magazine to TV talk show. At the same time, their actual published works have often become eclipsed by such media channels promoting literary product recognition.

Innovative literary assessments of contemporary social and political processes are no longer central to the literary mainstream; neither are teleologically oriented historical perspectives — owing to increased acceptance of views emerging from the application of chaos theory and similar concepts.[8] Rather, telos is being bent into a circle and linear concepts are increasingly replaced by cyclical perceptions, leading, in the case of literary production, to a large-scale abandonment of concepts deriving from or directly indebted to left-wing paradigms established in the works of Bert Brecht and his followers. More spontaneous, less class issue-oriented,[9] yet at the same time no less aggressive messages emerge. Aesthetically speaking, predominantly linear models of recounting are abandoned (e.g., traditional plays or novels) in favor of open forms of literary expression, including former fringe genres, especially genre-trespassing forms of literary expression). There are tendencies leading from typically mainstream German writers to groups long consigned to the periphery by the cultural center. Among them are "ethnic German" authors, who write in German while living abroad (as part of German-speaking minorities), or foreign authors living in Germany and writing in German, predominantly for a German audience (cases in point are Herta Müller and George Tabori, recipients of the Kleist and Büchner prizes respectively). In addition, there are authors of Jewish descent writing in German, such as Barbara Honigmann, Henryk Broder, Michael Wolffsohn, and Lea Fleischmann, gay and lesbian voices, including Dieter Schmutzer, Rosa von Praunheim, and Gudrun Hauer, as well as artists increasingly relying on regional dialects to spread their often bold messages in the media, thus becoming spokespersons of culturally long-dispossessed geographic margins: Georg Danzer, Hans Söllner, and Walter Moßmann.

These literary trends have been frequently discussed in critical assessments,[10] as have been contemporary issues of national identity,[11] and even a general discussion cannot be considered within the scope of this article. The interactive impact of two forces underlying these developments, however, has largely gone unexamined. It constitutes the main focus of this article. To understand the most recent developments in contemporary German literature (or is it, by now, literature in Germany?), two major trends must be kept in mind beyond the more obvious literary, philosophical, and cultural developments, including those linked to reunification: one is genre-related, the other involves the larger society, yet they both create the backdrop to much of contemporary writing in Germany, especially where German identity formation is at issue. The first trend would appear to be only marginally related to issues of national identity, the second only marginally related to literary issues, yet interacting together they have in recent years helped produce unique forms of literary expression that reach an ever growing clientele of consumers / recipients.

Out of the multitude of postmodernist trends and countertrends, there emerges a tapestry, the orthogonals of which all point in the same direction: away from a solidified notion of national identity and away from a traditional literary canon that was all too often the product of unquestioned constructs of national identity. In a two-pronged approach, this article will explore genre-related issues and address matters more directly related to the stated topic, the recent challenges to traditional concepts of national identity and their impact on emerging literary trends.

As regards literary genres: Along with the ongoing redefinition of national identity went an intensified redefinition of literature and the role of literature in a so-called *Kulturnation*. Continuing postmodernist trends, the concept of what constitutes literature has come under new scrutiny: German departments in Germany and abroad now often concern themselves with the issues that a few years ago were considered fringe phenomena or were attributed to different fields altogether. Cases in point for this change are the University of Marburg — once a symbol of the German *Bildungsuniversität* — which now sports a department of *Neuere Deutsche Literatur und Medien,* and the German Department of nearby University of Gießen, which offers a seminar analyzing various aspects of graffiti. In 1997, the *Germanistentag* finally acknowledged these trends and admitted media studies as a fully recognized branch of German studies. These developments may be considered a reaction to a literary elite and an elite literature that were often perceived as increasingly limiting and self-limiting. They may also represent a literary self-deconstruction or a trend toward increasing self-referentiality. The high-brow elements, the feeding on itself, as it were, literature's almost cannibalis-tic traits, directed the impatient and frequently frustrated and annoyed public toward more user-friendly forms of literature. Consequently, more popular forms of literary expression suitable for multimedia packaging have taken over (and in some cases have actually taken back) much of the terrain slowly abandoned by so-called high-brow literature. Amidst a continuing redefini-tion of the canon along postmodernist lines, recent years have seen an in-creased recognition of nonmainstream writing and the acceptance of former fringe genres like film, song, and popular art by the critical establishment.

A 1996 German survey showed that among all professional groups, writ-ers have recently taken the steepest nose-dive in social prestige. According to a 1995 German study on literacy, approximately four million Germans are presently to be deemed borderline illiterate (sekundärer Analphabetismus). A 1996 Dutch study echoed these findings, adding that fewer books are being read every year; recent Austrian figures show that fewer than 5 percent of so-ciety reads fiction of any type: In an increasingly librophobic climate, a newly emerging "high-stim"(ulation), "short-attention-span," "information over-load" computer generation would appear to want information and opinions served fast and in sound-bytes to suit the often hybrid lifestyles. After all, as we are often reminded these days, orality has always been a prominent fea-ture of human society: epic, theater, and lyric were originally oral media. Contemporary culture seems to be experiencing the "gradual end of the clas-sical age of reading."[12] It no longer has any use for conspiratory literary codes, for the cryptography that had characterized much of recent main-stream German literature. In a world that shows less and less interest not only in the written word, but in words altogether (often preferring icons in-stead), new and, at the same time, very ancient forms of communicating messages have emerged or reemerged.

At the end of our millennium, creative material has to a high degree be-come "societalized" — I am alluding to the virtually untranslatable Marxist term Vergesellschaftung, which portrays individual ownership, including that of intellectual / creative material, as eventually blending with the creative achievements of others into a commonly held property, into public domain. Today, this is, to some degree, true for literature, to a large degree for film, and to an even much larger degree for musical material. In its latest form, this phenomenon can be observed in the so-called rave or techno scene from Hamburg to New York and Tokyo, where disc jockeys craftily mix existing multimedia material from all over the globe into a virtual bombardment of acoustic and visual stimuli.[13] Contemporary artistic achievements would thus appear to have become part of a global reference pool on which self-proclaimed artists draw for their own creations — the ultimate form of "societalization." In the eyes of the younger generation, mining the extreme margins of human experience (even those perceived as freakish in the eyes of mainstream society) may lead to a better understanding of questions presently at the center of human experience. With its flashes of brilliance, its brief and forceful assertions of the creative spirit, more popular, multimedia-suitable culture may be filling a newly emerging void. Even when dealing with emotionally troublesome legacies, the genres of popular culture may turn that which is difficult to express, even the supposedly unspeakable,[14] into something that can be communicated and at times even mocked: a "carnivalization" of public German life, as envisioned — albeit toward different ends — in Marx's famous "Einleitung zur Kritik der Hegelschen Rechtsphilosophie" (1844, "Introduction to the Critique of the Hegelian Philosophy of Right")[15] has been under way for some time; it started in the late 1960s with the "carnivalization" of Western university life in the form of "go-ins," "sit-ins," and "teach-ins" and has since spread like wildfire through all areas of cultural life.

Among individual subgenres, it is especially songs and essays that have emerged or reemerged as prominent new forms of literary expression. As regards the former, the slogan runs in the tradition of Brecht: Words make you think, music makes you feel, and songs make you feel thoughts. Over the last quarter of this century, the song, political or not, has regained much of the position it held as a form of public discourse in earlier centuries. As regards essays in the proud tradition of Montaigne, Peter Schneider and Hans Magnus Enzensberger,[16] devout Europeans, have lifted the genre to new heights in the last decade and in the process challenged dated patterns of national identity formation.

Similarly, the recognition of film has been upgraded in recent years and has allowed cinema to be included as a topic of literary discussion. Relying on the universal language of film, this medium is capable of offering a degree of directness obviously beyond the ability of the written word. Often questioning national consensus, recent German films offer more multi- and transcultural aspects than any other medium. Many, particularly the ones by Wim Wenders,[17] have polylingual scripts; in the context of multicultural inclusiveness, Doris Dörri's 1995 *Nobody Loves Me*, for instance, costars an Afro-German. And many of the more recent German films, especially those by Dörri, manage to escape the cloud of doom plaguing much of earlier highbrow German cinematic production dominated by Wenderesque contrivance, as these new films tend to be funny in intelligent ways. No longer exists there a dichotomy between profitably entertaining and artistically valuable.

Not only the big screen offers new dimensions: Established writers, at times, try their hand at intelligent TV series. For instance, with "Liebling Kreuzberg," the recently deceased novelist Jurek Becker created one of the most successful series in German TV history; his screenplays made him more famous than any of his novels ever had.[18] And there are other, even more unprecedented forms of literary expression: talk show as theater, theater as talk show. Enzensberger's[19] most recent play, appropriately entitled *Nieder mit Goethe* (1996, "Let's Do away with Goethe"), staged in Weimar in the form of a talk show, constitutes an innovative affront not only to the *genius loci* and mainstream German literature, once referred to as *Nationalliteratur*,[20] but to cherished German concepts of the function of literature and the arts: After centuries of high-brow German achievements, there exists, according to Hanna Schygulla,[21] who plays a part in this talk show / play, "a yearning for mediocrity." (Does this spell enough apocalyptic, end-of-millennium doom for the German intellectual elite and traditional national concepts of *Bildung*?)

Moreover, there is increasing recognition for even the most popular forms of literary expression. A case in point is the popular singer Udo Jürgens, who was recently awarded the *Großes Ehrenzeichen der Republik*. Over time, more intellectually oriented singers, *Liedermacher*, had managed to (re)establish guitar poetry as a medium of social discourse and a literary subgenre in its own right. They were, so to speak, the thinking person's Udo Jürgens, who at their best can be seen as cultural philosophers who have their finger on the pulse of society. In recent years, some of these *Liedermacher* won prestigious national literary prices, most notably Wolf Biermann, who received the Büchner Prize, Germany's major literary award, in 1991 and the Heine Prize in 1993, and, as the first writer ever, the *Nationalpreis* in 1997. Of course, popular genres such as the ones mentioned here often have to compete head-on with Hollywood and other citadels of the global entertainment industry whose function is increasingly reduced to delivering demographic target groups to their respective advertisers.

In theory, the fact that some forms of literary production have revitalized or even given birth to increasingly popular fringe genres may constitute a challenge to the national literary canon, but it does not per se pose a challenge to concepts of national identity. Yet, as it turns out, the at times bold messages of unconventional fringe genres tend to question any seemingly preestablished consensus. Regarding national identity constructs, fringe genres frequently carry the messages of societal margins, of socially marginal, marginalized, or geographically disadvantaged groups.

As for the second issue, national identity: In a trend only at first glance unrelated to literary issues — and very much related to the subject of this article — the traditional concepts of what constitutes an individual's identity within society, his or her supposedly irreducible positionality, is presently being challenged on many fronts. Cities and regions, not nations, are becoming the principal site of identity for most people in Europe. Mentalities are changing fast. A more or less quiet revolution is under way, as lives are increasingly defined on two levels: locally / regionally and internationally / globally.

The rise of a global economy and a communications / transportation revolution have unleashed forces beyond the control of any nation-state. The nation-state is no longer the main economic and cultural reference point, as the faith in any national government's ability to respond to contemporary challenges is rapidly eroding. Europe is undergoing radical changes: Over-regulated nation-states are too big to manage the problems of daily life, yet at the same time too small to handle international challenges ranging from environmental problems to the task of negotiating with the only remaining superpower, the United States, on a more nearly equal basis. Already, member nations of the European Union (EU) have ceded some of their sovereign powers in the hope of becoming more competitive players on the world stage. People are no longer looking to their national capitals for guidance — they increasingly disparage them as havens for slothful bureaucrats and feckless politicians. In the past, a regional focus, of course, often entailed ethnic chauvinism — and for some areas of South-Eastern Europe it still (or again) does. Yet, regional issues, if linked with transnational or even global concerns, quickly lose their once potentially chauvinistic dimensions.

With the breakdown of the nation-state, Europeans are not only crossing the bridge to the next millennium, they are also returning to their historical roots. Life in Charlemagne's Franconian Empire, for example, was regional and at the same time contextualized within the continuation of a multinational and multicultural empire: Back then, even businesspeople, holding up the tradition of the West-Roman Empire, communicated in Latin, not (as generations of German teachers have tried to make students believe) in German. Europe's new focus on cities and regions is also reminiscent of a Europe based on city-states forming transnational and multicultural networks such as the Hanseatic League, the alliance of northern port cities that were sovereign entities in the fifteenth and sixteenth centuries. Once again, Europeans may identify themselves as Florentines or Venetians, Hamburgers or Amsterdamers, as they did prior to the emergence of nation-states in the eighteenth and nineteenth centuries. After all, the national paradigm and the nation-state proved mixed blessings at best. They produced the ugly, destructive demons of chauvinist nationalism. Incidentally, emigrants from and minorities living in Germany have, over time, also defined themselves in city or regional terms. As an example, a German-born Jewish person may identify him- or herself not as a German Jew, but as a Frankfurter or Wertheimer Jew.

One of the most prophetic statements of the late French President François Mitterand postulated that for Europe to truly grow together, it would have to become porous at its internal borders. Yet, active efforts to create a new Europe as envisioned by Mitterand have merely fed into, or gone hand in hand with, already emerging trends. For some time, transnational communities — for instance, across the Dutch, German, and Belgian borders — which had flourished in medieval times as major trading centers, have been revived. The Saarland, Luxembourg, and Lorraine have been forming into an economic and culturally homogenous supranational entity complete with border-crossing commuter trains. French Lyon, Swiss Geneva, and Italian Turin form a prosperous triangle, the Alpine Diamond, that has become a symbol for an ambitious effort to break the confines of the nation-state and shape a new political, cultural, and economic future.

But how does all of this relate to literature? Not only have some regionally conscious writers become strong advocates of regional empowerment, but they also address pan-European or international issues as well: "Act locally, think globally" is a recurrent slogan in the global village, even among writers.[22] In the nineteenth century, regional writers, or writers of the geographical margins, often attempted to transcend their regionalism while maintaining some local flavor. Earlier in the twentieth century, modernist urban literature and *Heimatdichtung*, regional literature, pursued opposing programs and points of view. The latter tended to extol the virtues of rural life with strong regional accents and proud use of respective dialects. In light of the recent European cultural and political developments, as described in this article, it would appear that this type of polarization has become obsolete. There is nothing provincial about thinking locally or regionally any more.[23] Even the literary use of dialect was by the mid-1980s no longer considered *drollig*, or cute, as it was in the 1950s, when H. C. Artmann experimented with various forms of Viennese dialects, including those of the working-class districts of Ottakring, which at that time carried a low-class stigma in literary circles. In 1997, Artmann ended up winning, somewhat belatedly, what is arguably Germany's most prestigious literary award, the Büchner Prize.

One striking example of present-day literary regionalism and of literature using dialect and relying on literary fringe genres is potentiated by another emerging phenomenon: border-crossing literary regionality. Among the geographical fringes, which, according to Mitterand, were to fray, the French Alsace and the German Upper Rhine region are paradigmatic. For decades, the entire region has been ablaze with political issues. First, of course, were the inevitable *Heim-ins-Reich* (back home to the Empire) calls following Alsace's reunification with France after the Second World War. Yet, more recently, this border-crossing region has been a feisty opponent to the demands of Paris and Bonn as well as to those of big business. In its continued struggle against the lobby of the nuclear industry, for instance, this supranational region has come together in unprecedented ways, and several writers there have managed to blend postmodernist trends moving toward multicultural pluralism with some of the rebellious counterculture sentiment of the late 1960s and early 1970s. French Alsatian writer André Weckmann, writing in German, ponders regional issues in novels like *Odile oder Das Magische Dreieck* (1986, "Odile, or the Magic Triangle"), while, on the other side of the Rhine River, Walter Moßmann and a handful of others, beyond pondering issues of national identity, have for years addressed the "little people" on both sides of the Rhine River, asking them to resist the dictates of grand economic schemes cooked up in some national capital or corporate headquarters, with their aggressive songs in Alemannic dialect. At times, these French and German writers have been joined by Swiss *Liedermacher*, young activist poets from across the border, who also use the Alemannic dialect. International chemical giants have their worldwide headquarters in that region. Their record is replete with incidents of poisoning the Rhine, which flows through several EU member states. This example shows that local issues are inextricably intertwined with global environmental concerns. The literatures of transcultural movements in these geographic border areas use the vernacular, often local German dialects, to mirror a larger cultural diversity and pluralism. In the Swiss context, some of the voices from the margins are the ultimate expression of a plurilingual culture characterized by a unique mix of unity and diversity.[24]

Combativeness, again expressing itself largely in dialect, also characterizes the works of several contemporary Bavarian singers, including one of the younger, very colorful figures of regionally based songwriting in Germany, the Upper Bavarian Hans Söllner, who is widely considered the most radical new voice. Labeled, not without reason, the "Rabid Dog of Reichenhall," Söllner, in an amalgam of biting satire and social commentary, hurls thinly veiled puns and insults at regional Bavarian and national authority figures. As a result, the young anarcho-*Liedermacher* with his caustic wit and his dreadlocks — an uncompromising advocate of cannabis legalization, a truly supranational issue — has already been the frequent target of (usually unsuccessful) litigation. Söllner is at his best when he challenges traditional German identity constructs[25] and parodies the arrogant bureaucratic discourse. In his irreverent ballads, he describes the interconnectedness between public officials, various industries, and special-interest groups. By 1997, and in ways not seen since the heyday of political songwriting in the late 1960s, some of his songs have already become classics for the young and disenchanted: Söllner speaks the language of the politically minded among the otherwise individualist and politically mostly passive postwall generation.

A similar rejection of the dictates of central government and a rejection of the literary canon also resounds from the songs of some dialect bands from

Bavaria, namely, cult groups such as "Die Biermösl Blosn" and other regional bands, including those of the so-called Hessian Wave of dialect songwriting, among them the "Rödelheim Hartreim Projekt" (consisting of two Hessians, one of them Afro-German); the pugnacious "da wedda" from picturesque Ladenburg, a town with Roman roots; and "bap" with Liedermacher Niedecken, who sings in Cologne dialect. Across the border, the Dutch "bots" sing in German against comfortable traditional European stereotypes; and in the North numerous Low German dialect bands represent a minority of approximately ten million Low German speakers from Bremen to Rostock, for a long time a silent minority. And then there is, of course, border-crossing rap and punk, the "4 Reeves" (four Afro-German siblings) or the furious "Anarchist Academy." These groups launch vicious attacks on traditional German concepts of national identity, such as the *jus sanguinis* (according to law, Germans are German by blood). It may not come as a surprise that for most of these fringe artists, German reunification did not constitute a unifying theme.

On the more sedate side, the newly emerging regionalism has produced various forms of fiction and film with quasi-documentary value (or which is even part documentary in nature) — fiction and films concerning themselves, for instance, with issues surrounding a given region's or city's experience during the Third Reich. Such works deal with complex issues from a local perspective and often constitute an affront to a nationally cherished consensus regarding a given matter. Among the by now better-known classics are the motion picture *Das schreckliche Mädchen* (released in the United States under the title *The Nasty Girl*, 1990) and the much-read novel *Herbstmilch* (1989, "Autumn Milk").

Distrust of the central government's ability to handle regional and transnational issues also characterizes many Germans' — and many German writers' — assessment of their national government's role in the reunification process, the most challenging task ever for most of those involved. According to Bielefeld sociologist Niklas Luhmann, organized society organizes itself: Reunification took its course without much input on the part of the citizens. "Der Mensch steht im Mittelpunkt und damit allen im Wege" is a witty popular slogan characterizing the so-called system theory. As graffiti, it can be read on city walls and highway overpasses throughout the reunified nation. Most writers give credence to the argument that, ultimately, people were allowed very little input in the course of events once reunification was imminent. In the opinion of many German writers, a new identity was imposed on the citizens of the German Democratic Republic (GDR) in much the same way as it had been imposed on Germans on earlier occasions — by the victorious powers of 1806, 1918, and 1945. Similarly, writers' opinions were, for the most part, studiously ignored in the process of reuniting Germany, as they presently are over the course of entering the third phase of the EU: There was no dialogue between *hommes de lettres* and politicians on how to achieve inner unity for a new German cultural state, and there is no democratic public dialogue on how to work toward a more cohesive German identity within the emerging New Europe.

In this context, it may have been especially hurtful to the cause of writers that many of them, both in the East and the West, had underestimated the resilience of capitalism / free-market societies and overestimated the viability of Real Socialism and its ability to metamorphose and regenerate. In disbelief, German writers witnessed the concrete-reinforced GDR collapse like a house of cards. The events of 1989 and thereafter made the existence of this fledgling alternative state, which, after all, had spanned much of a lifetime, appear in retrospect like a mere mirage, a footnote to history at best. Yet, the cultural and political explosion of Eastern Europe, although resulting in a return to diversity, pluralism, and social change, lacked, in the eyes of most writers, the utopian perspectives that had been so prevalent a generation earlier. Many of the altruistic ideas of the 1960s have by and large given way to concepts of enlightened self-interest and individualist cost-benefit thinking.

At the close of this century (and millennium), many Germans, not only writers — in the eastern and western parts of their reunited country — find themselves at a crossroads after the collapse of the ideologies that determined post–Second World War history. The present political establishment of the new Germany dismisses the utopian dreams as impractical and a hindrance to transforming Eastern Europe and the new German states *(Neue Bundesländer)* from bankrupt command economy to a lean (and mean), globally oriented free-market society, offering market solutions to deep-seated social problems. Although from different political perspectives, writers such as Günter Grass or Franz Josef Degenhardt view the emerging economic system as "casino-capitalism," in which companies merge rather than compete.[26]

When the "wrapping-up" of East Germany occurred, many writers felt forced into retrospective soul-searching to reassess their long-cherished socialist dreams: Hardly any one of them would have imagined a political ideology that promised so much to intellectuals and delivered so little, a paradigm that, as many authors have come to accept,[27] proved untenable in the end. Faced with an impasse, these thoughts led some authors to postulate a crisis of reason altogether,[28] bringing to an end a period shaped by the events of 1789 exactly two centuries after that date. According to Walter Benjamin, "art is the regent of utopia," and utopianism has often been called, not necessarily the cutting, but certainly the growing edge of society. Eras lacking utopian ideas traditionally may be considered the heyday of the philistine, times of sociopolitical rollback and atrophy in the arts. Yet, there was always reason to believe that writers of different generations and political persuasions, once no longer mesmerized by a frozen East / West dualism, would unleash a new intellectual pluralism, and the innate tensions between the forces of unity and diversity would ultimately culminate in dialectical progression.

After the official amalgamation of an affluent "capitalist" state with a relatively poor "Real Socialist" state, writing in Germany mirrors a German identity crisis not experienced to this degree since 1945.[29] Perhaps this crisis is the result of a long overdue act of self-reflection that, according to cultural critics and writers,[30] should have taken place in the postwar era. In a climate characterized by the waning of utopian energies and a mounting neoconservative cultural criticism that dominates much of the intellectual discourse, old issues of guilt and regret have been reactivated in 1989 and in the postwall era. The competing desires of stonewalling or assigning blame seem like a replay of the postwar scenario, Peter Schneider recently pointed out in one of the first German books seriously reflecting on reunification:

> If every advance in knowledge involves the exercise of memory, then in Germany our ability to learn is imperiled. Because German self-righteousness presents an insuperable obstacle to levelheaded reflection. People who openly admit that they have to rethink something or that they made a mistake are seen as intellectual cowards. Almost any turn of phrase that describes this process is either negative or strikingly theatrical in tone. We "confess a mistake," we "abandon our position," we "shift our stand." Even the relatively harmless "change of heart" sounds disreputable in political discourse. The archaic ideal of Nibelung loyalty still counts more than the desire for knowledge. Which is why major conceptual upheavals always tend to elicit two apparently very different reactions in Germany: stubborn persistence or energetic reversal. The latter is of course blood brother to the former — since every change of conviction is tainted with betrayal and consequently accompanied by heavy feelings of guilt. This is why these reversals happen so quickly, as people make their flying leaps onto the bandwagon.[31]

Franz Josef Degenhardt, a *juris doctor*, erstwhile law professor, and an ex-Catholic, may serve as an example for option one. He has become increasingly unpopular due to his defense of Real Socialism. His songs were often reduced to a primarily liturgical function among the ever dwindling number of orthodox Marxist / Leninists, and he lost much of his once substantial left-leaning liberal following. Yet, the polit-bard stuck loyally to his colors in an allegiance reminiscent of the Nibelungs, before and after the collapse of Real Socialism in the erstwhile GDR: "Man geht nicht von der Fahne ... erst recht nicht, wenn die Sache verloren ... das tut nur Pack."[32]

Degenhardt's critical, yet unwavering allegiance to the utopian Socialist cause is viewed by many as "dinosauric" and a prime example of a grim Teutonic resolve. Following Schneider's argument, it can be neatly juxtaposed with the attitude of writers such as Wolf Biermann, Degenhardt's longtime intimate foe (see Schneider's option two). Biermann's metamorphosis into a poet laureate of neoconservative bent and his path from the naive Communist cadre to the GDR's *enfant terrible* and international *cause célèbre* and finally, after 1989, to the role of national media celebrity and darling of the liberal (and at times, even of the conservative) press are well documented.[33] In his contributions to Germany's most serious conservative newspaper, the *Frankfurter Allgemeine Zeitung*, he now frequently ridicules his former allies on the left, accuses the German pacifist movement of a "merciless pacifism,"[34] and continues to uncover, with remarkable ease, former Stasi spies among his literary colleagues in the East — and, more recently, in the West as well.

Many East German writers and intellectuals have been blamed by their colleagues for their GDR past, perhaps in an honest attempt to prevent the suppression of yet another German recent past. It is, however, problematic that philosophical and moral guidelines are applied in the process that differ from the ones that are applied to West Germans with respect to their Nazi past. Since 1945, there has hardly been an honest, broad-based examination of the collective German memory. Few of those who are old enough to go that far back are asked the same questions about the Nazi period as the citizens of the former GDR. Concerning the attempts at self-defense by former GDR officials, it is again Peter Schneider who offers the wittiest assessment. He maintains that a much-sought phrase to cushion the slide into the post-Communist era was found in January 1990. It was introduced by Egon Krenz, former secretary general of the Socialist Unity Party, into the language of the day.

> When questioned about his role in the Leipzig election fraud of the previous spring, he stated for the record: "From the present perspective, it seems to me that our elections in East Germany were never really free and secret." Not one of the ever-dour participants at the meeting laughed or applauded Krenz's new application of the Heisenberg uncertainty principle. In lay scientific terms, the secretary's statement could be rephrased like this: The appearance of a given subject — say, electoral fraud — depends completely on the observer's perspective. Not being, but time (or, in fact, the exact date) determines consciousness! But it wouldn't have mattered if they had laughed, because the motto "From the present perspective" describes, with unprecedented conciseness, the intellectual balancing act that became a popular sport after November 9. Players must combine traditional school figures with new, diametrically opposed movements, all without falling off the bar. The goal of the exercise is a speedy and skilled descent — in sports language, this is called "landing on your feet."[35]

According to Schneider, the versatility of Krenz's phrase demonstrates its worth because it brings to mind countless examples and variants the minute one hears it.

> Dislocations, splits, and even withdrawals noticed in the media skirmishes suddenly make sense, language being one example. Speech and writing have changed almost overnight and whole areas of everyday political jargon have been abandoned, while others, long forgotten, are suddenly being rediscovered.[36]

Many writers in the former GDR, even those who are not stonewalling or in denial, have remained symbiotically joined or chained to the memory of the former system, even after its demise.[37] Dissidents who had opposed the oppressive political apparatus of "Real Socialism" now often share an inquisitorial zeal comparable only to that of their former oppressors. Former victims frequently turn into victimizers in an attempt of unmasking their former tormentors. In an air of a not altogether un-German role reversal and with considerable self-righteousness, some of these writers, including Hans Joachim Schädlich[38] and Erich Loest, have shown little taste for innovation and diversity. Many of them do not address current political and cultural issues such as the ongoing regionalization and multiculturalism, the migrations and the accompanying xenophobia, all of which are reshaping German society.[39]

In the absence of major unifying themes, the rapid diversification would, for the purpose of attaining a more coherent sense of self, suggest the need to develop a new sense of community and to redefine the cultural center and fringes so that center and margin can engage in a process of mutual redefinition in an atmosphere of trans- and multicultural awareness. Such a process would challenge the status quo and present notions as to which degree the literatures of different marginalized minorities deviate from the dominant value system. The recent tendency to focus on the paradoxical aspects of an existence on the outside is proof of German society's continued inability to tolerate difference and otherness. On a larger scale, the literary discourse on these key issues could and would contribute to answer the crucial question of Germany's place and cultural identity within the EU: Is there, culturally speaking, hope for a European Germany, or is there reason to fear a Germany-dominated Europe that defines itself predominantly in antiutopian economic terms?

By the summer of 1997, a discourse analysis of more or less public statements on these topics in the confines of the traditional *Streitkultur*, the public "culture of debate," reveals a spiraling brutalization of the literary dialogue in Germany.[40] In a country notorious for its inability to dispose of despotic figures, German writers and literary critics have, after the fall of the wall, shown a virtual obsession with ridding themselves of larger-than-life literary icons who could be considered a red thread running through the process of national identity formation. Any discussion of the castration of literary father figures, of course, would have to begin with Goethe; Enzensberger's aforementioned 1996 *Nieder mit Goethe* is a beginning. The literary patriarch Günter Grass was publicly ridiculed by Marcel Reich-Ranicki, and the matriarchal icon Christa Wolf retreated to California amidst a nasty controversy about her role in the former GDR.

Recently, the literary icon bashing has reached new heights with the deconstruction of literary figures who themselves had become famous by knocking national literary icons off their pedestals. John Fuegi's 1994 demolition of Brecht,[41] the ultimate literary father figure of Germany's progressive forces, was recently followed by the brutally critical lines of Biermann — a former Brecht disciple — about Heiner Müller.[42] The playwright Müller had been instrumental in deconstructing the German postwar self-image in plays like his three-part *Germania* cycle, premiering in 1978 with *Germanias Tod in Berlin* ("Germania's Death in Berlin"). In the process, he had become a mainstream German cult figure himself. Two years before his death, he was asked to direct *Tristan and Isolde* in Bayreuth, that mecca of old-time German identity formation. After Müller was barely in the ground, his statue was already knocked off the pedestal by an irreverent *Liedermacher*. The trend of icon bashing is continuing amidst devastating revelations concerning the career of a writer who was one of the GDR's most revered literary figures, Stephan Hermlin, the former vice president of the International PEN.[43]

At the threshold of the third millennium, are these processes to be seen as literary contributions to the attempts at national emancipation, as German contributions to the proclamations about the end of history, or are they mere manifestations of the relentless old-time German pettiness and self-righteousness?

Notes

1. Such as the ones following the ideas of the Greek philosopher Polybius and some of his contemporaries who at an earlier turn of a millennium subscribed to the idea of two-thousand-year cycles in history. Contemporary literary case in point is Kate Atkinson's 1997 novel *Human Croquet,* in which history repeats itself, backward and forward.

2. See, for instance, Francis Fukuyama's *The End of History and the Last Man* (1992) or John Updike's 1997 novel *Toward the End of Time.*

3. In regards to the recent emergence of violent militia groups and of end-time-cults, by now preaching their often apocalyptic mass-murder or mass-suicide messages even through web sites, see, for instance, E. J. Dionne Jr., "Heaven's Gate Cult Members," *The Philadelphia Inquirer,* April 5, 1997. "The most advanced forms of modernity join forces with darker impulses that go back to the caves" (A 9). Boston University now sports a Center for Millennial Studies, concerning itself with millennium-related activities.

4. At present, Germany is, according to many observers, experiencing "a far-reaching crisis in the self-understanding and public role of German intellectuals." Andreas Huyssen, "After the Wall: The Failure of German Intellectuals," in *Twilight Memories: Marking Time in a Culture of Amnesia* (New York: Routledge, 1995), 37.

5. Case in point: the speech delivered to the Federal Parliament by its seniority president, the renowned author Stefan Heym. The text of his address to the new *Bundestag's* opening session was, against all protocol, not printed in the next official government bulletin — the head of the German Press and Information Office, by his own admission, did not want to provide the writer, a member of the *Partei des Demokratischen Sozialismus,* with a public forum for his political views.

6. According to the president of the Goethe Institut (in 1996, interviewed in several German publications, among them *Die Welt*), Germany should, given recent educational trends, brace itself for possibly having to part with the concept of defining itself as a *Kulturnation.*

7. See, for instance, Otto Kallscheuer and Claus Leggewie, "Deutsche Kulturnation versus französische Staatsnation?" in *Nationales Bewußtsein und kollektive Identität,* ed. Helmut Berding (Frankfurt am Main: Suhrkamp, 1994), 112–62.

8. The emergence of the eristic movement with its belief that the universe is ultimately chaotic (Eris is the Greek goddess of discord) can be seen as one manifestation of this trend — particularly among younger people.

9. Over recent years, "class" would appear to have slipped out of the discussion of what once constituted the "holy trinity" of class, race, and gender issues.

10. On the topic of literature by foreigners, see Heinz Friedrich, ed., *Chamissos Enkel* (Munich: dtv, 1986).

11. See Claus Leggewie, "Ethnizität, Nationalismus und multikulturelle Gesellschaft," in *Nationales Bewußtsein und kollektive Identität* (Frankfurt am Main: Suhrkamp, 1994), 46–65.

12. Alvin Kernan, *The Death of Literature* (New Haven, CT: Yale UP, 1990), 134.

13. For details on the techno, industrial, and synthetic music scene, see Nicholas Saunders, *Ecstacy and the Dance Culture* (London: Turnaround, 1995).

14. This trend is by no means limited to Germany. Another example is Art Spiegelman's Pulitzer Prize winning comics on the Holocaust, entitled *Maus*, which are now available as interactive CD-ROM, marketed by the U. S. Holocaust Museum.

15. Karl Marx, *Early Writings*, trans. and ed. T. B. Bottomore (New York: McGraw-Hill, 1964), 41–60.

16. My assessment of the influence of Montaigne was recently confirmed by a piece of "inside information": During an interview with Peter Schneider on June 23, 1997, he told me that at a party in honor of his fiftieth birthday, Enzensberger appeared with a German copy of Montaigne's essays as a gift for the celebrant. As regards the new Europe, Hans Magnus Enzensberger (*Ach Europa*, in English published as *Europe, Europe: Forays into a Continent* [New York: Pantheon, 1989]) believes that the strength of a united Europe lies increasingly in diversity and differentiation, not in customary regimentation.

17. Wim Wenders, *Until the End of the World* (1991). For a sensitive appraisal of Wenders's work, see Robert Phillip Kolker and Peter Beicken, *The Films of Wim Wenders: Cinema as Vision and Desire* (Cambridge: Cambridge UP, 1993).

18. In her touching eulogy, Frauke Meyer-Gosan assesses the role the late Becker played in multimedia diversification: "So schaffte der DDR-Nationalpreisträger Jurek Becker einen Spagat, der seinen mit allen Westwassern gewaschenen Schreibkollegen sichtlich schwerfällt: die Kombination von U- und E-Literatur." Frauke Meyer-Gosan, "Hinweise, die den meisten zu winzig sind," *die tageszeitung*, March 17, 1997, 21.

19. Long before Alvin Kernan's *The Death of Literature* (1990), and even before Roland Barthes's "The Death of the Author" (in *Image, Music, Text*, trans. Stephen Heath [Glasgow: Olson, 1977]), Enzensberger had pronounced literature as dead in his legendary 1968 *Kursbuch* ("Course Book").

20. Goethe himself, earlier a proponent of national literature, had second thoughts about this concept. Instead, he stressed world literature embedded in regionality. See Ernst Beutler, ed., *Maximen und Reflexionen* (Zurich: Artemis, 1977), 603, 767, or his talks with Eckermann on Jan. 31, 1827, and July 15, 1827, in *Johann Peter Eckermann: Gespräche mit Goethe in den letzten Jahren seines Lebens*, ed. H. H. Houben (Munich: Kurt Desch, 1948), 170 and 207.

21. Interview with *Deutsche Welle*, aired July 9, 1996.

22. Thomas Steinfeld cursorily discussed both the rise of regionality and the loss of the literary canon, both of which result in an increased popularity of contemporary European literature: "In recent years, a smart and surprisingly readable literature has

reached us from the fringes of Europe. We are being seriously entertained by it. That is why these books sell so well." Thomas Steinfeld, "Earlier, the Day Used to Start in a Simple Past. About the Misconceptions Regarding Pure Literature," *Frankfurter Allgemeine Zeitung,* March 25, 1997, literary section, p. 1.

23. Even the marketing strategists of the American pop culture industry, which blankets the globe with its products, have come to realize this. According to Steve Clark, *Variety,* Nov. 11, 1996, MTV Europe has had to work hard to "retain its special identity in an increasingly localized … marketplace" (51). And Erich Boehm argues that "with pop music becoming increasingly localized around the world," Americans can no longer simply export American pop music. *Variety,* Nov. 16, 1996, 52.

24. John L. Flood, ed., *Modern Swiss Literature: Unity and Diversity* (London: Oswald Wolff, 1985); Walter Moßmann, "Gespräche mit Jurko," in *Tarzan — was nun? Internationale Solidarität im Dschungel der Widersprüche,* ed. Andreas Foitzik and Athanasios Marvakis (Berlin: Libertäre Assoziation, 1997). Alemannic is spoken on both sides of the upper Rhine, in the French Alsace, the German upper Rhine valley and Black Forest regions, and the very northern region of Switzerland.

25. In his songs "Der deutsche Tourist" ("The German Tourist") and "Moi Nega" ("My Black Fellows").

26. Günter Grass, *Der Schriftsteller als Zeitgenosse* (Munich: dtv, 1996) and Grass's 1997 Dresden speeches "Zur Sache: Deutschland."

27. There are dissenting voices defending the Marxist cause. See Christopher Norris, *What's Wrong with Postmodernism* (Baltimore: Johns Hopkins UP, 1992), 25–28.

28. Wolf Biermann, "Der Schlaf der Vernunft bringt Ungeheuer hervor" — in *Affenfels und Barrikade* (Cologne: Kiepenheuer & Witsch, 1986), 103.

29. Heiner Müller, *Zur Lage der Nation* (Berlin: Rotbuch, 1990); Volker Braun, *Der Wendehals* (Frankfurt am Main: Suhrkamp, 1995).

30. Henryk Broder, for example.

31. Peter Schneider, *The German Comedy: Scenes of Life after the Wall,* trans. Philip Boehm and Leigh Hafrey (New York: Farrar Strauss Giroux, 1991), 69–70. [Original, German title: *Extreme Mittellage. Eine Reise durch das deutsche Nationalgefühl.*]

32. Franz Josef Degenhardt, *Reiter wieder an der schwarzen Mauer* (Munich: C. Bertelsmann, 1987), 247.

33. Peter Werres, "Wolf Biermann und Brechts Dialektik," *Brecht Jahrbuch 21* (1996): 244–58.

34. Ibid., 258.

35. Schneider, *The German Comedy,* 66–67.

36. Ibid.

37. Rainer Eckert and Bernd Faulenbach, ed., *Halbherziger Revisionismus. Zum postkommunistischen Geschichtsbild* (Munich: Olzog, 1996).

38. Peter Werres, review of *Aktenkundig,* by Hans Joachim Schädlich, *Monatshefte* 87 (U of Wisconsin P, 1995): 276–78.

[39.] Many conservatives, feeling infringed upon by concepts of multiculturalism and anguished over the country's divisions are worried that the fringe unilaterally attempts to redefine the center, as national identity was in their eyes eroded and not enriched by multiculturality.

[40.] As recently as November 1996, more than a dozen writers left the West-German PEN in protest over the repeated suggestion that PEN-East and PEN-West should be united in the near future. Six years after German reunification, these PEN-centers still constitute separate entities.

[41.] John Fuegi, *Brecht and Company: Sex, Politics, and the Making of the Modern Drama* (New York: Grove, 1994), revised German edition *Brecht & Company* (Hamburg: Europäische Verlagsanstalt, 1997).

[42.] Wolf Biermann, "Die Müllermaschine," *Der Spiegel* 2 (1996): 154–61. As regards the previously mentioned brutalization of literary discourse, a subsequent Biermann poem on "des genialen Mackers [Müller's] Mickerleben" (on the genius dude's petty life) caused an uproar from Müller supporters. For details, see *Der Spiegel* 24 (1996): 184; Stephan Speicher, "Ein Wagen für die Fußkranken," *Frankfurter Allgemeine Zeitung,* Oct. 1, 1996, L1; Peter Walther, "The Ballad of Inge and Heiner," *die tageszeitung,* June 11, 1996, 17. On January 8, 1996, Biermann had announced in *Der Spiegel* his intent to attend Müller's funeral. On January 12, he received an anonymous call (which Müller taped): "Ich habe meine Waffe noch. Ich schieß dich ab, du Schwein, am Grab." Biermann decided not to attend the funeral.

[43.] Karl Corino, *Außen Marmor, innen Gips* (Düsseldorf: Econ, 1996). Hermlin suddenly died unexpectedly in April 1997 — within a few months after the allegations, just one day short of his eighty-second birthday.

GERNOT WEIß

The Foreign and the Own: Polylingual Literature and the Problem of Identity

THE CHARACTER OF LANGUAGE, THE NOTIONS of the foreign and the own, the concepts of ethnic and individual identity — this is an intricate agglomeration of philosophical problems playing its part in the judgments on the long European tradition of polylingualism within literary texts. Investigating polylingual literature, one has to reconstruct the connection drawn between language and identity, as done in the first part of this article. On the background of this reconstruction and its results, one goes further to the aesthetic judgments on polylingual texts presented by scholars during the nineteenth and the twentieth centuries. But the premises on which these scholars based their judgments have become dubious. Polylingual literature has changed as well. Authors like Tristan Tzara and Hugo Ball used polylingualism within literary texts in order to propose other concepts of identity, which contrasted with the common notions of the nineteenth century. These notions will now be reconsidered.

During the last decades of the nineteenth century, there was a remarkable movement in Germany: After the unification of the German states to the one nation-state, some ideologists demanded for excluding superfluous foreign words from the German language. Many a social group and its institutions, as, for example, the *Allgemeine deutsche Sprachverein*, the *Kriegerbund*, and even skat clubs, shared their intentions[1] and so a real hunt for foreign words began. Hundreds of French and, increasingly in the 1890s, English words were replaced by equivalent German terms. This was meant to be a contribution to the strength of the new empire, as a member of the *Sprachverein* announced: "Wem es gelingt, ein deutsches Wort an Stelle eines entbehrlichen fremden wieder in seine Rechte einzusetzen, der fügt ein Sandkörnchen zu den Grundfesten des Reiches."[2] The rejection of foreign words was based on the notion that the identity of a people is adequately expressed by its language. Language, one author declared, derives its essence from the unconscious impulses of a people, or rather, every people derives its essence, the spiritual work to ennoble its feelings and to enlighten the mind, its entire view of the world, from the language that is its own, and like the miner, it mines the gold of its ethnicity to the light from the dark shaft.[3] Thus, language became the "treueste Abbild des Volksthums," the truest reflection of the people.[4] The connection between ethnic identity and language was already drawn in the eighteenth century. In those days, the origin of language was heavily discussed by scholars throughout Europe. Johann Gottfried Herder pointed out that the development of languages results from the nature of man as both sensible and social being. Language reflects what a human being is. Also the ethnic character is mirrored by language. As an example, Herder juxtaposes a people who does not sharply differentiate its feelings and therefore will know only a few expressions to differentiate the nuances of its sentiments, whereas a hot-headed people will use a lot of different words for describing its passions.[5] Somewhat later, Wilhelm Humboldt speaks about language as the soul of the nation[6] and argues that language itself would be able to shape a people.[7] Thus, language and ethnic identity seemed to be interdependent. If one of them changed, then the other one changed too.

By vulgarizing Herder's and Humboldt's theories, one now could be convinced that introducing foreign words into the German language hinted at a crisis of identity, at the self-alienation of the German people. The only way to rescue German identity was to abolish foreign words. So the history of foreign words in Germany during the nineteenth century shows how the concept of identity works in general: It both excludes and includes, it excludes the foreign and includes the own.

The foreign does not match the own. For Friedrich Genthe, a scholar of the 1830s, this was quite clear. It is impossible, he writes, that a language acknowledges the structures and the words of a foreign language as its own.[8] Insofar Genthe's statement fits the common statements on foreign words. Yet, it has a special reference point for an argument on polylingual literature. Genthe describes the long European tradition of mixing languages within literary texts. While making verses, he tells, some Roman poets already made no difference between Greek and Latin, thereby witnessing the incorporation of Greek culture into Roman culture. Finally, since the eve of the Middle Ages and throughout the sixteenth and seventeenth centuries, several writers — including Molière in his *Le Malade Imaginaire* (1673, translated as *The Hypochondriack*, 1732) — elaborately assimilated their native language to the scholars' Latin idiom. This species of poetry is called macaronic because it was inaugurated by Tifi degli Odasi's *Maccharonea* in 1490.[9]

As bilingual literature, macaronic poetry is a striking phenomenon. It seems to demonstrate the possibility of blending one language with another, a possibility, however, strictly denied by Genthe. Different languages may be brought together, he argues, but their compatibility remains an illusion.[10] This argument tinges his aesthetic judgment. For him, it is ridiculous to pretend the realization of something impossible. Mixing languages is an attempt at such an impossible task, and, therefore, it provokes nothing but laughter. In consequence, macaronic poetry, and furthermore all polylingual literature, is thought to be mere satire. Even today, some critics still share this opinion. Just adopting Genthe's statements on the incompatibility of languages,[11] however, they do not reconsider the ideological roots of their position. Unconsciously, they still adhere to the very same concept of language and identity, to the same notions of the foreign and the own, as scholars did during the nineteenth century. But since then, these notions have become more than dubious, and, moreover, polylingual poetry itself has changed. Thus, a revision of attitudes toward polylingual literature must take place.

The use of foreign words in everyday communication and the writing of polylingual literature were judged on the premise that different languages express different identities. Blending languages was then doing something self-contradictory and indicating a schism within identity. The traditional concept of identity, however, did not tolerate any ruptures. Today the situation has changed. Postmodern thinkers talk about pluralism within identity, progressive German politicians even demand a multicultural society. Consequently, the differences between the foreign and the own do not play an important part any more. This point of view is the result of a long development whose origins can be traced back until the romantic period and whose first noisy literary culminations can be observed at the beginning of our century — during the times of Zurich dadaism, amidst the First World War, in 1916.

One of the most famous polylingual poems of this period is a cooperative work by Tristan Tzara, Marcel Janco, and Richard Huelsenbeck. On March 29, 1916, they delivered a *poème simultan* entitled "L'amiral cherche une maison à louer" ("The Admiral Is Looking for a House to Rent"). English, French, and German verses are spoken simultaneously. The poem is typographically arranged like a score and thus shows great similarity with a musical phrase. Indeed, the poem was characterized as "kontrapunktisches Rezitativ,"[12] and Huelsenbeck writes in an article: "Es ist ähnlich wie in der Musik, wo die Verschiedenheit der Instrumente die geschlossene Wirkung des Orchesters hervorruft, nur daß hier … jeder der Mitwirkenden in jedem Moment sein Instrument wechseln kann und so in absoluter Freiheit befähigt ist, nach seinen künstlerischen Einsichten die Idee des Vorwurfs zu reproduzieren."[13]

Reminiscent of a musical phrase, the structure of "L'amiral cherche une maison à louer" allows a manifoldness within a unity. The fact that the unity of a musical phrase is built upon diversity was already noted by a philosopher whose theories on simultaneity were heavily discussed by the members of the Club Voltaire: Henri Bergson.[14] No doubt, Bergson's philosophy proposes a new concept of identity. He distinguishes an outside ego from an inside ego. The outside one is measuring its perceptions, while the inside one is blending them. In his *Essai sur les données immédiates de la conscience* (1889, "An Essay on the Immediate Data of Consciousness"), Bergson describes this process. Trying to put the pell-mell of his perceptions in order, he has to notice that in the deeper layers of his consciousness, his impressions have run into one another and are not lined up successively. Therefore, he concludes that his "sensations ... , au lieu de se juxtaposer, s'étaient fondues les unes dans les autres de manière à douer l'ensemble d'un aspect propre, de manière à en faire une espèce de phrase musicale."[15]

Also composed like a musical phrase, the *poème simultan* of Tzara and his coauthors adequately illustrates the process of experience described by Bergson. A hierarchy of perceptions does not exist; even the competing languages are of same value. Thus, there is no difference between the foreign and the own language and the principles laid down by Tzara in his "Note pour les bourgeois" (1916) can be realized. These principles "consistent dans la possibilité que je donne à chaque écoutant de lier les associations convenables."[16] In this way, words from different languages can also be combined — a strategy more radically carried out by Hugo Ball.

At the zenith of dadaism, in 1916, on June 23, Hugo Ball wrote into his diary: "Ich habe eine neue Gattung von Versen erfunden, 'Verse ohne Worte' oder Lautgedichte. ... Die ersten Verse habe ich heute abend vorgelesen."[17] Since then, Ball's verses "Karawane" ("Caravan"), "Labadas Gesang an die Wolken" ("Labada's Song for the Clouds"), and "gadji beri bimba" have become well known. Nevertheless, they are still waiting to be understood.

Already their author felt the need for explanations. Thus, before delivering his verses, Ball pointed out to his audience that by producing sound poetry he wanted to do without a language spoiled and made unusable by journalism. Besides, he refused to compose poetry by means of secondhand words. Instead, he claimed to invent brand-new words for one's individual usage. He repeated his demands on July 14, 1916, in a manifesto: "Ich will keine Worte, die andere erfunden haben. Alle Worte haben andere erfunden. Ich will meinen eigenen Unfug, und Vokale und Konsonanten dazu, die ihm entsprechen."[18] Consequently, he intended to withdraw to what he considered the "innerste Alchimie des Wortes, man gebe auch das Wort noch preis, und bewahre so der Dichtung ihren letzten heiligsten Bezirk."[19] Altogether, Ball seemed to look for a language that belonged only to himself. Thus, the connection between identity and language seems to be closer than ever. But actually, in some of his texts that he performed on June 23, in "Karawane"[20] and in "gadji beri bimba," words can be identified. In "gadji beri bimba," "rhinozerossola," "elefantolim," and "affalo" are apparent derivatives of "Rhinozeros," "Elefant," and "Affe." Words from several other languages are also used. "Bimba" means "little girl" in Italian and "top hat" in Spanish. "Beri" is the plural form of beer in Romanian. And to add other examples, there are "gramma" for Latin "letter," "bin" for "container" in English or for the first person singular of the present tense of German "sein." The word "ban" is Romanian for "coin" or English for "to ban." "Velo" is a bicycle in French and a sail in Italian. "Da" means "yes" in Russian and other Slavic languages; in Italian, it is an imperative; and in German, an adverb of place. "Tor" is either a door or a stupid person in German. "Viola" stands for an instrument or a flower in German, while in Romanian it means rape. A mad person can be called "gaga" in French and in German. Finally, "zanzibar" alludes to the island off the coast of Tanzania or to a French game of cards. After all, Ball's compositions of what he claims to be "verses without words" are indeed interlarded with words from several languages. Thereby, it is a striking phenomenon that some of these words have a meaning in more than one language.[21] This is the case with the word "dada," which is also found in more than one language. "Dada stammt aus dem Lexikon. ... Im Französischen bedeutets Steckenpferd. Im Deutschen: Addio steigt mir bitte den Ruecken runter, auf Wiedersehen ein ander Mal! Im Rumänischen: 'Ja wahrhaftig, Sie haben recht, so ist es. Jawohl, wirklich. Machen wir.' Und so weiter. Ein internationales Wort."[22] In this sense, "gadji beri bimba" is also international and demonstrates that the foreign and the own may coincide.

Ball seemingly missed his aim to invent new words just for himself. But, of course, the words he used have lost all their meaning. Thus, their mere sound is important. Some of Ball's colleagues argued that this manner of composing a poem was influenced by Russian Futurism. Raoul Hausmann repeatedly discusses connections between Ball and the main representatives of Russian Futurism, Velemir Khlebnikov and Aleksej Kruchenykh. For Hausmann, it was Wassily Kandinsky who instructed Ball in the latest developments of Russian literature.[23] Examples of Khlebnikov's sound poems are likely to have been given by Kandinski at the Cabaret Voltaire in 1916.[24] In fact, neither the published parts of Ball's diary, nor his incompletely edited letters hint at a direct connection to Russian Futurism. Although Hausmann's argument therefore remains unproved,[25] similarities between Ball's poetry and the writings of Russian Futurism do exist. Both Ball and Khlebnikov used words with meanings in several languages. Khlebnikov gives an example: The name of the German philosopher Kant written outside of any context may be misunderstood by a Scot as the term for a shoemaker.[26] This is just the same technique as observed in "gadji beri bimba." In addition, Khlebnikov's *Zaum*-poetry[27] is interlarded with words from foreign languages.

Furthermore, Ball's manifesto of July 14, 1916, reminds one of a declaration by Kruchenykh. In 1913, Kruchenykh published a leaflet entitled "Deklaratsiya slova kak takovogo — Declaration of the word as such." Some sentences of Kruchenykh might have sounded familiar to Ball: "Thought and speech cannot catch up with the emotional experience of someone inspired; therefore, the artist is free to express himself not only in a common language (concepts), but also in a private one ... , as well as in a language that does not have a definite meaning."[28] Searching for such a private language, Ball also gave up the common language: "Warum kann der Baum nicht Pluplusch heissen," he suggested, "und Pluplubasch, wenn es geregnet hat?"[29] A similar proposal was made by Kruchenykh: "An artist has seen the world in a new way, and, like Adam, he gives his own names to everything. A lily is beautiful, but the word 'lily' is soiled with fingers and raped. For this reason I call a lily 'euy,' and the original purity is reestablished."[30]

A language of original purity, however, was found in the onomatopoetic verses of shamanist spellings. Like other contemporary Russian artists, as for example the painters Michail Larionov and Elena Goncharova, Kruchenykh and Khlebnikov were interested in folklore and ethnography[31] and thus Siberian Shamanism attracted them. In 1912, Khlebnikov published "Schamane und Venus" ("Shaman and Venus"); at the same time, Larionov and Goncharova printed several lithographs and book illustrations showing shamans in trance. Apparently, shamanism and magic practice were interesting topics for Ball, too. Indeed, the performance of his verses without words looked like a shamanist ceremony. "Ich hatte mir dazu," Ball recounts, "ein eigenes Kostüm konstruiert. Meine Beine standen in einem Säulenrund aus blauglänzendem Karton. ... Darüber trug ich einen riesigen, aus Pappe geschnittenen Mantelkragen, der innen mit Scharlach und außen mit Gold beklebt, am Halse derart zusammengehalten wurde, daß ich ihn durch Heben und Senken der Ellbogen flügelartig bewegen konnte. Dazu einen zylinderartigen, hohen, weiß und blau gestreiften Schamanenhut."[32] Wearing this costume, Ball was carried onto the dark stage. Then the solemn deliverance of the verses "gadji beri bimba" and of "Karawane" began. During the recitation, Ball's mental state changed in a significant manner. "Die schweren Vokalreihen und der schleppende Rhythmus ... hatten mir eben noch eine letzte Steigerung erlaubt," Ball describes his feelings. "Wie sollte ich's aber zu Ende führen? Da bemerkte ich, daß meine Stimme, der kein anderer Weg mehr blieb, die uralte Kadenz der priesterlichen Lamentation annahm, jenen Stil des Meßgesangs, wie er durch die katholischen Kirchen des Morgen- und Abendlandes wehklagt."[33] As if absorbed in a trance, Ball let his voice follow religious tunes. Thus, his performance became a mystical experience. In order to underline this, at the end of the performance somebody switched off the light and the room sunk into a mystical darkness, in which Ball disappeared as "magischer Bischof,"[34] transcending all identity and all differences between the foreign and the own.

No doubt, there are remarkable affinities between Ball's poetry of the dadaistic period and the work of Russian Futurists. But the knowledge about the poetry of Kruchenykh and Khlebnikov could only be from hearsay. Whether Kandinski told Ball is unproved. In fact, Kandinski had contacts to David Burliuk, a contributor to *Der Blaue Reiter* and the editor of Russian Futurist manifestos and poetry. Besides, four of Kandinski's poems appeared in *A Slap into the Face of Common Taste* (1912), where writings by Khlebnikov and Kruchenykh were edited. Thus, there might have been a stream of information via Kandinski. But even more so, Kandinski himself influenced Ball.[35] Ball did not doubt that Kandinski "als Erster den abstraktesten Lautausdruck, der nur aus harmonisierten Vokalen und Konsonanten besteht, gefunden und angewandt [hat]."[36]

Indeed, in "Der gelbe Klang" ("The Yellow Sound"), a stage composition, the sound of the human voice is used "ohne Verdunkelung desselben durch das Wort, durch den Sinn des Wortes."[37] Thus, "Singen ohne Worte"[38] is an important element of Kandinski's stage composition. Furthermore, his theoretical writings *Über das Geistige in der Kunst* (1912, "On the Spiritual in Art") and "Über die Formfrage" (1912, "On the Question of Form") contain the roots of a theory on modern literature.[39] Kandinski argues that depriving words of all their meaning is discovering their inner sound:

> Geschickte Anwendung (nach dichterischem *Gefühl*) eines Wortes, eine *innerlich* nötige Wiederholung desselben zweimal, dreimal, mehrere Male nacheinander kann nicht nur zum Wachsen des inneren Klanges führen, sondern noch andere nicht geahnte geistige Eigenschaften des Wortes zutage bringen. Schließlich bei öfterer Wiederholung des Wortes ... verliert es den äußeren Sinn der Benennung. Ebenso wird sogar der abstrakt gewordene Sinn des bezeichneten Gegenstandes vergessen und nur der reine Klang des Wortes entblößt.[40]

The inner sound is what Kandinski calls "Geist" (spirit)[41] or "die Seele der Form" (the soul of form).[42] *Geist* and *Seele*, however, are nonempirical, intelligible things. Thus, depriving words of their meaning is opening a transcendental world. This transcendental world shines through every word, whether without meaning or not. Kandinski points out that "jedes gesagte Wort (Baum, Himmel, Mensch) eine innere Vibration erweckt. ... Sich dieser Möglichkeit, eine Vibration zu verursachen, zu berauben, wäre: das Arsenal seiner Mittel zum Ausdruck zu vermindern."[43] Therefore, the artist is allowed to use every word.

And that is what Hugo Ball did while composing his "gadji beri bimba."
He used words deprived of their concrete meaning in order to reveal their
hidden inner sound, the "innerste Alchimie des Worts." Therefore, his poetry is transcendental; his approach to language is mystical. For him, words
are more than mere significations of things. One day, before a performance
of "gadji beri bimba," he wrote into his diary: "Wir haben das Wort mit
Kräften und Energien geladen, die uns den evangelischen Begriff des
'Wortes' (logos) ... wieder entdecken ließen."[44] Logos is an absolute, beyond
space and time, without any relation to things. In contrast, the words used as
significations of things are only relative. Therefore, Ball differentiates the absolute word from relative words. "Die großen Dichter und Sprachkünstler
sind nicht mehr innerhalb der Kirche zu finden," he notes in 1919. "Sie haben, wo sie mit den Ekklesiasten konkurrieren, mehr Sinn und Gewissen für
das Wort in seiner ursprünglichen Bedeutung als jene, die es ex officio haben
sollten, und die das absolute Wort verkünden. Wie kann man aber ... zum
ewigen Wort einen lebendigen Zugang haben, wenn man das zeitliche und
relative Wort brutalisiert?"[45] Already in 1916, the difference between the absolute word and relative words is a decisive argument in Ball's "Eröffnungs-
Manifest." He criticizes the poets who only use words but have never had a
connection to the word as such. "Verehrteste Dichter," he addresses them,
"die ihr immer mit Worten, nie aber das Wort selbst gedichtet habt." In opposition to them, dadaist poets are evangelists[46] whose poetry aims at the logos.[47]

Verses like "gadji beri bimba" should reveal the logos. Therefore, the
performance of Ball's verses became a mystical ceremony: Like a shaman, the
poet incarnated a transcendental authority, as the foundation and basis of all
language logos emanated in words. Consequently, the use of words from
several languages, deprived of any meaning, is to be explained as an attempt
to show the hidden unity of the human tongue — a unity never touched by
questions of ethnic or individual identity.

Notes

[1.] "Kleine Mitteilungen," *Zeitschrift des Allgemeinen deutschen Sprachvereins* (1888), 1007.

[2.] Felix Rudolph, "Die nationale Bedeutung unserer Sprache," *Zeitschrift des Allgemeinen deutschen Sprachvereins* (1888), 157.

[3.] Anton Frank, "Die Sprache ein Spiegel des Volkes," *Zeitschrift des Allgemeinen deutschen Sprachvereins* (1887), 131–32.

[4.] Wilhelm Scherer, "Die deutsche Spracheinheit," *Preußische Jahrbücher* 24 (1872): 1.

[5.] Johann Gottfried Herder, *Abhandlung über den Ursprung der Sprache*, ed. Hans Dietrich Irmscher (Stuttgart: Reclam, 1981), 64.

[6.] Wilhelm Humboldt, "Über die Natur der Sprache im allgemeinen," *Schriften zur Sprache*, ed. Manfred Böhle (Paderborn: Schöningh, 1959), 7.

[7.] Wilhelm Humboldt, "Über den Nationalcharakter der Sprache," *Bildung und Sprache. Eine Auswahl aus seinen Schriften* (Paderborn: Schöningh, 1959), 78.

[8.] Friedrich W. Genthe, *Geschichte der Macaronischen Poesie und Sammlung ihrer vorzüglichsten Denkmale* (1836; reprint, Wiesbaden: Sendig, 1966), 9–10.

[9.] Jürgen Dahl, *Maccaronisches Poetikum oder Nachtwächteri veniunt Spießibus atque Laternis* (Ebenhausen: Langewiesche-Brand, 1962) also summarizes the history of macaronism. Günther Hess, *Deutsch-lateinische Narrenzunft. Studien zum Verhältnis von Volkssprache und Latinität in der satirischen Literatur des 16. Jahrhunderts* (Munich: Beck, 1971), 234–40 lists some examples of macaronic poetry in Germany.

[10.] Genthe, 10.

[11.] Dahl, 9; Hess, 236; see also Ernst Robert Curtius, *Europäische Literatur und lateinisches Mittelalter* (Bern: Francke, 1984), 249.

[12.] Hugo Ball, *Flucht aus der Zeit* (Zurich: Limmat, 1992), 87.

[13.] Richard Huelsenbeck, *Tristan Tzara: Dada siegt! Bilanz und Erinnerung* (Hamburg: Nautilus Nemo, 1985), 24–25.

[14.] Ball, *Flucht aus der Zeit*, 192–93.

[15.] Henri Bergson, *Essai sur les données immédiates de la conscience* (Paris: P. U. F., 1926), 96–97. Translation: [His] impressions, instead of being opposed to one another, were grounded within one another in such a way as to present the entirety of a particular angle, in such a way as to create a particular kind of musical phrase.

[16.] Tristan Tzara, "L' amiral cherche une maison à louer. Note pour les bourgeois," in *Œuvre complètes*, vol. 1 (1912–1924), ed. Henri Béhar (Paris: Flammarion, 1975), 493. Translation: These principles enable the listener to link his / her associations in a suitable manner.

[17.] Ball, *Flucht aus der Zeit,* 105.

[18.] Hugo Ball, "Eröffnungs-Manifest, 1," Dada-Abend, Zurich, July 14, 1916, in *Dada total. Manifeste, Aktionen, Texte, Bilder* (Stuttgart: Reclam, 1994), 34.

[19.] Ball, *Flucht aus der Zeit,* 106.

[20.] See Harald Henzler, "Die 'Karawane,'" *Hugo-Ball-Almanach* (1993): 99–100.

[21.] This has been noticed already by Eckhard Philipp, *Dadaismus* (Munich: Beck, 1980), 195 and Henzler, "Karawane," 97.

[22.] Ball, "Eröffnungs-Manifest," 34.

[23.] Raoul Hausmann, "Zur Geschichte des Lautgedichtes," in *Am Anfang war Dada,* ed. Karl Riha and Günter Kämpf (Gießen: Anabas, 1980), 39; see also Raoul Hausmann, "Note sur le poème phonétique: Kandinsky et Ball," *German Life and Letters* 21 (1967/68): 58.

[24.] As for Karl Riha, the hints given by Hausmann are "useful and revealing." Karl Riha, "Zur Lautpoesie," *Sprache im technischen Zeitalter* (1975): 263.

[25.] See Velemir Khlebnikov, *Werke,* vol. 2, ed. Peter Urban (Rowohlt: Reinbek, 1972), 581.

[26.] See Vladimir Markov, *Russian Futurism: A History* (Berkeley, CA: U of California P, 1968), 130–31.

[27.] The term "*Zaum*-poetry" is derived from "Zaumny jazyk," which, according to Victor Ehrlich, describes a language transcending any meaning and sense (see Victor Ehrlich, *Russian Formalism. History-Doctrine* [s'Gravenhage: Mouton, 1955]).

[28.] Markov, 130–31.

[29.] Ball, "Eröffnungs-Manifest," 34.

[30.] Markov, 131.

[31.] For Khlebnikov, see Henryk Baran, "Chlebnikov's Poetics and its Folkloric and ethnographic Sources," in *Velimir Chlebnikov (1885–1922): Myth and Reality. Amsterdam Symposium on the Centenary of Velimir Chlebnikov,* ed. Willem G. Weststeijn (Amsterdam: Rodopi, 1986), 15–73; see also Anthony Parton, "Avantgarde und mystische Tradition in Rußland 1900–1915," in *Okkultismus und Avantgarde. Von Munch bis Mondriaan 1900–1915* (Frankfurt am Main: edition tertium, 1995), 199–200.

[32.] Ball, *Flucht aus der Zeit,* 105.

[33.] Ibid., 105–6.

[34.] Ibid., 105.

[35.] See Henzler, 101–3.

[36.] Hugo Ball, "Kandinsky. Vortrag, gehalten in der Galerie Dada," Zurich, April 7, 1917, printed in Hugo Ball, *Der Künstler und die Zeitkrankheit. Ausgewählte Schriften,* ed. Hans Burkhard Schlichting (Frankfurt am Main: Suhrkamp, 1984), 54.

[37.] Wassily Kandinsky, "Über Bühnenkomposition," in *Der blaue Reiter,* ed. Wassily Kandinsky and Franz Marc; reedited by Klaus Lankheit (Munich: Piper, 1987), 208.

[38.] Wassily Kandinsky, "Der gelbe Klang," in *Der blaue Reiter,* 209–39.

[39.] Hausmann, "Note sure le poème phonétique," 58. Kandinski's influence on Ball is well known. See Dietmar Kammler, "Die Auflösung der Wirklichkeit und deren Vergeistigung der Kunst im 'inneren Klang'. Anmerkungen zum Material-, Künstler- und Werkbegriff bei Wassily Kandinsky und Hugo Ball," *Hugo-Ball-Almanach* (1983): 17–55.

[40.] Wassily Kandinsky, *Über das Geistige in der Kunst* (Bern: Benteli, 1952), 45–46.

[41.] Wassily Kandinsky, "Über die Formfrage," in *Der Blaue Reiter*, 145.

[42.] Philipp, *Dadaismus*, 183. He writes on the *lingua divina*, to which Ball seems to point in his lecture about Kandinski.

[43.] Kandinsky, *Über das Geistige in der Kunst,* 76.

[44.] Ball, *Flucht aus der Zeit,* 102.

[45.] Ibid., 255.

[46.] Ball, "Eröffnungs-Manifest," 34.

[47.] Ibid., 30.

MICHAEL S. BRYANT

I Say Coffee, You Say Inkwell: Normalizing the Abnormal in Kafka's *The Castle*

I sit down in a cafe, I order a light coffee, the waiter makes me repeat my order three times, and repeats it himself in order to avoid any chance of mistake. He rushes off, transmits my order to a second waiter, who scribbles it in a notebook and transmits it to a third. Finally a fourth waiter appears and says: "Here you are," setting an inkwell down on my table. "But," I say, "I ordered a light coffee." "And here you are," he says as he walks away. If the reader supposes, reading tales of this sort, that what has occurred is no more than a trick played by the waiters or some collective psychosis, we have failed. But if we have been able to give the reader the impression that we are speaking to him of a world in which these preposterous manifestations figure as normal behavior, then he will find himself plunged at one fell swoop into the heart of the fantastic.

— Jean Paul Sartre, "Aminadab,
or the Fantastic Considered as a Language"

THE TEMPTATION TO READ FRANZ KAFKA'S *Das Schloß* (*The Castle*, first translated in 1930) figuratively has been a seductive one for scholars ever since Max Brod essayed a theological interpretation of it in his afterword to the first edition of *Das Schloß* in 1926. According to Brod, K.'s efforts to settle in the village in the shadow of the castle were tantamount to a quest for "die Verbindung mit der Gnade der Gottheit." The opacity of the castle to K.'s understanding was symbolic of "die Inkommensurabilität irdischen und religiösen Tuns," the utter disconnection between human ethical thought and the categories of religion.[1] This view was reproduced in Thomas Mann's assessment of K.'s futile striving for contact with the castle as evidence of "the grotesque unconnection between the human being and the transcendental."[2]

Brod and Mann's interpretations of the castle as a symbol for something other than itself, namely God, was taken up by other critics. For Herbert

Tauber, the castle and the village represent God and the world respectively, while Barnabas symbolizes the intermediary between the sacred and profane realms.[3] Ronald Gray can decipher Kafka's work only if "the castle and its officials are taken to represent the relationships of men with the supernatural world."[4] This theological line of interpretation would appear to differ markedly from the interpretations of Marxist critics, but both groups share a common emphasis on the symbolic character of the novel. Beginning in the 1960s, Marxist scholars urged a reconceptualization of the castle as a seemingly omnipotent but, in fact, all-too-human product of human manufacture, a monstrous institution that exercises near total domination over the lives and thoughts of the village people but is nonetheless of human origin. In keeping with this immanentist / sociological reading, scholars like Marthe Robert and Walter Sokel have seen the castle as an anachronism, a vestige of a feudal system that miraculously and inexplicably continues to rule the village.[5] Like the theological views of Brod and Mann, these secular interpretations are premised on a tropological reading of *The Castle*: Whether it is God, repressive bourgeois authority, or an archaic hierarchy that has outlived its time, the castle is a sign referring to something other than itself.

I would like to challenge this figurative approach to the text, which makes of the castle a purely symbolic construct whose referent lies outside the novel. Instead, I would contend that the castle is precisely what it is, no more and no less. The castle is not a trope for God, dehumanizing bourgeois government, feudal hierarchy, or stifling bureaucracy; it is the universe transformed into a nightmarish insane asylum by the creative powers of Franz Kafka, one that exists solely within the pages of the novel, referring to nothing save itself. In the novel, the castle and the world merge to become a single baffling, appalling reality. The two so become one that it cannot be said the castle has a referent beyond itself, beyond what it has become; the world of Kafka's novel *is* the castle, with all of the terrifying implications that equation entails. This article examines why the castle resists a figurative reading and how Kafka's artistry creates a nonfigurative, highly literal reality that never ceases to disconcert the reader.

The temptation to levy on Kafka's fiction a premature closure has beguiled some of his more astute interpreters, who otherwise appear to appreciate the nonreferentiality of his work. Walter Sokel, for example, regards Kafka as belonging to a modernist aesthetics beginning with Kant and Baudelaire and culminating in the foundational expressionism of the playwright August Strindberg. Characteristic of this form of modernism is an antirepresentational theory of art, holding that the autonomy of art frees it from the shackles of mimesis and didacticism. Instead of representing the world outside the artist or ennobling the consumer with lofty moral instruction, modernist art presented a "created world" obeying "no logic other than that imposed by its own expressive process."[6] For Baudelaire, the artist's task was to invent a "counterworld," or "antinature," by drawing on elements from the existing world and twisting and deforming them through the creative imagination — an imagination that demonstrated its power "by its refusal to be bound by plausibility and habitual expectation."[7]

An outgrowth of the modernist revolt against mimesis is a "poetics of indeterminacy, or undecidability, of meaning." Sokel calls the poetics of indeterminacy an "extreme branch of modernism" that "eschews even hidden referential meaning and restricts itself to the 'direct presentation' of the image, to pure description or evocation that discourages the reader's hermeneutical attempt to 'understand.'" Kafka's *Die Verwandlung* (1915, translated as *Metamorphosis,* 1946) is Sokel's exemplar: In its "discrepancy between the represented world and the world of the reader," in the absence of a recognizable causality from its fictional world, and in its luminously evocative images, *Die Verwandlung* follows the modernist, antimimetic poetics of indeterminacy — but only to a degree. The "undecidability" of Kafka's fiction is balanced, Sokel maintains, by another tendency, a "mimetic narrativity" typical of modernism, which represents existence in a way "that elicits the reader's empathy with the represented world. Kafka is a storyteller as well as a modernist."[8] In this manner, Sokel posits a bipolarity in Kafka's fiction: at one pole, the "hermetic nonreferentiality" of the poetics of indeterminacy, thwarting all efforts to comprehend the text; at the other, a representational mimesis that "enables the reader to fill in missing links in the representation of an action that, though empirically impossible, achieves psychological and sociological plausibility and thus a meaningful connection with the world outside the text. Without officially consenting to it, the text — unofficially, as it were — invites the reader to reestablish referentiality."[9]

Sokel's notion of bipolarity is in diametrical opposition to the argument of this article. Not only does he affirm a metaphorical continuity between the grotesque world of Kafka's fiction and our own, but he goes on to argue that Kafka challenges his readers "to participate in and … to continue the writer's activity." Sokel's pacific view of Kafka's work reaches its acme in his remark that Kafka belongs to a tradition of art "in which art is not a representation of the world but a tonic for the soul."[10]

Plausibility, empathy with the represented world, a meaningful connection with the world outside the text, reestablished referentiality, invitations to closure, a tonic for the soul — these are the features of the narrativity pole Sokel believes to have located in Kafka's work. They are also unsupported by anything found within the precincts of Kafka's fictional world. In *The Writer in Extremis* (1959), Sokel weaves between the opacity of Kafka's literature and the tendency to coax meaning out of Kafka's texts. On the one hand, Sokel writes: "Kafka never connects the miraculous event [of Gregor Samsa's metamorphosis into an insect] with anything whatever outside itself. The reader yearns for such a connection with a larger world, for an explanation, a ray of light from anywhere outside to break into the dim prison of Gregor Samsa's frightful existence. ... But nothing is allowed to pierce the boundaries of this enigmatic universe."[11] On the other hand, Sokel insists that Gregor's metamorphosis is a metaphor, a "hieroglyphic sign" expressing, "without revealing, the essence of a hidden situation." From that point of view, the "hidden situation" that the metamorphosis expresses is Gregor's secret desire, concealed even from himself, to escape the crushing burdens of his familial responsibilities and regain his parents' spontaneous love. Confounding empirical causality, Gregor's wishes are realized in his transformation into a giant insect.[12]

An extended discussion of *Die Verwandlung* would steer this essay far afield from its subject. We are not given privileged access to Gregor's conscious or unconscious mind. We are never informed how Gregor's metamorphosis was brought to pass. The narrator does not dwell on the mechanics of this truly prodigious occurrence any more than Gregor does. If it is a transformation Gregor consciously longed for, his external behavior upon discovering the change does not betray it: His only concern upon awakening is to get out of bed and dress himself so as to catch the morning train on time. If it is a transformation Gregor unconsciously longed for, there are no psychological cross-sections in the text to support this view. In short, a psychological / metaphorical reading does not depend on anything within the text, but on the need for order, coherence, and intelligibility, which an implied reader brings to the text.[13]

Kafka also does not elicit our "empathy with the represented world" of the castle. How can we empathize with an authority that is both seemingly omnipotent and contemptuous of the struggles of those who, like flies writhing in a spider's web, are hopelessly entangled in the castle's inscrutable reality? How do we construct a bridge across the gulf separating our own world, where logic and illogic exist in equal ratios, from the world of the castle, from which logic has been erased and illogic elevated as the first principle? Sokel considers this resistance in Kafka's fiction an "invitation" to the reader "to reestablish referentiality," an errand made possible by the "psychological and sociological plausibility" of Kafka's art. Yet, Kafka is vexingly parsimonious in his portrayals of K.'s state of mind; we know little or nothing about him. We encounter none of the psychologically "plausible" stream-of-consciousness techniques in *The Castle* that we find in James Joyce or William Faulkner. On the contrary, the reader is annoyed that K. persists in his desultory pursuit of contact with the castle despite every indication of its continued futility. As for "sociological plausibility," we have already seen how little of it Kafka's novel contains. The castle's inaccessibility, its habit of sending arcane letters to job applicants offering them nonexistent jobs, its capricious willingness to hire a land surveyor to work as a school janitor all attest to the sociological implausibility of Kafka's fictional reality when measured against our quotidian experiences. Far from an invitation to complete the reading of the text, *The Castle* flouts the reader's efforts to correlate the action of the novel with everyday life. It is this disparity between our efforts "to fill in the missing links,"[14] as Sokel puts it, and Kafka's refusal to allow such closure, which induces the unsettling feeling we experience as we read Kafka.

The allure of allegorical or symbolical readings of Kafka, as typified by some earlier Kafka scholarship, is more readily understood if we consider *The Castle* in view of theories of reader reception developed by Wolfgang Iser. According to Iser, works of fiction are, in contrast to our experience of the natural world, profoundly underdetermined, riven with gaps that readers must themselves fill in if the text is to make sense. "As we read," Terry Heller, following Iser, comments, "we engage in a process of creating provisional unities; we hypothesize wholes, practicing for the final concretization of the work. This description emphasizes the importance of wholeness to our experience of the work of art because it shows reading to consist mainly of projecting possible wholes out of the fragments given at any specific point." In Iser's schema, what emerges from this process of gap filling is the "implied reader" for a particular text. "The implied reader," Heller continues, "consists of inferences about the connections between presented elements, inferences in which the reader is 'invested' or to which he is committed."[15] For Iser, a text offers the reader "a particular role to play, and it is this role that constitutes the concept of the implied reader."[16] The text both offers and creates this role of the implied reader, but its construction is collaborative with the reader. Both the reader and the text construct this "implied reader" (different from the actual, or real, reader), who possesses the moral or cultural attitudes necessary for the text to achieve its maximum effect. As Heller relates, the text "may determine points of view from which I am to look. It specifies, to some degree, my world, its events, its inhabitants, its mysteries, and its culture for the duration of the reading. In the process of reading, I pretend to occupy a fictional world as an observer of and … as an actor in that world."[17]

There is a potential tension, however, between these two halves of the reader (implied and real). If a text resists the imposition of order and the search for wholeness by the implied reader, the boundary separating the implied from the real reader may be eroded, and the real reader, sheltered behind his or her alter ego, may find him- or herself drawn into the perverse universe of a text that does not admit of closure. It is closure — the sense of resolution at the end of a literary work achieved by means of making inferences — that the implied reader strives for. Some texts, however, may with-hold closure from the implied reader by disallowing the imposition of unity or arrangement of the textual elements into a meaningful order. As some lit-erary scholars have noted, works that resist the closure sought by the implied reader tend to invite allegorical or symbolical interpretations. Without re-course to such interpretations, the text may lapse into sheer incomprehensi-bility.[18]

I would submit that *The Castle* is just such a work that resists implied readers in their effort to find closure. The very impenetrability of the world portrayed in this novel — as Irving Howe notes, everything in it, "language, events, characters," is clear, except for the "world itself" — is a spur to the figurative readings sketched here. Interpreting the castle as a symbol of the divine or as an antiquated feudal system reflects the natural cognitive impulse to complete the reading of the text — and, at the same time, to remove the noose that Kafka has knotted around the neck of the real reader. The figura-tive reading may preserve the real reader from the hangman and keep the world of intelligibility and order intact, but it does so at the risk of misread-ing the novel.

For it is the perverse, even demonic, illogicality of *The Castle* that defies the order mongering and symbol seeking of the implied reader. The aesthetic distance between the real reader and the text lowers as the boundary be-tween them, formed by the implied reader, dissolves. When the novel has been read cover to cover, closure still eludes the implied reader; the real reader cannot simply put the work aside as one could a traditional novel. The detachment normally facilitated by the buffer of the implied reader is gone, and the real reader experiences the anxiety that gave birth in the English lexi-con to the word "Kafkaesque."

How does Kafka shrug off the implied reader and draw the real reader into his literary cosmos? The answer is: by conjuring a nightmarish world synonymous with the castle authorities, a world that, in the words of Tzvetan Todorov, "obeys an oneiric logic" that "no longer has anything to do with the real."[19] There is no extratextual referent beyond the castle; it refers only to itself and to the universe it has devoured and made over into an image of itself. There is no reality in *The Castle* other than the castle. "It is often said of Kafka," writes Todorov, "that his narratives must be read above all *as nar-ratives*, on the literal level."[20] When *The Castle* is so read, the implied reader disappears into the maw of its anticlosure, leaving the real reader exposed to the peculiar horror of Kafka's nightmare.

On one level, the narrative flow is straightforward. K. arrives in the vil-lage, alleging to have a commission to serve as a land surveyor for the castle. The plot thickens as K. discovers the inaccessibility of the castle authorities; despite their absolute hegemony over the village, they are, with some minor exceptions (such as Klamm's secretary, Momus), virtually invisible, and certainly unavailable to K. K. is assigned a pair of harlequinesque assistants who neither work, nor are they asked to work. K. is eventually informed that there has been no need for a land surveyor in the village for years, but that he can work as a janitor in the local school if he wishes. The rest of the novel recounts K.'s pointless endeavors to establish contact with the castle, especially with its representative in the village, the mysterious Klamm. In the course of his futile wheel spinning, K. is unable to divine anything about the castle authorities' intentions, purposes, or the nature of their interests in the village (except for concubinage with its young women).

So much for the narrative story line. It is in the episodes themselves, however, that Kafka confounds the implied reader's search for closure and intelligibility. K.'s interview with the superintendent is an example. K.'s entire claim to any status whatsoever in the village is Klamm's first letter, offering him the job of land surveyor. On this slenderest of reeds, K. has built his future and burnt all bridges behind him: He has sacrificed everything at home to work as land surveyor in the village. With this letter and a few tenuous contacts who may or may not be able to intercede for him with Klamm (including Frieda), he stakes his hopes for getting on in the village. The superintendent, however, discounts Klamm's letter as not being an official correspondence, but merely a private letter. He informs K. that to a person versed in reading official correspondences (and for this reason more adept at reading unofficial letters) this fact would be more than clear.[21] K. counters that he has established contacts in the village that provide him with a link to the castle — a ray of hope the superintendent quickly extinguishes by citing K.'s ignorance of the castle's institutions. He claims that due to his ignorance, K. may mistake apparent contacts with the castle for actual ones (71). There is an air of malevolent exultation in the superintendent's dismissal of K.'s grounds for hope as he gloats over K.'s failure to distinguish between an official and unofficial letter.

A bewildering logic — or, by the standards of the real and implied reader, a disturbing *illogic* — prevails in this encounter, as it does in so many others in the novel. Letters from functionaries offering jobs are in the normal course of events exactly what they purport to be: invitations to employment. If there has been some misunderstanding — if, for example, the job opening has suddenly and unexpectedly closed, or a mistake has been made in calculating personnel needs — the implied reader expects this information to be disclosed, giving the text a sense of completeness, permitting one to fill in the gaps. Yet, this is what Kafka refuses to provide the reader. In the universe of the novel, nothing is as it should be for the reader: apparently clear letters do not mean what they say (and are in fact meaningless); bureaucrats who offer jobs to prospective civil servants are permanently inaccessible to them when they finally arrive; other bureaucrats in the same organization mock the efforts of job applicants from a position of superior, but recondite, knowledge instead of furnishing helpful guidance; contacts cultivated by job applicants are discounted as illusory. And why is this? Is it a matter of the authorities' conspiratorial malice or their incompetence? The superintendent reveals the reason for the imbroglio: "Sie aber halten sie infolge Ihrer Unkenntnis der Verhältnisse für wirklich" (90). The fault lies with K., the apparent victim; if he only knew "the circumstances," or were able to read letters properly, it would all be clear to him!

Despite the superintendent's assurances, it is far from certain that the fault resides in K.'s ignorance. As we accompany K. through the novel, we are as puzzled as he is by the deceptive, constantly shifting permutations in what we had assumed were fixed points. Klamm is not merely unavailable to K. (except through his letters, which are indecipherable to K. as well as outdated) but may not even be the person K. had assumed him to be (he may be Momus, Olga cautions). Arthur and Jeremias, the apparently innocuous and ineffectual assistants, turn out to be Klamm's messengers (according to Frieda). Jeremias, apparently a young man, is revealed as a much older man who poses a threat to K.'s relationship with Frieda. And Frieda's love for K. is revealed by Pepi to be a scheme to attract attention to herself in the village. The effect of reading *The Castle* for the reader is like driving in a strange city on a main street with detour after detour, and detours from the detours, none of which ever reconnect with the streets of which they are detours, so that one drifts helplessly further and further from the intended destination, with neither compass nor atlas to show the way back.

But is there a way back? Kafka suggests that, within the world of his novel, there is not. Sartre's parable about the waiter and the inkwell (quoted at the beginning of this article) sums up Kafka's fictional world brilliantly. If we can rest assured that the bizarre logic of this world is simply the result of bad faith on the part of malicious or incompetent bureaucrats, or a "bad trip" after K. has taken a hit of LSD, the disturbing effect of the novel is dissipated. The reader then has a base line of normality and reason; a degree of closure is possible. If, on the other hand, the world conveyed to the reader is "a world in which these preposterous manifestations figure as normal behavior," then all that is familiar to the reader based on his / her own life experience becomes problematic. All ties to lucidity — to the reality most of us inhabit — are abolished. Our only recourse is to identify with the novel's "hero," K.; yet of him we know little, except that he has staked everything on the job offered him and that he longs for an interview with Klamm. In short, K. is almost as incomprehensible to the reader as the village and the castle. To identify with K., Todorov asserts, is to "exclude oneself from reality," plunging "our reason, which was to right the topsy-turvy world, ... into this nightmare."[22]

By now, it should be clear why a figurative interpretation of the castle misses the mark. Interpreting the castle as a symbol of God or an allegory of class oppression represents an imposition of forced closure on a work that fundamentally resists closure. Figurative interpretations insist that the novel *is* consonant with the reader's life experience, that Kafka's oneiric cosmos *can* become transparent to our understanding, if only we find its referent outside the text. Such a view can dilute Kafka's nightmare into a plea for social or political reform, as Paul Oppenheimer, writing in 1956, observed regarding *Der Prozess* (1925; *The Trial*):

> If Kafka's novel, and Welles' cinematic treatment of it, were simply allegories of bureaucratic frustration, if 'kafkaesque' simply meant ... a social misery and futility born of purely human pointlessness, stupidity, and redundancy, then the resemblance to actual nightmares would be very slight indeed. The significance of the novel, and indirectly of the film, would be scarcely greater than that of a campaign for good government, or a more humanely super-vised civil service. Kafka's genius, however, lies in his creating a lucid, essentially simple prose with more impressive implications — in his deliberate confusion of governmental bureaucracy with the universe itself, as though Josef K.'s arrest ... were the natural result of a physical or divine madness at the heart of reality.[23]

There is no indication in *The Castle* that Kafka intended his work as a cautionary tale, a political polemic, or a theological statement. It may be comforting to view the novel in any one of these lights; but to do so hardly does justice to the text itself, which presents to the reader an amoral world wherein all value systems are obsolete, just as, in a parallel sense, all yearnings for closure founder on the unassimilable structure of the text.

In *The Castle*, the abnormal and the fantastic have become the rule, not the exception. There is no way to come to terms with the fictional world of the novel; no Rosetta stone can decode these hieroglyphics; no all-illuminating symbol can annex the work to a recognizable framework. Herein resides the peculiar horror of Kafka's art. Stripped of the implied reader construct, the real reader experiences an anxiety akin to that described by William F. Fischer in his account of responses to psychological danger: "My world, my relations, my situation no longer speak to me in the familiar language. I am no longer at home. The situation seems dissonant, inappropriate, even meaningless. ... The situation is collapsing and I am caught in the here-and-now of its destruction. ... Who, where, and what I am are no longer clear. My wants mingle in confusion. The past seems uncertain as it ceases to support the present and it surrounds me without revealing avenues of escape."[24]

This intransitivity in Kafka's art — this refusal to gesture toward an extratextual referent, but instead to create in the text a perverse world that signifies nothing but itself — is the source of our disquietude as we read *The Castle*. By the end of the novel, Kafka's tortuous nightmare has, in Todorov's words, "swallow[ed] up the entire world of the book and the reader along with it."[25]

Kafka does not merely withhold meaning from the reader of his text, however; he also refuses to allow himself this solace. Unlike many of his contemporaries, Kafka did not try to pierce the cloud of unknowing by resorting to occult ideas, which he then incorporated into his fiction. Whatever his personal spiritual yearnings may have been, *The Castle* does not point toward a higher dimension of consciousness, nor does it hint at a metaphysical solution to existential riddles. In order to appreciate the degree to which Kafka resisted the flight from ambiguity into the arms of mysticism, it is helpful to recall just how tempting occult ideas were to many intellectual figures of Kafka's era.

East and Central Europe at the fin de siècle was a cauldron of esoteric doctrines, secret societies, and mystical teachings. Why did the occult appeal to artists during this period? One explanation is a reaction against the tough-minded positivism and scientism of the mid- to late nineteenth century. The pragmatic materialism so characteristic of the age — represented in politics by Bismarck's *Realpolitik*, in the arts by realism and naturalism, in the life sciences by the works of Herbert Spencer and Charles Darwin, in the social sciences by Auguste Comte's atheistic positivism, in foreign affairs by nationalist and racist forms of imperialism, and in religion by the corrosive theologies of Bruno Bauer, David Friedrich Strauss, and Ernest Renan — made a thorough housecleaning of traditional spiritual practice. Old certitudes were shaken to their foundation, leaving many Europeans bereft of the faith of their fathers.[26] The allure of esoteric, anti-Enlightenment movements at the fin de siècle is in part explained by the perceived spiritual emptiness of nineteenth-century scientific culture.

The Russian mystic Helene Petrovna Blavatsky brought her mystical teachings known as "Theosophy" to international renown during this period. While Theosophy fused magic, alchemy, Renaissance Neo-Platonism, study of the Kabbalah, Tarot cards, necromancy, and Buddhism into a single occult creed, its political message of pacifism and internationalism found a receptive audience among the English and American middle classes. Blavatsky's Theosophy was rich in offspring in Central and Eastern Europe, notably Rudolf Steiner's Anthroposophy.[27] Like Theosophy, Anthroposophy was an antiscientific set of beliefs, teaching that nature contains secret powers unglimpsed by modern science — powers that a suitably trained adept could control through magic. It was primarily through Steiner's Anthroposophy that the mystical currents in Theosophy affected so many among Kafka's generation.

It is truly striking how many of Central Europe's preeminent intellectuals were influenced by Theosophical / Anthroposophical ideas at the turn of the century. The list reads like an artistic honor roll: Wassily Kandinsky and the *Blaue Reiter*, Gustav Mahler, Arnold Schönberg, August Strindberg, Alfred Kubin, Gustav Meyrink, Piet Mondrian, and Kafka's friend Max Brod were all involved, to varying degrees, in Theosophical speculation. Occult ideas intrigued even the self-styled "Enlightenment" exponent Sigmund Freud, whose psychoanalysis never lost its "gnostic" overtones.[28] For our purposes, the noteworthy feature of these engagements is how the occult affected the artistic products of the fin de siècle. Schönberg described his work as a "deciphering method" that would enable us to "draw nearer to God, since then we no longer insist that we should understand him." By abandoning the rational project of understanding God, we can enter into a fuller experience of the unknowable other.[29] Kandinsky's book *Über das Geistige in der Kunst* (1912, translated as *The Art of Spiritual Harmony,* 1914) dealt in part with Anthroposophy and referred to Steiner's journal, *Lucifer-Gnosis* (published between 1903 and 1908). Patrick Werkner argues that August Strindberg's work was permeated with the Swedish mystic Immanuel Swedenborg's writings.[30]

Two of the more interesting occultists among the Central European intelligentsia of this period were the Austrian artist Alfred Kubin and the Czech writer Gustav Meyrink. Kubin, who was very likely introduced to Eastern mysticism and the occult by Meyrink, was candid about the relationship of mysticism to his art, as he revealed in a stream of letters to Fritz von Herzmanovsky-Orlando: "In general, I am more mystical than ever. I live in fact in a general aura of mysticism, without individual or specific experiences. ... I seek exclusively a deepening of my awareness, only that. I will struggle to experience this secret realm, which is so deeply rooted in my humanity, and to pour the results of that experience into the mold of art."[31] Gustav Meyrink shared Kubin's early enthusiasm for Buddhism, to which Meyrink finally converted in 1927. Long before then, however, Meyrink had entertained a fascination with a variety of occult practices, including secret teachings, Theosophy, parapsychology, and alchemy. Meyrink's primary interest was Yoga, which he regarded as a means of promoting spiritual development. According to Muriel W. Stiffler, the aim of Meyrink's fiction, which is replete with supernatural beings and events, was "to shock his fellow citizens out of their complacency," "to awaken them to the possibility of spiritual integration on a higher level." The type of alchemy Meyrink envisioned was not merely the kind that turned lead into gold, but a type that transformed "animal human beings" *(Tiermenschen)* into "golden human beings" *(Gold-*

menschen). He strove to present this secret alchemical knowledge in his fiction.[32]

Meyrink's work is an exotic amalgam of personal occult experience and his own poetic imagination. In *Der Uhrmacher* (1937, "The Watchmaker") and *Der weiße Dominikaner* (1921, translated as *The White Dominican,* 1994), Meyrink wove such mystical symbolism into his text as the Hermaphrodite, an ancient symbol of the coincidence of opposites fundamental to mystical experience. His reference in *Der weiße Dominikaner* to a brotherhood of higher spiritual beings possessing esoteric knowledge and controlling human destiny evokes parallels with Blavatsky and Steiner.[33] It may have been this belief in a transcendent realm of higher consciousness expressed in these and other works that attracted the young Max Brod, who found in Meyrink a model for his own literary efforts, describing him as the "non plus ultra aller modernen Dichtung."[34]

The examples of Schönberg, Kandinsky, Strindberg, Kubin, Meyrink, and Brod demonstrate the pervasive influence of occult ideas on the art, music, and literature of the fin de siècle. They also remind us how unlike them Kafka was. Kafka may have been a *Gottsucher* in private life, as Brod claims, but *The Castle* does not in any way lend itself to occult interpretations. We encounter in the novel no "deciphering method," as we do in Schönberg; we find no "struggle with the secret realm" that we find in Kubin's disturbing art; we see none of the gestures toward mystical conceptions that pervade Meyrink's fiction. *The Castle* sheds no light, reveals no secret, conveys no truth. It dissolves the reader's sense of orientation to a familiar world, yet refuses to substitute for it a higher reality. It is Kafka's unflinching refusal to resolve ambiguity through secret brotherhoods, spiritual hierarchies, and mystical wisdom that sets his work apart from his contemporaries.

This refusal, moreover, shields Kafka from the charge of involvement in the development of Nazi racialism. The same cannot entirely be said of Kafka's contemporaries. The connections between Nazism and occult movements of the fin de siècle have been widely noted.[35] While Blavatsky's Theosophy was politically progressive, internationalist, and pacifist, it contained within itself the potential for a sinister reinterpretation. With its mythology of the Earth's seven "root races," its glorification of "the Aryan" as the race with the greatest spiritual potential, and its belief in a prehistoric "fall," or primal degeneration caused by racial interbreeding, Theosophy contributed to a nineteenth-century vein of Nordic racialism that Adolf Hitler would later appropriate. An intermediary between Theosophy and Nazism was the Austrian writer and Ario-Sophist Jörg Lanz von Liebenfels, who proclaimed "a coming era of German world rule" dominated by the *Armanen*, an ancient brotherhood of Aryan man-spirits.[36] Kubin, Strindberg, Herzmanovsky, and Hitler were all attracted to Liebenfels's Theozoology — Strindberg and

Herzmanovsky going so far as to join Liebenfels's mystic society, the "Order of the New Temple."[37] Peter Washington has pointed out how the occultism of Georges Gurdjieff, emphasizing primitivism, irrational surrender to authority, and confrontational combativeness, suggests a subtle opening of Theosophical ideas to an authoritarian politics.[38] Finally, Meyrink's fiction, stressing esoteric rites of initiation, secret societies of higher spiritual beings, and the values of hierarchy and unconditional obedience have more than a passing affinity with fascist modes of thought.[39] In view of such evidence, it is hard not to agree with Werkner's observation that these "powerful currents of metaphysics and mysticism," reflecting a "turbid and disillusioned attitude toward life and society," helped "prepare the way for Fascism."[40]

Despite his own disillusionment, the fact that Kafka avoided this flight into occult solutions to his problems absolves him from complicity in Nazi barbarism. Kafka's reaction to Meyrink's fiction, as related by the Meyrink enthusiast Max Brod, is surely telling in this respect. Kafka reportedly found "die blendend geschriebene Satire einfältig."[41] For Kafka, the *Einfalt,* the simple-mindedness, of Meyrink's work, we may surmise, was the retreat into mysticism as a means of escaping the torture of ambiguity. Kafka affords his readers no such outlet from the cul-de-sac of his fictional nightmares. The figure of the castle, like Gregor Samsa's metamorphosis, is as opaque to our understanding at the beginning of the novel as at the end. In *The Castle,* as in all of his fiction, Kafka presents us with a knot — one that resists being untied with the fingers of metaphor or cut with the blade of occult gnosis.

Notes

[1.] Max Brod, "Nachwort zur ersten Ausgabe des Schloß-Romans," *Das Schloß* (Munich: Kurt Wolff, 1926), 530.

[2.] Quoted in Irving Howe, "Introduction to Franz Kafka," in *The Castle,* trans. Willa Muir and Edwin Muir (New York: Everyman's Library, 1992), xviii.

[3.] Herbert Tauber, *Franz Kafka* (New Haven, CT: Yale UP, 1948), 170.

[4.] Ronald D. Gray, *Kafka's Castle* (Cambridge: Cambridge UP, 1956), 121.

[5.] Marthe Robert, *L'Ancien et le Nouveau* (Paris: Payot, 1963), 243; Walter H. Sokel, *Franz Kafka: Tragik und Ironie* (Munich: A. Langen, 1964), 397.

[6.] Walter H. Sokel, "Kafka and Modernism," *Approaches to Teaching Kafka's Short Fiction* (New York: Modern Language Association, 1995), 23.

[7.] Ibid., 23. Sokel likens this alembic power of the imagination to Freud's "work of the dream." He writes: "In dreams, too, the individual elements come from the empirical world but are deformed and transformed according to rules unknown to the dreamer's consciousness. Each dream element, even though taken from waking reality, functions according not to the rules of that reality but to the 'thought' that the dream seeks to express." In dreams, as in many of Kafka's texts (such as "Das Urteil," [1913, translated as "The Judgment," 1948]), the thoughts of the dreamer are magically transformed into events — a phenomenon Sokel calls the "wish-fulfilling function" of dreams. This is one aspect of modernism, Sokel contends; the other is the "poetics of indeterminacy" (25–26).

8. Sokel, "Kafka and Modernism," 26–28.

9. Sokel finds sanction for his bipolarity thesis in a letter Kafka wrote to Felice Bauer discussing his short story "Das Urteil." In this letter, Kafka asked Bauer if she had found "some straightforward, coherent meaning that one could follow" in the story, then confessed he was wholly unable to understand it. Kafka pointed out that some features of the story, such as the similarity of the characters' names to their own, suggested a possible autobiographical / allegorical meaning. Sokel cites this tentative remark by Kafka as evidence for his claim that a streak of referentiality runs through Kafka's fiction cheek by jowl with its antimimetic qualities. Sokel's "evidence," in this case, can just as easily prove that Kafka, like most readers, craved the blessings of closure. The irony is that Kafka here imposed closure after the fact on his own work.

10. Sokel, "Kafka and Modernism," 34.

11. Walter H. Sokel, *The Writer in Extremis: Expressionism in Twentieth-Century German Literature* (Stanford, CA: Stanford UP, 1959), 47.

12. Ibid.

13. Other commentators have run afoul of this nettlesome contradiction in Kafka interpretations. Margit M. Sinka, for example, believes that Kafka's fiction reflects an "untiring quest for meaning. Because he cannot, he does not supply the 'truth.' But he always intimates its existence." Several pages later, Sinka undercuts her earlier statement with the observation that Kafka's *Metamorphosis* represents "the end of the so-called canon" insofar as "there are no redeeming ideas or redeeming love" in it; instead, Gregor "dies and diminishes into nothing as he is swept out of the world." Even without the artifice of a bipolarity thesis, the contradiction in which Sinka mires herself is clear, made possible by her very human need to extract human meaning from a text that fundamentally resists such an operation. Margit M. Sinka, "Kafka's *Metamorphosis* and the Search for Meaning in 20th Century German Literature," in *Approaches to Teaching World Literature* (New York: Modern Language Association, 1995), 107, 112.

14. Sokel, "Kafka and Modernism," 29.

15. Terry Heller, *The Delights of Terror: An Aesthetics of the Tale of Terror* (Urbana: U of Illinois P, 1987), 4.

16. Wolfgang Iser, *The Act of Reading* (Baltimore: Johns Hopkins UP, 1978), 34–35.

17. Heller, 4–5.

18. See Tzvetan Todorov, *The Fantastic: A Structural Approach to a Literary Genre* (Ithaca, NY: Cornell UP, 1973); see also Howe, xiv; see also Heller, 123.

[19.] Todorov, 173.

[20.] Ibid., 172.

[21.] Franz Kafka, *Das Schloß* (Berlin: Fischer, 1996), 71. Further page references to this book will appear in parentheses in the text.

[22.] Todorov, 174.

[23.] Paul Oppenheimer, *Evil and the Demonic: A New Theory of Monstrous Behavior* (New York: New York UP, 1996), 115.

[24.] William K. Fischer, "Towards a Phenomenology of Anxiety," in *Explorations in the Psychology of Stress and Anxiety*, ed. Byron P. Rourke (Don Mills, Ontario: Longman Canada, 1969), 110–11.

[25.] Todorov, 174.

[26.] Several prominent artists in the late nineteenth century were afflicted with this sense of bereavement over science's disenchantment of the world. Many, like William Butler Yeats, turned toward Theosophy for spiritual guidance. Yeats not only remained a student of the occult until the end of his life, but his literary work reflected his mystical leanings, as Yeats himself wrote in 1892: "The mystical life is the centre of all that I do and all that I think and all that I write." Yeats regarded Theosophy as the glimmerings of a higher mass consciousness, and he regarded himself as "a voice of what I believe to be a greater renaissance — the revolt of the soul against the intellect — now beginning in the world." For Frederick Crews, Theosophy was an inspirational force in Yeats's writing, without which "Yeats would have been deprived of the prophetic strain and several of the odd but passionately held beliefs that helped to lend his verse its unique rapt quality." Frederick Crews, "The Consolation of Theosophy," *The New York Review of Books*, Sept. 19, 1996, 26.

[27.] The first German Theosophical Society was founded in 1884; a Theosophical Lodge was established in Prague in 1891. Before he developed his own variant, Steiner was general secretary of the German branch of Theosophy. Patrick Werkner, *Austrian Expressionism* (Palo Alto: Society for the Advancement of Science and Scholarship, 1993), 181.

[28.] Following Frederick Crews, I am using the word "gnostic" loosely to refer to "the intuitive apprehension of deep truth without a felt need for corroborating evidence," not to the numerous religious sects in the history of Christianity that bear the name. Although the link between Freud and Theosophy / Anthroposophy is at best tenuous, his lifelong fascination with the occult is well documented. He related to Ernest Jones his belief in clairvoyance, ghosts, numerology, and telepathy. See Ernest Jones, *The Life and Work of Sigmund Freud*, vol. 3 (New York: Basic Books, 1957), 381. The "talking cure" itself reflected Freud's mystical preoccupations, as Frederick Crews notes: "A gnostic tendency lay at the very heart of analytic work as the mature Freud conceived it. In drawing on a privately determined symbology to assign thematic meanings to dreams, associations, errors, and symptoms ... and then in leaping inferentially from those arbitrary interpretations to putative childhood 'scenes' that had to be 'recalled' or at least acknowledged if a cure was to occur, classical analysis didn't just resemble divination: it was the very thing itself. And in this light, Freud's lifelong paranormal sympathies — almost always treated as a minor biographical curiosity — deserve to be considered an integral part of the record." Crews, "The Consolation of Theosophy II," *The New York Review of Books*, Oct. 3, 1996, 41.

29. Letter, Aug. 19, 1912, Schönberg to Kandinsky, 69. Patrick Werkner speculates that Schönberg likely encountered Theosophy during his first stay in Berlin (1901–1903). His evidence is the presence of Schönberg and Steiner in Berlin contemporaneously, at a time when Steiner lectured on "Christianity as a Mystical Fact." Subsequently, Schönberg referred to his *Theory of Harmony* as a "secret science," a title reminiscent of Steiner's earlier *Secret Science in Outline* and Blavatsky's *Secret Teaching*, both published in 1899.

30. Werkner, 171, 181; see also Sixten Ringbom, *The Sounding Cosmos: A Study in the Spiritualism of Kandinsky and the Genesis of Abstract Painting* (Abo: Abo Akedemi, 1970). As Werkner comments, Anthroposophic jargon was not uncommon among the members of the *Blaue Reiter* circle; he cites a letter by August Macke referring to the "astral stare" in Schönberg's pictures — an allusion, as Werkner interprets it, to the Anthroposophical notion of the "astral body" serving as a link between humans and higher spiritual beings.

31. Quoted in Werkner, 205. Kubin's interests in the outré ran the gamut from spiritualism, seances, alchemy, and esoteric lore to Theosophy and Anthroposophy, the Indian Vedas, Lao-tse, and medieval mysticism. Kubin recommended to Herzmanovsky the works of Blavatsky, Annie Besant, and Steiner, as well as the bizarre "Theozoology" of Jörg von Liebenfels, whose Ariosophic mysticism would intrigue Strindberg, Herzmanovsky, and Adolf Hitler (Werkner, 206).

32. Muriel W. Stiffler, *The German Ghost Story as Genre* (New York: Peter Lang, 1993), 111. Where Yeats sought in the occult a surrogate for a doctrinal religion he no longer could believe in, Meyrink's motivation would appear to stem from the turbulent circumstances of his life. He grew up poor, went to jail as a banker for questionable financial doings, declared bankruptcy, contracted a form of spinal tuberculosis his doctors deemed fatal, saw his first marriage end in divorce, and lost a son in an accident. He loathed bourgeois culture, from which he felt permanently estranged. The occult furnished Meyrink an escape into a higher reality far removed from these traumatizing experiences.

33. Gustav Meyrink, *Der Weiße Dominikaner* (Munich: Langen Müller, 1977), 244.

34. Max Brod, *Streitbares Leben* (Munich: Kindler, 1960), 291; Peter Cersowsky, *Phantastische Literatur im ersten Viertel des 20. Jahrhunderts* (Munich: Fink, 1983), 171. In Brod's essay "Höhere Welten," dealing with the contrast between material reality and a "higher" dimension of experience, Brod recounts his interest in Blavatsky, Steiner's *Luzifer-Gnosis*, and Meyrink. The reader will take note that Brod, the first scholar to interpret Kafka as a moralist and seeker after God, was influenced by occult ideas of the fin de siècle. Brod, "Höhere Welten," in *Über die Schönheit häßlicher Bilder. Ein Vademekum für Romantiker unserer Zeit* (Vienna: Zsolnay, 1967); see also Cersowsky, 181.

[35.] See, e.g., Nicholas Goodrick-Clarke, *The Occult Roots of Nazism: Secret Aryan Cults and Their Influence on Nazi Ideology; The Ariosophists of Austria and Germany, 1890–1935* (New York: New York UP, 1985); see also Crews, "The Consolation of Theosophy II." Crews cautions us "not to overlook the broad epistemic likeness between Theosophical dreamers and the idealogues who smoothed the way for the terroristic Nazi state. The common factor was their shared rejection of rational empiricism. By pretending that reliable knowledge can be obtained through such means as clairvoyant trances and astrological casting, the original Theosophists encouraged their German colleagues to 'uncover' in prehistory just what they pleased; and the resultant myth of how Aryan hegemony was broken by quasi-simian races formed a template for the infectious post–World War I story of betrayal by Jewish materialists and the vindictive Allies. The whole visionary apparatus — the vitalistic sun cult, the mystic brotherhood, the pygmy usurpers, the lost ancient continents, the millennial cycles, even the idea of a conspiracy by a cabalistic 'Great International Party' of diabolical anti-traditionalists — was already there in *The Secret Doctrine*" (39).

[36.] Goodrick-Clark, quoted in Crews, "The Consolation of Theosophy II," 38.

[37.] Werkner, 206. According to Werkner, the source of their attraction to Liebenfels's ideas was "the elitist cultural attitudes and racist content" of Theozoology.

[38.] Quoted in Crews, 28–29. Washington writes of Gurdjieff: "If Theosophy represents the idealistic tendencies in early-twentieth-century Europe — the currents of feeling which gave birth to the League of Nations, social democracy and youth movements — Gurdjieff is part of the complementary fascination with barbarism and primitivism which colours the politics of Fascism and works of art from Lawrence's novels to Stravinsky's early ballets. Gurdjieff's doctrine was war and his method of teaching was to stir up productive strife with all the means at his disposal." Peter Washington, *Madame Blavatsky's Baboon: A History of the Mystics, Mediums, and Misfits Who Brought Spiritualism to America* (New York: Schocken, 1993), 170.

[39.] In this connection, see Marzin's discussion of *Der Weiße Dominiker*. "Doch die Berührungspunkte zwischen dem Faschismus und dem Okkultismus zu untersuchen ist nicht die Themenstellung dieser Arbeit, obwohl viele Einzelaspekte — Initiationsriten, bedingungsloser Gehorsam, hierarchischer Aufbau — zu durchaus interessanten Rückschlüssen führen." Florian F. Marzin, *Okkultismus und Phantastik in den Romanen Gustav Meyrinks* (Essen: Blaue Eule, 1986), 98.

[40.] Werkner, 246; see also Klaus Jeziorkowski, "Empor ins Licht: Gnostizismus und Licht-Symbolik in Deutschland um 1900," in *The Turn of the Century: German Literature and Art 1890–1914*, ed. Gerald Chapple and Hans H. Schulte (Bonn: Bouvier, 1981), 171–96. Whatever Kafka's contacts with Theosophy or other occult ideas, however, there is no evidence of their registration in *The Castle*.

[41.] Brod, *Streitbares Leben*, 237.

DAGMAR C. G. LORENZ

Transcending the Boundaries of Space and Culture: The Figures of the Maharal and the Golem after the Shoah — Friedrich Torberg's *Golems Wiederkehr*, Leo Perutz's *Nachts unter der steinernen Brücke*, Frank Zwillinger's *Maharal*, and Nelly Sachs's *Eli. Ein Mysterienspiel vom Leiden Israels*

IN NUMEROUS ESSAYS AS WELL AS IN HIS recollections of Central Europe's German-Jewish culture, *Die Tante Jolesch* (1977, "Aunt Jolesch"), the politically conservative Austrian-Jewish intellectual Friedrich Torberg (1908–1979) discusses the milieu of German-speaking Jewish interwar writers and journalists in Vienna and Prague, and their indebtedness to the cosmopolitan legacy of the Austro-Hungarian Empire. According to him and other critics who fashioned the concept of a German-Jewish symbiosis to describe the close ties between Central European Jewish and Gentile culture, the k. and k. monarchy was imbued with Jewish thought and tradition.[1] As one who had actively participated in the Central European literary and critical tradition, Torberg returned from exile to Austria after the Second World War to keep its legacy alive by transmitting it to the post-Shoah generation of German-speaking Jewish writers. In the Second Austrian Republic, he represented a strong, decidedly Jewish voice, albeit a controversial and often solitary one, which made him a role model for some Jewish intellectuals of the post-Shoah generation. Like the pro-Western critic Hans Weigel, a major force in the rebuilding of Austrian literature in the postwar era, he was a virulent anticommunist. His rejection of Bert Brecht, Thomas Mann, Hilde Spiel, and Elias Canetti, whom he considered "fellow-travelers," earned him the epithet of an "Austrian McCarthy," and the journal *FORUM*, founded by him with the support of the Rockefeller Foundation and the CIA, was viewed by many with suspicion.[2]

Nonetheless, precisely because he was a controversial figure, Torberg stood out and found a following among younger Jewish intellectuals who resisted assimilation and accepted neither religious orthodoxy nor Zionism.[3] Some of the Jews growing up in post-Shoah Austria may have seen their own identity crisis reflected in the ambiguous personality of Friedrich Torberg. As a former sportsman and member of the Vienna and Prague HAKOAH, a cosmopolitan — until his death, he retained his U. S. citizenship, which he had acquired in exile — with close emotional ties to the centers of the former Habsburg monarchy, Vienna, Prague, and Budapest, he was a decidedly European Jew and a supporter of Israel.[4] A representative and an advocate of the European *galut*, Torberg validated the multifaceted culture of his youth and its traditional supranational and pacifist ideals, and he continued to champion the model of the multination-state long after the demise of the Danube monarchy. His work, including his postwar writings, is an integral part of the sphere from which emanated a phenomenon termed by Claudio Magris the "Habsburg Myth," a myth created and expanded by authors such as Torberg.

To some extent, Torberg's views on history and culture correspond with those of other exiles, including Frank Zwillinger and Leo Perutz. Torberg writes:

> Die Geschichtsbücher, mit gewohnter Oberflächlichkeit, legen diesen Untergang auf das Jahr 1918 fest. In Wahrheit ist er erst 1938 erfolgt. Was in Wahrheit österreichisch war am alten Österreich, was die wahren Eigenheiten, die unvergleichlichen und unersetzlichen Qualitäten dieses seltsamen Staatengebildes ausgemacht und den einstmals schwarzgelben Kulturkreis zusammengehalten hat: damit, meine ich, war es erst 1938 endgültig vorbei. Zwar hatte jenes Österreich, das 1938 auch formal zu existieren aufhörte, nicht als Erbe und nicht einmal als Abbild des alten Österreich gelten können; aber es hatte immer noch gewisse Kontinuitäten zu wahren vermocht, es war, wenn schon kein Zentrum, so doch eine Art Knotenpunkt, wo die noch nicht restlos abgespulten Fäden von dermaleinst zusammenliefen. Prag und Budapest standen noch immer in regster Wechsel- und Austauschbeziehung mit Wien, geistig, künstlerisch, atmosphärisch.[5]

Like other authors and critics associated with Habsburg culture, Torberg confirmed the interconnectedness of Jewish and Gentile imagination and made the German- or Austrian-Jewish symbiosis a central theme of his work.[6]

In his analysis of the Jewish assimilation process, Torberg characterizes the position of Jewish speech, the so-called Jargon, as paradigmatic of the situation of Central European Jewish bourgeoisie. By the turn of the century, the assimilated middle class avoided this colloquial idiom reminiscent of the language of the *shtetls* outside of the private sphere, because it stigmatized them as being different. Distinct from Yiddish and Standard German, it set them apart from the Gentile Germans and Austrians as well as from the unassimilated Eastern European Jews. But even the High German of completely assimilated Jews continued to reflect Jewish usage and concepts. German texts by Austrian-Jewish writers negotiate the experience and sensitivities of individuals whose families made the transition from the Jewish languages spoken in the Habsburg Empire: Hebrew, Yiddish, and Ladino.[7] By doing so, they also transformed the discursive practices of the Gentile language, creating a multicultural medium accessible to Jews and Gentiles alike.[8]

The literary and oral tradition of Prague's Rabbi Loew, the Maharal — the Exulted One — is as much a part of Habsburg culture as the popular legends about Christian emperors and saints. Peter Demetz writes that some of the best-known myths about the "mystery-laden epoch of Rabbi Loew, Rudolph II, and the Golem" were widely popularized at the fin de siècle when the latent conflicts caused by Jewish-German assimilation, rising anti-Semitism, as well as emerging Jewish nationalism were coming to a head.[9] It is no coincidence that the multivalent Golem myth was rediscovered during this disquieting era, receptive to modern and medieval ideas alike. Figures such as the Wandering Jew Ahasver and the Golem have traditionally provided models to accommodate the most diverse ideological positions, pro-Jewish and anti-Semitic, as is the case in one of the most widely known versions of the Golem story, Paul Wegener's highly acclaimed film *Der Golem: Wie er in die Welt kam*.[10] The propagandistic use of the blood libel and accusations of an occult Jewish world conspiracy by anti-Semites and the pogroms in Russia seem incongruous with the advent of modernity.[11]

The revival of Prague's legendary Jewish past reflects the unresolved conflicts between modern and medieval thought and the encounter between assimilated and nonassimilated Jews, Jews and non-Jews, creating a widespread popular interest in Jewish mysticism.[12] The sixteenth-century cabalist Jehuda Loew ben Bezalel (1513?–1609), imputed with having created a Golem, an *homme machine*, occupied the imagination of twentieth-century authors like few other historical figures did.[13] Dealing with various kinds of Jewish and Gentile interaction, issues of identity, and the problems of violence, self-defense, and pacifism, the Maharal stories became an expression of the ambivalence of the modern Jewish experience and the resentments of pre–First World War Gentile society.

Realizing that the stronghold of Jewish culture in Central Europe, the multinational Habsburg monarchy, was at the brink of collapse, the Jews, whose safety depended on its existence, observed its demise with a sense of impending doom. The period of Rudolph II and Rabbi Loew, a period of transition ending in the fall of Habsburg's most enigmatic monarch and imputed friend of the Jews, lent itself to be interpreted as a mirror image of the k. and k. monarchy at the eve of its destruction, with the powerful cabalist Jehuda Loew as a symbol of hope against hope. In 1917, one year prior to the end of the First World War, Gustav Meyrink's fantastic novel *Der Golem* appeared, preceding Chayim Bloch's popular version of the Golem stories, *Nifloet Mhrl* (1917, "The Miracles of the Maharal"), followed by their English version, *Legends of the Ghetto of Prague,* in 1925.[14] Halpern Leivick's Yiddish poem *Der Golem* (1921), Egon Erwin Kisch's novella *Den Golem wiederzuerwecken* (1925, "Reawakening the Golem"), and Paul Wegener's film *Der Golem: Wie er in die Welt kam* (1927, "The Golem: How He Came into the World") are among the numerous Golem versions of the interwar era.

After the Shoah, the Maharal, the Golem, and Emperor Rudolph II were reconfigured by Jewish authors into paradigms of the destroyed Jewish culture of Central Europe. They became literary devices to examine the Holocaust experience.[15] The experience of the Nazi terror had challenged basic Jewish tenets, as is obvious from the frequently articulated assumption that Jews, by adhering to their traditional way of life and by complying with the Nazi authorities, had contributed to their own demise.[16] As Inge Strobl points out, there was even doubt about the existence of a Jewish resistance movement despite the fact that there were armed underground organizations in forty East European ghettos, comprised of men, women, and children.[17] Moreover, the worldwide indifference toward the plight of Jews in Palestine had drawn into question many of the patterns inherent in Central European Jewish culture, such as the traditional, largely apolitical, urban, civilian lifestyle.

A large number of exile authors and Holocaust survivors grappled with two opposing models of Jewishness, one pacifist and cosmopolitan, associated with traditional European Jewry, the other nationalistic and militaristic, reflecting the programmatic views of Theodor Herzl, Max Nordau, and Vladimir Jabotinski. The concept of the Jewish fighter, epitomized by the Warsaw ghetto uprising, and the idealized Zionist soldier-farmer were incorporated into Israeli culture, whereas Yiddish and German-Jewish culture tended to be dismissed because of their association with the old ghetto culture, a supposedly shameful chapter in Jewish history. The modern Jewish state was configured as the very antithesis of the *galut,* with which German-speaking authors of different generations, including Nelly Sachs, Edgar Hilsenrath, Friedrich Torberg, and Ruth Beckermann still identified, unable to reconcile Jewish militarism with their concept of Jewishness, which was indebted to Central European history in geographic, cultural, and linguistic terms.

Among the authors who revisited the rich tradition of Rabbi Loew and the Golem after 1945 in light of Nazi history and the Holocaust were Friedrich Torberg, Leo Perutz, and Frank Zwillinger, Austrian authors of Jewish descent.[18] Leo Perutz's fantastic novel *Nachts unter der steinernen Brücke* (1953, "At Night under the Stone Bridge"), written during the author's exile and later rejected by the Zsolnay Publishing Company because of the "virulent anti-Semitism" after the Second World War, as Margarita Pazi asserts,[19] Frank Zwillinger's post-Shoah drama *Maharal* (1960), and Friedrich Torberg's narrative *Golems Wiederkehr* (1963, "Golem's Return") are examples of the different ways in which authors transformed the Maharal stories to express their views and experiences with twentieth-century history.[20] Even after the reorganization of eastern Europe in the late 1980s, the myths and images of the Maharal complex continue to provide reference points in a reality defying human reason and control.[21]

The majority of the literary works dealing with Prague, ancient or modern, focuses on the mysteries of the awe-inspiring city and the locations associated with the Maharal and his creature: the few remaining streets of the Jewish quarter, the *Altneuschul*, the Jewish community building, and the old cemetery with the tombs of Rabbi Jehuda Loew and Mordecai Meisl, the famously wealthy mayor of the Jewish community.[22] Twentieth-century authors have represented Rabbi Loew as a mystic, an alchemist, or a magician, although these roles seem to contradict historical evidence; Demetz argues that Prague never held a rank even remotely approaching that of other mystical sites, Safed and Gerona, for example.[23] On the other hand, Moshe Einstadter poses questions suggesting that Demetz's point of view is debatable: "Was there a Golem that waked the ghetto streets during the last quarter of 16th century Prague? Did Maharal indeed create a homunculus-like man to serve and protect a victimized Jewish populace? ... Whether he *could* have created a Golem is no matter for debate at all."[24] By considering the manuscript by R. Yitzchak Katz, the Maharal's son-in-law, as well as the latter's claim of having participated in the construction of a Golem as authentic, Gershon Winkler confirms the historical validity of the Golem stories.[25] Moshe Idel in his scholarly analysis of mystical texts regarding the Golem, on the other hand, mentions the Maharal only in passing.[26] Idel focuses on esoteric Golem literature for a specialized elite readership rather than dealing with popular legends.

In contradiction to the popular Golem tradition, Idel maintains that the reason for creating a Golem was neither the attainment of a mystical experience, nor a "practical magical purpose."[27] In his view, "the Golem practices" constituted "an attempt of man to know God by the art He uses in order to create man."[28] Hence, a man's degree of perfection could be assessed by the Golem he produced. "The man of God, or the Divine Man can induce a speaking soul into the Golem, provided he has realized a state of union with the Divine Intellect,"[29] Idel writes. Popular tradition does reflect the latter theme as well, but in general, it highlights the manipulation of the material world through magic. The fact that the Maharal creates an imperfect Golem, one that is mute, begins to malfunction, and ultimately has to be deactivated by his maker implies lack of perfection on the part of the Maharal himself.[30] This not withstanding, Rabbi Loew has been celebrated in popular tradition as the savior of his community. Occasionally, it has been suggested that his resolve to lay the Golem to rest enhanced his spiritual progress, since he succeeded to avert the threat to his community by his power of persuasion.[31]

Leo Perutz, Frank Zwillinger, and Friedrich Torberg were familiar with the popular Maharal tradition and Gustav Meyrink's fantastic novel *Der Golem*, which blends occult themes, psychoanalysis, melodrama, romance, and naturalist elements. The horror in Meyrink's novel, produced by an artfully evoked feeling of disorientation resulting from a purposefully diffuse narrative perspective, influenced most of the later works, including Torberg's novella. In Meyrink, the self and the other merge, foiling traditional expectations and challenging the notions of permanence and identity. Indeed, the way in which Meyrink's protagonist experiences Prague calls to mind Kafka's characterization of his native city as a "little mother with claws."[32] Simona Brolsma-Stancu argues that mystery and the uncanny are part and parcel of the image of Prague and the Maharal motif. However, the fantastic elements ascribed to Bohemia's capital vary greatly in quality and intent: Johannes Urzidil in his stories from old Prague was concerned with the magic of the ancient K'hille, whereas Egon Erwin Kisch used the Golem myth parabolically to expose the devastating effects of modern technology.[33] In yet other works, the Golem-Maharal motif is a variation on the *Doppelgänger* motif, the Maharal representing the positive hero and the Golem his negative "shadow" figure. Occasionally, parallels between Jewish and Gentile tradition are established, namely, by emphasizing the parallels between the Maharal and the Faust figure.[34] Brolsma-Stancu contends that texts with the latter tendency reflect the German-Jewish dichotomy that shaped Prague's culture. The growing conflict between Prague's Czech, German, and Jewish inhabitants complicated matters in the interwar period.[35]

The changing role of the Maharal motif, different in any given text, reflects the changes in Prague Jewish culture. Depending on the focal point of a text, different aspects and moods of the Maharal tradition come to the fore: The story of the creation and neutralization of the Golem, who usually goes by the name of Joseph — since he is not a normal living being, he cannot be killed — carries portentous and tragic overtones; the humorous anecdotes detailing the misuse of the Golem as a robot display misogynistic tendencies, which affirm patriarchal values — usually the rabbi's wife is cast as the culprit;

the accounts about the relationship between Rudolph II and the Maharal, culminating in the audience at the imperial palace or other meetings between the rabbi and the emperor, underscore the exceptional status of the Jewish community and its leader, as well as the close ties between German and Jewish culture.[36] Sherwin points out that the alleged encounters between the Maharal and the emperor "stimulated popular Jewish imagination" and inspired several Christian legends.[37]

Yet another motif occurs in Leo Perutz's fantastic novel *Nachts unter der steinernen Brücke*: the romance between Rudolph II and Esther, the wife of the philanthropist and mayor of the Jewish community, Mordecai Meisl, who according to tradition owed his life to the Golem.[38] The love between the beautiful Jewish woman and the emperor, which Rabbi Loew tries but fails to facilitate in such a way as to keep the lovers free of sin,[39] may be a carryover from other romances associated with the Maharal complex, such as the love story of Rahel and Ladislaus.[40] At the same time, Perutz's romance must be read as a Golem story in disguise; in the absence of the actual Golem, Esther's function corresponds to that of the Maharal's creature. In the presence of powerful gothic motifs, including the plague and the dance of the dead children in the old cemetery, the sacrificial death of the virtuous Jewish woman creates a profound horror effect. Esther is instrumentalized against her will and without the knowledge of her husband in a variety of ways: The object of the emperor's desire, she is the Maharal's tool to appease the Christian ruler, but later she is destroyed as atonement for the intrigues of the powerful as the Maharal makes her the scapegoat to save his community from divine wrath. The mind-body problem that is implied but contained in the traditional Golem stories unfolds fully in Perutz's novella. Esther and Rudolph are united in their dreams only, but since these dreams are sinful, they must be avenged. The emperor being outside the jurisdiction of the Jewish god, the Jewish woman bears the consequences of the Maharal's magic spell. Much like the supposedly soul-less Golem is deactivated once his presence poses a problem, Esther is also eliminated when it transpires that her soul wishes to join that of a Christian.

Aside from adding new perspectives to the Maharal tradition, *Nachts unter der steinernen Brücke* is concerned with the memory of Bohemia's destroyed Jewish culture, which Perutz mourned until the end of his life. Focusing on the romances and mysteries of Prague allowed the author to remember and pay tribute to the famous Jewish quarter and its immortal characters, to celebrate this tradition, and to convey it to future generations.[41] At the same time, the novella indicts the mighty, Jews and non-Jews, for carrying out their high-handed designs at the expense of the innocent. In Perutz's work, the Golem is reconfigured into a symbol of the socially, sexually, and spiritually disempowered. By assigning Esther a Golem-like role, Perutz questions the very notion of a humanlike automaton. Revealing the realistic aspects of the Golem legend, the reification of women and the "other," he pleads for compassion with the oppressed and abused. At the same time, he condemns those who arrogate complete power over human lives, in this case a high-status Jew and a Gentile monarch. Told in the mode of a medieval fairy tale, Perutz's narrative is nonetheless informed by the history of the Holocaust and addresses the moral and ethical issues relevant to this context.

Contrary to *Nachts unter der steinernen Brücke*, Frank Zwillinger's *Maharal* invites the reader / viewer to identify with the predicament of those in power. The drama examines the conflict and, ultimately, the understanding between Rudolph and the Maharal, the ruler of the Christians and the leader of the Jews. Emblematic of the power of the world and that of the spirit, these two characters are the dramatic vehicles to bring about the collision and, ultimately, the resolution of two antithetical forces. The title of the vol ume, *Maharal, Geist und Macht*, containing spirit and power, is indicative of the tendency of Zwillinger's traditional drama of ideas *(Ideendrama)*. *Maharal* addresses well-known themes, the blood libel, the threatened extinction of the Jewish community, the making and deactivating of the Golem, the disparities between men and women, Jews and Christians, and it features the traditional characters of the Maharal stories, Rudolph II, Jehuda Löw, and his wife, Perele, Isaak Kohen, his student and son-in-law, Mordechai Meisel, and others. However, the philosophical and cultural differences between the two protagonists are the focal point of the play, culminating in a dispute about power, mental and physical. Approaching his subject matter *sub specie aeternitatis*, Zwillinger contextualizes the Maharal stories in the framework of a baroque *Welttheater* — world theater — as Jewish history and world history. In accordance with its motto, "In gratitude to my dear fathers," his drama is an affirmation of Judaism and Jewish life. Zwillinger's Maharal is twice victorious: He avoids delivering the Golem into Rudolph's power, and he convinces the worldly ruler that "a spiritual power in the service of life" is worth more than an entire army of robots.[42] Like Perutz, Zwillinger employs historical themes to explore recent events, the Second World War and the Holocaust. However, in contrast to the profound skepticism of *Nachts unter der steinernen Brücke*, *Maharal*, in keeping with its Hegelian structure, is permeated by a sense of confidence in the human spirit and the historical process.

Validating Jewish mysticism and German Idealism, Zwillinger's drama is positioned at the intersection of two hierarchical, male-dominated traditions, whereas Perutz's novella subverts the Golem myth by eroticizing and personalizing it. Perutz questions the Maharal's integrity by casting him as a mystical procurer and killer, thereby undermining his credibility and that of the powers he serves, Jewish and Christian. Perutz's novella lacks the faith in

progress and the spirit that emanates from Zwillinger's drama, which transcends personal and collective destruction. The latter confidence is possible
only from a decidedly idealistic vantage point, which discounts the suffering
of the average person.[43]

With the Maharal tradition as its background, Friedrich Torberg's *Golems
Wiederkehr* deals with the Holocaust, which, in keeping with the author's
own refusal to repudiate the German-Jewish symbiosis "just because of Hitler," is characterized as the most radical threat to Jewish existence in history,
but not at all as a unique event.[44] The main plot being set during the Nazi
occupation of Prague, which the Nazis had chosen as the site of a museum
and documentation center for the soon-to-be eradicated Jewish culture,
there is no room in Torberg's narrative for nostalgic romantic elements such
as the ones featured in *Nachts unter der steinernen Brücke*. Likewise, the
brutality and insanity of the genocide preclude a detached intellectual approach such as Zwillinger's. Yet, much like Zwillinger's play, *Golems Wiederkehr* is driven by a utopian perspective. The setting of the narrative frame is a
future era so far removed from the Shoah that the narrator, an archivist or
historian, finds it impossible or unnecessary to recount details of the Nazi
era, which is even more foreign to him as Rabbi Loew's sixteenth century.
But while Hitler's name has sunk into oblivion (*Golem*, 138) — be it that it
was forgotten, be it that it is not mentioned in order to eliminate it from the
annals of history — the legends of the Maharal and the Golem live on: The
latter's body is still believed to rest in the famous room without a door in the
attic of the *Altneuschul*. The twentieth-century chronicle recounted by Torberg's narrator is no less fantastic than the original legend: It suggests that
the Golem returned to save the venerated synagogue from destruction,
thereby validating the legend of its indestructibility from which the Jews derived the strength to resist their enemies through the centuries.

In order to contextualize the miraculous salvation of the *Altneuschul*,
Golems Wiederkehr surveys the traditional Golem stories. At every historical
disaster, it is implied, there were enough Jewish survivors to tell their story
and preserve their tradition, the Holocaust being no exception. Torberg, like
Zwillinger and Perutz, selects those elements of the Maharal legends to support his view of Jewish history and identity. He defines Jewishness against the
enemy image of the Nazis, but also against the possibility of an aggressive
Jewish resistance. The concept of the Jewish fighter is excluded from his text
on several levels. By exposing the destructive and self-destructive nature of
the perpetrators, it is suggested that the Nazis succumbed to their own wick-
edness rather than to the physical force of the Golem-like Knöpfelmacher. It
remains a mystery why the two rivaling Nazi officers, Vorderegger and Kac-
zorski, shoot each other to death (183) and how the torches intended to destroy the *Altneuschul* were, in fact, extinguished; a sense of mystery is sus-

tained throughout the text. Thus, the short story supports the notion that mysterious powers have protected the Jewish people throughout history. By showing Knöpfelmacher both as ignorant and inspired, Torberg places him into the realm of the sacred paradox. Coming into his own at the moment of his brutal destruction by the Nazis, the mute valet instills the otherwise realistic plot with significance. The capacity of sensing the mystery is ascribed to the Jewish character, including the narrator, whereas oblivion to the metaphysical realm, caused by the cynical use of reason, is an attribute of the Nazi characters. Vorderegger, the scholarly director of the Nazi ghetto project, is unaware of the significance of Knöpfelmacher's name, Joseph, which suggests the giant's true identity. Ironically, so is Knöpfelmacher himself until Vorderegger inadvertently activates him by causing him to pronounce the Hebrew-Yiddish words "kodausch — kodausch — kodausch — adonaj zewoaus" ("Holy, Holy, Holy is the Lord of Hosts"), inscribed on a crucifix on the Charles Bridge (*Golem*, 175).

In the absence of a Maharal, the Hebrew word alone, no matter the context, suffices to instill the mute Jewish servant with the spirit of resistance. By disobeying several of Vorderegger's orders, he leads the latter to his death at the hands of a rival Nazi officer. In Torberg's story, the powers of Jewish mystical tradition, so blatantly defied and ridiculed by the Nazis, supersede those of Nazism — even a Nazi may inadvertently become their tool. Like Zwillinger, Torberg celebrates the superiority of Jewish culture over Nazism in a text that "proves" that despite repeated attempts to wipe out the Jewish people, Jewish tradition will prevail in the end, materially and spiritually; the *Altneuschul,* "whose indestructibility was a comfort to the Jews and inspired them with the strength to endure" (184) is spared, and the names of the Maharal and Joseph, the Golem, outlive those of the Nazis. The language of the narrator, one of humility and piety, furthermore indicates that the irreverent rationalism of the Nazis has been overcome.

To avoid any possible parallel between victims and perpetrators, Torberg's text also discredits Jewish germanophilia, represented by Max Wellemin, and it refrains from addressing Jewish, armed resistance or featuring Jewish leftists, least of all, women fighters. The Jewish characters in Torberg's Holocaust story are fundamentally peaceful civilians, middle-aged and older. This choice of characters, including the fear-inspiring, but nonviolent Golem figure, allows to set up clear distinctions between those who kill and those who do not, the guilty and the innocent, good and evil, Nazis and Jews. These binary oppositions, thoroughly undermined in Perutz's novella, are an important aspect of other Holocaust literature by Jewish authors. They provide a definitive ideological and spiritual framework similar to the one constructed in Nelly Sachs's play *Eli. Ein Mysterienspiel vom Leiden Israels* ("Eli: A Mystery Play about the Suffering of Israel"). Written in 1943, when the author had heard about the mass-murders in eastern Europe but did not know about the extent of the genocide, *Eli* provides a utopian vision of a time "after the martyrdom." A brief comparison between Sachs's text and Torberg's *Golems Wiederkehr* will help to illustrate certain common themes as well as the differences between the works of two authors deeply committed to the traditions of European Jewry and the *galut*.

Set in an eastern European soulscape among the survivors of a shtetl that the Germans have laid to ruins, Sachs's drama, like Torberg's *Golems Wiederkehr*, is inspired by Jewish mysticism, in her case, the book of *Zohar*, the central text of the *Kabbalah*.[45] Sachs's assumption that after the defeat of the Nazis, the reconstruction of Jewish culture will be possible, coincides with the message of Torberg's *Golems Wiederkehr*. Furthermore, both texts represent the Nazi terror as a divine test that is followed by the redemption of the faithful and the reconstruction of Jewish life. Contrary to *Golems Wiederkehr*, which does not raise this issue directly, *Eli* expresses serious concerns about the spiritual condition of the Jews who experienced the genocide as children, as well as the following generations. Her play suggests that males in particular may have become permanently tainted by the violence they witnessed, as is indicated by the games the children play: The girls dream of weddings, but the boy Jossele wants to reenact a rape. The way in which Sachs and Torberg deal with the characters functioning as the tools of divine justice suggests a profound concern about the reproduction of violence: Both Michael and Knöpfelmacher vanish once their mission has been accomplished lest violence remain in the world.

In Zwillinger's drama, the main issue is the supremacy of the intellect over the material world. The Maharal triumphs over political, social, and material demands and pressures on his path toward perfection as a spiritual leader. He does so as a Jew; hence, Judaism emerges as victorious over the powerful Christian realm. Sachs, on the other hand, and later Torberg, assign spiritual preeminence to humble characters: Michael is a shoemaker and Joseph Knöpfelmacher a simple-minded servant. Both of these Golem figures, chosen by the Highest One to perform a Jewish mission, validate the simple folk. Written from a critical perspective and commenting explicitly or implicitly on the problem of the corruptibility of the privileged, both Sachs's and Torberg's texts praise the long-suffering, anonymous average Jew. Despite his political views and affiliations, Torberg's story validates Brecht's view that the need for heroes bespeaks troubled, chaotic times. Like Sachs's Hasids, who quietly carry on Jewish tradition, his hero remains anonymous. He may or may not be the resurrected Golem created by the Maharal, and the Maharal's legacy may not have any bearing on the events during the Nazi occupation at all; rather than calling for direct connections, *Golems Wiederkehr* only points at possible parallels. While the intervention of a divine force is not disputed — there are hints that an intervention may in fact have taken place — Torberg's multilayered text lacks the certainty of Zwillinger's drama, where great minds determine the fate of the common people by assuming the role of pacesetters and leaders. The logical extension of the hierarchy of characters manifest in *Maharal* is a hierarchically ordered spiritual universe presided over by a supreme being. In the absence of such certainty, Torberg focuses on the spiritual principles and traditions on which the continuity of the Jewish people is based. Joseph Knöpfelmacher is the embodiment of collective powers, an entity that will arise from the community when necessary in desperate situations. Pervaded by universal mistrust and uncertainty, Leo Perutz's novella, although calling to mind an intact religious and cultural cosmos, does not conform to traditional belief systems. By humanizing the traditional Golem, Perutz not only dismantles the mystery associated with the Maharal, he questions the philosophy underlying the Maharal stories, despite their allure and beauty. Not only does *Nachts unter der steinernen Brücke* fail to yield an interpretation of Jewish suffering, the text shows the fate of every individual to be overshadowed by tragedy.

Perutz's, Zwillinger's, and Torberg's works, written under the immediate impression of the Shoah and its aftermath, relate to the experience of destruction in vastly different ways. They reflect the Jewish experience from the point of view of authors who, close in age and background, relate markedly differently to their situation as Jews who were born and raised in Central Europe. The three texts are examples of the changed significance of the Golem myth in a twentieth-century context. While in mystical texts the making of a Golem was a process in which the believer emulated the divine, he imitated the act of creation in order to become like the creator in much the same way as the Buddhist, by imitating the activities of the Buddha in sitting and walking meditation, strives to become Buddha-like. In that sense, a mystic's preoccupation with the Golem is an act of religious contemplation. From this perspective, the purpose of producing a Golem is the believer's spiritual progress, and the quality of the actual product provides evidence about its producer's spiritual condition. Popular tradition and literature, on the other hand, have focused on the social and political function of the Golem. As a result, they revealed problems arising from the production of an *homme machine* with superhuman powers, such as the ambivalent role of its maker.

In light of twentieth-century history, Zwillinger draws a logical conclusion from both traditions: *Maharal* shows that producing a Golem may be a great feat, but Rabbi Loew's true greatness lies in his ability to conquer the minds without magic or violence. Torberg and Perutz, like Zwillinger keenly aware of the ethical problems posed by modern science and technology, treat the Golem theme critically as well. Perutz configures a female character as a

Golem. Esther is a symbol of the material world, traditionally cast as female in Jewish and Christian tradition. He questions and indicts Christian and Jewish spirituality as a spirituality represented by men who arrogate absolute power over women, animals, and the inanimate realm. By constructing the relationship between Rudolph and the Maharal in such a way as to make them accomplices rather than opponents, Perutz criticizes privileged men of both cultures. Rather than casting Jews and Christians as victims and perpetrators, Perutz exposes different levels of oppression in both groups. Torberg, on the other hand, less radical in his outlook, suggests that there is a fundamental difference between Nazis and Jews, Gentiles and Jews. His Golem, an expression of brute force as far as he allows such a force to surface in a Jewish context, is more spiritual, "human," and at the same time more powerful than even his moderate Nazi characters.

The problems arising in all three contemporary Maharal stories reflect upon the ideology of the respective author as well as on the usefulness of the traditional myth for the interpretation of the Shoah. Clearly, Torberg's business-as-usual attitude presents a dilemma, and so do Zwillinger's holding on to the lofty ideas of times past and Perutz's bypassing of the problem of genocide altogether, at least on a literal level. Moreover, however, it is obvious that the Golem myth, created in and for a different historical era, fails to provide a comprehensive structure for the representation of the post-Shoah world. The fact is that there was no Golem to protect twentieth-century European Jewry, and no gentle Esther would have appeased the Nazi leaders. In the case of Torberg and Zwillinger, the frame of reference and textual structures are strikingly incongruous with the larger context of the literary text.

Notes

[1.] Günter Nenning in "Mit seinem kreisrunden Gamsbart," *Die Zeit*, Nov. 10, 1989, 552 refers to Torberg as the "probably last German-Jewish author." Reviewing various assessments of Torberg, however, reveals the divergent elements in the image this author projected. Erich Dummer in "Musterknabe des Kraus-Onkels," *Neue AZ*, Oct. 21, 1989, 27 emphasizes Torberg's Zionist tendencies and his resistance to assimilation. Alfred J. Fischer in "Israel ist keine Lösung der Judenfrage," *Berliner Allgemeine Jüdische Wochenzeitung*, Sept. 1988 further differentiates Torberg's position by highlighting the author's rejection of postwar German and Austrian philosemitism and his conviction that Israel was the spiritual and cultural center of the Jewish world without representing a solution to the "Jewish Question." Torberg did not believe such a solution possible.

[2.] Frank Tichy, "Der Fünfspalt," *Wochenpresse* 23, June 10, 1988, 48–49. Günter Nenning, "Die vier Welten des Friedrich Torberg," *Profil* 32 (1988): 56–57.

[3.] Dagmar C. G. Lorenz, "The Legacy of Jewish Vienna," *Insiders and Outsiders. Jewish and Gentile Culture in Germany and Austria*, ed. Dagmar C. G. Lorenz and Gabriele Weinberger (Detroit: Wayne State UP: 1994), 298.

[4.] See David Axmann, "Torbergs jüdisches Selbstverständnis," *Illustrierte Neue Welt* (June / July 1988): 6-7. He quotes Torberg's often-reiterated phrase: "Ivri anochi" — "I am a Hebrew man." At the same time, Axmann writes, Torberg refused to give up on the German-Jewish interrelationship "just because of Hitler." Peter Pelinka discusses Torberg's career, then "Schani" Kantor, as a waterball player in the HAKOAH in "Hakoah," *Arbeiter-Zeitung*, Oct. 21, 1987, 18–19.

[5.] Friedrich Torberg, *Die Tante Jolesch* (Munich: dtv, 1977), 220.

[6.] An anecdote recounted by Torberg is a case in point. It encapsulates both the self-confidence and the self-irony characteristic of many German-Jewish texts: During a hike close to the imperial resort of Bad Ischl, Torberg noticed the Jewish journalist and critic Heinrich Eisenbach. The latter approached Torberg and proclaimed: "Sir, from this very location the ancient Jews used to contemplate the *Dachstein* [one of the local mountain ranges]" (*Tante Jolesch*, 80).

[7.] As discussed in Gilles Deleuze and Félix Guattari, *Kafka: Toward a Minor Literature*, trans. Dana Polan (Minneapolis: U of Minnesota P, 1986).

[8.] Neil G. Jacobs, "On the Investigation of 1920s Vienna Jewish Speech: Ideology and Linguistics" (Ohio State University, Columbus, Ohio, July 3, 1995, photocopy), 14–16.

[9.] Peter Demetz, "Die Legende vom magischen Prag," in *Bridging the Abyss. Reflections on Jewish Suffering, Anti-Semitism, and Exile*, ed. Amy Colin and Elisabeth Strenger (Munich: Fink, 1994), 378–79; see also Peter Demetz, *Alt-Prager Geschichten* (Frankfurt am Main: Insel, 1980).

[10.] Lester D. Friedman, "The Edge of Knowledge: Jews as Monsters / Jews as Victims," *Melus. The Journal of the Society for the Study of Multi-Ethnic Literature of the USA* 2/3 (1984): 54–55. Demetz mentions as authors inspired by Prague's Jewish past George Eliot, Wilhelm Raabe, the radical anti-Semite Hermann Goedsche, the author of *Biarritz*, and Sergej Nilus's infamous *Protocols of the Elders of Zion* (Demetz, 378).

[11.] The 1882 show trial in Tisza Eszlar, Hungary, in which a Hungarian Jew was accused of the ritual slaughter of a young girl, was one of the earlier instances. Nilus's 1905 *Protocols* are largely based on century-old superstitions, including the myth of an occult Jewish world conspiracy. The 1915 lynching of Leo Frank in Atlanta, Georgia, involving the accusation of ritual slaughter proves that these ideas were also eagerly received in the United States.

[12.] Bazalel Safran, *Hasidism: Continuity or Innovation?* (Cambridge, MA: Harvard UP, 1988), 47 asserts that there is an affinity between Hasidic thought and the Maharal's teachings.

[13.] Byron L. Sherwin, *Mystical Theology and Social Dissent. The Life and Works of Judah Loew of Prague* (London: Associated UP, 1982), 27–29 writes that the Maharal was born in Posnan or Worms no earlier than 1512 and no later than 1526. He spent his childhood in Posnan or Prague and at the age of thirty-two married Pearl, the daughter of Samuel Schmulke Reich. Jehuda Loew arrived in Prague in 1541 after the threat of expulsion in 1520 and the fire in 1541. His famous audience with Rudolph II took place in 1592. He died August 12, 1609, in Prague and was survived by five children.

[14.] Chayim Block, *The Golem. Legends of the Ghetto of Prague*, trans. Harry Schneidermann (Vienna: John N. Vernay, 1925), 31.

[15.] Sherwin, in *Mystical Theology and Social Dissent,* examines the wider ramifications of the Maharal myth and establishes a link between the Holocaust experience and Prague history. Prague's "Jews are gone, but their presence survives," he asserts (13) and proceeds to relate an episode about a group of Jews praying in the *Altneuschul* who were miraculously saved from deportation (14).

[16.] Bruno Bettelheim, "The Ignored Lesson of Anne Frank," in *Surviving* (New York: Knopf, 1979), 246–57.

[17.] Ingrid Strobl, *"Sag nie, du gehst den letzten Weg. Frauen im bewaffneten Widerstand gegen Faschismus und deutsche Besatzung"* (Frankfurt am Main: Fischer, 1989), 181.

[18.] Friedrich Torberg was born in Vienna in 1908. He studied philosophy and law in Vienna and Prague. Having relocated to Prague in 1924, he commuted between both capitals as a journalist. He was the editor of *Prager Mittag,* but he also wrote for other Czech, German, and Austrian papers, including the *Prager Tablatt, Der Tag, Die Weltbühne.* In 1938, he moved to Switzerland and joined the Czech army in 1939. In 1941, he escaped to the United States via Mexico and entered a contract with Warner Brothers. In 1944, he directed German language courses at the University of California at Los Angeles, then he moved to New York and wrote for

Time Magazine. After his return to Vienna, he wrote for *Die Neue Rundschau, Der Turm, Süddeutsche Zeitung, Wiener Kurier, Die Presse* (Vienna) and was the editor-in-chief of *Forum.* Leo Perutz, a descendent of the Perezes of Toledo, was born in 1882 close to Prague. In 1894, his family moved to Vienna, where he later studied mathematics. From 1915 to 1918, he served as a reserve officer, was wounded, and eventually became a freelance writer. His most productive period was in the interwar period, from 1918 until 1933. He was recognized by Hermann Broch, Siegfried Kracauer, Alfred Polgar, and Kurt Tucholsky and had connections with Egon Erwin Kisch and Franz Werfel. (See Ilse Unruh, "Der österreichische Schriftsteller Leo Perutz in einer Ausstellung der Deutschen Bibliothek," *Börsenblatt für den deutschen Buchhandel* 10,600 II (1989): A433–A436; see also Margarita Pazi, "Das war Leo Perutz," *Israel Nachrichten,* July 30, 1993, 6–11. In 1934, he joined the conservative *Bund der legitimistischen jüdischen Frontsoldaten* despite certain socialist proclivities. In 1938, he and his family emigrated to Palestine, where he had difficulty adjusting (Pazi, 8). He died in Bad Ischl in 1957. Frank Gerhard Zwillinger was born in Vienna in 1909. As a high school student, he wrote poetry for German-language Czech publications as well as for the *Wiener Zeitung.* Having published his *Dalmatinisches Bilderbuch* ("Picture Book of Dalmatia") in 1938, he emigrated to Italy and fought in the French army in Indochina beginning in 1939. In 1946, he moved to France and spent 1948/49 in the United States, but he continued to make frequent visits to Austria. Similar to Joseph Roth, Zwillinger had close connections to the Catholic resistance and royalist circles aside from being proud of his Jewish heritage, hence his interest in Habsburg culture and history. He died 1989 in Paris.

[19.] Pazi, 11.

[20.] Outside of Europe, Isaac Bashevis Singer and Cynthia Ozick, as well as Elie Wiesel's *The Golem. The Story of a Legend* (1983) are to be mentioned. For further discussion, see Arnold Goldsmith, "Elie Wiesel, Rabbi Judah Loew, and the Golem of Prague," *Studies in American Jewish Literature* 5. *The Varieties of Jewish Experience,* ed. Daniel Walden (Albany: State U of New York P, 1986), 15–28.

[21.] Demetz writes that upon a trip to Prague, he was surprised to hear more talk about "the magical site of the Golem than about the former residence of T. G. Masaryk." Peter Demetz, "Die Legende vom magischen Prag," 367, 371.

[22.] A recent film about Prague in the early 1990s deals with the legacy of the Czech avantgarde of the interwar period. Nonetheless, the Jewish sites figure as significant points of reference. Nadja Seelich, *Sie saß im Glashaus und warf mit Steinen,* produced by Nadja Seelich and Bernd Neuburger (Vienna: Extrafilm, 1992).

[23.] Demetz, 373.

[24.] Moshe Einstadter, "Introduction," in *The Golem of Prague,* by Gershon Winkler (New York: Judaica Press, 1980), xxi.

[25.] Winkler, 4. André Neher, *Faust et le Maharal de Prague. Le Mythe et le Réel* (Paris: Presses Universitaire de France, 1987), 125 refers to the "explosion of Golem legends at the end of the 16th century" and defines the Golem as a "monster," a "phantom," and an "automaton" (126, 127, 129). Lester D. Friedman, "The Edge of Knowledge: Jews as Monsters / Jews as Victims," *Melus. The Journal of the Society for the Study of Multi-Ethnic Literature of the USA* 11/13 (1984): 49–62 defines the Golem as "matter without shape, a yet unformed thing" (51).

[26.] Moshe Idel, *Golem* (New York: State U of New York P, 1992), 108. He attributes to R. Yehuda Loew ben Bezalel of Prague the view that "magical activity is presented as following a mystical state," which would correspond to Zwillinger's view that the Maharal ultimately rejects the Golem. "The Maharal discusses the talmudic statements that the righteous can create worlds, explaining it by the 'total cleaving to Him,' which ensures the possibility of creating worlds," Idel elaborates.

[27.] Idel, xxvi.

[28.] Ibid., xxvii.

[29.] Ibid., 107.

[30.] Arnold Goldsmith, "Elie Wiesel, Rabbi Judah Lowe, and the Golem of Prague," *The Varieties of Jewish Experience*, ed Daniel Walden (Albany: SUNY Press, 1986), 16–17.

[31.] Bloch, 77, 212.

[32.] Simona Brolsma-Stancu, "Der Prager Golem, ein Polygänger," in *Kontroversen, alte und neue*, ed. Albrecht Schöne, vol. 5 of *Akten des VII. Internationalen Germanisten-Kongresses* (Tübingen: Niemeyer, 1985), 189.

[33.] Ibid., 192.

[34.] Rabbi Loew and the Golem are configured in a similar way as Faust's two souls in one bosom, as Faust and his demonic counterpart Mephisto, and as Faust and his humanoid creation, Homunculus. Gershon Winkler in *The Golem of Prague*, 64 points out that some critics believed that the Golem story was inspired by Mary Shelley's *Frankenstein* (1818).

[35.] Brolsma-Stancu, 187.

[36.] Sherwin, 14.

[37.] Ibid., 16.

[38.] Leo Perutz, *Nachts unter der steinernen Brücke* (Munich: dtv, 1978); see also Bloch, 77.

[39.] Perutz, 194.

[40.] Bloch, 106.

[41.] Leo Perutz made annual visits to Austria and died in the legendary imperial resort of Bad Ischl in 1957.

[42.] Frank Zwillinger, *Maharal. Schauspiel in 5 Akten*, in *Geist und Macht. Vier Dramen. Österreichische Dramatiker der Gegenwart*, ed. Friedrich Geyer (Vienna: Österreichische Verlagsanstalt, 1973), 81.

[43.] Zwillinger's dramatic practice, the contextualization of contemporary problems in a historical setting, and his showcasing of individual conflicts as symbols of historical processes is developed even more succinctly in *Wiener Welttheater* (1965). Dagmar C. G. Lorenz, "Frank Zwillinger: *Wiener Welttheater*," *Modern Austrian Literature* 21, no. 1 (1988): 61–82.

[44.] David Axmann, "Torbergs jüdisches Selbstverständnis," *Illustrierte Neue Welt* (Juni / Juli 1988): 6–7. Axmann quotes Torberg as saying, "That is precisely your mistake, to consider Hitler the first Hitler. ... Hitler did not invent anything, especially regarding the Jews."

[45.] In a letter to Berendson of May 23, 1946, she states that too much tragedy entered her "entirely overwhelming material, the mystery of the eternal," which to express she consulted Martin Buber and *Zohar* (Nelly Sachs, *Die Briefe der Nelly Sachs*, ed. Ruth Dinesen and Helmut Müssener [Frankfurt am Main: Suhrkamp, 1984], 57). *The Book of the Zohar* is one of the central cabalistic texts from thirteenth-century Spain. It is written in thirteenth-century Aramaic, in other words, a reconstructed language just as Sachs attempts to reconstruct a Jewish language beyond her own native German. Further information on this topic, Sachs and cabala, in Elisabeth Strenger, "Nelly Sachs and the Dance of Language," in *Brücken über dem Abgrund,* ed. Amy Colin and Elisabeth Strenger (Munich: Fink, 1994), 228–29; see also Gershom Scholem, ed., *Zohar, the Book of Splendor. Basic Readings from the Kabbalah* (New York: Schocken Books, 1995).

Index

Abdel-Qadir, Ghazi 227, 229, 231, 234, 235
  Die sprechenden Steine, 229, 235
abortion, 63
Abraham, 135, 144
abuse, 5, 26, 121, 137, 147, 148, 151, 215, 292
acculturation, 85, 165, 166
achtziger Jahre (1980s), 236
Adelson, Leslie A., 233, 236
Adorno, Theodor W., 20, 152, 153
  Dialektik der Aufklärung, 20, 152
adventure, 69, 83, 116, 119, 124, 126, 127
Africa, 23, 33, 38, 134
African American, 233, 164
Afro-German, 234, 236, 242, 247
aggression, 9, 149, 150, 172, 207, 208
agnosticism, 138
Ahasver, 287
Aichinger, Ilse, 188, 213
Die Aktion, 94, 101
Al-Hilali, Huda, 227, 228, 235
  *Von Bagdad nach Basra.
    Geschichten aus dem Irak*, 234
Al-Maaly, Khalid, 228, 235
Alafenisch, Salim, 227, 233, 234
  Das versteinerte Zelt, 234
alchemy, 14, 277, 278, 283
Algeria, 30
Allen, Woody, 216
Allgemeiner Deutscher Sprachverein, 257, 265
Aloni, Jenny, 85
Alsace, 94, 245, 246, 255
alterity, 3, 4
Altneuschul (Prague), 289, 293, 294, 299

Amado, Jorge, 216
Améry, Jean, 89
Amselles, Jean-Loup, 165
Amsterdam, 79, 82, 86, 244, 266
Anatolia, 148, 149
ancestry, 135, 145
Andalusia, 229
Anderson, Benedict, 2, 20, 167
androgyny, 40
animals, 1, 5, 9, 18, 21–27, 33, 36, 37, 47, 49, 56, 63, 72, 146–148, 150–152, 154, 278, 297
Anschluß (annexation of Austria), 22, 173, 184, 200
anthroposophy, 14, 277, 278, 283
anti-Semitism, 1, 10, 14, 58, 65, 132–136, 151, 159, 171–174, 179, 191, 287
antifascism, 27, 86
apostate, 8, 132, 133, 138, 141–143
Appiah, Kwame Anthony, 163, 167
Arabs, 2, 3, 12, 227–234
Arab-Germans, 3, 12, 217, 227, 228, 230, 231, 234
Aramaic, 191, 302
Arbeiter Zeitung, 298
Arendt, Hannah, 53
aristocracy, 23, 52
Armageddon, 148
Arnds, Peter, 11, 12, 215
Arp, Hans, 34
Artmann, H. C., 245
Ashkenazic culture, 10, 11, 149, 153, 185, 187, 189, 190, 193–195, 198
Assefa, Samuel, 226
assimilation, 98, 163, 176–179, 189, 286, 287, 298
Aston, Louise, 104

Augustin, Elisabeth, 85, 105
Auschwitz, 22, 26, 188
Ausländer, Rose, 7, 85, 86
Austria, 2, 7, 10, 11, 15, 17, 83, 87,
    120, 169, 171–184, 199–207,
    208–212, 214–216, 218–220,
    224, 284, 286, 298, 300–302
Austrian literature, 200, 217, 285
Austro-Hungary, 202, 203, 285
autobiography, 8, 30, 31, 63, 68, 69,
    75, 87, 88, 94, 103–107, 110–
    114, 138, 153, 156, 159, 203,
    213, 181
Axmann, David, 298, 302
Ayerst, W., 133

Bahr, Hermann, 210
Ball, Hugo, 13, 257, 260–267
    gadji berri bimba, 260–262, 264
    Karawane, 260, 261, 262, 266
baptism, 133, 137–139, 144
Barthes, Roland, 40, 70, 80, 254
Baudelaire, Charles, 35, 36, 209, 270
Bauer, Felice, 281
Bauer, Bruno, 277
Baum, Vicki, 85
Baur, F. C., 144
Bauschinger, Sigrid, 6, 44
Bavaria, 246, 247
Bavarian Academy of the Arts, 229
Bayreuth, 134, 135, 252
beauty, 34, 38, 49, 64, 121, 296
Becker, Jurek, 188, 242, 254
    Liebling Kreuzberg, 242
Beckermann, Ruth, 188, 201, 288,
    183, 184
    Unzugehörig: Österreicher und
    Juden nach 1945, 183
Beer-Hoffmann, Richard, 210
Belfellah, Abdellatif, 228, 235
Beller, Steven, 184
Benjamin, Georg, 58
Benjamin, Walter, 4, 20, 25, 26, 28,
    58, 64, 89, 248

Über den Begriff der Geschichte, 20,
    28
Berdahl, Daphne, 181, 182
Berg, Alban, 210
Bergson, Henri, 13, 260, 265,
Berlin, 8, 17, 22, 23, 31, 45, 58, 62,
    64, 82–86, 90, 94, 95, 103, 109,
    133–135, 155, 157, 158, 176,
    283
Berliner Allgemeine Jüdische
    Wochenzeitung, 298
Berliner Tageblatt, 160
Berliner Morgenpost, 212
Bernhardt, Sandra, 32
Bettelheim, Bruno, 299
    The Ignored Lessons of Anne Frank,
    299
Bhabha, Homi, 2, 20
Bhagavat-Gita, 24
Bible, 27, 34, 139, 143, 189, 190
Bielefeld, 247
Biermann, Wolf, 243, 250, 252, 255,
    256
    Affenfels und Barrikade, 255;
    Die Müllermaschine, 256
Bildungsroman, 12, 191, 217, 218,
    220, 222–225
biography, 4, 8, 19, 23, 48, 63–65,
    67, 94, 148, 243, 283
Biondi, Franco, 230, 235
    Ein Gastarbeiter ist ein Türke, 235
Der blaue Reiter, 263, 267
Blavatsky, Helene Petrovna, 277,
    279, 283, 284
Bloch, Chayim, 288
    Nifloet Mhrl, 288
Bloch, Ernst, 68, 80, 84
    Das Prinzip Hoffnung, 68, 80
Bloch, Karola, 84, 87, 91
blood libel, 287, 292
Bloom, Harold, 35
Blum, Klara, 85
Bodnar, John, 182

body, 1, 4, 9, 23–25, 39, 41, 49, 69, 70, 75–77, 94, 119, 126, 146–151, 173, 238, 282, 291, 293
Boehm, Philip, 234, 255
Bohemia, 11, 196, 203, 290, 291
Bonaparte, Napoleon, 47, 49, 53, 60, 110, 186
Bonn, 245
Bonsack, Hans Joachim, 124
Born, Nikolas, 232, 236
    Die Fälschung, 232, 236
Bornemann, Ernest, 88, 92
Börsenblatt für den deutschen Buchhandel, 300
Boston, 175, 253,
Botz, Gerhard, 184
Bowman, Derek, 109, 114
Boyer, John, 109, 114
Braun, Volker, 255
    Der Wendehals, 255
Brazil, 12, 15, 204, 209, 214, 216–223
Bremen, 247
Breslau, 137, 155
Bridge, Charles, 294
Brinker-Gabler, Gisela, 128
Britain, 35, 67, 80, 86, 148, 115, 155
British Broadcasting Corporation (BBC), 156
Broch, Hermann, 300
Brod, Max, 13, 14, 145, 268, 269, 278, 280, 283, 284
Broder, Henryk, 239, 255
Broslma-Stancu, Simona, 290, 301
Brooklyn, 98, 99
Bryant, Michael, 13, 14, 268
Buber, Martin, 192, 197, 302
Buber-Neumann, Margarete, 87
Bubis, Ignaz, 159
Büchner, Georg, 46, 52, 58, 239, 243, 245
    Dantons Tod, 46, 52
Büchner Prize, 239, 243, 245
Buddhism, 23, 27, 122, 277, 278

Bund der legitimistischen jüdischen Frontsoldaten, 300
Bunzl, Matti, 10, 169, 182, 184
Bunzl, John, 181, 183, 201, 210
    Antisemitismus in Österreich, 183
Burger, Rudolf, 200, 201, 210
Busch, Eva, 87

Cabala, 302
Cabaret Voltaire, 261
California, 87, 252, 299
Canetti, Elias, 5, 17, 21–24, 26–28, 153, 228
    Die Blendung, 22, 28
    Das Geheimherz der Uhr, 22, 28
    Die gerettete Zunge, 153
    Masse und Macht, 21, 23, 28
    Die Stimmen von Marrakesch, 228
canon (literary), 1, 41, 62, 64, 103, 233, 234, 236, 237,240, 241, 243, 246, 281
Cargas, Harry, 144
Carmelite, 9, 141, 145
carpe diem, 27
Carrol, Lewis, 216
    Through the Looking-Glass, 216
Cassel, Selig, 8, 132–145
    Der Judengott und Richard Wagner, 143
Castonier, Elisabeth, 87
Catholicism, 9, 137–139, 141, 142, 145, 249, 300
Celan, Paul, 88, 89, 228
Celje, 120, 123, 124, 130
Central Europe, 3, 4, 14, 16, 18, 172, 177, 178, 190, 277, 278, 285–288, 296
Central Intelligence Agency (CIA), 286
Central Jewish School Organization of Poland, 192
Cetinski, Ursula, 115, 128–130
Charlemagne, 244
chauvinism, 18, 136, 177, 244
Cherokee nation, 149

Chicago, Judy, 32
Chicago, 83
children, 16, 23, 25, 38, 40, 47, 52,
    55, 56, 63, 67, 75, 77, 81, 83, 85,
    90, 93, 96, 103, 111, 119, 136,
    141, 148, 174, 175, 179, 180,
    185, 186, 188, 208, 209, 214,
    221, 222, 229, 288, 291, 295,
    299
China, 85, 96–100
Chlebnikov, Velimir, 226
    Schamane und Venus, 262
Christ Church (Berlin), 8, 133, 134,
    143
chronicle, 293
church, 8, 26, 114, 133–137, 139–
    143
cinema, 242, 254
citizenship, 67, 95, 130, 165, 172,
    286
City of Benares, 86
civil rights, 15, 16, 146
Cixous, Hélène, 5, 29, 30, 31–33,
    35, 37, 38, 41, 42
    La jeune née, 29, 42
coffeehouse (Kaffeehaus), 10, 176–
    179, 178, 179, 180, 230, 235
Cold War, 16, 17
Colin, Amy, 65, 78, 214, 219, 225,
    302
Cologne, 145, 247
colonialism, 149
Columbus, Christopher, 119, 120,
    123
Comte, Auguste, 277
concentration camps, 58, 82, 86,
    148, 152
Conrad-Martius, Hedwig, 139
Cooper, Gabriele von Natzmer-
    Cooper, 35, 78
Corday, Charlotte, 50, 53, 60
Corino, Karl, 256
    Außen Marmor, innen Gips, 256
Crews, Frederick, 282–284
crimes against humanity, 149

Critical Theory, 17
crusades, 149
Cuba, 82
cultural boundaries, 3, 7, 215, 217
cultural diversity, 12, 164, 234, 246
cultural code, 12, 164, 234, 246
cummings, e. e., 35
Curtius, Ernst Robert, 265
    Europäische Literatur und
        lateinisches Mittelalter, 265
Czech language, 203, 207, 278, 290,
    299, 300

Dachstein, 298
Dadaism, 13, 259, 260, 261, 265,
    266
Dahl, Jürgen, 265
Dallas, 230, 232
Danton, Georges, 45, 48, 49, 51–54
Danzer, Georg, 240
Darwin, Charles, 277
Davis, Natalie Zemon, 181
De Cillia, Rudolf, 183
De Le Roi, Johann F. A., 134, 143
deconstruction, 17, 29, 35, 36, 64,
    224, 240, 252
Degenhardt, Franz Josef, 248–250,
    255
Deleuze, Gilles, 2, 20, 298
Delitzsch, Franz, 136. 137
Demeter, 40
Demetz, Peter, 287, 289, 298–300
    Die Legende vom magischen Prag,
        298, 300
democratization, 3
desire, 6, 8, 33, 34, 37–40, 64, 69–
    71, 74–77, 80, 85, 106, 1180121,
    129, 130, 140, 145, 147, 150,
    192, 204, 208, 249, 254, 271,
    291
Desmoulins, Camille, 48
detective story, 217
Deutsche Welle, 46
Deutsches Theater, 46
dialect, 157, 192, 193, 245–247

dialectics, 4, 26, 221
Diamond, Alpine, 245
diary, 2, 31, 68, 69, 84, 108, 125, 260, 261, 264, 269
Dickens, Charles, 220
    David Copperfield, 220, 222, 223
Dijon, 45
Diner, Dan, 229, 235
Dinesen, Ruth, 302
Dinter, Artur, 152
Diogena, 103
Dionne, E. J., 253
disability, 1, 126
disc jockey, 241
discourse analysis, 116, 251
discovery, 71, 73, 105, 117, 118, 123, 125, 127
dissidents, 251
diversity, 4, 12, 151, 164, 176, 177, 227, 234, 246, 248, 249, 251, 254, 255, 260
Doderer, Heimito von, 216
    Die Dämonen, 216
Döhl, Reinhard, 61
Dörrie, Doris, 242
    Nobody Loves Me, 242
drama, 33, 46, 50, 55, 155, 156, 214, 256, 289, 292, 295, 296
Dresden, Sem, 152
Dummer, Erich, 298
Duplay, Eléonore, 46, 48, 50, 52, 56, 57

East Prussia, 110
Eastern Europe, 163, 167, 175–177, 189, 190, 193, 244, 248, 277, 289, 295
Eastern Bloc, 17
eating, 21, 230
Eben, Michael C., 33, 43
Eckermann, Johann Peter, 254
Ecklbauer, Michaela, 212
ecofeminism, 149, 151
écriture féminine, 38

education, 83, 101, 110–113, 127, 138, 155, 174, 220, 231
ego, 40, 118, 260, 272
Ehrlich, Victor, 266
Einstadter, Moshe, 289, 300
Eisenbach, Heinrich, 298
Eliot, T. S., 215
Eliot, George, 103, 299
emancipation, 38, 65, 11, 133, 136, 143, 176, 179, 188–190, 252
Embacher, Helga, 183, 184
emigration, 85, 87, 90–93, 101
Ende, Michael, 232, 233, 236
    Momo, 232, 233, 236
Engelmann, Bernt, 92, 153
English language, 8, 17, 44, 67, 84–86, 96, 101, 106, 113, 115, 122, 136, 140, 144, 211, 226, 254, 257, 259, 261
Enlightenment, the, 1, 10, 15, 106, 114, 118, 123, 147, 153, 164–167, 170, 187, 188, 190, 102, 208, 230, 248, 277, 278
environment, 149, 244, 246
Enzensberger, Hans Magnus, 164, 166–168, 242, 243, 252, 254
epic, 33, 47, 105, 218, 241
epistolary novel, 124
Erdle, Birgit R., 78, 79
Erfurt, 133
eros, 60, 68, 75
Espin, Oliva M., 142
ethnicity, 1, 3, 4, 6, 7, 9, 10, 13, 15, 17, 18, 65, 130, 133, 141, 146, 148, 151, 163–167, 174, 195, 216, 227, 229, 239, 244, 257, 258, 264, 299, 301
Études sur Robespierre (Studies on Robespierre), 60
European Union, 11, 200, 244
execution, 48, 49, 52, 56, 57, 142
exile, 4, 6, 7, 17, 18, 22, 81–100, 155, 156, 159, 161, 162, 204, 285, 286, 288, 287, 295, 297
Existentialism, 17

Exodus, 38, 190
exploitation, 26, 73, 97
Expressionism, 89, 94

fairy tales, 23, 149, 195
faith, 51, 114, 133, 135, 137, 139,
    140, 141, 159, 244, 275, 277,
    292
Faktor-Flechtheim, Lili, 90, 92
family, 7, 23, 37, 56, 80, 84, 86, 98,
    120, 137–141, 144, 145, 149,
    157, 166, 167, 179, 190, 205,
    206, 209, 217, 229, 231, 271,
    300
fantasy, 124, 149, 179, 186
fatherland, 63
Federal Republic (of Germany), 9,
    16. 155, 158, 160, 277
Felden, Tamara, 128
Feldhay-Brenner, Rahel, 144
female voice, 69, 74
female writing, 5, 8
feminism, 5, 6, 8, 16, 29, 30, 32, 62,
    64–67, 75, 78, 79, 104–107, 115,
    116, 119, 138, 146, 147, 149
femme fatale, 188
Feuchtwanger, Martha, 87
Feuchtwanger, Lion, 85
feuilleton, 9, 66, 160, 212
Fichte, Johann Gottlieb, 168, 187,
    196
Henry Fielding, 223
    Tom Jones, 223
fifteenth century, 244
film, 12, 15, 81, 85, 91, 101, 156,
    161, 182, 206, 216, 241, 247,
    154, 176, 177, 180, 287, 288,
    300
fin-de-siècle, 10, 139, 142, 169, 172,
    174, 180, 181, 184
final solution, 58
First World War, 44, 94, 95, 118,
    124, 149, 159, 192, 201, 259,
    187, 188
Fischer, William F., 276

Fischer, Bernd, 10, 163, 168
Fittko, Lisa, 87
Fleischmann, Lea, 239
folklore, 123, 233, 262
Fontane, Theodor, 44, 114, 187, 188
    Schach von Wuthenow, 114
    Vor dem Sturm, 41
food, 5, 21, 25, 74, 88, 177, 178
Formosa, 116
Forum Stadtpark, 214
Foucault, Michel, 170, 171, 182, 183
    *Discipline and Punish: The Birth of
    the Prison*, 183
France, 63, 87, 101, 102, 120, 155,
    162, 165, 182, 188, 233, 245,
    300
France-Amérique, 95
Frank, Anne, 85, 86, 188, 299
Frank, Anton, 265
Frankfurt, 16, 82, 185, 196, 200,
    202, 210, 212, 213, 224, 226,
    244, 250, 255
Frankfurter Allgemeine Zeitung, 250,
    255, 256
Frankfurt School, 16
Frauen im Exil, 91
French Revolution, 6, 44, 45, 46, 50,
    52, 53, 230
Freud, Sigmund, 5, 30, 210, 220,
    222, 278, 280, 282, 283
Freytag, Gustav, 152, 187, 188
Friedan, Betty, 32
Friedman, Ellen G., 236, 237
Friedman, Lester D., 299, 301
Friedrich, Caspar David, 73
    Der Mönch am Meer, 73
Frisch, Max, 7
    Homo Faber, 215
Frischmuth, Barbara, 225
Fuchs, Anne, 128
Fuchs, Miriam, 236
Fuegi, John, 252, 256
Fürnberg, Louis, 228, 235
Fuhrmann, Robert, 8, 103
Fukuyama, Francis, 253

Die Furche, 212, 213
Furst, Lilian, 42
futurism, 261, 266

Gal, Susan, 181
Galanda-Bailer, Brigitte, 183
Gallop, Jane, 40, 43
galut, 198, 286, 288, 295
Gärtner, Reinhold, 214
Gates, Henry Louis, 163, 165, 167
Gättens, Marie-Luise, 62
Gauß, Karl-Markus, 225
Geiger, Ludwig, 113
gender, 1, 4–9, 17, 18, 21, 26, 31,
    65, 69, 74, 81, 84, 105,106, 112,
    117, 118, 123, 144, 151, 163.
    183, 237, 253
Geneva, 94, 245
genius, 107, 143, 243, 256, 276
genocide, 9, 146, 147, 149, 150,
    151, 172, 194, 203, 195, 297
Genthe, Friedrich W., 258, 259, 265
geography, 67, 119, 176–179, 189
German Democratic Republic
    (GDR), 16, 247–252
German Studies, 1, 11, 185, 186,
    197, 133, 136, 240
German Empire, 200
Germanistik, 3, 10, 11, 79, 185–187,
    191, 195, 233, 236
German Life and Letters, 43, 266
Gerona, 289
Gershoni, Israel, 182
ghetto, 23, 148, 155, 185, 186, 189,
    193, 196, 198, 229, 288, 289,
    294, 299
Gilje, Nils, 266
Gilman, Sander, 214
Giorgione, 217, 221
Girondists, 50, 52, 53, 56
Glatzer, Nahum, 144
Gnosis, 78, 278, 280, 283
God, 12, 23, 24, 27, 51, 52, 55, 56,
    134, 135, 137, 139, 141, 145,
    268, 269, 276, 278, 283, 291

goddess, 40, 150, 253
Goedsche, Hermann, 299
    Biarritz, 299
Goethe, Johann Wolfgang von, 5, 8,
    34, 37, 39, 40, 80, 104, 105,
    107–111, 113, 216, 218, 243,
    252–254
    Dichtung und Wahrheit, 8, 80,
        104, 107, 109, 110
    Faust, 39, 216, 290, 300, 301
    Heidenröslein, 34
Goethe Institut, 253
Goldhagen, Daniel Jonah, 142
    Hitler's Willing Executioners, 142
Goldmann, Emma, 31
Goldsmith, Arnold, 300, 301
Golem, 14, 285, 287–297, 299, 300,
    301
Golgatha, 57
Goll, Yvan, 96
Goll, Claire, 2, 7, 93–96, 98, 99,
    100, 101, 102
    Arsenik, 101, 102
    Eine Deutsche in Paris, 95, 101
    Education Barbare, 101
    Die Frauen erwachen (Claire
        Studer = C. G.), 101
    Der gestohlene Himmel, 102
    Der gläserne Garten, 101
    Ich verzeihe keinem, 101
    Laverie Chinoise, 102
    Le cirque de la Vie, 102
    Le ciel volé, 101
    Ménagerie sentimentale, 102
    Ein Mensch ertrinkt, 101, 102
    Der Neger Jupiter raubt Europa,
        95, 101
    Le nègre Jupiter enlève Europe, 95,
        101
    Die Reise nach Italien (Claire
        Studer = C. G.), 7, 98, 102
    Der Rote Hahn (Claire Studer = C.
        G.), 101
    Die Stunde der Frauen, 94, 101

Tendres impots à la France (Claire Studer), 101
Le Tombeau des Amants Inconnus, 101
Goncharove, Elena, 262
Goodman, Katherine, 104, 108, 113, 114
Goodrick-Clarke, Nicholas, 284
Goslar, Lotte, 83, 91
Gospel, 135, 136
Gothenburg, 82, 85
Göttingen Circle, 139
Götz, Franziska, 222
Gottlieb, Lynn (Rabbi), 32
Grass, Günter, 161, 188, 248, 252, 255
Gray, Ronald D., 269, 280
Graz, 176
Greco-Roman culture, 34, 137
Greek language, 222, 253, 258
Greenblatt, Stephen, 125, 129, 131
Greenstein, Edward L., 125, 129, 131
Gretchen, 39, 40
Greuling, Robert, 216, 225
Gribetz, Judah, 43
Gruber, Helmut, 183
Grubitzsch, Helga, 128, 131
Grundig, Lea, 87
Gryphius, Andreas, 35
Gstätter, Egyd, 213
Guattari, Félix, 2, 20, 298
Gugelberger, Georg, 236
Gurdjieff, Georges, 280, 284

Habermas, Jürgen, 210
Habinger, Gabriele, 117, 128, 129
Habsburg Empire, 118, 130, 176, 177, 179, 199, 202, 203, 286, 287, 288, 300
Hackl, Erich, 217, 225
Hafrey, Leigh, 255
Hage, Volker, 158, 161, 162
Hahn-Hahn, Ida von, 103
HAKOAH, 286, 298

Halbwachs, Maurice, 181
Halle, 155
Halperin, David, 183
Hamburg, 67, 68, 155, 190, 241
Hamburger, Käte, 82, 85
Hameln, Glückel von (= Hamil, Glikl), 31, 189, 190, 196, 197
Hammer, Elke, 235
Hammer, Stephanie, 5, 29
Handler, Richard, 182
Hannich-Bode, Ingrid, 92
Hanseatic League, 244
Hanukkah, 140
Harden, Maximilian, 159
Harden, Theo, 128
Hardenberg, Henriette, 89
Hart, Gail, 42
Hasenclever, Walter, 89
Hasid, 295, 299
Haskalah, 10
Haskole, 10, 188, 189
Hauer, Gudrun, 239
Hausmann, Raoul, 262, 266, 267
Hebrew, 17, 31, 138, 142, 187, 189–191, 198, 287, 294, 298
Heilbrun, Carolyn, 105, 113
Heimann, Moritz, 156, 161
Die Wahrheit liegt in der Mitte, 161
Heimat, 90, 92, 203, 209, 212
Heine, Heinrich, 68, 104, 111, 186, 191, 228, 243
Heller, Terry, 272, 281
Heller, Erdmute, 234
Henzler, Harald, 266
Herbst, Ingrid, 91
Herbstrith, Waltraud, 145
Herder, Johann Gottfried, 168, 258, 265
Abhandlung über den Ursprung der Sprache, 265
Herf, Jeffrey, 153
Hermann, Ute, 213
hermaphrodite, 279
Herrick, Robert, 34, 40, 43

Herz, Henriette, 104
Herzl, Theodor, 288
Herzmanovsky-Orlando, Fritz von, 278–280, 283
Herzog, Wilhelm, 158, 162
Heschel, Susannah, 144
Hess, Günther, 265
Hessayon, D. G., 43
heterosexuality, 5, 9, 34, 41, 146
Heym, Stefan, 253
high culture, 1, 170
High German, 192, 194, 195, 287
Hilsenrath, Edgar, 2, 9, 146–153, 188, 288
    Jossel Wassermanns Heimkehr, 152, 153, 295
    Das Märchen vom letzten Gedanken, 152
    Nacht, 148, 152
Hinduism, 27
Hippie movement, 16
Hirsch, Karl Jacob, 145
historians, 4, 82, 85, 89, 120, 134, 135, 142, 149, 150, 163, 201, 293
Hitler, Adolf, 7–10, 17, 23, 44, 59, 76, 81–86, 89, 91, 142, 67, 81, 86, 106, 111, 116, 123, 133, 137, 142, 143, 146, 148, 149, 151, 152, 158, 163, 165, 170, 171–173, 178, 180–183, 187, 189–192, 197, 198, 201, 202, 204, 210, 217, 221, 224, 225, 229, 238, 243, 248, 252, 253, 258, 265, 266, 282, 286, 288, 289, 292, 293, 294, 299, 300
Hofmannsthal, Hugo von, 210
Hollywood, 84, 243
Holocaust, 9, 14, 17, 27, 32, 62, 132, 144, 146, 147, 149–151, 159, 172, 173, 182, 187, 228, 254, 288, 289, 293–294, 299
Holy Roman Empire, 186, 195
Holzer, Gabriele, 210
homelessness, 15

homme machine, 287, 296
homunculus, 289, 296
Honigmann, Barbara, 239
Hopkins, Leroy T., 234, 236
Horkheimer, Max, 20, 152
    Dialektik der Aufklärung, 20, 152
Hörner, Karin, 235
Howard, Richard, 182
Howe, Irving, 273, 280, 281
Huelsenbeck, Richard, 259, 265
Hugo-Ball-Almanach, 266, 267
human condition, 13, 99, 152
Humanism, 9, 26, 65, 66, 166
Humboldt, Wilhelm, 258, 265
Hungarian language, 120, 173, 174, 201, 203, 285, 299
Husserl, Edmund, 138, 139
Hutcheon, Linda, 226
Hutton, Patrick, 182, 183
Huyssen, Andreas, 182, 183

identification, 5, 6, 22, 26, 48, 59, 99, 171, 175, 179, 180, 181, 184, 186, 202, 220
identity politics, 164, 165, 167
illiteracy, 241
Illustrierte Neue Welt, 298, 301
immigrants, 18, 96–99, 173, 180
immortality, 25, 48, 51
incest, 116, 145
independence, 164, 222
Indian culture, 23, 121, 126, 167, 283
insects, 119, 271
insecurity, 81, 164, 118
Insel-Almanach auf das Jahr 1930, 67
intermarriage, 121, 190
Iran, 227
Iraq, 227, 228
Iser, Wolfgang, 243, 272, 281
Israel, 14, 133, 144, 148, 175, 182, 286, 294, 298, 300
Italy, 96, 98, 300
ius sanguinis, 247

Jabotinski, Vladimir, 288
Jacobs, Friedrich, 108
Jacobs, Neil G., 194, 198, 298
Jacobsohn, Sigfried, 162
   Der Fall Jacobsohn, 163
Jäger, Ludwig, 78
Jaiser, Constanze, 92
   Das Schweigen hütet die
     Schicksalsspur, 92
Jameson, Frederic, 217, 225
Jargon (Jewish-German), 251, 283,
   286
Jauss, Hans Robert, 234, 237
Jehuda Loew ben Bezalel (Rabbi
   Loew), 14, 287, 288, 289
Jelinek, Elfriede, 188
Jelinek, Estelle, 105, 106, 113
Jerusalem, 84, 85, 114
Jesus, 571, 133, 135–137, 143, 144,
   187, 231
Jewish culture, 14, 86, 87, 89, 191,
   192, 285, 287, 288, 291, 294,
   295
Jewish quarter, 291
Jewish question, 132, 142, 143, 185,
   298
Jewishness, 51, 63, 141, 193, 195,
   196, 198, 288, 293
Jeziorkowski, Klaus, 284
Jhering, Herbert, 45, 160
Jones, Ernest, 282
Jong, Erica, 32, 75
   Fear of Flying, 73
Joyce, James, 215, 271
Judaism, 5, 8, 21, 32, 51, 54, 132,
   133, 136, 138–140, 142, 144,
   145, 187, 189, 197, 292, 295
Judt, Tony, 211, 213
   Die Krise der Intellektuellen, 213
Jürgens, Udo, 243

Kafka, Franz, 2, 13, 14, 20, 22, 28,
   145, 234, 268–284, 290
   Brief an den Vater, 145

   Das Schloß (*The Castle*), 12, 268–
     184
   Das Urteil, 281
   Die Verwandlung, 270, 271
Kaléko, Mascha, 84, 91
   Höre Teutschland, 91
Kallscheuer, Otto, 253
Kalmar, Stephen S., 911
Kämpf, Günter, 14
Kandinsky, Wassily, 266, 267, 278,
   279, 283
   Der gelbe Klang, 263, 267
Kann, Emma, 82, 85, 86
Kannonier-Finster, Waltraud, 182,
   183
Kant, Immanuel, 165, 261, 269, 298
Kantor-Berg, Schani (= Friedrich
   Torberg), 298
Karasholi, Adel, 228, 229, 231, 235,
   236
   So wollen sie uns sehen, 231, 236
   Wenn Damaskus nicht wäre, 236
Karlin, Alma Maximiliana, 115–131
   Einsame Weltreise, 115, 116, 129
   Im Banne der Südsee, 123, 130
Kasack, Hermann, 62, 63, 67
Katz, Dovid, 191, 192, 197
Katz, Jakob, 132, 142, 143
Katz, Judith, 216
Katz, R. Yitzchak, 289
Kaus, Gina, 81
Keilson, Hans, 82, 91
Keller, Gottfried, 206, 220, 222
   Der grüne Heinrich, 206, 220,
     222,
Keller, Josef, 67
Kernan, Alvin, 254
Kerr, Alfred, 9, 155–162
   Die Diktatur des Hausknechts, 162
   Empfindsame Flucht, 158
   Godwi, 161
   Die Sucher und die Seligen, 161
Keun, Irmard, 88, 92
Khalil, Iman O., 12, 227, 236

Khlebnikov, Velemir, 261, 262, 263, 266
Kiev, 192, 197
Kisch, Egon Erwin, 288, 290, 300
Klapdor-Kops, Heike, 87, 91, 93, 94, 100, 101
Kleine Zeitung, 212, 213
Kleist, Heinrich von, 30, 168, 239
Klier, Walter, 211
Klimt, Gustav, 210, 149
Klinger, Ruth, 87
Klüger, Ruth, 42, 85, 91, 196
    weiter leben, 85, 91
Knapp, Gerhard P., 183
Knight, Robert, 183
Kohen, Isaak, 292
Kolb, Annette, 87
Kolker, Robert Phillip, 254,
Kolmar, Gertrud, 2, 4, 5, 7, 21–86
    Das Bild der Rose, 5, 33, 41
    Das Bildnis Robespierres, 45, 56, 60
    Briefe an die Schwester Hilde, 78, 80
    Cecile Renault (Gertrud Chodziesener = G. K.), 48, 55–58, 61
    Dark Soliloquy, 43, 78
    Devorah, 33
    Die Frau und die Tiere, 22, 23, 28, 63
    German Sea, 6, 62, 63, 67–69, 74–78, 80
    Jener Abend, 48
    Eine jüdische Mutter, 65
    Die Kröte, 25
    Ludwig XVI, 48, 61
    Das lyrische Werk, 28, 60
    Nacht, 52, 53
    Napoleon und Marie, 53
    Preussische Wappen, 25, 74
    Robespierre, 6, 44–60, 68
    Susanna, 22, 23, 25, 26, 28, 65, 78
    Der Tag der großen Klage, 24

    Das weibliche Bildnis, 23, 26
    Das Wort der Stummen, 44, 56, 60, 79
Königsberg, 103, 108
Konzelmann, Gerhard, 228, 235
    Allahs Plagiator, 235
Kos, Wolfgang, 201, 206, 211, 214
    Eigenheim Österreich, 214
Koshar, Rudy, 182
Kosinski, Jerzy, 147
    The Painted Bird, 147
Kowalewski, Michael, 69, 80
Kracauer, Siegfried, 300
Kraus, Karl, 159, 210, 298
Kraus, Werner, 45
Krenz, Egon, 250, 251
Kristeva, Julia, 215, 225
Kruchenykh, Aleksej, 261, 262, 262
Kubin, Alfred, 14, 278, 279, 284
Kugelmass, Jack, 181
Kursbuch, 254

La Voix de France, 95, 101
Lacan, Jaques, 220, 226
Lamott, Franziska, 214
Landau, Lola, 87, 192, 197
Landshoff-Yorck, Ruth, 87
Langer, Lawrence, 58, 61
Lao-tse, 283
Larionov, Michail, 262
Lasker-Schüler, Else, 7, 42, 51, 61, 78, 85
Latin, 54, 138, 172, 181, 191, 205, 212, 231, 233, 244, 258, 261, 265, 274
Latin America, 258, 261, 265, 274
Latvia, 192
Lawrence, Karen, 69, 80
Laws of Nature, 150
Lawson, Richard H., 22, 28
Le Fort, Gertrud von, 140, 145
Le Goff, Jaques, 181
Le Rider, Jaques, 199, 210
Lebanese, 232, 236
Leda, 69, 70, 71, 74, 75

legends, 19, 25, 123, 149, 287, 258, 289, 291, 293, 299, 300
Leggewie, Claus, 253, 254
Leipzig, 133, 136, 141, 250
leitmotif, 70, 219
Leivick, Halpern, 288
Lemon, Alaina, 181
Leninism, 249
Lenz, Jakob, 109
Leo Baeck Instiute Yearbook, 61, 197, 142
Lesbianism, 32, 146, 299
Lessing, Gotthold Ephraim, 185, 187–189
  Nathan the Wise, 185, 187–189
letters, 31, 63, 68, 73, 76, 78, 82, 85, 87, 88, 94, 103, 111, 134, 137, 138, 140, 145, 272, 274, 275, 278, 281, 283
Levenson, Alan, 8, 132, 145
Levi, Primo, 89
Levine, Lawrence W., 20
Levy, Sara, 109, 110
Lewald, Fanny, 2, 8, 31, 103, 114, 186, 196
  Clementine, 103, 111, 114
  Für und wider die Frauen, 111
  Jenny, 103
  Meine Lebensgeschichte, 103, 111, 112, 113
  Prinz Louis Ferdinand, 114
liberation, 11, 152, 165, 172, 201
Liebenfels, Lanz von, 279, 280, 283, 284
Liedermacher, 239, 243, 246, 247, 252
Liepmann, Ruth, 87
Liessmann, Konrad Paul, 225
  Donquichotterie des Geistes, 255
Lind, Jakov, 147
  Eine Seele aus Holz, 147
Linz, 176
Literatur des Exils. Eine P.E.N.-Dokumentation, 53, 92
Literatur und Kritik, 199, 225

Lithuania, 192, 193
Llosa, Ilse, 85
Locke, John, 223
  Essay Concerning Human Understanding, 223
Lodgers, Helen (= Gertrud Kolmar), 67, 80
Loest, Erich, 251
Löffler, Sigrid, 202, 212
London, 3, 20, 22, 85, 91, 115, 122, 133, 134, 142, 143, 155, 175, 176, 178
Lorenz, Dagmar C. G., 1, 5, 9, 10, 11, 14, 21, 42, 43, 51, 61, 78
Lorenz-Lindemann, Karin, 65, 66, 79
Lorraine, 94, 245
Lorris, Guillaume de, 34
  Roman de la Rose, 34, 39
Low German, 247
Lübeck, 67, 68
Lublin, 82
Lukács, Georg, 216
Ludwig XVI, 50, 53, 56
Lueger, Karl, 172, 183
Luhmann, Niklas, 247
Lützeler, Paul Michael, 213, 214, 225, 231, 236
Luxembourg, 245
Luxemburg, Rosa, 31, 198
Lyotard, Jean-François, 1, 20, 210

Macaronic (Maccaronic), 258, 259, 265
Maccabees, 137
Mach, Ernst, 210
madness, 182, 276
magic, 13, 20, 76, 82, 119, 123, 195, 246, 262, 277, 281, 289, 290, 291, 296, 300, 301
Magris, Claudio, 23, 28, 202, 282
Maharal (Rabbi Loew), 285, 287, 297, 299, 300
Mahler, Gustav, 210, 278
Maier, Charles, 182
Malinowski, Bronislaw, 124

Manisch, Philipp, 192
mankind, 26, 153
Mann, Erika, 83, 87, 91, 92
Mann, Klaus, 89, 92
Mann, Thomas, 13, 68, 82, 84, 268,
    269, 285
    Buddenbrooks, 68
manuskripte, 212, 214
Marbacher Literaturarchiv, 61, 62
Marbacher Magazin, 67, 78, 79, 80
Marburg, 194, 240
Marc, Franz, 267
marginalization, 65, 117–120, 124,
    126, 172, 181, 185, 206, 233,
    234, 243, 251
Marin, Bernd, 183
    Antisemitismus in Österreich (by
        John Bunzl and Bernd Marin),
        183
Markov, Vladimir, 266
marriage, 35, 89, 95, 110, 114, 121,
    126, 138, 151, 190, 220, 283
Marxism, 13, 16, 26, 150, 241, 249,
    255, 269
Marzin, Florian F., 284
Masaryk, T. G., 300
masculinity, 5, 8, 29, 31, 32, 33, 34,
    38–41, 103, 120
masochism, 116, 183
Mason, Mary, 105, 113
mass media, 169
mass production, 232, 234
materialism, 20, 136, 151, 208, 230,
    233, 277, 284
Mathiez, Albert, 45, 46, 57, 59, 60,
    61
matura, 174, 184
Maurer, Doris, 104, 113
    Nähe nicht — lebe!, 113
McHugh, Kathleen, 42
meat, 21, 56
Meaun, Jean de, 34
media, 15, 160, 161, 169, 170, 176,
    202, 227, 232, 236, 239, 240,
    241, 242, 251, 254

Mediterranean countries, 16
Meerbaum-Eisinger, Selma, 85
Meisel (Meisl), Mordechai, 292
Meissl, Sebastian, 183
memoirs, 85, 87, 94, 96, 98, 103,
    106, 189, 197
memory, 8, 10, 14, 15, 57, 64, 69,
    88, 107, 116, 151, 163, 169, 170,
    184, 204, 205
Menasse, Robert, 2, 11, 12, 199,
    201–204, 206, 207, 212–226
    Das Land ohne Eigenschaften, 203,
        212, 215, 225
    Phänomenologie der Entgeisterung,
        212, 216, 221, 224
    Schubumkehr, 11, 200, 203, 213,
        214
    Selige Zeiten, brüchige Welt, 11, 21,
        213–226
Mendelssohn, Felix, 135, 137
Mendelssohn, Moses, 114, 189, 190,
    197
mental health, 26
mentality, 121, 125, 166, 202, 203,
    231, 243
Menz, Florian, 182
Mephisto, 301
Messiah, 53, 55–57, 59, 136
metamorphosis, 5, 23, 73, 271
Metis, Eduard, 139, 140, 145
Mexico, 86, 299
Meyer-Gosan, Frauke, 254
Meyerbeer, Giacomo, 137
Meyrink, Gustav, 14, 278–280, 283,
    284, 288, 290
    Der Golem, 14, 288, 290
    Der weiße Dominikaner, 279, 283,
        284
Miami, 228
Michaels, Walter Benn, 163, 167
Middle Ages, 105, 120, 132, 258
Middle East, 3, 49, 228, 229, 230,
    231, 232
Middle High German, 192, 194, 195
middle class, 9, 22, 111, 277, 287

migrant authors, 7, 12, 18, 230, 233, 234, 236
military, 15, 44, 229, 230
millennium, 11, 15, 146, 149, 150, 152, 185, 202, 238, 241, 243, 244
Miller, Alice, 214
Mills, Sarah, 117
mimesis, 269, 270
minor literature, 2–5, 7, 10, 11, 12, 14, 20, 234, 298
Mishnah, 145
misogyny, 27, 147
missionaries, 8, 132, 133, 137, 141–143
Mitten, Richard, 182, 183
Mitterand, François, 244, 245
modernism, 10, 165, 167, 269, 213, 253, 369, 270, 280, 281
Moeller, Susanne, 153
Moi, Toril, 65, 66, 79
Molière,
    Le Malade Imaginaire, 258
Mondrian, Piet, 378
money, 84, 87, 88, 97, 98, 127, 134, 160, 202
Montaigne, Michel Eyquem, 242, 254
Moore, George, 105
Moravia, 178, 189, 196
Mosbahi, Hassouna, 227, 234
    So heiss. So kalt. So hart. Tunesische Erzählungen, 234
Moses, 39, 50, 135
Moßmann, Walter, 240, 246, 255
mother, 3, 31, 40, 41, 48, 56, 65, 82, 85, 86, 120, 137, 138, 140 141, 144, 148, 153, 180, 188, 205, 216, 219, 222, 223, 290
mother tongue, 86, 98
mourning, 35, 63, 74, 77, 87
Muir, Edwin, 28, 280
Muir, Willa, 28, 280
Müller, Joachim, 47, 60
Müller, Herta, 239

Müller, Heiner, 252, 255, 256
Mulley, Klaus-Dieter, 183
multiculturalism, 10, 17, 63, 64, 165, 227, 229, 230, 236, 251, 256
Munich, 229
Murath, Clement, 128
museum, 170, 182, 195, 293
music, 33, 84, 112, 135, 159, 178, 179, 210, 228, 241, 242, 254, 255, 259, 260, 265, 279
Muslim, 2, 227–230
Musner, Lutz, 181
Müssener, Helmut, 302
mysticism, 14, 119, 277, 278, 280, 283, 287, 292, 295
mythology, 5, 23, 30, 70, 75, 100, 167, 279

Naoum, Jusuf, 229–233, 235, 236
    Die Kaffeehausgeschichten des Abu al Abed, 235
    Der Scharfschütze: Erzählungen aus dem libanesischen Bürgerkrieg, 232, 236
Napoleon, 53, 69, 110, 186
The Nasty Girl (film), 247
Nathorff, Hertha, 84, 87, 91
nation, 11, 15, 16, 20, 74, 114, 221
Nation of Islam, 167
national identity, 11, 12, 98, 100, 144, 173, 182, 195, 200, 202, 213, 238, 240, 241, 243, 246, 247, 252, 256
national literature, 4, 192, 194, 215, 243, 252, 254
National Socialists (Nazis), 3, 5, 7, 11, 14–18, 22, 23, 26, 44, 58, 62, 63, 67, 82, 86, 87, 96, 118, 150, 158, 159, 172, 194, 201, 250, 274, 277
nationality, 9, 68, 122, 190, 210
Native American nations, 164
nature, 146, 147, 150, 151, 152, 169, 204, 258, 270, 274, 277
Natzmer-Cooper, Gabriele von, 78

Der Nazi und der Friseur (Edgar Hilsenrath), 148, 152
Negev, 227
Neher, André, 300
Nenning, Günter, 298
neocolonialism, 230
neoconservatism, 249, 250
neopaganism, 142
Netherlands, 190
Neuburger, Bernd, 300
Neue Bundesländer (new German states), 248
Neue Rundschau, 300
Neue Schaubühne, 94
neutrality, 83, 201, 202
new historiographer, 45
New High German, 134
New Testament, 56, 57, 135, 144
New York, 7, 75, 84, 91, 95, 96, 148
New Right, 165
Nibelungenlied, 195
Nieder mit Goethe (Hans-Magnus Enzensberger), 243, 252
Nietzsche, Friedrich, 30, 148, 153
  Also sprach Zarathustra, 153
Nilus, Sergej, 299
  The Protocols of the Elders of Zion, 299
Nobel Prize, 21, 86
Nooteboom, Cees, 215
  Philip en de anderen, 215
Nora, Pierre, 181
Nordau, Max, 288
Norris, Christopher, 255
nostalgia, 104, 105, 121, 249, 151, 184, 293
novelists, 31, 103, 140, 242
novella, the, 22, 26, 28, 65, 94, 96, 102, 203, 256, 288, 290, 291, 292, 294, 296
Nowak, Peter, 183
nuns, 56, 140
Nussbaum, Marth, 42,

Occident, the, 12, 227

occultism, 280
Offner, Richard, 89
Ohnesorg, Stefanie, 129
Old Testament, 132, 134–136, 144
Olden, Ika, 86, 91
Olden, Rudolf, 86, 91
oligarchy, 46
Oliver, José F. A., 235
opera, 156, 176, 195, 230, 241
Oppenheimer, Paul, 282
oppression, 5, 21, 126, 146, 149, 189, 276, 197
orality, 241
Orient, the, 12, 15, 86, 227, 229, 230, 231
orientalism, 20, 38, 195, 234, 236
otherness, the Other, 1, 2, 4–9, 13, 17–19, 22, 63, 105, 109, 114, 116, 118, 119, 125, 127, 147, 173, 175, 204, 205, 219, 220, 223, 224, 242, 251, 268, 278, 291
Ottakring, 245
outsiders, 2, 16, 17, 31, 116, 124, 151, 153, 198, 204
Ozick, Cynthia, 300
O'Keefe, Georgia, 39

pacifism, 250, 277, 287
panting, 39, 73, 84, 85, 262
Palestine, 227–229, 231, 236, 288, 300
pan-European issues, 245
paradise, 74, 77
pariahs, 140, 170
Paris, 3, 38, 48, 54, 95, 99, 101, 102, 175, 176, 178, 179, 245, 300
Parton, Anthony, 266
Pasha, Enver, 266
Pasha, Kemal (Atatürk), 150
Passover, 138, 229
Patai, Raphael, 234
Patterer, Hubert, 212
Pauli, Hertha, 87
Pazi, Margarita, 189, 300

pedagogue, 25
Pelinka, Anton, 200, 201, 211, 214
Pelinka, Peter, 298
Pelikan, Johanna, 183
Pelz, Annegret, 119, 126, 128, 130, 131
PEN, 256
Penthesilea, 30
periodization, 163
perpetrator, 53, 150, 172, 188, 293, 294, 297
persecution, 7, 9, 26, 44, 58, 85, 86, 88, 90, 150, 152, 173
Persephone, 30, 40, 41
personas, 63, 185
Perutz, Leo, 14, 285, 289–294, 296, 297, 300, 301
    Nachts unter der steinernen Brücke, 14, 285, 289, 291, 292, 296, 301
Peterson, Linda, 106, 113
Petrarch, 35, 105
petty bourgeoisie, 45, 56
Pfaff, William, 211
Philipp, Eckhard, 266, 267
philology, 32, 187, 192–194, 298
philosemitism, 8, 132–134, 138, 140, 141, 143, 186
Pickerodt, Gerhart, 12
Piehler, Kurt, 182
Plan (ed. Otto Basil), 214
Plaskow, Judith, 32, 35, 47
playwrights, 57, 151, 160, 269, 252
pleasure, 31, 34, 39, 40, 41, 45, 74, 125, 150, 152, 175
Plett, Heinrich F., 225
pluralism, 10, 164, 176, 177, 239, 246–249, 259
pogroms, 149, 190, 282
Poland, 9, 137, 155, 190, 192
Polgar, Alfred, 300
Polish language, 155, 159, 173
Pomo Palace Casino, 167
Pope Pius XI, 141
    Mit Brennender Sorge, 141, 145

popular culture, 12, 32, 242
Porter, Dennis, 69, 80
Portugal, 85
positionality, 3, 66, 238, 243
post-Shoah issues, 9, 10, 14, 17, 147, 188, 265, 285, 286, 289, 297
postemancipation, 138
Posthofen, Renate, 1, 6, 7, 11, 93, 199
Prager Tablatt, 299
Prager Mittag, 299
Prague, 287–291, 293, 299, 300, 301
Pratt, Mary Louise, 129
Praunheim, Rosa von, 239
press, the, 100, 120, 124, 158, 160, 250, 253
Die Presse, 300
primitivism, 280, 284
prisons, 56, 88, 171, 183. 271
prisoner-of-war camps, 44
Profil, 214
prostitution, 111, 126, 220
Protestantism, 8, 139, 141
Prussia, 110, 187
Psalms, 190
Psychoanalysis, 17, 11, 278, 290
Pulitzer Prize, 254
Pulzer, Peter, 183
Puritans, 50, 55

Quakers, 87, 106

Raabe, Wilhelm, 152, 220, 222, 299
    Der Hungerpastor, 220, 233
Rabbi Loew, 14, 287, 288–193, 296, 300, 301
race, 5, 6, 10, 15, 26, 31, 33, 117, 121, 122, 163, 164, 167, 228, 232, 253
racialism, 136, 279
racism, 10, 121, 129, 149, 164, 208
radio, 96, 158, 161
Die Rampe, 214
Ranke, Leopold, 133

Rathenau, Walter, 156
rave scene, 241
Real Socialism, 239, 248, 249, 251
Realism, 108, 277
reason, 148, 182, 248, 275, 289, 294
regionalism, 12, 251, 254
Reich, Schmule Samuel, 299
Reich-Ranicki, Marcel, 9, 55, 62, 252
   Das literarische Quartett, 160, 161
   Über Ruhestörer. Juden in der
      deutschen Literatur, 162
   Der Verreißer, 161, 162
Reinach, Adolf, 139
Reinach, Anna, 139
Reinecke, Sabine, 128
Reinerova, Lenka, 87
Reinhardt, Max, 45, 46
remigration, 89, 90, 92
Renaissance, 277, 282
Renan, Ernest, 135, 277
Renner, Karl, 172
reunification (German), 12, 62, 238–
   240, 245, 247, 249, 256
Rhine River, 245, 246, 255
Rich, Adrienne, 421, 242
   Of Woman Born, 421
Richter, Trude, 87
Rieger, Berndt, 212
Riha, Karl, 266
   Am Anfang war Dada, 266
Rilke, Rainer Maria, 5, 34, 35, 43
   Sonnets to Orpheus, 34
Ringbom, Sixten, 283
ritual slaughter, 21, 299
Robert, Marthe, 269, 280
Robespierre, Maximilien-Marie
   Isodore de, 6, 44–60
Rockefeller Foundation, 286
Rödelheim Hartreim Projekt, 247
Rolland, Romain, 45, 45, 51, 58
Roman Catholicism, 9, 142
Roman influences, 34, 137, 186,
   189, 195, 244, 247, 258
Romania, 148, 153, 173, 175, 179,
   261

Romanticism, 31, 187, 238
Rome, 111, 167
roses, 5, 29, 33–35, 37–41, 43
Rose, Paul Lawrence, 142
Rosenkranz, Herbert, 184
Rosenzweig, Franz, 138, 139, 144
Rostock, 247
Rotenberg, Robert, 181
Rotenberg, Stella, 85
Roth, Gerhard, 213
Roth, Joseph, 180, 192, 198, 300
Rotter, Gernot, 235
Rougement, Denis de, 34, 43
Rousso, Henry ,182
Rubinstein, Hilde, 87
Rudolph II, 14, 287, 288, 291, 292,
   297, 299
Rudolph, Felix, 265
Rufeisen, Oswald, 133
Rühle, Günther, 60
Rühle-Gerstel, Alice, 86, 87, 91, 92
   Der Umbruch oder Hanna und die
      Freiheit, 86, 87, 91
rural settings, 153, 204, 227,231,
   245
Russell, Bertrand, 225
Russia, 190, 229, 261, 287
Ruth (biblical), 32
Rüthel, Else, 88

Saarland, 245
sabbath, 136, 139
Sachs, Nelly 86, 295, 302
   Eli. Ein Mysterienspiel vom Leiden
      Israels, 14, 285, 294
sadism, 147
Safed, 289
Said, Edward, 2, 20, 195, 227, 234,
   236
Salmony, Georg, 159, 162
Salomon, Charlotte, 85
salons, 31, 103, 180
Salten, Felix, 210
Sammons, Jeffrey L., 225
San Francisco, 123, 130, 145

Sand, George, 103
Sao Paulo, 216, 217, 222
Sappho, 29, 34
Sartre, Jean-Paul, 268, 275
satire, 103, 148, 152, 230, 246, 259, 280
Saunders, Nicholas, 254
Schädlich, Hans Joachim, 251, 255
    Aktenkundig, 255
Schami, Rafik, 227–236
    Das Murmeln meiner Kindheit-Geschichten aus Damaskus, 235
    Damaskus Nights, 228, 229, 234, 235
    Der ehrliche Lügner, 229, 235
    Ein Gastarbeiter ist ein Türke, 235
    Der Fliegenmelker und andere Erzählungen, 235
Scheler, Max, 139
Scherer, Wilhelm, 265
Schiele, Egon, 210
Schindel, Robert, 188, 213
    Gebürtig (Born — Where), 213
    Selige Zeiten, Brüchige Welt (Blissful Times, Fragmentary World), 216, 218
Schlenstedt, Silvia, 78
Schmeichel-Falkenberg, Beate, 7, 81, 91
Schmickl, Gerald, 226
Schmidt-Dengler, Wendelin, 214
Schmutzer, Dieter, 239
Schneider, Peter, 242, 249–251, 254, 255, 299
Schnitzler, Arthur, 180, 210
Scholem, Gershom, 302
Scholl-Latour, Peter, 228, 235
Schönberg, Arnold, 14, 279, 278, 283
Schönerer, Georg, 183, 172
Schutzhaft (protective custody), 58
Schwandt, Erhard, 99, 101, 102
Schwarz, Susan, 212
Schygulla, Hanna, 243
science fiction, 23, 33, 124

Second District (Vienna), 177
Second Republic (Austria), 172, 201, 203, 211
Second World War, 3, 7, 15, 15, 89, 95, 120, 125, 245, 248, 285, 289, 292
secularism, 9, 136, 139
Seelich, Nadja, 189, 300
Seghers, Anna, 7, 82, 85, 91, 93, 100, 101, 188
    Post ins gelobte Land, 100
    Transit, 100
Seidler, Irma, 216
Semitic heritage, 134–136
Sephardic heritage, 30
sermons, 133, 190, 191
seventeenth-century, 189, 191, 258
sexuality, 4, 15, 18, 21, 38, 65, 70, 71, 74, 75, 79, 150, 171
Shafi, Monika, 6, 43, 50, 53, 58–62, 78–80
Shaheen, Jack J., 232, 236
shamanism, 13, 262, 264
Shchukin, Mark B., 167
Shelley, Mary, 30
    Frankenstein, 301
Sherwin, Byron L., 291, 299
Shiach, Morag, 42
Shoah, the, 9, 10, 14, 17, 147, 149, 152, 188, 285, 186, 188, 289, 296, 297;
    survivors of, 9, 32, 40, 81, 146, 148, 149, 172, 173, 190, 288, 193, 195
short story, 96, 102, 203, 124, 125, 156, 232, 281, 294
shtetl, 287, 295
Siberia, 262
Siebert, Ulla, 129
Sieburg, Friedrich, 46, 60
Das Silberboot, ed. Ernst Schönwiese, 214
silence, 22, 44, 74, 151
Silesia, 137, 155
Simon, Heinrich, 103

Simson, Alexander von, 91
Simson, Louise von, 83
Singer, Peter, 9, 146, 248, 151–154
Singer, Isaac Bashevis, 21, 146, 148, 151–154
Sinka, Margit M., 281
sixteenth century, 191, 244, 258, 287, 293
sixties (1960s), 219
Skirbekk, Gunnar, 226
Slibar, Neva, 8, 115
Slibar, Vlado, 130
Slovenia, 115, 116, 120, 122, 128, 130
Smith, Sidonie, 105, 113
Smith, Henry A., 33, 43, 78
Snow White, 37
soap opera, 230
social criticism, 96
socialists, 86, 95, 202, 249, 250, 300
socialism, 150, 183, 201, 239, 248, 249, 251
socialization, 2, 220, 221, 224
Sodom and Gomorrah, 135
Sokel, Walter H., 269–272, 280, 281
Söllner, Hans, 240, 246
    Der deutsche Tourist, 255
    Moi Nega, 255
song, 33, 136, 195, 241, 242, 246, 249, 255
sonnet, 33–37, 41, 43, 47
Sonntags Zeitung, 213
Sorbonne, 45
Soudah, Wadi, 227, 234
South America, 115
Soviet Union, 85, 174, 193
Spanish, 261
speciesism, 149, 152
Speicher, Stephan, 256
    Ein Wagen für die Fußkranken, 256
Spencer, Herbert, 277
Spenlow, Dora, 222
Der Spiegel, 160, 161, 256
Spiegel, Marjorie, 147, 152

Spiegelmann, Art, 254
    Mouse, 254
Spiel, Hilde, 87, 285
Spinoza, Baruch, 33
Spira, Steffi, 87
spirituality, 9, 42, 283, 297
Springer, Ulli, 212
Stadttempel (Vienna), 191
Stahr, Adolf, 103, 111
Der Standard, 213, 225
Stanonik, Janez, 120, 125, 130, 131
Stasi, 250
Stefan, Verena, 75
    Häutungen: Autobiographische Aufzeichnungen, 75
Stein, Auguste, 138
Stein, Edith, 8, 9, 132–145
    Aus dem Leben einer jüdischen Familie, 144, 145
Stein, Gertrude, 29, 31, 42
Stein, Regina, 43
Stein, Siegfried, 136
Steinbach, Erwin von, 107
Steiner, Rudolf, 277–279, 282, 283
    Luzifer-Gnosis, 278, 279, 282, 283
Steinfeld, Thomas, 254, 255
Stephan, Inge, 50, 60, 61
Stephanus, Paulus, 133
Stern, Frank, 142, 182
Sterne, Lawrence, 216, 223
    Tristram Shandy, 216, 223
Stiffler, Muriel W., 278, 283
Stockholm, 82, 86
Stocking, George, 181
storyteller, 230, 270
Strack, Hermann, 134, 137, 142
Strauss, David Friedrich, 277
stream-of-consciousness, 271
Streisand, Barbara, 32
Strenger, Elisabeth, 298, 302
Strindberg, August, 14, 269, 278, 279, 283
Strobl, Inge, 196, 288, 299
student movement (German, 1960s), 16

Studer, Claire (Goll), 94, 101
Studer, Heinrich, 94
Stunde Null (Point Zero, 1945), 172
Styx, 40
subjectivity, 31, 34, 66, 69, 217, 218, 219, 221, 224
Süddeutsche Zeitung, 159, 162, 300
Suderberg, Erika, 42
Sudermann, Hermann, 157, 158
suicide, 49, 89, 92, 96, 253
Sulaiman, Abdel Qadir, 234, 253
Summer of Love (1967), 16
superstition, 12, 26, 119, 123, 127, 230, 299
supranationality, 176, 190, 245, 246, 286
Sweden, 82
Swedenborg, Immanuel, 278
Switzerland, 15, 82, 95, 101, 102, 155, 200, 210, 255, 299
synagogues, 8, 133, 138, 293
Syria, 227–230, 233
Szondi, Peter, 89

taboo, 27, 75, 116, 164, 202, 206
Tabori, George, 239
die tageszeitung, 254, 256
Der Tag, 299
Der Tagesspiegel, 213
talk shows, 239, 243
Talmud, 136, 137, 145
Tanzania, 261
tarot, 277
Tauber, Herbert, 269
Taufiq, Suleman, 233, 236
Tel Aviv, 175
television, TV, 157, 158, 160, 161, 228, 230, 232, 236, 239, 242, 243, 252, 253
Tergit, Gabriele, 85, 87
terror, 6, 45, 46, 52, 52, 56, 151, 154, 231, 181, 184, 188, 195
theosophy, 14, 282–284
Théot, Cathérine, 55–57
Theweleit, Klaus, 17, 20, 151, 154

Männerphantasien, 154
Third World, 217, 231, 232, 236
Third Reich, 23, 153, 2159, 247
Thirty-Years-War, 190
Thomas, Adrienne, 83
Thomas, Nicholas, 228
Tichy, Frank, 298
   Der Fünfspalt, 298
Tiedemann, Rolf, 20, 28
time, 6, 12, 19, 57, 83, 86, 232, 253
Time Magazine, 300
Todorov, Tzvetan, 273, 275, 277, 281, 282
tolerance, 142, 143, 165, 177, 189
toleration, 189, 196
Toller, Ernst, 89
Torah, 27, 32, 33
Torberg, Friedrich, 14, 83, 185, 286, 288–290, 294–299
   Golems Wiederkehr, 14, 285, 289, 293, 295
   Die Tante Jolesch, 285, 298
trance, 13, 262, 284
transformation, 5, 7, 14, 23, 63, 68, 71, 76, 140, 178, 197, 206, 220, 271
Transit. Europäische Revue, 210, 211, 213, 214
trauma, 63, 81, 97, 200, 205, 283
Travemünde, 67, 67, 71–74
Treitschke, Heinrich von, 134–136, 138, 143
Trenkler, Thomas, 213
Tshernovits Conference, 193
Tucholsky, Kurt, 89, 156, 161, 300
Tunisia, 227
Turin, 245
Turks, 149
Der Turm, 300
turn-of-the-century, 138, 150, 153, 179, 184
twentieth century, 47, 103, 157, 159, 176, 177, 180, 182, 183, 192–194, 200

Tzara, Tristan, 13, 257, 259, 260, 265

U. S. Holocaust Museum, 254
Ukraine, 177
Umansky, Ellen M., 42
United States, 10, 15–17, 31, 42, 83, 90, 94–98, 13, 144, 228, 230, 233, 244, 247, 299, 300
Unruh, Ilse, 300
Die Unterrichtspraxis, 236
Updike, John, 253
Urzidil, Johannes, 290
    Alt-Prager Geschichten, 298

Varnhagen, Rahel, 31, 104, 186
Vaughn, Billy, 181
Vedic literature, 24
vegetarianism, 21
Venice, 217, 219, 221, 223
Venske, Regula, 103, 111, 113, 114
Verein für Cultur und Wissenschaft der Juden, 191
Vetrih, Polona, 115
Vienna, 10, 20, 22, 23, 79, 92, 130, 152, 169, 171–184, 191, 196, 202, 210–214, 216, 217, 219, 220, 222, 225, 226, 283, 286
Viertel, Salka, 87, 91
    Das Unbelehrbare Herz, 91
Viertel, Berthold, 88, 92
    Das graue Tuch, 92
Vietnam War, 15, 16, 182
Viëtor-Engländer, Deborah, 9, 155
Vilna, 190
Von Wangenheim, Inge, 87
Von der Lühe, Irmela, 91
Von Mayenburg, Ruth, 87

Wagner, Frank, 100
Wagner, Heinrich, 109
Wagner, Richard, 134–136, 138, 143, 195
    Das Judenthum in der Musik, 134, 135

Waldheim, Kurt, 173, 183, 184, 202
Wall, the (Berlin Wall), 12 17, 140, 239, 246, 249
Walther, Peter, 256
Wandering Jew, 287
Warsaw Ghetto, 155, 288
Washington, Peter, 280, 284
Wasserstein, Wendy, 32
Waterstradt, Berta, 85
Weber, Max, 167
Weckmann, André, 246
Wegener, Paul, 187, 188
    Der Golem: Wie er in die Welt kam, 287, 288
Weichmann, Elsbeth, 87
Weigel, Hans, 285
Weigel, Sigrid, 60, 78, 131
Weil, Grete, 82, 86, 91
Weil, Simone, 31
Weimar Republic, 5, 9, 63, 153, 159, 160, 243
Weininger, Otto, 147, 152, 210
    Geschlecht und Charakter (*Sex and Character*), 147, 152
Weinzierl, Erika, 211
Weiß, Gernot, 13
Weischedel, Wilhelm, 226
Weiss, Ernst, 89
Weiss, Peter, 147
    Die Ermittlung, 147
Weiss, Ruth, 85
Wellemin, Max, 294
Welles, Orson, 276
Die Welt, 253
Die Weltbühne, 161, 299
Die Weltwoche, 226
Wenders, Wim, 242, 254
    Until the End of the World, 254
Wenzel, Hilde, 22, 60, 63
Wenzel, Peter, 63
Werfel, Franz, 94, 300
Werkner, Patrick, 278, 280, 282–284
Werres, Peter, 12, 13, 255
Wespennest, 214

West Germany, 15, 16, 248, 250, 256

West, Cornel, 167

Westbank, 229

Wiegler, Paul, 46, 47, 60

Wiener Zeitung, 300

Wiener Kurier, 300

Wiesel, Elie, 300, 301

Winkler, Gershon, 289, 300, 301

Winsloe, Christa, 87

Winter, Jay, 182

Wischenbart, Rüdiger, 200, 210

Wistrich, Robert, 183

witches, 27, 31, 123, 249

Wodak, Ruth, 181–184

Wolf, Christa, 100, 252

Wolfenstein, Alfred, 89

Wolff, Charlotte, 87

Wolffsohn, Michael, 239

Wollf, Kurt, 94

Woltmann, Johanna, 60–65, 78–80

Women in Exile, 7

workers, 16, 94, 206, 245

world history, 187, 292

world conspiracy, 287, 299

Wort in der Zeit, 199, 214

Wunberg, Gotthart, 181

xenophobia, 111, 136, 207, 251

Yeats, William Butler, 35, 282, 283

Yiddish, 10, 11, 84, 185, 187, 189–191

Yiddishist, 192–194

Yinglish, 84

YIVO, 192

yoga, 278

Yom Kippur, 138, 229

Young Turkish Revolution, 150, 153

Young, James E., 182

Zaum poetry, 262, 266

Zaumny jazyk, 266

Die Zeit, 104, 113, 167, 212, 225, 298

Zeit-Echo, 262, 266

zeitgeist, 110, 129, 194, 225

Zerubavel, Yael, 182

Ziegler, Jean, 231, 235

Ziegler, Meinrad, 182, 183

Zinner, Hedda, 87

Zionism, 132, 141, 286

Zohar, 295, 302

Zrouki, Mohamed, 234

Zuckmayer, Carl, 91, 159, 162
  Als wär's ein Stück von mir, 162
  Der fröhliche Weinberg, 160

Zur Mühlen, Hermynia, 85

Zurich, 13, 22, 85, 102, 159

Zweig, Arnold, 192, 198

Zweig, Stefan, 89

Zwiefelhofer, Barbara, 212

Zwillinger, Frank Gerhard, 14, 285, 286, 289, 292–297, 300–302
  Dalmatinisches Bilderbuch, 300
  Geist und Macht, 292, 301

UNIVERSITY LIBRARY
NOTTINGHAM